A Battle for Neutral Europe

A Battle for Neutral Europe

British Cultural Propaganda
during the Second World War

Edward Corse

BLOOMSBURY
LONDON · NEW DELHI · NEW YORK · SYDNEY

Bloomsbury Academic

An imprint of Bloomsbury Publishing Plc

50 Bedford Square	175 Fifth Avenue
London	New York
WC1B 3DP	NY 10010
UK	USA

www.bloomsbury.com

First published 2013

British Library Cataloguing-in-Publication Data
A catalogue record for this book is available from the British Library.

ISBN: HB: 978-1-4411-9963-8
PDF: 978-1-4411-5330-2
ePub: 978-1-4411-4336-5

Typeset by Deanta Global Publishing Services, Chennai, India
Printed and bound in Great Britain

Contents

List of Figures

List of Tables

List of Abbreviations

ABF	*Arbetarnas Bildningsförbund* (Workers' Education Association).
AG	*Archivo General*, at MAEC.
AGA	*Archivo General de la Administración*, Madrid, Spain.
APN	*Anglo-Portuguese News.*
BCPHA	British Council Portugal, Historical Archive CD-ROM.
BLM	*Bonniers Litterära Magasin.*
BRCO	Day Files of Sir Malcolm Robertson, Chairman of the British Council, 1942–5 at CAC.
BT	Records of the Board of Trade and successor and related bodies, at TNA.
BW	Records of the British Council, at TNA.
CAC	Churchill Archives Centre, Churchill College, University of Cambridge.
DO	Records created or inherited by the Dominions Office and of the Commonwealth Relations and Foreign and Commonwealth Office, at TNA.
FD	Records created and inherited by the Medical Research Council, at TNA.
FO	Records created and inherited by the Foreign Office, at TNA.
HKRC	Hyman Kreitman Research Centre, Tate Britain, London.
HLG	Records created and inherited by the Ministry for Housing and Local Government and of successor and related bodies, at TNA.
HO	Records created and inherited by the Home Office, Ministry of Home Security and related bodies, at TNA.
HS	Records of the Special Operations Executive, at TNA.
INF	Records created and inherited by the Central Office of Information, at TNA.
JDH	The Papers of John Davy Hayward, at KCA.
KCA	King's College Archive, King's College, University of Cambridge.
KNAT	The Papers of Sir Hughe Knatchbull-Hugessen, at CAC.
KV	Records of the Secret Service, at TNA.
MAEC	*Ministerio de Asuntos Exteriores y de Cooperación*, Madrid, Spain.
MAF	Records created and inherited by the Agriculture, Fisheries and Food Departments and of related bodies, at TNA.
MALT	The Papers of Sir Victor Mallet, at CAC.
MEPO	Records of the Metropolitan Police Office, at TNA.
MEW	Ministry of Economic Warfare.
MOI	Ministry of Information.

MSN	*Medical Science News.*
PN	The Papers of Philip Newman, at RNCM.
PREM	Records of the Prime Minister's Office, at TNA.
PWE	Political Warfare Executive.
RAS	*Riksarkivet*, Stockholm, Sweden.
RBTN	The Papers of Sir Malcolm Robertson, at CAC.
RI	Royal Institution Archive, Royal Institution, London.
RNCM	Royal Northern College of Music, Manchester.
SIS	Secret Intelligence Service (MI6).
SOE	Special Operations Executive.
STE	The Papers of John Steegman, at KCA.
T	Records created and inherited by HM Treasury, at TNA.
TGA	Tate Gallery Archive, at HKRC.
TNA	The National Archives, Kew (formerly the Public Record Office).
W L BRAGG	The Papers of Sir Lawrence Bragg, 1890–1971, at RI.

Acknowledgements

My research on the British Council started in the summer of 2007 for my PhD thesis, 'Cultural Propaganda: the British Council's activities in neutral Europe 1939-1945', at the University of Kent. This book is based on that thesis with a number of additions. The book draws on sources from a number of British and overseas archives and I would like to take the opportunity to acknowledge the work and help provided by the staff of those archives. Their help has been invaluable in tracking down new sources and shortening the amount of time required to conduct research. I have also been fortunate to have been in contact with individuals who were connected with the work of the British Council during Second World War as well as friends and relatives of those individuals. All of these contacts have, I believe, helped to make this book a thorough examination of the British Council's work in this period from a variety of different perspectives.

In particular, I would like to note the help from the following individuals, in alphabetical order: Henrik Arnstad, Dr Robin Baker, Manuel Balson, Chris Bastock, Alexandra Blair, Peter Bloor, Anthony Bottrall, Jane Bramwell, Sue Breakell, Leonora Collins, Mary Ann Davison, Elizabeth Ennion, Angela Faunch, Andrew Gent, David Gordon, Antony Grant, Jane Harrison, Caroline Herbert, Professor Frank James, Peter Jones, Kerstin Jonsson, Ingrid Eriksson Karth, Siobhan King, Britt-Marie Lagerqvist, Sofia Leitão, Pilar Casado Liso, Lucinda Mahony, Philip Mallet, Patricia McGuire, Luis Mesas, Tim Pate, Raúl Lopez Renau, Alison Roberts, Nicola Roberts, Lynsey Robertson, Betty Thirsk, Elizabeth Wells, Emily White, Claire Whitfield and Lars Wickström.

I would also like to thank Professor David Welch and Professor Ulf Schmidt for their guidance over the past few years as well as the History Office staff at the University of Kent, other History academic staff and fellow postgraduate students for useful and thought-provoking discussions. Added to this should be Professor Mark Connelly and Dr Sian Nicholas as my examiners for my PhD who gave a useful challenge at my viva. Also, I have had very interesting discussions since completing my PhD at a conference held in the memory of Philip M. Taylor at the Institute of Communication Studies at the University of Leeds in December 2011. Discussions and papers presented by Professor James Chapman, Professor Jeffrey Richards, Professor Nicholas J. Cull, Dr Robin Brown, Professor David Ellwood, Professor David Culbert, Professor Nicholas Pronay and Dr Kate Utting, to name a few, were very useful in developing my final thoughts while transforming my manuscript into this book.

I should also thank my colleagues at my employer – the British Government (at the Department for Environment, Food and Rural Affairs (Defra) until October 2008 and then at Department of Energy and Climate Change (DECC)) – for their flexibility and understanding while undertaking research alongside my day job of playing a small part in saving the world. Also thanks to the staff at Continuum for being so enthusiastic about my first book and for their professionalism in taking the project forward.

Special thanks to my family who have given me unwavering moral support and encouragement throughout my studies.

Finally, I should point out that all the translations in this thesis are my own – with the originals available in the notes for anyone who wishes to check the original language quotations.

Edward Corse
Paddock Wood, Kent
March 2012

1

Introduction

When research for this book began in the summer of 2007, the British Council was an organization that many people in Britain had never heard about. It was far better known outside Britain through its activities of teaching the English language and promoting British culture abroad so much so that, in many places, it was, and remains, the most tangible British asset overseas – rivalled only by the British Broadcasting Corporation (BBC). Since the summer of 2007, however, the British Council has become much more of a household name within Britain as well, but not in ways the British Council would have chosen. In December 2007, the Russian Government demanded the closure of the Council's offices in Yekaterinburg and St Petersburg, claiming that the Council had not paid adequate taxes. The closures were widely suspected, in Britain at least, to be part of the wider diplomatic tension between Britain and Russia at the time. This tension had stemmed from the murder of Alexander Litvinenko in London in November 2006, the refusal of the Russian Government to extradite the KGB agent Andrei Lugovoi, who was suspected of murdering Litvinenko, and the ensuing expulsion of diplomats from the two countries' respective Embassies. The British Council suddenly became much better known across Britain as its name and role became displayed on the front pages of British newspapers and in the headlines of television news.[1] Just over a year later, events in February 2009 provided a similar story of the British Council's staff and offices being threatened because of a wider tension between Britain and a foreign country – this time Iran (though compared to the events in 2011 appeared quite a small affair).[2] The British Council's premises in Kabul in Afghanistan were also attacked in August 2011 making, again, front page news.[3] The events in Russia, Iran and Afghanistan in the early twenty-first century demonstrate some of the many tensions in the British Council's role which have been present ever since it was established in 1934, and these tensions will become familiar in the following chapters.

In this book, the British Council's role and activities in neutral Europe during Second World War will be examined in detail. The British Council's broad aim is worth stating at the outset – which was to promote British life and thought abroad. In 1935, it published an official statement of its aims and objectives, which will be examined in more detail later:

> To promote abroad a wider appreciation of British culture and civilisation, by encouraging the study and use of the English language, and thereby, to extend a knowledge of British literature and of the British contributions to music and the fine arts, the sciences, philosophic thought and political practice. To encourage

both cultural and educational interchanges between the United Kingdom and other countries and, as regards the latter, to assist the free flow of students from overseas to British seats of learning, technical institutions and factories, and of the United Kingdom in the reverse direction. To provide opportunities for maintenance and strengthening the bonds of the British cultural tradition throughout the self-governing Dominions. To ensure continuity of British education in the Crown Colonies and Dependencies.[4]

As a shorthand, the term 'cultural propaganda' has often been associated with its work, as it attempted to promote British culture through institutions and other media to foreign countries.

The first time that an in-depth study on the British Council had been undertaken was in the 1980s by Philip Taylor in his *The Projection of Britain*, which considered the role of pre-Second World War British Council. Taylor's work, referenced particularly in the 'Learning from the past' chapter of this book, was ground-breaking in its attempt to understand why the Council was established, what its role was meant to be and how it operated within the machinery of the British Government.[5]

Shortly after Taylor's study, D. W. Ellwood and Diana Eastment focused on the war period itself with a similar scope to Taylor's work, centering on the operations of the Council in a British organizational context and then, in 1984, Frances Donaldson wrote the British Council's official history covering the first 50 years of its existence.[6] All of these studies focused primarily on the plans that the Council drew up for implementing its work, agreements reached between various Government bodies, the struggle that the Council faced to secure funding and the struggle for recognition against the view promoted by certain influential individuals – primarily Lord Beaverbrook – that its work was a waste of money.

Other studies conducted by authors overseas have focused on particular countries and aspects of the British Council's work during Second World War, such as Jacqueline Hurtley's *José Janés: editor de literatura inglesa*, Jean-François Berdah's *La 'Propaganda' Cultural Británica en España durante la Segunda Guerra Mundial a través de la acción del 'British Council'* and Samuel Llano's *Starkie y el British Council en España*. Interestingly, they have relied heavily on British sources from the National Archives in Kew, rather than files from the local country's national archives.[7] Studies of related organizations, such as Ian McLaine's *Ministry of Morale* – studying the work of the Ministry of Information – do not mention the British Council's work, largely because the focus has been on home front propaganda rather than on work overseas.[8]

All of these aspects of study are important – the value for money of all public sector organizations is particularly pertinent in today's political climate – but none of the studies above really focused on the propaganda work of the British Council itself, how it operated on the ground, or how that propaganda work was received – particularly across all of the European countries that the Council operated in. For example, Ellwood concluded, without detailed analysis in his chapter on the British Council's wartime work, that

Turkey took the largest single slice of the Council's budget, and in fact it seems reasonable to suggest that nowhere outside the Empire itself was so much British influence concentrated in any one spot for such a sustained length of time. And all to very little avail. Neither the threat of Hitler nor the blustering of Churchill nor the systematic blandishments of the British Council were enough to get the Turks' co-operation when it mattered.[9]

It is this lack of understanding of the achievements and importance of the British Council's cultural propaganda work that this book attempts to challenge and overturn. The British Council's work was about creating long-term sympathy and spreading British influence among the neutral elites. It was not, as Ellwood suggested, about bringing those neutral countries into the military war, but instead was about aiming to create enough sympathy in those countries primarily to prevent them from joining the Axis and to increase knowledge of Britain's culture and values.

This book, by contrast, focuses on the propaganda work of the Council and has reached out beyond the National Archives (though highly important) to examine the private papers of individuals such as the correspondence of Sir Malcolm Robertson (Chairman of the British Council, 1941–1945) in the archives of Churchill College at the University of Cambridge, the diaries of John Steegman at King's College, Cambridge, the Hyman Kreitman Archive Centre at Tate Britain and the Royal Institution's archive in Albermarle Street in London for the papers of Sir Lawrence Bragg. Also examined have been Spanish, Portuguese and Swedish newspapers at the British Library's Newspaper Archive at Colindale, London, as well as archival material from the *Ministerio de Asuntos Exteriores y de Cooperación* and the *Archivo General de la Administración* in Madrid and the *Riksarkivet* in Stockholm to gauge the 'view from the other side'. Not until now has the 'view from the other side' been examined at all. Access to the Swedish secret police file on Ronald Bottrall, the British Council's representative in Sweden, has uncovered a number of interesting, previously unknown, points. For example, this has shown that the Swedish secret police followed Ronald Bottrall and other British Council personnel, that the Swedes were aware of the German view of the Council being used as a centre for the secret services, as well as uncovering the anti-Semitic prejudices in their descriptions of Bottrall himself. On the Spanish side, access to the previously unseen files has shown how the Spanish Foreign Ministry agonized over whether to allow Walter Starkie, the British Council's representative in Spain, to be appointed and to travel to Madrid. They needed the recommendation of the Duque de Alba, the Spanish Ambassador in London, to invite him and there were attempts by Ramón Serrano Suñer, the Spanish Foreign Minister, to prevent any publicity about the Council during his tenure of the post of Foreign Minister.

Archival material has been analysed in conjunction with published memoirs such as those written by Michael Grant, the British Council's representative in Turkey during the war period, and Peter Tennant, the British press attaché in Stockholm, as well as my own correspondence with people who were involved with the Council's work at the time, and relatives and friends of the main actors in this book. This broad basis for the book, particularly on primary sources, I believe makes this book robust and substantial, and enables the model of cultural propaganda, developed in the final chapter, to be built on a strong foundation.

The contribution of this book will not be limited to showing how the British Council operated and the analysis of the Council's work in Europe in isolation, but it will also demonstrate how the British Council's cultural propaganda work can be put within a wider context. This will range from putting the Council's work on a higher level of importance within the wider framework of propaganda carried out by Britain during Second World War, but also by attempting to examine the Council's work in the context of existing propaganda and social transmission theories. This book will not only examine the work of Jacques Ellul and Leonard Doob, in particular, in terms of propaganda analysis – pre- and sub-propaganda, sociological propaganda and rumour spreading – but will also look at theories outside the discipline of academic history, to identify and examine linkages with meme theory, the Zahavi Handicap Principle and the Reputation Reflex, the social cognitivism work of Rosaria Conte and the 'soft power' theory of Joseph S. Nye.[10] It will show that the cultural propaganda work of the British Council, seen in this wider academic context, was far more important for Britain's war effort, through effective and profound influence of the elites of neutral countries, than it has been given credit. The techniques it employed – particularly word-of-mouth propaganda in the margins of cultural events – were perhaps the most effective form of propaganda deployed by Britain to neutral Europe during the war. This book will also put the British Council's work in a wider context of the history and development of communications around the world – particularly its place in the growing role of cultural diplomacy during the twentieth century.

I will first consider the Council's work from a conceptual point of view – what cultural propaganda is (with an examination of previous research on cultural propaganda), what the British Council's aims were, what broad constraints the Council faced and how it planned to operate. Second, how the Council interacted with other British organizations and individuals will be discussed – for example, its interaction with other Government Departments (the Foreign Office and Ministry of Information, in particular) and British cultural figures and how its institutions and personnel interacted with British Embassies on the ground. Third, the book will look at the cultural propaganda work of the Council itself and consider what techniques the Council employed when promoting British culture. This will focus on the exhibitions the Council organized, the touring lecturers who were sent out to foreign countries, as well as the ways in which the Council achieved its aim of sympathy creation among neutral peoples. Next, the book will, for the first time, examine how the Council was viewed by people in the countries where it operated – whether it was viewed as a haven for pro-British elites, how it compared with other belligerents' cultural work and how the changing course of the war affected how the Council was treated. Lastly, the book will be summarized with an assessment of the level of success that the Council was able to obtain, with an attempt to draw together a model of cultural propaganda that can be applied to other situations and time periods.

Before the main arguments of the book begin, it is worth taking a moment to understand two aspects over the next two chapters. First, it is important to consider propaganda and cultural transmission theories and how these might help in understanding the work of the British Council in Second World War – this is covered in the following chapter titled 'Cultural propaganda theories and definitions'. Second, it is vital to understand the British Council's history from 1934 to the outbreak of Second World War – its antecedents and foreign competitors, why the Council was established and what it hoped to achieve – these points are covered in the chapter titled 'Learning from the past'.

Cultural Propaganda Theories and Definitions

The British Council's view

A key point that will appear many times in this book regarding the British Council's work and its method of operation, was its aim of being notably different in tone and forcefulness compared with other types of propaganda – particularly propaganda from other countries. The Council often shied away from using the word 'propaganda', as the word already had negative connotations associated with it stemming from First World War, the Bolshevik Revolution and Nazi and Fascist use of the word in the 1930s. The word 'propaganda' in the English language had (and still has) a much darker undertone than it does in the Spanish, Italian and Portuguese languages (where it translates more neutrally as 'publicity' or 'promotion'), and this difference in definition should always be kept in mind when analysing the use of the word. This difference has roots all the way back to the effects of the Protestant Reformation, when the word 'propaganda' was first used in a positive sense in 1622 by the Roman Catholic Church for propagating the Catholic faith.[1] The fact that Spain, Italy and Portugal are primarily Catholic countries and that Britain has had a history over the past few hundred years of being anti-Catholic, or at least being suspicious of Catholicism, accounts in large part to the different understandings of what the word 'propaganda' means. The Council's 1935 statement of aims and objectives outlined in the previous chapter avoided the use of the term 'propaganda' and Sir Malcolm Robertson, the British Council's chairman from 1941 to 1945 (and Member of Parliament (MP) for the Mitcham Division of Surrey), was one of the greatest advocates of avoiding the use of the word propaganda altogether to describe its work. For example, in 1943, he was furious with HM Treasury for viewing the Council's work as propaganda and wrote to a fellow MP:

> The Treasury's idea that the British Council is 'itself a part of the immediate "propaganda offensive"' is complete anathema to me. 'Propaganda' is exactly and precisely what we are not doing. Our aims are essentially long-term. We are endeavouring at long last to explain abroad the British attitude towards life and we are urging other nations to explain to us their attitude towards life. The general idea is solely to build us the basis for a real understanding of the peoples by the peoples of the world.[2]

It, of course, all depends on how one defines the word 'propaganda' whether the British Council's work can fit into its definition. It is somewhat futile, therefore, to argue for or against whether the Council's work can be described as propaganda or not, because the definition of the word is relatively loose. In this book, the word propaganda is used in very broad terms to cover any attempt to influence others and reinforce or change opinions of other people. The British Council's work clearly falls into this broad definition of propaganda. Robertson himself had previously accepted, in 1942, that the work of the Council in supplying articles on British culture to the neutral press could be seen as propaganda but not

> in the generally accepted derogatory sense of that word. They [the articles] aim at holding up a mirror to British ways of life and thought, and are making overseas readers better acquainted with the 'make-up' of the British people. Whenever possible, these articles are accompanied by sets of first-class illustrations, since the picture makes an almost greater appeal to the imaginations than the written word, especially when readers are comparatively unfamiliar with the subject discussed in print.[3]

What is clear from Robertson's statements is that he was aiming for the Council to be very different from the *political* propaganda bodies that had made the word propaganda so repulsive. Lord Lloyd, the Council's previous chairman (from 1937 to 1941), had been less worried about the term propaganda than Robertson, but was still keen to demonstrate that the Council's work was different from political propaganda – and this largely rested on an emphasis of the difference in tone and style.[4] Lord Lloyd stated early on in the war that

> As a race we [the British] have too long been content to remain aloof and misunderstood. Our strength and our wealth have in the past won us respect; we have never sought sympathy or understanding . . . . We have in many places a critical audience to convert, but our opponents' lack of discretion has worked largely in our favour. Everywhere we find people turning in relief from the harshly dominant tones of totalitarian propaganda to the less insistent but more responsible cadences of Britain. We do not force them to 'think British'; we offer them the opportunity to learn what the British think.[5]

Lloyd's statement has a number of important points to bear in mind when analysing the British Council's view of its work and why it was different from other forms of propaganda. Speaking in 'responsible cadences' was clearly a key part of the British Council's method of delivery. The aims of the Council should not, just therefore, be seen in terms of *what* it was trying to promote, but also *how* it was trying to promote it. The *what* and the *how* are intrinsically linked in all propaganda forms – it is very important that if someone wishes to persuade someone else to think or act in a certain way, they must speak in a manner to which the other person is receptive. The *what* must determine the *how*, but the *how* also affects the *what*. Lloyd was clear here that the Council's propaganda was being promoted as an offer only and foreign people could take it or leave it. It is also clear that Lloyd was setting no timeframe in which people had to 'take' the Council's propaganda and there was a deliberate lack of immediacy. This lack of immediacy meant that the Council's work would be a specific and important departure from political propaganda which was often far more prominent, as it needed an instant (or at least short-term) action. Also, the short-term nature of political propaganda was, in the words of William Mackenzie, the historian of the Special Operations Executive (SOE), a 'writ in water', as the circumstances in which it would be disseminated would be only there at that particular time and the propaganda would only make sense for a short period.[6] As, in Lloyd's and Robertson's view, the Council's work was aiming to be incremental, on a 'gently, gently' approach, accumulating sympathy on a long-term basis, the propaganda it produced had to be designed to make sense over that longer period of time and not just there for a particular moment in time. It had, therefore, to be necessarily timeless. Bombastic and fast-moving political propaganda was more obvious perhaps, but not necessarily more effective. Looking for short-term action meant the effect of political propaganda was limited to a superficial level. The idea was that the Council's propaganda, on the other hand, may have been slower to produce results, but should have a more profound effect. Being timeless also meant that the Council's propaganda had by necessity to be, to a large extent, historically based and 'telescopically' inspired, in the sense that it has to show a road to the present through various milestones of progress. Views about Britain's history and place in the world were, likely therefore, to be tried and tested, old-fashioned and conservative. The knock-on effect of this was that the Council's work would essentially be more attractive to the conservative pro-British elites than to the wider masses – and elites were, in many ways, easier to reach through direct contact and word-of-mouth propaganda than through a mass media approach – a concept that will be returned to in the following chapters. Although as we shall see (and as demonstrated in Figure 1 (a model of influence for the British Council's work in neutral Europe) which I have developed) once the elites had been exposed to British Council propaganda their existing networks and influence could allow the Council to reach a wider audience over time.

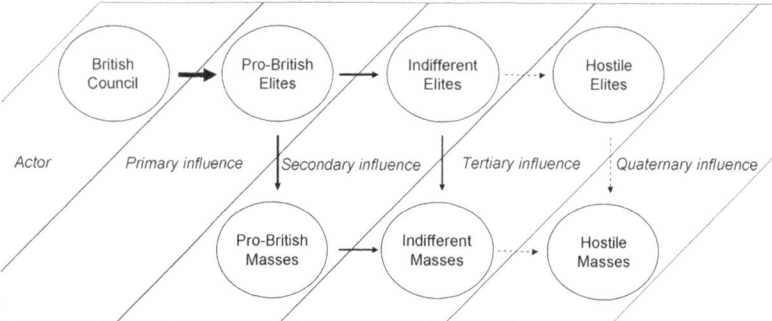

Figure 1 A model of influence for the British Council's work in neutral Europe.

Existing definitions of 'cultural propaganda'

The phrase 'cultural propaganda' has often been used to describe the Council's work in order to distinguish it from the political propaganda that Robertson and Lloyd despised. As the phrase 'cultural propaganda' still contained the word 'propaganda' the Council was also wary of its use to describe its work – but there is a question about what exactly is the definition of 'cultural propaganda'.

Philip Taylor, in his study of the Council in the 1930s, defined cultural propaganda as 'the promotion and dissemination of national aims and achievements in a general rather than specifically economic or political form, although it is ultimately designed to promote economic and political interests'.[7] While Taylor was right to state that cultural propaganda 'is ultimately designed to promote economic and political interests' (i.e. it is very much aligned to the overall aims of political propaganda), his definition did not demonstrate the difference that exists between cultural and political propaganda in style, tone, pervasiveness and intended time to produce an effect, and which Robertson and Lloyd were trying to promote in the quotes above, nor the ability of the intended audience to subsequently influence secondary audiences. The difference of tone was also absent from the definition given by Nicholas J. Cull, David Culbert and David Welch in their encyclopaedia of propaganda and mass persuasion, though the emphasis on the long term nature of cultural propaganda was recognized as was the secondary effect of the 'pressure of public opinion' on policy makers:

> Cultural propaganda is a long-term process intended to promote a better understanding of the nation that is sponsoring the activity . . . . Such activity involves the dissemination of cultural products – films, magazines, radio and television programs, art exhibitions, traveling [sic] theater [sic] groups and orchestras – as well as the promotion of language teaching and a wide range of 'educational' activities, such as student exchange schemes. Over a period of time, these activities are designed to enhance the nation's image among the populations of other countries, with a view to creating goodwill and influencing the polices [sic] of their governments through the pressure of public opinion.[8]

As Cull, Culbert and Welch note, the aim of cultural propaganda, as opposed to political propaganda, is to create sympathy on a long-term basis through a range of techniques designed to make that sympathy profound, rather than aiming for a desired short-term action on the part of the audience. However, the difference in style, tone and pervasiveness is very important in the definition of cultural propaganda that Robertson and Lloyd recognized – and is not fully recognized in historical definitions so far.

Cull has developed his consideration of cultural propaganda further in his book *The Cold War and the United States Information Agency*, as part of a wider analysis on public diplomacy. Cull has stated that 'public diplomacy is an international actor's attempt to conduct its foreign policy by engaging with foreign publics'.[9] Interestingly Cull demonstrates that the term 'public diplomacy' was a convenient way of sidestepping the term 'propaganda' for the United States Information Agency (USIA), and a term that Robertson would probably have approved to show its difference from the propaganda he despised.[10] His analysis has concluded that there are five core components of public diplomacy:

> *listening*: research, analysis, and the feedback of that information into the policy process – an example would be the commissioning of opinion polls by a foreign ministry; *advocacy*: the creation and dissemination of information materials to build understanding of a policy, issue, or facet of life of significance to the actor, which might take the form of an embassy press conference; *cultural diplomacy*: the dissemination of cultural practices as a mechanism to promote the interests of the actor, which could include an international tour by a prominent musician; *exchange diplomacy*: the exchange of persons with another actor for mutual advantage, as in the exchange of college students; and *international broadcasting*: especially the transmission of balanced news over state-funded international radio.[11]

Like the terms 'public diplomacy' and 'propaganda', 'cultural diplomacy' and 'cultural propaganda' are also essentially interchangeable terms. As we shall see, from its activities in this book, the British Council's work clearly falls within the Cull's 'cultural diplomacy' component, with many artists being deployed to neutral Europe to promote British culture. The British Council's activities would also fit within the component of 'exchange diplomacy', with students and journalists being offered opportunities to visit Britain – although the opportunities during wartime were very limited for practical reasons. To an extent too, the Council's work was about listening to what neutral people wanted to know about Britain and then providing it through its cultural propaganda work. However, the Council's work was less about advocacy of British Government policy – particularly wartime policy – although there were some exceptions. Broadcasting was something largely left to the BBC although, on occasion, broadcasts were co-ordinated with Council events and some musical events were performed on local radio. Cull's framework of analysis, therefore, is useful in demonstrating that the British Council's work was part of wider public diplomacy effort by the British Government, but was not the full picture in itself, and that it heavily concentrated on cultural propaganda – and did not get involved in the political work that Robertson feared.

The British Council's work also fits within the definition of 'soft power' promoted by Joseph S. Nye, which he has defined as 'the ability to get what you want through attraction rather than coercion or payments. It arises from the attractiveness of a country's culture, political ideals, and policies'.[12] Although Nye only mentioned the British Council briefly, it is clear from the other examples that he gave – the *Alliance Française*, the United States' Office for Wartime Information (OWI) and the like – that he would see the British Council's work fitting into a story of efforts to wield soft power.[13] In Nye's view, soft power is what results from a number of sources such as culture, domestic values and policies, and the substance and style of foreign policy – and policies of public diplomacy can enhance soft power.[14] Nye has set out his view that there are three dimensions of public diplomacy, the first being daily communications, second, strategic communication, 'in which a set of simple themes is developed', and third, the development of lasting cultural relationships with key individuals.[15] The British Council's work clearly fits within Nye's third dimension and, as Nye demonstrated in his work, the soft power which cultural propaganda can produce can be just as important, if not more important, than hard power which is more obvious and familiar. Nye did not agree that public diplomacy and propaganda are interchangeable terms (and by extension would not agree that cultural diplomacy and cultural propaganda are interchangeable), but that all, of course, depends on the definition of propaganda – and it is the meaning behind the terms used which is important. Both Cull's and Nye's work have been important in setting out where cultural propaganda should sit in a spectrum of other forms of influence, and in demonstrating that cultural propaganda is an important source of power. However, both Cull's and Nye's frameworks do not concentrate on exactly how cultural propaganda works to be effective and how it interacts with other forms of propaganda – and do not emphasize enough that difference in tone that Robertson and Lloyd recognized. These are points that this book will draw together in a model of cultural propaganda in the last chapter.

Related theories of propaganda and social transmission

It is worth considering some other theories of propaganda and social transmission to get a better understanding of how the long-term, positively toned, sympathy-creating and essentially conservative cultural propaganda definitions set out above fit within a broader landscape of ideas about propaganda. The first of these theories is the Bolshevik distinction between 'agitators' and 'propaganda', both in terms of nomenclature and the applicability of the word 'propaganda'. 'Agitation' in the Bolshevik model meant preparing a group vigorously, on a short-term basis, for a particular action. 'Propaganda', on the other hand, meant a long-term educational programme to prepare the ground for agitation.[16] This is a somewhat different definition to the meaning that is usually associated with the word 'propaganda' as if it is something prior to, but essential for, propaganda (in today's sense) to take place. Essentially, in the Bolshevik model, 'agitation' takes the place of what would usually be recognized today as being propaganda. In terms of word-of-mouth propaganda, therefore, the Bolsheviks used oral agitators to spread messages drawing on sympathies and prejudices that had already been instilled through a long-term educational programme promoting Marxist-Leninist doctrine. However, the British Council could be seen as covering aspects of both roles in the Bolshevik model. On the one hand, its official aims were to teach the English language, provide schooling and organize cultural events, all of which were aimed at long-term sympathy-creation (i.e. 'propaganda' in the Bolshevik model). Yet, on the other hand, the Council could also be seen to be aiming to directly influence those same people that attended the cultural events through talking about life (particularly cultural life) in wartime Britain, using those cultural events as a conduit for direct influence (i.e. 'agitation' in the Bolshevik model). Whether it can be said to have influenced them directly 'to action', as the Bolshevik model suggests it should, is perhaps less clear and depends on the action that the British Council was expecting to induce and the type of action demanded by the Bolshevik model. In many cases, the scope for 'action' in neutral countries was rather limited. Action could simply mean that sympathetic elites took on the role of influencing other elites and masses within the neutral countries – in places where the British Council or British influence generally could not reach directly.

A more appropriate model to how the British Council operated is perhaps provided by Leonard Doob's analysis of propaganda techniques. Doob effectively expanded the Bolshevik model, and made a distinction between 'sub-propaganda' and 'main propaganda', stating that:

> Many sub-propaganda campaigns are postulated on the assumption that final action must be postponed until the propagandees [the audience] are psychologically prepared or find themselves in a situation which provides the appropriate stimuli. . . . No action need be indicated in a sub-propaganda campaign, for here the aim is simply the learning of an attitude to facilitate the main propaganda itself.[17]

There is a subtle difference here between the Bolshevik model in the sense that, in the Bolshevik model, word-of-mouth propaganda only really fits with 'agitation' and is outside the scope of the educational programme defined in 'propaganda'. In Doob's analysis, there is no attempt to rule out the role of an agitative method of propaganda (such as word-of-mouth propaganda) in the psychological preparation of the audience. Instead, Doob simply described the two layers of propaganda – in reality, propaganda aiming for long-term and short-term effects – rather than the methods employed to achieve those effects. Because of this subtle difference, Doob's model is closer than the Bolshevik model to the British Council's method of operation that Lloyd and Robertson envisaged. He also described a formal disconnection between the 'main propaganda' and the 'sub-propaganda' by stating that 'the aim is simply the learning of an attitude' which can be taken to mean that the sympathy-creation aim of the Council could fit into the description of 'sub-propaganda' without being directly related to how that sympathy was going to be manipulated. The two concepts of 'main propaganda' and 'sub-propaganda' are still related however, if more remotely, and Doob implied that the main propaganda required the sub-propaganda to be already embedded within the audience in order to be effective, and therefore would work on currents and themes which were already familiar to the audience.

Jacques Ellul's concept of 'sociological propaganda' is also worth considering in this context. Ellul himself started his description of sociological propaganda by stating that sociological propaganda is a type of propaganda that does not have an organization directing it – it is something built into the culture of a country about how people in that country should live their lives. He stated 'sociological propaganda springs up spontaneously; it is not the result of deliberate propaganda action. No propagandists deliberately use this method, though many practice it unwittingly, and tend in this direction without realizing it'.[18]

What Ellul suggested was that sociological propaganda provided the themes of existing currents of thought in a culture which were constantly being reinforced by that culture. Propagandists must comply with this sociological propaganda in order to make their propaganda effective. Ellul combined his view, of there being existing sociological propaganda within a society, with the view of Doob, that sub-propaganda (or, in Ellul's words, 'pre-propaganda') was essential for direct propaganda to work. Sub-propaganda, Ellul believed, must complement the existing sociological situation if it were to be successful. He postulated:

> Direct propaganda, aimed at modifying opinions and attitudes, must be preceded by propaganda that is sociological in character, slow, general, seeking to create a climate, an atmosphere of favo[u]rable preliminary attitudes. No direct propaganda can be effective without pre-propaganda .... Sociological propaganda can be compared to plowing [sic], direct propaganda to sowing; you cannot do the one without doing the other first.[19]

Sociological propaganda is therefore not just something circulating around a society which cannot be influenced by propaganda organizations, but it is already there in existence and has to be worked with and moulded.[20] Sociological propaganda cannot be invented solely from scratch by a propaganda organization to meet its own purposes. Nevertheless, Ellul went on to state that there are complex issues surrounding the implanting of sociologically based propaganda themes into a different society: 'The more conscious sociological propaganda is, the more it tends to express itself externally, and hence to expand its influence abroad.'[21] Ellul was specifically referencing the influence of post-war American culture on Europe (and particularly France) and the fact that the American culture was not intended to be propagandistic in a political sense – it was merely showing America in the way that Americans believed to be accurate (there is clearly a link here with Robertson's belief, stated above, that the British Council did not do propaganda – the Council simply tried to show Britain for what it was). The complexity arose when the French saw this American culture partly as a good thing – where technological advantages, in particular, were obvious – but also exasperating, where they sensed an American 'superiority complex' that seemed to express the opinion that the American way of life was the *only* way of life.[22] In other words, true sociological propaganda, replicating a way of life without the need for a propaganda organization, can only work successfully within societies where there is an existing, or perhaps latent, acceptance of its benefits promulgated by that propaganda. The people within those societies do not regard it as propaganda because they see it just as their way of life (or a way of life which they wish to emulate) and have no reason to question its propagandistic nature. Generally outside that society, it cannot work as pure sociological propaganda, because the context is not right and there is much more need for a directing organization to ensure it can be accepted, or at least understood, in another culture.

Ellul's idea that there is a current of self-perpetuating propaganda within a society which helps hold a culture together links strongly with what Richard Dawkins and Susan Blackmore, to name a few academics looking at this area, have described as 'memes' – cultural equivalents to genes in the sense that they evolve over time through a process of natural selection. Memes are defined as units of a culture which replicate within a society from one person to the next, slowly becoming more and more refined (unintentionally) to meet the needs of the succeeding generations.[23] Dawkins originally gave the following examples that could be described as memes: 'tunes, ideas, catchphrases, clothes fashions, and ways of making pots and arches'.[24] Blackmore has developed the idea and has stated:

> Everything that is passed from person to person in this way [by imitation] is a meme. This includes all the words in your vocabulary, the stories you know, the skills and habits you have picked up from others and the games you like to play. It includes the songs you sing and the rules you obey. So, for example, whenever you drive on the left (or the right!), eat curry with lager or pizza and coke, whistle the theme tune from *Neighbours* or even shake hands, you are dealing in memes. Each of these memes has evolved in its own unique way with its own history, but each of them is using your behaviour to get itself copied.[25]

Meme theory (or memetics) takes the view that all units of culture are constantly competing against each other and only the useful ones or the 'fittest' ones get replicated. There is not, however, a grand design or designer orchestrating the process, and it continues unintentionally (or at least without purposeful direction). Blackmore has stated that not all thoughts and learning should be considered as memes, but only those that can be copied by imitation and therefore passed on to someone else.[26] It would be hard to argue that the British Council's actions were unintentional and undirected, but there is an interesting connection here between sociological propaganda and the spreading of units of culture, which should be explored further. Hearing a story and passing it on would be something on which a cultural propaganda organization (like the British Council) would rely in order to influence audiences they could not reach directly (as demonstrated in Figure 1). It is conceivable that the Council's work could be seen as being a conduit for feeding memes into a new society, and that they had to compete with other memes already existing in that society, together with memes being introduced by the Axis countries – and there is a term for this too in memetics: 'meme vehicles'.[27] The idea that units of culture will compete with each other and the successful ones will be the ones that get replicated is fine in one society, but in another society, for new units of culture to stand a chance of competing with units already embedded within another society, they need a directing organization to make their survival viable. The British Council's work fits this idea of a vehicle very well – the Council was there specifically for propagating British culture (a group of memes complementing each other) and used institutions, schools and individuals to try to implant ideas from one society to another. I would like to suggest that specifically, this is where cultural propaganda comes into play. Cultural propaganda differs from Ellul's sociological propaganda because it needs a vehicle to perpetuate it. Sociological propaganda becomes cultural propaganda once it is outside of the society where it originates and is being directed to penetrate a different society. This idea of needing an organizing body will be developed further in the last chapter when this book attempts to draw together a model of cultural propaganda.

Memetics has been debated and argued over for the past couple of decades, with the theory receiving significant criticism. Much of the criticism has surrounded the concept of the meme as a unit, and whether this unit can really be defined and isolated. Critics have largely dismissed the theory on this basis describing memetics as a 'pseudoscience' because the item of study 'appears to grow indefinitely and arbitrarily'.[28] This is an unconvincing argument as many concepts like 'ideas', 'thoughts', 'information' and even 'culture' cannot be defined easily and many authors will have differing views of what these are – nevertheless that does not mean that any of them do not exist. Other more serious criticisms have revolved around the 'horizontal' (i.e. person-to-person) transmission of memes as opposed to the 'vertical' (i.e. generation-to-generation) transmission of genes; whether memetics is truly Darwinian (in the sense that fitness is determined by a meme's predisposition to survive in new and changing environments) rather than being affected by environmental feedback; the lack of room in the theory for innovation by individuals; and the view that when memes transfer from one person to the next, they are changed too significantly by that person to be analogous to genetic evolution.[29] Social psychologists, such as Rosaria Conte, have criticized Blackmore's work for ignoring other forms of social transmission, and focusing solely on imitation and so perhaps a future definition of memetics will fit the British Council's work better than that provided by Blackmore.[30]

Only one book exists to date – Michael Drout's *How Tradition Works* – that has attempted to apply meme theory to a historical period. Drout provides a convincing rebuttal to the criticisms above, to show that none of them really undermine the core elements of the theory, though he does accept Conte's argument that memetics ignores forms of social transmission outside of imitation, and that memetics should therefore not over-claim its universal applicability. In Drout's case, the historical period studied was tenth century Anglo-Saxon England and the Benedictine Reforms, and he traced changes to the Rule of St Benedict through various influences over time which he analysed through the theory of memetics. He put forward a claim that 'tradition' is a concept that develops when ideas, tunes and catchphrases are passed from one person to the next but no one can remember their origin, but that they fit well with the situation in which they are replicated (Drout's Word-to-World Fit concept). Over time, Drout suggests, a 'Universal Tradition Meme' develops that is used to justify traditional actions when their origin is forgotten – which translates as 'because we have always done so' – and becomes automatic.

Drout's ideas are useful additions to this analysis of propaganda theories and to the situation of the British Council in Second World War for a number of reasons. First it suggests that tried and tested, conservative (or 'traditional') elements of culture are more likely to be safely accepted by the recipient audiences, than new ideas, as they usually need less explanation and fit better with an audiences' expectation. While *they* may not 'have always done so', in the sense of Drout's Universal Tradition Meme, the audiences in neutral Europe could potentially be convinced that, if the *British* had always done something and it had been successful, they should follow the British lead.

Second, it shows that all the memes that the British Council promoted in neutral Europe had to fit with the pre-existing views of Britain and other influences the audiences were being subjected to (the Word-to-World condition) – in other words, the British Council had to understand and complement the perceptions of the audiences it wished to influence and work with them (that also connects with Cull's first component of public diplomacy – listening).

Lastly, by highlighting the 'University Tradition Meme' concept, Drout provides a useful way of hooking ideas transferring from one person to the next, onto a real antecedent situation and a reason for why this transfer should take place. Previously memetics has suffered from appearing inert and static, in the sense that though 'tunes, ideas, catchphrases' and the like were recognized as memes, and things which were transferable, there seemed little reason for any of them to actually be transferred.

Other theories connected to memetics and genetics are also worth a mention at this point – that of the 'Handicap Principle' developed by Amotz and Avishag Zahavi and the 'Peacock's Tail and the Reputation Reflex' put forward by Robin Wight. Both Wight and the Zahavis have questioned why in nature certain characteristics, such as the peacock's tail, have developed without appearing to have any practical use, and, indeed, handicap the animal which has developed it. The answer put forward is that the ability to 'waste' resources on a feature which has no practical use is a way of signalling genetic, or cultural, fitness and enhancing reputation. Both the peacock's tail and the sponsorship of art are considered in this context – in the sense that neither have practical uses, but both produce responses, in what Wight terms the 'Reputation Reflex', in the amygdala part of the brain.[31] The British Council's work could be seen as having no practical value, and could therefore be seen as 'wasteful', but highly important in terms of maintaining and advancing the reputation of Britain.

Towards a new definition of cultural propaganda

This chapter has demonstrated that the existing definitions of cultural propaganda (and its role within wider public diplomacy), written and expanded upon by Taylor, Cull, Culbert, Welch and Nye, do not fully describe the aims and purpose of the British Council as viewed by its two wartime chairman – Lord Lloyd and Sir Malcolm Robertson. It has also demonstrated that there are a number of other theories of propaganda and social transmission, written and developed by Ellul, Doob, Blackmore, Drout, Wight and the Zahavis, which could add a lot of value into a broader understanding of how cultural propaganda can produce long-term effects, why it is necessary and how it can be successful. The book will attempt to compare and contrast aspects of these definitions and theories, with a view to developing them through an analysis of actual activities of the British Council during Second World War. In the final chapter, a new model of cultural propaganda will be outlined that I hope will add significant value to the understanding of the British Council's activities but importantly also be applicable to other eras and organizations, such as the *Alliance Française*, United States Information Agency and the *Goethe Institut*.

Learning from the Past

Roots and antecedents of the British Council in Britain

The British Council's establishment in 1934 was overdue. It had been recognized by the British Government in First World War that aiming cultural propaganda at opinion-forming elites in neutral countries was effective, if done well. Increasing pressure during the 1920s and early 1930s for the establishment of an organization, like the British Council, for the promotion of cultural propaganda abroad was something the Foreign Office in London could not put off forever. Prior to First World War, the British Government had taken the view that British achievements were self-evident – the British Empire's size and diversity was unprecedented and could be simply illustrated by the reddish-pink colour on the world map – no one, it was argued, need go any further in telling foreigners how great Great Britain was.[1] That view changed with the outbreak of war in 1914 as Britain showed for the first time since the days of Napoleon, just how vulnerable it was on its own doorstep. The reddish-pink colouring-in of India, Australia, Canada and much of Africa meant very little when the guns of the Somme could be heard, quite literally, in southeast England. As the war drew on, and the stalemate of the western front became seemingly more and more permanent, Britain needed to find ways of bringing in resources from outside the Empire in order to win the war – that area outside the Empire, of course, being primarily the United States of America.

Isolationist, over the other side of the Atlantic, and far from having the special relationship with Britain in the post-Second World War period, the United States was not an easy partner to coax into joining the Anglo-French alliance against Germany. But clearly there was a way that this was achieved, as in 1917, the formerly neutral Americans joined the war – so how did that change take place? There were many reasons for this change, but the main reason was the very significant and important role played by an organization in creating sympathy for British culture in American minds, yet it was so secret at the time that only a very select few knew that it existed and operated at all.[2] That organization was known as Wellington House – a secret wartime propaganda office functioning under its chief, Charles Masterman.[3] At Wellington House, Philip Taylor had stated,

> [i]t was . . . decided that the best propagandists for the Allied cause [in the United States] were sympathetic Americans, particularly those in influential positions

in government, business, education, and the media. The principle here, as one document put it, was 'that it is better to influence those who can influence others than attempt a direct appeal to the mass of the population.'[4]

This principle, as will be shown in the following chapters, is one which could very easily be applied to the work of the British Council during Second World War. Wellington House set many of the precedents that the British Council would eventually pick up at its establishment in 1934, and its memory lived on in the minds of Foreign Office officials during the 1920s as an example of using effective techniques for influencing opinion-forming elites. Even some of those involved with the work of Wellington House, such as Eric Maclagen and Muirhead Bone, became later involved in British Council activity.[5]

Work at Wellington House was directed primarily at neutral countries and was split into sections on a linguistic basis – Scandinavia, Holland, Italy and Switzerland, and Spain, Portugal and South America and lastly, with a special focus, the United States of America.[6] 'Any recipients of official British propaganda were to receive it through unofficial sources. It was a general policy that a definite nexus should exist between sender and recipient, thus avoiding any impersonal or wholesale distribution', noted M. L. Sanders, who wrote an account of the work of Wellington House in 1975.[7] Wellington House may have initially employed more traditional techniques of propaganda such as the creation of pamphlets and cartoons, and dealt with the war situation more directly than the case would be with the British Council – although 'conventional literary propaganda' was still deemed to be dominant[8] – but the principle of creating sympathy among neutral elites through promoting British culture, was a proto-example that Wellington House provided for the Council to emulate. Wellington House started to arrange lecture tours for Britons on specialist subjects, but the lecturers were 'not to reveal their connexion [sic] with the British Government'.[9] Trips for British theatrical companies, educational exchanges, the fostering of the Boy Scout movement abroad and the establishment of Anglophile societies were all supported by Wellington House, as were the establishment of propaganda bureaux in foreign countries.[10] Masterman stated that the materials were

> [n]ot circulated promiscuously but . . . either . . . sold or sent with a personal letter
> to some man or woman of importance, placed in public libraries or distributed
> amongst a selected list of those to whom the particular literature was suitable.[11]

All of these methods of propaganda have, as we shall see, clear parallels to the work of the Council a few decades later, although the British Council was more open about the sources of the materials it was distributing.[12]

Masterman was keenly aware of the potential criticism that his propaganda organization could attract due to its focus on cultural, and understated, propaganda techniques and stated that '[i]t is in the nature of the case that we cannot expect to be rewarded to any great extent by realizing definite and overt results'.[13] As Masterman predicted, Wellington House received significant criticism. For example, Sanders stated '[t]he person-to-person distribution of propaganda in North America was considered inferior, as the recipients were selected from Britain', and 'the report condemned as unnecessarily wasteful the policy of Wellington House of buying published works for distribution as propaganda'.[14] The importance of 'wastefulness' in Wight's Reputation Reflex was clearly not recognized in this report. According to Sanders, towards the end of the war, the new Ministry of Information (formed in March 1918) under Lord Beaverbrook decided that the secret nature of Wellington House was

> no longer believed to be necessary. Instead of the indirect appeal, the ministry sought to be direct in every way. To Beaverbrook and those around him, the most direct and effective forms of publicity were propaganda by films, by wireless and cable and by the press. It was very much a newspaperman's view of propaganda. Where Wellington House hard largely aimed at an intellectual élite, the Ministry of Information sought mass response.[15]

This view of Beaverbrook, as we shall see, affected how he viewed the creation and development of the British Council – campaigning almost tirelessly for its closure because, he believed, it wasted money on ineffective propaganda. But, overall, the work of Wellington House was deemed successful, at least by the Foreign Office, and the reforms enacted by Beaverbrook were, in effect, too late to make any impact on the part Wellington House played on influencing the United States to enter the war. As Taylor stated

> In sharp contrast to the methods employed in 1918 [by Beaverbrook's Ministry], direct mass activity was not considered to be an effective approach [by the Foreign Office]. Yet it was entirely compatible with the Foreign Office's somewhat limited concept of 'public opinion' and its preference for allowing others to conduct propaganda on its behalf; the emphasis upon secrecy was not simply a device to prevent clean hands from getting dirty, but derived from a genuine belief in the value of disguised, indirect propaganda.[16]

Outside the realms of direct wartime propaganda, First World War also prompted British policymakers in Government to examine the state of Britain's reputation at a cultural level in foreign countries more generally. A committee was established in August 1917 under Sir Henry Newbolt to examine the state of the circulation of British books and periodicals abroad. It also drew conclusions about the level of knowledge of British cultural achievements overseas. The committee members noted in their report that:

> Apart from the inadequate methods of [book] distribution, we have been impressed by other causes of the general depreciation of the intellectual impulse which British thought can claim to have given the world at large, and of the general misapprehension of the facilities which British invention and enterprise can offer to the trade and manufacture of foreign countries.[17]

Clearly the committee was stating that there was a general need for promoting British culture abroad, which was not just limited to the war needs being serviced by Wellington House. There was a general lack of understanding of Britain outside of the British Empire which meant that not only were British cultural achievements widely unknown, but was beginning to affect Britain's commercial and economic interests with the wider world. Britain's large and diverse Empire now not only meant very little with hostilities on Britain's doorstep, but it also had little meaning generally to a world that was unengaged with the British Empire on a cultural level.

If only Beaverbrook, or the Treasury, had seen the commercial and economic arguments for promoting British culture abroad, it could be speculated that there could have been enough momentum at the end of First World War for a British cultural propaganda organization to be established. But they did not, and in 1919 the Treasury promptly ruled that cultural propaganda was too wide and too vague to be of any profitable value.[18] This ruling, however, has to be seen in the wider context of the post-First World War atmosphere. There are three broad points to understand here. First, propaganda had become a dirty word during and particularly soon after the war, largely because of the spread of atrocity stories during the war period which turned out not to be true – exposed more fully by Lord Ponsonby in 1926. Second, there was a lack of money, and a seemingly less urgent need, to spend money on propaganda of any type, when Britain had spent so much of its wealth on winning the war. Third, Britain had won the war and the mind-set of the British Government quickly turned back to the understandable, but flawed, position that the Empire again spoke for itself – and now, of course, with the defeat of Germany, covered an even larger geographical area.[19] Even when the Foreign Office attempted in 1920, supported by the committee of Sir John Tilley, to consider it had a moral obligation to support British communities abroad and to promote British culture within its own Empire, Treasury officials were still not interested in changing their position.[20]

For the Foreign Office, a raw disparity of funding between French, Italian, German and British cultural propaganda was obvious. The fact that the French Government was spending around £500,000 per annum, and the German and Italian Governments around £300,000 per annum each, on cultural propaganda activities was rather shocking when compared to the British Government which was only permitted to spend up to £10 – yes, just ten pounds. And this was only allowed in exceptional circumstances, which usually meant only being able to send a few books to Central and South America, despite the continual requests from British communities abroad to the Foreign Office for more cultural activities to take place.[21] The Foreign Office was unable, without hard evidence on the effect that this shocking statistic was having on British fortunes abroad, to make any progress on cultural propaganda until the end of the decade.

The Treasury's intransigence was broken finally in 1929 when it, at last, opened its eyes to the fact that a lack of promotion of British culture was damaging British commercial and economic interests and that foreign opinion-forming elites were unaware of developments in Britain which might make them more sympathetic to British interests. The impetus for this change came from an official in the Foreign Office's News Department, and one of the founding fathers of the British Council – Rex Leeper. In 1929, a highly influential report landed on Leeper's desk. It was a godsend for Leeper. And it was damning for the British Government. The report was authored by Viscount D'Abernon who had just returned from a trade mission to South America, and tore to shreds the Government's (and, more particularly, the Treasury's) negative attitude towards cultural propaganda. D'Abernon's report recommended a clear case for the interdependency of commercial and cultural interests, stating:

> To those who say that this extension in influence has no connection with commerce, we reply that they are totally wrong; the reaction of trade to the more deliberate inculcation of British culture which we advocate is definitely certain and will be swift.[22]

Frances Donaldson, who wrote the official history of the British Council for its 50th anniversary, noted that the final chapter of the D'Abernon Report titled 'The Commercial Importance of Cultural Influence' was particularly hard-hitting for Government officials, and had 'far-reaching consequences'.[23] D'Abernon expanded on his views at an address given on 29 October 1929 at the Royal Institute of International Affairs:

> Turning now to propaganda, I refer mainly to propaganda in the commercial sphere rather than in the political sphere, for, after all, our interests in these countries are, and should be, economic rather than anything else. It is common ground that more active propaganda by England is required, but propaganda needs not only to be more active but more subtle. The 'puff' direct is not sufficient, you have to begin further back; you must train your public to appreciate English taste and English goods. For this purpose, cultural influence is also important. Other nations are working hard in this direction. America is offering free education in engineering and other departments to South American youths who will go to the United States for three to four years; France has developed an intensive cultural propaganda, sending every year distinguished professors to South America to carry out a course of lectures on literary and scientific subjects. All this intellectual propaganda, or so-called intellectual propaganda, is intended to have, and will have, wide commercial results. We must not be behindhand . . . .[24]

D'Abernon would clearly have agreed with Ellul's and Doob's proposition that pre- or sub-propaganda was vital for political, and other forms of direct, propaganda to work effectively. The effect of the report on changing opinions in the British Government cannot be overstated. It was not the only report to have influence, but most definitely led the way. Further evidence was later supplied from a young British lecturer who had just taken up a post at the University of Coimbra in Portugal. He could not believe that, though the Portuguese were willing to engage with Britain, the British had made no attempt to extend cultural relations to Portugal, and any British influence was crowded out by German, French and Italian concerns. He went to the British Ambassador in Lisbon, Sir Claud Russell, to make his views known and supplied a written report of which forty copies eventually arrived at the Foreign Office from the different sources that Russell's staff had sent on to Universities in Britain. The lecturer, Sidney George West, would later become the British Council's representative to Portugal, and Lisbon would be one of the first foreign cities to host a British Institute under the auspices of the Council.[25]

Rex Leeper collated the evidence from the D'Abernon Report and made the case for increasing the grant for cultural activities to support British commercial interests, and to counter the 'aggressive propaganda of other countries', to the Labour Foreign Secretary Arthur Henderson. Henderson in turn approached the Treasury for £10,000 per annum – a significant increase on that £10 previously allowed, though still minute compared with the expenditure of France, Germany and Italy. In late 1930, the Treasury agreed to a sum of £2,500 per annum – not what the Foreign Office had asked for, but it was a start, and the principle of the Treasury's 1919 ruling had been overturned.[26] Even the £2,500 was not safe though, as the economic crisis unfolding at the time meant that the decision was reversed in 1931, though one-third of the money had already been spent. Instead, the Foreign Office's News Department went into planning mode for when the money returned in the 1932/1933 financial year. There was enough confidence to do this as the News Department believed that the value of British cultural propaganda work had been recognized, together with the cost of other countries' cultural propaganda on British commercial interests. It was now just a matter of time before their cultural propaganda work began in earnest.

In June 1934, after some detailed planning work and some initial cultural propaganda work itself, Leeper proposed the establishment of a Cultural Relations Committee to co-ordinate the work of various bodies already in existence within and outside the Foreign Office – such as the Board of Trade, the Travel Association and the Empire Marketing Board – to be funded by private sources. He proposed that its work, aimed at promoting British culture abroad, be divided into five categories:

1. the provision of prizes and scholarships to foreign schools and universities in order to increase the study of the English language;
2. the establishment of British libraries abroad;
3. the arrangement of lecture tours by distinguished British speakers;
4. sponsored visits to England of prominent journalists and professional men;
5. films.[27]

These five areas of work do not match exactly with the British Council's statement of aims the following year, but they are very close to it, and are a good reflection of what the British Council actually did in practical terms, with the same broad aim of promoting British culture abroad in a general sense. The exception, as we shall see, was the focus on films, which the Council did not really concentrate on until well into Second World War, and often in collaboration with the Ministry of Information (MOI). The Cultural Relations Committee was established, then closed due to a debate over its constitution and some 'office politics' regarding whose vision of the committee would prevail. The majority of those involved, led by Leeper, wanted to see the Foreign Office as the leading actor in the committee instead of private, commercial interests. The Committee was re-established into what was initially called the 'Advisory Committee for the Promotion of International Relations' in November 1934 with a stronger emphasis on Foreign Office control over the committee. Lord Tyrell, the recently retired British Ambassador to France and former head of the Foreign Office's News Department, was invited to chair the first meeting held on 5 December 1934, which then changed its name at the meeting itself to 'The British Committee for Relations with Other Countries'. This committee was still firmly a committee, among many other committees, in the Foreign

Office and an annex of the News Department, but soon became more independent of its master – adopting the name 'British Council' in 1936.[28]

Developments in other European countries

The French, through the *Alliance Française*, had been operating in foreign countries since the nineteenth century and it had been expanding its work throughout the period of the French Third Republic. The French Government, noted Philip Taylor in his analysis and comparison of how Britain projected an image of itself abroad in the 1930s,

> regarded cultural relations as an effective method of creating an atmosphere favourable to the extension of political and commercial interests by bringing the full weight of the national cultural heritage to bear in support of its foreign and economic policies and of its political prestige abroad.[29]

All of the major European powers, as well as Japan, had similar organizations to the *Alliance Française* by the time of Second World War, and the British Council, representing Britain in a similar capacity, had to be there fighting Britain's corner against the backdrop of a range of competing national interests. Germany had the *Auslandschulen* and the *Deutsche Akademie*; the Soviet Union had the *V.O.K.S.* (All-Union Society for Cultural Relations with Foreign Countries); Italy had the *Dante Alighieri* Society; and Japan had the *Kokusai Bunkwa Shinko Kwai* (Society for the Promotion of International Cultural Relations).[30] All of these cultural organizations had been established prior to the British Council's inauguration in December 1934 and so the Council was always playing a game of catch-up in fighting Britain's corner. Just to give a sense of the scale of the British Council's task, the *Deutsche Akademie* had over 250 language schools in Europe during Second World War.[31] Admittedly, it had a lot more of Europe available in which it could operate, and most of it was not neutral territory, but still it gives a good feel for the extent of the German cultural propaganda at this time. The Germans already had four language institutions in the Franco-controlled areas of Spain by 1938, during the civil war, well before the British Council arrived with just one institute in 1940.[32] The Germans had been heavily influenced by the French model of first promoting its language, with the aim of following that knowledge of its language abroad with the promotion of other forms of its culture. A German study of French cultural propaganda by Karl Remme and Margarete Esch, published in 1927, had been highly significant in the German development of cultural propaganda, even prior to the Nazi takeover of power in 1933.[33] Ironically, the German expansion of cultural propaganda actually slowed down in the mid to late 1930s, as the Nazi Government did not see it as a priority against other spending demands (particularly the money being spent on rearmament). It was the expansion of the British Council's work in the late 1930s, as well as continued French influence, that spurred the Nazi Government into expanding its cultural work exponentially again. In 1940, the former head of the *Deutsche Akademie*, Franz Thierfelder, wrote a booklet titled *Englischer Kulturimperialismus: Der 'British Council' als Werkzeug der geistigen Einkreisung Deutschlands* (translated as: 'English[34] Cultural Imperialism: The "British Council" as a tool for the mental encirclement of Germany') in an attempt to demonstrate the threat posed by the British Council to Germany, which Thierfelder thought was politically inspired.[35] Thierfelder had been sidelined by the Nazis in 1937, and was restricted to only writing publications at this time, so this booklet should be viewed partially as an attempt to reassert his influence in the field of German cultural diplomacy. Nevertheless, it also must be viewed as having the tacit agreement of the Nazi Government, otherwise it would not have been published nor had such influence in (re)forming Nazi cultural policy.[36] Clearly, the British Council was seen within Nazi Germany as a force to be reckoned with and in response, during Second World War, the *Deutsche Akademie*'s budget rose from 1 million Reichmarks (R.M.) in 1940 to 7 million R.M. in 1944.[37] The Council, though feared by the Nazi Government, was clearly not going to be operating in a vacuum in any of the neutral countries in Europe.

As the biographer of Lord Lloyd, Colin Forbes Adam, concluded, the British Council's rise, though helping to promote an understanding of Britain in the period just prior to the war, had not begun early enough to make a real difference immediately. It is no small point to state that though the D'Abernon Report had overturned the British Government's attitude to cultural propaganda it took another five years before the British Council was established, and longer still to turn the Council into a viable and proactive cultural propaganda organization under Lloyd's chairmanship. Forbes Adam stated '[t]he important and melancholy fact was that the Council started too late in the day in a race where the competitors, Germany and Italy, had several laps start and infinitely greater resources'.[38]

Clearly, in Forbes Adam's view, the procrastination and delays evident after First World War in establishing a British Council-like organization, as described earlier in this chapter, failed to provide a basis on which the British Council could succeed in helping to prevent Second World War. Harold Nicolson, the Member of Parliament and someone who later went on lecture tours under the auspices of the British Council, summed up the reason for the delay in an article for the British Council's 21st anniversary in 1955. His words, even with a bit too much artistic licence, help summarize the situation the British Council found itself in, in the 1930s:

> In the nineteenth century there may have been some justification for this imperturbability. Great Britain was regarded abroad as the champion of liberal institutions and the pioneer of technical progress and invention . . . . The excellence of our institutions, the honesty of our middle class, the contentment of our proletariat, the amicable tolerance of all our ways, persuaded us that we were universally liked, respected and admired . . . .
>
> Our complacency was pierced by intimations that our best markets were being invaded by persistent and ingenious competition; even our self-assurance became clouded by the suspicion that foreigners did not invariably regard us as either so charming or so intelligent as we seemed to ourselves; and once aeroplanes came to crowd the sky above our island we realised that we had ceased to be the most invulnerable of the Great Powers and had become one of the most vulnerable . . . .
> It was then that we first realised that our foreign competitors had been devoting

effort, skill and large sums of money to rendering their languages, their type of civility, their scientific or technical resources and inventions, and the desirability of their exports, familiar to students and buyers overseas.[39]

However, it was as clear to the British Government as it was to many observers, that both the Axis powers and France (first as a British ally, then under the guise of the Vichy Regime) were going to be conducting propaganda abroad in a variety of ways – both politically and culturally. Just by being there, located on neutral territory, would be very much a political statement that they expected to be listened to, which would have an impact in some way on the local populations. The Axis powers would be very keen to take the initiative and take their message to neutral peoples in this way, and, either convince them to join the war when it came, or ensure their neutrality was benevolent towards the Axis. The British, through the guise of the British Council, simply had to do the same – even if they were latecomers compared with the Axis powers. To use a well-worn phrase that it was there to 'fly the flag' does not begin to describe its role of cultural relations, but this concept did play a role in its existence and purpose. Of course there were other organizations, not least the British Embassies and Consulates, that were also part of this role, and the British Council was there as part of that wider machinery of British presence in foreign countries. It was not just a matter of being seen to be there that was important. Ensuring (or at least trying to ensure) that British interests in the cultural field were treated in the same way as Axis interests, and preferably given favourable treatment, was a vital task. Britain had to be seen to be winning the (non-military) struggles against the Axis on neutral territory on the cultural battlefield – in a battle for neutral Europe.

The early years of the British Council

The British Council's establishment in 1934, though a direct result of the fear of, and the need to counter, German and Italian cultural propaganda, was still in a time of peace. In 1934, the threat from Germany in a military sense did not appear particularly great to the vast majority of observers. The Council's official statement of aims reproduced earlier in this book dating from soon after its establishment in 1935 may, therefore, seem to emanate from a period which had little in common with the wartime situation the Council found itself a few years later. Indeed, although Britain's declaration of war on Germany in September 1939 had only a very modest effect militarily until the following spring, it had two direct effects on the British Council. First, through the changing of the machinery of British Government with the establishment of the MOI in particular, the propaganda landscape within Whitehall was transformed overnight and the British Council's position was precarious and its continued existence in doubt. This situation, as shall be shown in later chapters, was resolved through intra-Governmental negotiations even though the decision to maintain the British Council in existence was to be revisited a number of times during the war. The second direct effect, and a more important effect from a conceptual point of view, was that the British Council necessarily became part of the British wartime propaganda armoury. Whether the Council liked it or not, the collective aim of that armoury, of which it was part, was to ensure everything necessary was done from a propaganda point of view to secure Britain's victory in the war against Germany. The outbreak of war, it seems, had changed everything.

An official statement of aims from 1935 may, at first then, seem somewhat irrelevant in September 1939, as the national political landscape had changed so significantly, yet it was this statement of aims that the Council tried to keep to throughout its wartime existence. In fact it did not just stop with Second World War. In 1984, Frances Donaldson, the author of the official version of the British Council's first 50 years, noted that the official statement would 'still serve as a fair description of the aims and objects of the British Council' with the exception of the terms 'Crown Colonies and Dependencies'.[40] As another point of comparison, in 2010 the British Council's purpose was stated in just one sentence – 'We build engagement and trust for the UK through the exchange and knowledge and ideas between people worldwide' – which reflects the age of the 'sound bite', but was still along the same lines, if more generalized, as the statement of aims from 1935.[41] It can be concluded that although the 1935 statement was lengthier than the statement of aims today, it was clearly not detailed enough to act as a blueprint for action relevant only to the year 1935, and deliberately so. The aims as expressed here were primarily aspirational and could be juxtaposed into a multitude of situations and time periods. By stating a high-level framework such as this, the Council gave itself inherent flexibility. That is not to say that this high-level statement was not important, or that the British Council assumed that its working environment would change so significantly in less than half a decade. However, it made its statement intentionally flexible enough to be applicable to the majority of countries in the world, and gives important clues to the overall strategy that the British Council aimed to follow and the type of person the British Council was aiming at then, and indeed throughout much of its history. But it does not provide a list of aims specific to the conditions of Second World War. To understand these it is essential to look at its target audience, the conditions it was working in and its proposed methods of operation.

The British Council's history from its establishment in late 1934 to the outbreak of war in 1939 was one of expansion in terms of grant increases, scope and geographical remit, and the influence of its third Chairman, Lord Lloyd, who dramatically changed the course of the Council in the late 1930s, after his appointment in 1937. The Council initially established sub-committees and advisory panels on special subjects, to draw in expertise from British cultural figures who were asked to become members. The first committees to be established in 1935 were: the Students committee – designed to bring foreign students to Britain; the Lectures committee – for organizing lecture tours on a range of cultural subjects in foreign countries by prominent British figures; the Fine Arts committee – for organizing British art exhibitions abroad; the Music Advisory committee – for organizing music concerts abroad involving the likes of distinguished British composers Ralph Vaughan Williams and Arthur Bliss; the Books and Periodicals committee – not only for supplying books abroad, but also to try to promote positive reviews of British books in foreign newspapers; the British Education Abroad committee (which closed in 1936, shortly after it had been established); and the Ibero-American committee stressing the emphasis at the time on Latin America, taking over the Ibero-American Institute of Great Britain. Before, or just after, the outbreak of war these were joined by the Near East committee led by Lord Lloyd before becoming Chairman in 1937, Drama and Dance committee, Films committee (preceded by a joint venture between the Travel Association and the British Council) and the Resident Foreigners committee.[42] All of these were aligned to the official statement of aims set in 1935.

Lord Lloyd transformed the Council from being a Committee of the Foreign Office at the time of his appointment in 1937 to an independent body secured by Royal Charter in the autumn of 1940. Lloyd was headstrong and determined to make the Council very much his own organization. He developed the Council into a structure that was capable of supporting its own work, and no longer needed to rely on the Foreign Office. Under his tenure of the Chairmanship, the Council became far more active and went out into the world by establishing institutes in Cairo and Lisbon and elsewhere in 1938. A. J. S. White, the Secretary-General of the British Council during Second World War, stated that

> the cause of the British Council attracted him [Lord Lloyd] above all other causes because of his deep belief in the value of British influence overseas and his realisation that this influence could be exerted no longer politically but only through such work as that of the Council. Lord Lloyd had a great capacity for infecting others with his own enthusiasm and it can be understood that with his own deep belief in the Council's aims, his great drive and his powerful contacts both at home and overseas, he was an almost ideal head of the Council in its youthful days. It is difficult to overestimate the stimulus given to the Council and its cause from having a man of Lord Lloyd's stature as its leader and most devoted adherent.[43]

As will be shown later in the book, Lord Lloyd's enthusiasm and drive for success were key reasons for the Council's survival at the outbreak of Second World War. At the time of Lloyd's appointment it was becoming increasing clear that the threat from the Fascist powers was real, and that the British point of view needed to be argued against the cultural propaganda of other countries. The D'Abernon Report had really started this process, of course, but it was now becoming obvious that British cultural propaganda was crucial. Apparent Italian ascendancy in the Mediterranean around the time of, and following, the Abyssinian Crisis alarmed Britain. Britain was particularly concerned that its influence in its own possessions – Egypt, Palestine, Malta and Cyprus – was under threat from Italian cultural propaganda. Appeals to the Treasury were now becoming more successful in increasing its grant from £5,000 in the 1935/36 financial year steadily increasing during this period to £330,249 in the 1939/40 financial year.[44]

The Council made its arguments for funding not only on the basis that cultural relations were necessary for promoting commercial interests, but for promoting an understanding between countries which would, in turn, be vital in preventing a repeat of First World War. It was an argument that seems to have gone down well with the Chancellor of the Exchequer, Neville Chamberlain.[45] Though it would be wrong to equate the rise of the British Council during this period with the rise of the policy of Appeasement – the details of the two were very different in many ways – their overall aim of promoting British interests through non-aggressive and non-military means can be seen as complementary. The Council's approach to the Treasury could be said to reflect Chamberlain's desire to find innovative ways to avoid conflict with Germany and an increase in the grant was always going to be likely with Chamberlain as Chancellor, even though he always took a cautious approach whenever the word 'propaganda' was involved.[46] Lloyd himself was certainly no fan of Appeasement, despite being on good terms with Chamberlain, having advocated rearmament since the early 1930s and seeing the British Council as another weapon in the armoury of British defences.[47] Anthony Eden too was one of the key players arguing for an increase in the Council's grant and influence in both his pre-war and wartime stints as Foreign Secretary, as will be shown later.[48] Eden's support for the Council is perhaps the best illustration of the difference between the Council's approach and the policy of Appeasement, but the arguments made to the Treasury during the late 1930s for an increase in the British Council's budget rested firmly on the basis that the Council could help prevent wars, not that it was an alternative weapon of war. This was an argument that changed, of course, as soon as the Munich Conference had failed and war broke out in September 1939.

By stating in 1935 that it was choosing to concentrate on 'British literature . . . music and fine arts, the sciences, philosophic thought and political practice' the British Council was showing that it was aiming at people who had the time to appreciate that kind of culture. To a great extent, the Council had little choice about its target audience – it was largely determined by the circumstances of war that the only people who were going to have the time to think about being pro-British actively in any meaningful way in neutral countries were the elites. The masses, partly through censorship restrictions, and partly because of the need to survive in whatever circumstances they found themselves, either did not have the time to think about where their sympathies lay or, if they did, did not have the influence or resources to act upon their sympathies. The people who had the time were necessarily elites and it can readily be assumed, therefore, that the Council was aiming at elites in preference to the masses – and this fits very well with the propaganda theories discussed in the previous chapter and the model of influence constructed in Figure 1.[49]

If the Council was not targeting the elites where (to cite one obvious example missing from its 1935 list of cultural forms) was the greatest and newest cultural mass medium phenomenon of the 1920s and 1930s – film? To be fair, the Council did sponsor a number of short films during the war, but it appears very much as an afterthought compared with music and fine arts (the Films Committee was established in 1939 whereas the Music Advisory Committee and the Fine Arts Committee were both established in 1935).[50] Excluding newsreels, there are 67 British Council films listed on the British Film Institute catalogue, with a per annum total of 12 produced in 1941, 1942, 1944 and 1945 (with less in other years) which averages as less than one a month in the whole war period.[51]

Equally, one could question whether the working classes in foreign countries really going to be interested in British 'philosophic thought' and 'fine arts'? Some may well have been, but it seems clear (at least from the official statement) that this was not who the British Council was aiming at, and 'cultural propaganda' as defined by the

British Council itself was not intended to be propaganda about popular culture, but so-called high culture. Good (i.e. effective) propagandists always keep their audience in mind and try to see how their propaganda will be viewed by their audience. There was little point in trying to promote popular culture to elites, or high culture to the masses, as the propaganda would sit uncomfortably with the respective audiences. This argument sits very well with Drout's 'Word-to-World Fit' proposition – that is, that the propaganda being promoted had to fit well with the audience's pre-existing views, and be credible for them to be influenced by it. It can be deduced that the elites were the key audience for the British Council to target and the Council's aim of promoting high, and more traditional, culture sat very well with the target audience. It will be tested throughout this book whether this assumption about its audience is a reasonable assumption to make, and how closely the 1935 official statement of aims can be said to have been followed.

From certain points of view, to aim solely at elites does seem somewhat surprising because the British Council was, from very early on, supported across all political parties. Clement Attlee, the leader of the Labour Party, for example, was on its Executive Board from 1936 to 1940 as were a number of Conservative MPs.[52] As we have seen, Arthur Henderson, the Labour Foreign Minister, was one of the key people who recognized the importance of cultural propaganda to commercial interests around the time the D'Abernon Report was produced. It was deliberately non-political in a partisan sense. Perhaps a pragmatic approach was taken by Attlee and other Labour politicians who realized that the leaders of many of the countries in Europe at the time (particularly Franco in Spain and Salazar in Portugal) were unlikely to be appreciative of purportedly left-wing propaganda. In the war itself there was the more important aim of keeping these right-wing dictators out of the war, rather than presenting a full picture of British culture – both high and popular – to the diverse audiences in the countries where the Council operated. While this pragmatism would be understandable during the war itself, it does seem to be somewhat paradoxical that Labour MPs would support an elite targeting organization during the pre-war period. Perhaps Labour MPs thought it best to work with an organization which may not immediately correspond with their aims but could be morphed over time to be a more mass targeting establishment once they were in a position of power. It is certainly important not to look at Labour's position solely from a twenty-first-century viewpoint with the knowledge that they would win the 1945 general election by a landslide – in the mid-1930s. Labour was still a young and inexperienced party that had held power only twice for very brief periods and could not be said to be a credible 'alternative Government' at this point. Labour MPs had to work with what existed in the mid-1930s. To examine this paradox in detail would take this book off at a tangent and out of its scope of concentrating on the war period. However, the important point to note here is that all political parties supported the British Council and clearly saw value in the Council having the aim purportedly of targeting elites for foreign countries and to spread British high culture abroad. So what value was there in targeting the elites?

Concentrating on the elites had a number of advantages. It had been already noted in First World War by British propagandists that 'it [was] better to influence those who can influence others than attempt a direct appeal to the mass of the population' when the British were trying to influence neutral American opinion.[53] It was 'better' in three senses. First, if there was pre-existing pro-British sympathy in neutral countries, there was likely to be a high proportion of it residing in the elites. As has been stated the elites were more likely to have the time to think about where their sympathies lay and to have vested interests in their sympathies. It is true that this also means that the elites also had the opportunity to think about whether their sympathy should lie with Britain's enemies – but at least there should be a pocket of genuine pro-Britishness among them due to the elites having more ability to be free thinking. The masses by contrast would not have the same amount of time to think about where their sympathies lay and would be more subject to political propaganda in neutral countries telling them where their sympathies should lie. The second reason was that those pro-British elites were likely to have networks of influence which they already used and knew worked (otherwise they were unlikely to be in the position of an elite – elites generally, by definition, are influential and opinion-forming) – if one can persuade an elite, they can generally induce sympathy elsewhere in the population both in terms of the indifferent and hostile elites as well as the masses. The model of influence that I constructed in Figure 1 demonstrates how influencing the pro-British elites could have a chain reaction effect to influence these other groups, and demonstrates how meme theory that was described earlier could work in practice. The primary audience here was viewed as a channel to reach a wider audience rather than solely as a receptacle itself.[54] Also by using pre-existing networks of influence the Universal Tradition Meme described by Drout would naturally become more dominant in the sense that the connection to the original motives behind spreading information will become less and less obvious the further down the network the information spreads. The third reason why it was better to influence the elites was that, as elites were by definition less numerous than the masses, concentrating on a small number of people would allow a very effective method of propaganda to be utilized – propaganda by word-of-mouth, which will be explored a little later.

The Council has often been under pressure throughout its history with regard to the image of Britain that it is trying to promote, usually from those areas of society which do not feel they are being adequately represented by the Council, or think other areas of society are being over-represented. In the following chapter, this issue will be explored in detail with regard to how the Council dealt with the competing array of interests that were vying for influence. This will particularly reference the criticisms levelled by Lord Beaverbrook, both newspaper proprietor and Minister of Aircraft Production (May 1940–May 1941) – and a former Minister of Information from the First World War period. The Council's concentration on the elites produced one consistent theme of criticism. Many have viewed this concentration as a problem because it missed out a large section, indeed the majority section, of British society and therefore produces a distorted image of Britain to foreign countries. Other critics have usually questioned the value of cultural propaganda in any sense, high or popular. The *Daily Mirror*, which was aimed at a mass working class readership, ran an article in November 1944 which crystallized the essence of many of the complaints about the British Council's work in both its early years, and the wartime period, and reinforced the impression that the British Council was providing a skewed 'high culture' image of Britain to foreign elites, and was not worth supporting. The article is worth quoting at some length:

> . . .they [The British Council] have in the past week rendered yeoman service to the Empire by finding a deerstalking expert willing to teach his art to the Spaniards, and a scholar from Brighton ready to enlighten the natives of Cyprus on the works of Aristotle on which he is an authority . . . .
>
> The Swedes have had some real treats. Here are a few of them:
>
> Mr. T. S. Eliot lectured to them on 'Poetry, Speech and Music.'
>
> Professor Holford delivered five lectures on British architecture.
>
> Dr. Darlington spoke on 'Cylology' and 'For more general audiences, on Darwinism.'
>
> Even Iceland was not forgotten. The Council sent a pianist there who gave 'five very successful concerts.'
>
> The Council is probably the only institution which has ever been paid by a Government to propagate snobbery. If you don't believe me, listen to this statement by one of its ex-chairmen:
>
> 'We are not catering for the lower type who might like a cup of cocoa or a sing-song. We are proposing to entertain the more intellectual . . . those who would appreciate and understand a higher type of British culture.'
>
> I know that our export trade is in a dreadful state, but snobbery is the one thing we cannot afford to send abroad. Not even as reverse Lend Lease.[55]

It is not possible to verify the accuracy of the 'ex-chairman's statement' as this is not documented elsewhere and if said, is unlikely to have been a written statement. Second, the writer clearly was not aware of the history of cultural propaganda in a wider sense when stating that '[t]he Council is probably the only institution which has ever been paid by a Government to propagate snobbery' – as we shall see, if this type of work was indeed 'snobbery', the *Alliance Française* had been at it since the 1880s. However, the point of view held by the *Daily Mirror* was one that was commonly uttered by the mass press. Newspaper proprietors believed that propaganda was better focused on enemies directly and that sympathy for the British cause in neutral countries would be created naturally by the awe of military success against the enemy. There was no need, in their view, to spend money talking about British culture (high or popular) abroad, as it would have little effect compared to that sympathy created by military success. Admittedly cultural propaganda is primarily a long-term phenomenon and cannot expect to have the same immediate effect as military success in changing opinions, but its effect can be more profound in the long term. It was mentioned above that effective propagandists keep their audiences in mind when creating propaganda. High culture being promoted to elites could be effective (on the assumption that it was promoted well). Mass audiences (in Britain or indeed abroad) were unlikely ever to see the value of the British Council promoting high culture however well it was presented as they were not the intended audience. Lord Beaverbrook in particular, and the late Lord Northcliffe's family (both Lords had been active in the British propaganda campaign in First World War), knew this perfectly well. Beaverbrook in particular knew that focusing on the 'snobbish' elements of the Council's work was more likely to sell newspapers to a mass audience (an audience to whom the Council's propaganda was not aimed and would therefore irritate), and provide momentum to his view that the Council should be closed down. If the Council was promoting snobbery, it is equally true that it was aiming at snobs, not the masses. As one analysis of targeting intellectuals through propaganda has concluded,

> [t]here are not many intellectuals in the world, and therefore an intellectual is flattered by intellectual approaches. . . . They can be approached with more subtle arguments, greater cando[u]r, more direct discussion of the opponent's ideology, longer commentaries, more discussion of the relative credibility of courses, and distinctions between what is certain and what is merely probable.[56]

In other words, though the terms 'elites', 'intellectuals' and 'snobs' are arguably not entirely synonymous, the Council's propaganda had to be designed to fit with the needs of its elitist audience, and could not be fully understood by the masses as its propaganda was not designed to be received by them. Many of the Council's critics took the Council's work out of context and did not give credit to the wider benefits of its work. For example, stating the rather bland fact that 'Mr. T. S. Eliot lectured to them [the Swedes] on "Poetry, Speech, and Music"' does not even attempt to describe the impact that his visit made on Swedish opinion. It does not describe the tone of the Council's work, and how this tone compared with what the Swedes were used to receiving in terms of propaganda from other sources. Nor does it begin to allow the reader to understand how his visit, while not turning the tide of Swedish opinion on its own, was one of many, by a variety of different British personalities, which incrementally accumulated increasing pro-British feeling among the Swedish population. Eliot's visit will be examined in detail in the chapter titled 'On the front line', but the important point here to note is that the Council's aims cannot simply be described as wanting to 'entertain' neutral elites. There was a far deeper aim of sympathy-creation which was a key, if under-recognized, part of the British propaganda effort and war effort in general. Targeting elites in the 'language' they understood was the cornerstone of that effort.

The British Council and the approach of war

The war situation necessarily limited the field of operation for the British Council in a geographical sense. Having opened its first overseas institute in Egypt in 1938, followed closely by others in Portugal, Poland and Romania in the same year, the Council had plans to expand rapidly across the Middle East, Europe and South America.[57] Though the war had not changed the aspirations of the Council, the war most definitely changed the extent to which those aspirations were achievable. First, the Council could not operate in what were now enemy countries – Germany first, then Italy and Japan – and had to quickly withdraw operations in countries that were invaded by the Axis powers. Table 1 outlines the institutes that were opened and closed in Europe during the war period. It shows that the Council's work ceased in the institutes it had already established in Poland, Italy, Yugoslavia, Greece, Bulgaria and Romania in quick succession as those countries were invaded or submitted to Axis influence. British Council staff had to be evacuated along with the staff of the British Embassies. In Europe, this left nine countries where the Council could possibly operate: Spain, Portugal, Sweden, Turkey[58], Switzerland, Malta, Cyprus, Iceland and Eire (the part of the island of Ireland today constituting the Republic of Ireland). Malta, Cyprus and Iceland were all either part of the British Empire or were under British control during the war, and so were not, or cannot be regarded as, neutral. They are consequently not within the scope of this book except in passing. Eire, though regarded by the British Government as part of its Empire, *was* officially neutral but, as we shall see, was not considered as a location for operations by the British Council to the same extent as other neutral countries because of the political difficulties that existed there, particularly with regard to Anglo-Irish relations. These difficulties arose especially as a result of the Irish Civil War and the Partition between Northern Ireland and Eire – the limited extent of the Council's operations in Eire will be examined in more detail in the next chapter. Switzerland was very difficult to travel to, owing to the fact that it was surrounded by Axis and Axis-occupied countries, and consequently the Council's work there was restricted to utilizing British materials already in the country (lantern slides, literature etc.) and notionally supporting the work of pro-British communities to promote the British cause.[59] This left only four countries in Europe – Spain, Portugal, Sweden and Turkey – where the Council could, and did, operate in any meaningful way for the majority of the war period. All four of which, of course, were neutral countries but being neutral did not mean that they were in any way immune from the effects of Second World War. Neutrality was rarely a passive notion and had to be enforced through censorship restrictions and trade agreements. Spain, for example, had recently emerged from a civil war and its new leadership, under General Franco, had relied on German and Italian assistance in order to be victorious. Spain, it appeared at least, looked on the verge of joining the Axis a number of times during Second World War, though Spanish-Axis relations were far more complex than is often realized.[60] Turkey feared that it would go the same way as much of the Balkans and be invaded by German or Italian forces which it was not in a position militarily to resist.[61] Sweden had only been spared invasion by Germany during the Scandinavian campaign in early 1940 because it did not have a North Sea coast (and therefore unlikely to be invaded by Britain) and Germany considered that it would be easier to obtain the raw materials it needed for its war effort (of which Sweden had many) from a 'free' country than from an occupied country. By being surrounded by Axis-occupied or aligned countries (in the case of Finland), Sweden was always going to be wary of irritating Germany so it could maintain its neutral position. Sweden also feared the Soviet Union, which until 1941, was a German ally.[62] Only Portugal can be said to have been in a position geographically where the Council could operate without fear of German troops marching across the border directly. However, politically Portugal was still wary of antagonizing Germany and Portugal's leader, Oliveira Salazar, had sympathies with many aspects of Nazi political thought. Within each of these four countries there were also separatist movements (for example Catalans and Basques in Spain, and Armenians and Kurds in Turkey) and an array of internal political and social differences which meant the Council had to act very carefully and have a good understanding of the position on the ground to ensure it did not antagonize these different elements to the detriment of the British cause.

Table 1 The British Council's presence in Europe (1938–45)

	1938–39	1940	1941	1942	1943	1944	1945
Countries in which the British Council opened an institute	6	6	1	0	0	5	8
	Greece	Bulgaria	Sweden	–	–	Belgium	Czechoslovakia
	Italy	Cyprus				France	Denmark
	Malta	Iceland				Gibraltar	Finland
	Poland	Spain				Greece	Hungary
	Portugal	Turkey				Luxembourg	Italy
	Romania	Yugoslavia					Netherlands
							USSR
							Yugoslavia
Countries where the British Council had to close institutes	1	2	3	0	0	0	0
	Poland	Italy	Bulgaria	–	–	–	
		Romania	Greece				
			Yugoslavia				
Net opened	5	4	–2	0	0	5	8
Total number open	5	9	7	7	7	12	20

Source: Figures calculated from list of countries in Donaldson, 1984, pp. 373–6 (Appendix 3: 'Countries in which the British Council is or has been represented').

The Council's field of operation in Europe, therefore, did not look particularly propitious. Its choice of audience was severely limited by circumstances, both geographically and politically. Not only were there merely four countries where it could operate, therefore, but it was evident that within all four there were always likely to be restrictions in the way the Council could operate. Yet, there was pro-British sympathy in all four countries – partly from an ideological point of view and partly because of commercial and trade reasons.[63] The British Council could, and had to, nurture that pro-British sympathy if it was to make any headway in these countries. It is also reasonable to assume that just as extreme pro-British feeling was rare, so was extreme anti-British feeling. Indifferent feeling was far more common, and could be reached if propaganda was directed carefully.[64] The Council had to think very carefully about its methods of operation in order to make a pervasive impact which could contribute significantly to the war effort through keeping those four countries out of the war.

Just existing on neutral territory was clearly not enough from both the point of view that it needed to compete with other countries and also the need to actively sell the image of Britain abroad. It had to organize cultural events in order to be noticed and to win those propaganda battles against the Axis powers. Its organization of cultural events was an attempt to meet two key separate, though linked, objectives. First, it genuinely wanted to satisfy interest (and create it, if it did not already exist) in British culture within the neutral populations. It has already been discussed what type of neutral person the Council was aiming at – that is, the elites – and it will be discussed in later chapters how far that interest already existed in neutral populations, and how those populations reacted to the British Council's activities. As has already been mentioned, it was a reasonable assumption that there would be some kind of interest in the background of Britain as the only country holding out militarily against Germany for a significant proportion of the war. It may not necessarily have been entirely a sympathetic interest, and that interest may have been shaped by a whole range of other influences – historical knowledge, political propaganda, censorship and the like – but it was an interest that would most definitely have been there. As was mentioned earlier, George West, who became the British Council's representative in Portugal, had for some time been urging the British Government that there was a need among the Portuguese population for cultural interchange with Britain.[65] The opening of the British Council's institute in Lisbon prior to the outbreak of war showed that this need had already been recognized in Portugal. There were similar needs elsewhere, although less obvious than they had been in Portugal. The main events that the Council would organize were lecture tours (from eminent figures in British academic life – historians, scientists, musicians and artists in particular), art exhibitions, music concerts, book exhibitions and the teaching of the English language (which gave neutral peoples the tool to find out more about Britain and the English-speaking world). The type of cultural event that would be organized stemmed directly from its 1935 statement of aims and these events will be examined in detail in the chapter titled 'On the front line'.

The second objective that the Council had to meet in organizing cultural events was to draw people together. The Council well understood that the cultural events created the perfect excuse for British people to meet with neutral peoples to discuss a wide range of issues. Indeed, it would not really matter what the cultural events actually consisted of and could be lacking in a specific theme (a cocktail party to welcome a particular lecturer to the country was as good a cultural event as an art exhibition or music concert), as long as it achieved the objective of drawing people together. This objective can be split into two sub-sections. First, by establishing institutes and organizing events, the Council could provide a much-needed focus for people who were already sympathetic to Britain, and those who became sympathetic during the war, to meet. Second, it was mentioned earlier that targeting elites allowed word-of-mouth propaganda to be utilized by the Council staff because of the small numbers of people involved and this could be very effective.

The British Council's aim to spread propaganda via word-of-mouth was not a new, nor a unique idea. Bolshevik Agitators had been very active before, during and after the Russian Revolution in 1917. Word-of-mouth techniques were also used in a number of ways in Second World War by Joseph Goebbels's 'rumour-mongers', and the British 'sib' (whispering) campaign, to disseminate rumours in neutral countries.[66] But the British 'sib' and German *Flüsterpropaganda*, campaigns were clandestine, and often aimed at the masses to try to spread discontent among them – something quite different from the British Council's way of operating. The British Council's audience, as we have seen, was an elitist one, and so the word-of-mouth propaganda could be more overt, though restricted to a smaller initial audience (which also meant there was more control over the initial message), and designed to spread a more positive image of British culture abroad. Nevertheless, there are a number of points which relate the British Council use of word-of-mouth propaganda in the margins of cultural events to rumour-spreading in its aim of promoting the British way of life – and will be explored in 'On the front line'.

Conclusion

There are a number of themes in the previous chapters which need to be summarized and drawn into a framework in which the work of the British Council can be analysed over the following chapters. It can be concluded that the 1935 statement of aims outlined at the beginning, although a useful aspirational summary, does not give enough detail to be seen as a blueprint for wartime objectives. Nevertheless, it gives important clues as to the type of propaganda that the British Council was aiming to produce and the type of person it was aiming at. Its aim was to present an image of Britain to neutral countries which the Council thought was a truthful and accurate one and was not seen as 'propaganda' in a derogatory sense – they were presenting Britain as they thought it actually existed. This links very well with the sociological propaganda model that Ellul produced in which he demonstrated that cultures are already made up of self-perpetuating currents of thought which do not need a propaganda organization to promote them as the people within that society just think of it as their way of life. The British Council employees were clearly not naïve enough to think that British culture had only to be exposed abroad, and would be readily consumed without any direction and promotion by the Council itself. The Council was not working in a vacuum and there were plenty of other cultural organizations promoting other nations in the neutral countries. Neutrality in those countries, too, was not a passive policy and the Council would have to actively fight against it as well as Axis influence to become successful. The British Council had to fight Britain's corner on the cultural battlefield and make sure the culture that the Council was presenting was heard above the furore of other interests. Having said that, the Council was going to have to produce propaganda that was acceptable to the audience it was trying to persuade. Its propaganda had to mould into the existing sociological contexts. By aiming for influential pro-British elites, and in order to reach indifferent and hostile elites who effectively ran the neutral countries (as well as eventually reaching the masses through a chain of secondary influences), the Council was going to have to create propaganda that they would be interested in. This would mean that the projection of timeless, conservative themes of high culture was absolutely necessary to reaching these elites. The elites were the people who had the time to appreciate the propaganda and creating propaganda that they were interested in was essential. Those high culture events could then also be used for word-of-mouth propaganda which, as will be shown, is one of the most effective forms of propaganda both in terms of ability to persuade, but also in circumventing censorship restrictions and being difficult to trace. The cultural propaganda of the British Council, if conducted effectively, was going to be instrumental in persuading the elites of the neutral countries to take a more sympathetic view of wartime Britain through the range of techniques that the Council was aiming to deploy. The Council's story, which will unfold in the following chapters, is one of battling on a long-term, incremental basis for the hearts and minds of neutral Europe with an attempt to achieve a widespread influence slowly penetrating more deeply into the existing sociological situations. Other more direct and immediate propaganda may be better known and more impressive in terms of being more tangible and having an immediate and visual impact. The Council, as has been shown and will continue to be shown, has often been criticized for carrying out propaganda that was only 'entertaining snobs'. Its work could be seen as a waste of taxpayers' money at any time, let alone at a time of war, but critics only had a very narrow understanding of the Council's work during the war. Its wider implications had the potential to be profound. Political and more immediate and visual propaganda could not have been as successful in neutral Europe at critical points in Second World War without the work of the British Council, behind the scenes, preparing the ground for direct action.

At Home: The British Council's Relationships with Other Organizations

Relations with the British Government

The Foreign Office was the British Council's patron. In a letter to the Foreign Secretary, Anthony Eden, in August 1942, the British Council's Chairman, Sir Malcolm Robertson, described Eden as the British Council's 'godfather'.[1] And it was true – the Foreign Office had created the British Council in 1934 and had championed its cause ever since its creation. The Foreign Secretary had the role of appointing the Council's Chairman, many of their staff were seconded from the Foreign Office, and the Foreign Office had a dedicated member of staff responsible for overseeing the Council's affairs.[2] The extent to which it supported the Council is evidenced by the role that the Foreign Office played in September 1939 and February 1941 when its very existence appeared in doubt.

In September 1939, at the outbreak of war, the Council was in danger of being swallowed up by the newly created Ministry of Information. Detailed planning for the Ministry's formation had begun a number of months prior to the outbreak of war, and relations between the British Council and the embryonic Ministry got off to a bad start – and got worse before they improved later in the war.[3] When rumours started spreading in June 1939 of its intended formation, Lord Lloyd was embarrassed to admit to his Executive Committee that he 'had not in fact been informed or consulted on the subject by anyone', to which his Committee 'expressed surprise' that the Council 'should not have been consulted'.[4] Worse still for the Council, it was far from guaranteed that it would survive and even if it did there was a real possibility that it would only survive as a shadow of its former self. It was generally assumed that with the outbreak of war there would be an immediate bombing campaign by Germany over Britain, and London in particular, and that the Council would be unable to carry on its work independently as its staff would be on Territorial Army duty. The most likely outcome, it was assumed, would be a mothballing of the Council until after the war.[5] A minute by a Treasury official in September 1939 stated the belief that the 'best course would be for the Ministry [of Information] to assume effective control over the Council's expenditure', and that the Foreign Office would be 'acting on the advice of the Ministry'.[6] A couple of weeks later the same Treasury official formally acknowledged that 'the Ministry are now the Department responsible for the Council'.[7] Lord Lloyd, however, was having none of it. A few days after the outbreak of war he was back in the Council's offices determined not only to ensure the survival of the Council, but also to actually expand its activities during the war.[8] He even had the audacity to suggest to Lord Macmillan, the first Minister of Information, that far from the Ministry absorbing the British Council, the British Council should take over parts of the Ministry.[9] At any rate, Lloyd was anxious for the Council not to be 'under' the Ministry (to the dismay of the Treasury), even if it had to work with it.[10]

Many months of political haggling followed involving the Ministry of Information, the British Council, the Foreign Office and the Treasury. Lord Lloyd was fully supported by the Foreign Office in defending the Council's remit.[11] Lord Halifax, the Foreign Secretary at this time, made his views clear when he wrote to the Chancellor of the Exchequer, Sir John Simon, stating that he and the Foreign Office were not only fully behind the continued existence of the British Council, but also that the British Council was a major weapon in the war:

> To my mind the Council's cultural work is just as important as the political propaganda of the Ministry of Information. Our cultural achievements are one of our greatest assets in presenting our case against Nazi Germany: and it is surely vital that we should keep them constantly in evidence in neutral countries, so that they can see that we are able to maintain, and even to extend, our cultural influence in spite of the strain of war. The British Council is the proper body to do this, and I think that they should be given every encouragement in their task.[12]

Halifax's view that there was a difference between political and cultural propaganda, and that these two elements of propaganda should not be mixed, became the focus of the negotiations and also the main tenet of the Foreign Office's defence of the British Council's continued existence throughout the war. Halifax, however, left Lloyd to settle the issue with Sir John (and soon to be, from October 1940, Lord) Reith, who replaced Lord Macmillan as Minister of Information in January 1940. Halifax regarded Lloyd and Reith as 'two wasps . . . fighting one another' due to their equally matched ferocity when defending their territory, and had no wish to get involved with the detail.[13] Sir Robert Bruce Lockhart, a Foreign Office official, noted in his diary that 'Reith's terms were too hot for Lloyd', and that Lloyd feared that there would never be an agreement when there was such a lack of goodwill from Reith.[14] Without an agreement, the whole of the Council's work in the 1940/41 Financial Year was under threat, as the Treasury took 'the line that they [would] not settle his [Lord Lloyd's] estimate . . . until agreement [had] been reached as to the respective spheres of the Ministry and the Council'.[15] With this in mind, no doubt, eventually Lloyd and Reith did reach an agreement. They agreed that there would be a demarcation of duties between them with the Ministry in charge of political propaganda, and the Council in charge of cultural propaganda, just as Halifax had suggested. There always remained 'boundary disputes' (as has been noted earlier, the definition of 'cultural propaganda' is not clear cut, so the split between cultural and political propaganda would always be somewhat arbitrary), but these were settled through close liaison and regular meetings between the Council and the Ministry throughout the war.[16] Figure 2 (the British Government's propaganda organizations during Second World War) shows the complicated relationship between the MOI and the British Council, and indeed, other organizations within the British Government's structure with an interest in propaganda.

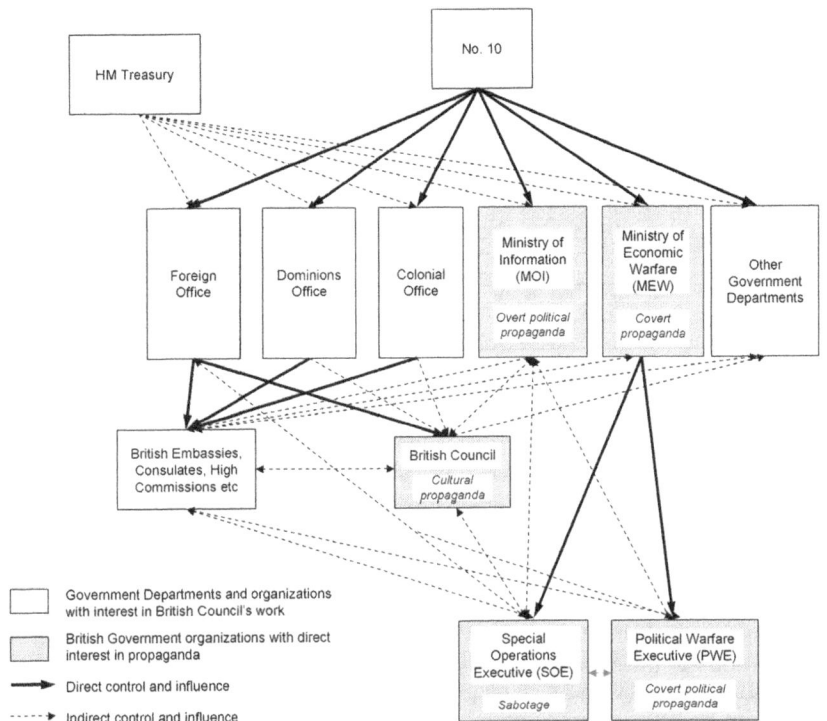

Figure 2 The British Government's propaganda organizations during Second World War.

Between this agreement and the British Council's next threat to its survival in February 1941, there were many varying views within the British Government as to the value of maintaining the Council. For example, a number of powerful personalities such as Lord Beaverbrook, as mentioned earlier, campaigned for the Council to be closed down. Bruce Lockhart noted that '[c]ultural propaganda, admittedly not much use in wartime – is beyond [Beaverbrook's] comprehension and attitude to life!'[17] As is clear from Bruce Lockhart's quotation, he too had his doubts as to the value of the British Council's work. Both Beaverbrook's and Bruce Lockhart's views reflected a wider unease about the British Council within the British Government. The problem was that during the summer of 1940, when Britain's very survival was at stake, spending money on cultural propaganda did not seem the best use of Britain's resources – as cultural propaganda was something for the long term, it should take a lower priority in the short term. Clearly, the Zahavi and Wight theories, mentioned previously, would have meant nothing to Lord Beaverbrook. The Beaverbrook newspaper, *Daily Express*, wrote, just prior to the outbreak of war, that

> Which is the best propaganda for us – the roar of . . . British bombers and fighters, or the melody of madrigals broadcast by the British Council? If we save the money wasted by the Council, we could have three extra squadrons of fighters to join the display.[18]

Beaverbrook's opinions about the Council, which were reflected in his newspapers, had a profound effect on the Council's work throughout its history, not just during Second World War. Frances Donaldson, in her official history of the Council published in 1984, noted that

> throughout its history it [the Council] has been able to attract the services of original and talented people who have been unconcerned with this consistent, cleverly-directed attack [by the Beaverbrook press]; but the [Beaverbrook] propaganda has in general had an appallingly weakening effect. Lord Beaverbrook died twenty years ago, but at the time of writing it is almost impossible to be in the company of a British Council officer of any length of service without his name coming up.[19]

Donaldson outlined the many criticisms made by Lord Beaverbrook in her book, who she described as 'one of the few deliberately wicked men in British history', so there is no need to repeat them here.[20] It is ironic that one of the greatest propaganda advocates from First World War should be the Council's greatest critic for carrying out cultural propaganda work, but it was something the Council would have to learn to bear and deal with. Of course, it was not just Beaverbrook who was opposed to the Council's work, and other newspapers certainly made their anti-Council views known as the article from the *Daily Mirror* mentioned previously demonstrated, but Beaverbrook was the most vocal opponent.[21] Some non-Beaverbrook papers like the *Daily Telegraph* noted, however, that 'reports of the [British] Council being possibly absorbed by the war-time Propaganda Ministry in London have produced most unfavourable reactions in a number of foreign countries where British institutes are already in being'.[22] This view was echoed within many areas of the Government – and, increasingly, in the Ministry of Information itself, as one of its officials commented, '[w]e must remember that the name of the British Council is established and that it may be a good cover for activities parallel to those of the Ministry of Information'.[23] It was this view, that it would be an own-goal in propaganda terms to close down a British institution that was becoming firmly established abroad (and it could be an advantage to the MOI to keep the British Council separate), and the steadfast nature of Lord Lloyd's personality, that saw the British Council survive through its first year of war. The attacks of Reith and Beaverbrook had been thwarted and in October 1940 the British Council's existence was secured (at least in theory) by a Royal Charter.[24]

The sudden death of Lord Lloyd in February 1941 deprived the Council of its greatest asset, particularly with regard to its defence against the likes of Beaverbrook, but also in advocating an expansion of its work. Once again, the Council's future appeared precarious – and this was only four months after its Royal Charter had been published, which was meant to secure its future. The Prime Minister, Winston Churchill, was sceptical of the British Council's continued worth, stating 'I should have thought that with the M[inistry] of E[conomic] W[arfare] on one side and the M[inistry] of I[nformation] on the other there was very little place for it [the British Council]'.[25] 'On the whole', Churchill went on, 'I am inclined to think that its usefulness ended with the death of Lord Lloyd'.[26] Churchill was considerate enough, however, to seek the views of Eden, now Foreign Secretary, and a number of other Cabinet members, and was not going to close down the Council unilaterally. In reply to Churchill's letter to him, Eden stated

> I attach great importance to the work of the British Council. I was responsible for the early development of its work when I was last Foreign Secretary. In my view it would be a grave error to close it down now after all the effort that has been put into it.[27]

Without the Foreign Office's support, and in particular Eden's support, it was probably unlikely that the British Council would have survived. The Foreign Office's defence of the British Council had many reasons, and was not merely a personal 'pet project' of the Foreign Secretary, as the above quotation could suggest. There was a genuine belief in the Foreign Office that the British Council was an organization worth patronizing owing to its attempts, and apparent success, in promoting good relations with foreign countries through cultural exchange. As a minute by R. A. Butler, Under Secretary of State for Foreign Affairs, described:

> . . .the success of the Council's work in Greece, where a cultural convention has been signed between our two countries, in Turkey, in Portugal and in Spain, to take only four examples, makes the Foreign Office attach vital importance to the distinction between cultural propaganda and education on the one hand and political propaganda on the other. We think it essential that the former kind of activity, if it is to maintain its influence, should be carried out independently of the wartime political propaganda, and in close association with the general lines of our foreign policy.[28]

There are clearly strong similarities here between what Butler was describing and the models of propaganda examined earlier – specifically the Bolshevik, Doob's sub-propaganda and Ellul's sociological propaganda models – which proposed that short-term political propaganda should build on the foundations laid by long-term cultural propaganda, if it is to be successful.

Yet, genuine though Butler's views were, there was also a strong element of a power struggle within the British Government, which influenced the Foreign Office's hand. The Foreign Office believed that as it was the British Government's primary actor abroad, it should control all of Britain's publicity and propaganda abroad, particularly in wartime, to ensure that a coherent British point of view was communicated to foreign countries. However, with the creation of the Ministry of Information, as well as other organizations that played a role in propaganda abroad – such as the Ministry of Economic Warfare, the Political Warfare Executive and the Special Operations Executive – the Foreign Office's control over propaganda had become diluted. The British Council, therefore, was the only organization over which the Foreign Office had complete ownership and it fought fiercely to protect it and its interests from other Government Departments. The complicated nature of the British propaganda machine is demonstrated in Figure 2.

The Foreign Office's complete ownership of the British Council was an issue for more than just the Ministry of Information, for more practical reasons. Although the Foreign Office was the Government's primary actor abroad, 'foreign' at this time excluded the Colonies (the remit of the Colonial Office) and the Dominions (the remit of the Dominions Office). The British Council operated not only in 'foreign' countries, but also in the Colonies and Dominions, where the Foreign Office had no jurisdiction and, in the words of a Ministry of Information official, the Council could 'not be regarded as experts in propaganda there'.[29] The British Council also had a hand in organizing events within Britain itself, such as organizing lectures for Prisoners of War and on food rationing.[30] Although this is largely an issue that is outside the scope of this book in concentrating on neutral Europe, it also had an effect on the arguments about whether the Foreign Office should maintain control of the Council, and is important to consider. The Colonial and Dominions Offices were represented on the British Council's Executive Committee, but there was still a concern that '[t]here is practical evidence of the failure of the British Council to consult the Dominions Office or Colonial Office in regard to their activities in the Dominions or Colonies'. The MOI argued that it should at least have a veto over material sent by the British Council to the Empire, even if it did not absorb the Council.[31]

As mentioned earlier, Eire was a neutral country during Second World War like Spain, Portugal, Sweden and Turkey. However, unlike those countries, it did not have relations with the Foreign Office. As part of the British Empire (at least from Britain's point of view, if not Eire's) it had relations with the Dominions Office and so presents an interesting anomaly. However, though the British Council did operate in Eire, it did so to a much lesser extent than in other European countries, basing its lack of involvement on its reluctance to 'have to justify the risk of expenditure . . . on nothing more valuable than the entertainment of a hostile population'.[32] This excuse appears a little strange, as Eire was far from being the only neutral country that could be described as 'hostile', but it may have been due to a number of reasons. First, as Eire was not a country that had relations with the Foreign Office, the British Council felt uncomfortable operating there. Second, because the Dominions Office had made no secret of the fact that it wished to use a visit by theatrical actors, under the auspices of the British Council, as a cover for political propaganda – the cultural aspect was clearly a lower priority. As R. B. Pugh of the Dominions Office wrote to an official in the British Council:

> They [the actors] should be, or should consist of, people pre-eminently suited to the purposes which we have in view, namely to convince the Irish that we are certain to win the war and that our victory will be to their advantage. *In addition*, of course, such persons and groups should be professionally well qualified, since an important *secondary consideration* is to maintain and strengthen the cultural bonds between the two countries [My emphasis].[33]

Third, the Irish Censorship had intercepted a letter in July 1941 from the British Council to the Gaiety Theatre in Dublin, suggesting theatre performances 'for goodwill propaganda purposes', and the Irish authorities, being nervous of the term 'propaganda', became reluctant to allow the British Council in.[34] The most likely reason, however, was that as Eire was so close to Britain geographically, there was a concerted effort within the British Government to do as little propaganda in Eire as possible, whether that be of a cultural or of a political kind, as it was fearful of that propaganda backfiring and threatening Britain's security. The Irish Civil War and the Partition were very much open wounds at this time. Most British propaganda that was conducted in Eire was left to John Betjeman, the Press Attaché, who had an eye for the sensitivities of the Irish people and Government during this period.[35] In other Empire countries, Anthony Eden, in his last week as Dominions Secretary before becoming Foreign Secretary in May 1940, made it clear to Reith that 'the British Council have limited their propaganda within the oversea [sic] Empire to a proposal to establish Dominion studentships for study in this country and subsidies to theatrical tours'.[36] In other words, the Ministry's arguments for taking over the Council, on the basis that it operated substantially in countries other than those that had relations with the Foreign Office, were exaggerated.

Perhaps instrumental in persuading Churchill not to close down the Council following the death of Lloyd were the views of the new (and third) Minister of Information, Alfred Duff Cooper, who was also against its abolition. Duff Cooper's basis for arguing that the Council should be maintained was that 'it has built up a good working organisation', and shutting it down would send out all the wrong messages – a view that had been aired by an increasing number of ministers and officials. Nevertheless, he did not agree that the British Council should be independent of the Ministry, stating that

> [t]he supposition ... that the British Council exists only for cultural, and not for political propaganda ... [is] at the best of times mere camouflage since no country would be justified in spending public money on cultural propaganda unless it had also a political or a commercial significance.[37]

Duff Cooper's view of cultural propaganda being ultimately to support commercial or political interests, dovetails with Philip Taylor's definition of cultural propaganda mentioned earlier. The two bodies, Duff Cooper argued, should be brought 'under one control' – that is, 'the Minister of Information should in future be ex officio Chairman of the British Council'.[38] Churchill's protégé, Eden, however, had the casting vote on the independence and survival of the Council, deeming the Ministry 'as a body quite unsuited for this type of work', and the British Council maintained its full independence from the Ministry.[39] Eden also appointed the new Chairman of the Council, Sir Malcolm Robertson, as was his duty under Article 20 of the British Council's Royal Charter. Reports in the *Daily Express*, *Evening Standard* and the *Daily Mirror* clearly saw the Foreign Office's appointment of Robertson as a coup for the Foreign Office over the Ministry of Information, as the press believed it was done 'without any consultation'.[40]

The British Council's relations were not always smooth with the Foreign Office however, and, on a number of occasions, relations teetered on the brink of collapse. In July 1943, after a tour that Sir Malcolm Robertson made to the Middle East a few months previously, Robertson came to his Executive Committee with proposals for a 'Middle East Review' of the British Council's work in that region. The Foreign Office official on the Executive Committee, Kenneth Gurney, who was responsible for overseeing the work of the Council from the Foreign Office's perspective, flatly turned down his proposals in such a way that Robertson seriously considered his position. 'Never in a long life', Robertson exclaimed,

> have I received such a rebuff, let alone so discourteous a one. No Chairman that I
> know of would retain his position in such circumstances. . . . I am too old and too
> experienced a man now to be willing to continue in a position which apparently
> carries with it no authority, and in which my considered and supported opinions
> are just turned down.[41]

Clearly still smarting after this rebuff, the next day Robertson lashed out against the Treasury and the Ministry of Information in a letter to Richard Law, Parliamentary Under Secretary of State for Foreign Affairs. The Treasury's ideas, Robertson stated, were a 'complete anathema' to him, and that the Treasury had 'only the very haziest notion of the effect that the work of the British Council is, in point of fact, having on foreign minds'. The Treasury's suggestion that the Council's work was 'philanthropy' really lit Robertson's touch-paper. He even point blank refused to work with the Ministry of Information abroad claiming that 'we shall eternally be tarred with the political propaganda brush and shall lay ourselves open to the suspicions which the cultural propaganda of the Germans and Italians have really justly brought upon them'.[42] Robertson was evidently perturbed and exasperated by how he was treated by other Government Departments.

It is a little unclear exactly what happened next, but plainly Robertson was persuaded to remain as Chairman and it appears that such rebuffs were only associated with certain sections of the Foreign Office. A couple of months later, Robertson began distinguishing in his letters between the 'sceptics' and the 'more enlightened spirits in the Foreign Office'.[43] He retained a particular dislike for 'young Gurney' as he dismissively called Kenneth Gurney, but his letters were noticeably less strongly worded.[44] Perhaps, it was more of a 'civil war' within the Foreign Office, between the sceptics and the more enlightened officials, that led to the downturn in relations, rather than a Foreign Office-British Council quarrel, but nonetheless Robertson appeared far more wary of the British Council's patron from that point on.

In a letter to Eden in December 1943, Robertson described some of his reasons for his continuing frustration with the bureaucratic nature of the Council's relationship with the Foreign Office, his apparent disenfranchisement, and suggested that the British Council should become a Government Department:

> At present I am Chairman of the Executive Committee without any authority at
> all or any powers of decision. I have to refer practically everything either to the
> Foreign Office, the Treasury, the British Council's Finance and Agenda Committee
> or the Council's Executive Committee, or all four. The result is that questions are
> dealt with piecemeal and decisions are interminably delayed. There is no real
> plan, no order of priority as between parts of the world or countries. . . . In these
> circumstances I would urge you to consider whether the time has now come for
> the setting up of a special Cabinet Committee to consider the whole organisation
> and future of the Council and whether it should not become a Department of
> His Majesty's Government annexed to the Foreign Office like the Department of
> Overseas Trade.[45]

Robertson appears to have been confused about what he really wanted for the Council. One Foreign Office official noted that this was 'most surprising' as it was out of step with Robertson's previous views, and would pose 'the danger of its [the British Council's] activities being dismissed as propagandist'[46] – clearly something which Robertson had been working hard to avoid. Indeed, in his unpublished autobiography, written soon after Second World War, Robertson pleaded the case for the Council to remain independent of politics and *not* become a Government Department. In fact, his autobiography made it clear that he later agreed with the views of that Foreign Office official:

> It is . . . vital for the [British] Council's aims and ideals that it should never become a Government Department manned by Civil Servants, and still more that it should never be absorbed by the Foreign Office. It would then be universally regarded as a mere 'propaganda' Agency, which it is not now and never must be allowed to be. . . . The functions of the F[oreign] O[ffice] in regard to it are supervisory only. . . . [A]ll political influences should be eliminated.[47]

Robertson's letter to Eden, therefore can be seen as an aberration – but an important one. He clearly was having great difficulties with parts of the Foreign Office around 1943, and his suggestion to make the Council a Government Department shows just how low relations had become with certain areas of British Council's 'patron'.

As for the British Council's relations with the Ministry of Information, they generally improved within the machinery of Whitehall. This was partly due to the more positive relationship that ensued with Brendan Bracken, the new, and more lasting, Minister of Information. Bracken was less interventionist in his relations with organizations like the British Council and the BBC, though as Ian McLaine shows in his book *Ministry of Morale*, relations with the Foreign Office always remained somewhat difficult.[48] As will be shown later, Bracken had also helped in securing Professor Walter Starkie's agreement to be the British Council's representative in Madrid, prior to becoming Minister of Information, which probably helped a great deal in his general feeling towards the Council.[49] But the improvement there was nothing compared to the improvement in relations in the countries within which they both operated. Indeed, Eastment has stated that '[o]verseas, the Council and the MOI acted so closely together in some areas that they became almost indistinguishable'.[50] In Sweden, the de facto British Council representative until 1941, and the Press Attaché (employed by the MOI), were the same person – Peter Tennant.[51] Largely this was due to the need to pool a limited amount of resources and to ensure that there was as little waste as possible in both organizations in making similar products, such as films.[52] In Tennant's case, difficulties in travelling to and from Sweden made the sending of a full time representative impossible until late 1941.[53] Clearly, Robertson's point-blank refusal to work with the MOI in July 1943 did not materialize in the countries in which they operated. Relations had become so good, in fact, that the Foreign Office was concerned and the Council was instructed not to become too closely identified with the MOI.[54]

The British Council's relations with the Treasury centred around the Council's budgets for each Financial Year. This involved each of the Council's representatives in the operational countries supplying cost estimates. These were to be combined with the estimates of the Council's costs in Britain, to be challenged first within the

Council itself, and the Foreign Office, and then by the Treasury who would agree the Council's budget.[55] The Council's budget increased considerably during the war, costing the Treasury in total over £6 million. Partly this can be explained by inflation, which was significant throughout the war period, and the increase in expenditure is not, therefore, quite as rampant as it may appear at first.[56] It is nevertheless sizeable and reflects the huge expansion in the Council's work. Taking inflation into consideration, the Council's expenditure increased by between 20 per cent and 50 per cent from one year to the next, during the war period. It should be noted, however, that this expansion rate was less than the pre-war period when the Council's expenditure increased by over 100 per cent from one year to the next. Throughout the war period, the Treasury was the main provider of funds for the Council – only in one year did the Treasury's proportion of the British Council's funding fall below 90 per cent – and therefore the Council was heavily dependent on good relations with the Treasury. Just as a point of comparison, the British Council today is far less dependent on public funds, with the majority of funds coming from fees and services it provides – particularly the provision of English language classes.[57] Also, it should be noted that much of the Treasury's grant to the British Council was unallocated to specific projects, to enable the British Council to respond quickly to changing events with the required funds.[58] Its expenditure was considerably less than its grant and any amounts not used were returned to the Treasury.[59]

As mentioned already, it was the Treasury's insistence that the British Council's budget for the 1940/41 Financial Year would not be settled until there had been an agreement with the Ministry of Information over their respective spheres of influence that ultimately drove Lord Lloyd to an agreement with Sir John Reith.[60] The Treasury noted that lack of settlement was 'handicapping him [Lord Lloyd] seriously'.[61] However, the Treasury was also keen to tighten the controls on the Council's expenditure – the procedures that the Foreign Office and the British Council had in place for monitoring expenditure were not designed for such a large increase in budget, or increase in responsibility. The Treasury's view was that the Council kept on asking it for more and more funds with the excuse that, as Germany was expanding its influence in neutral countries Britain should too, without any strategic thinking about whether spending extra money would be of benefit to Britain.[62] Though competing with Germany was part of 'flying the flag', the Treasury did not want that aspect to trump all consideration of value for money. Part of the problem with cultural propaganda was that it did not give a tangible return for the money invested and, as one of its representatives pointed out, that issue has always dogged the British Council throughout its history, whether in times of war or peace.[63] The Treasury was acutely aware 'that the activities of the [British] Council are watched with a jealous eye by some of the organs of the Press and by Lord Beaverbrook, who has consistently attacked the Council in his papers . . .', and that any suggestion that the Council was frittering away money on unproductive propaganda would be instantly seized upon.[64] Their aim, C. G. L. Syers, an official in the Treasury stated, was 'to produce a figure which will present the least surface to attack'.[65] The Treasury did not trust the Foreign Office's scrutiny of the British Council's expenditure plans – '[t]his is, of course, the familiar Foreign Office rubber stamp', noted another Treasury official.[66] They quizzed Reginald Leeper, who was then the Foreign

Office's official responsible for the British Council, as to why 'prima facie, it seemed odd that there should be so large an increase when the disappearance of neutrals alone must restrict the activities of the British Council and the general International situation must end to restrict them still more'.[67] Leeper gave reasons along the lines that if a neutral was overrun by Germany, the British Council's budget would be directed to supporting refugees of those countries, so there would only be a minor saving.[68] The Treasury seemed to be satisfied with this excuse but got Leeper to agree that the Foreign Office would watch the Council more closely, to ensure that funds allocated for expenditure in one country were not diverted elsewhere without the Treasury's prior agreement and to ensure the Treasury sanctioned any large projects.[69] The Treasury got its way and under the direction of a new Finance Officer, Reginald Davies, the British Council's expenditure was much more rigorously controlled, and the Treasury was involved at all the necessary decision points.[70]

By 1943, the Treasury even began to see the British Council as a vital part of the 'immediate "propaganda offensive"', much, as was shown earlier, to Sir Malcolm Robertson's annoyance – 'our aims are essentially long-term' – but it goes to show how essential the Treasury had begun to see the British Council's work by this time.[71] The Treasury defended the British Council at the Public Accounts Committee in July 1944, which claimed that there were 'serious defects in the control of the Foreign Office and of the [British] Council over its own organisation', by stating that the Council had improved its financial procedures and that financial control was 'fairly watertight'[72] – the most flattering a statement the Treasury was likely to give. Robertson had recognized the problems of the Council's financial management, and had worked hard to turn around the finances in 1943 and 1944. Tellingly he stated to the Council's representative in Turkey, Michael Grant, that 'the Treasury . . . constantly complain, and confess, *with some justice*, that our finances have been badly managed and that we are unnecessarily wasting public money in a dozen almost minor ways' [My emphasis].[73] He knew he had to act, and he did. However, towards the end of the war it became clear that the Treasury and other departments including the Foreign Office were still not satisfied with how the British Council was being run and how its budget was controlled. During the war this was left largely unchecked, barring the efforts of Robertson, due to the exceptional circumstances of the war, but with the end of the war in sight, there were calls for the British Council to be restructured, and its future became uncertain once again.[74]

On a number of occasions, there is evidence that the Foreign Office and the SOE attempted to persuade the British Council to take a more secretive role in the war. As stated before, one official in the Ministry of Information had suggested that, as the British Council was already established, it would be a 'good cover' for other activities.[75] Gladwyn Jebb, the SOE's Chief Executive Officer, wanted to take this a step further and in late 1941 or early 1942 he asked the Foreign Office to pursue any possible avenues for using the British Council as a cover for infiltrating Turkey with secret agents.[76] Around this time, there were increasing fears that Germany would invade Turkey, and records in the British Council files show that the Council were seeking assurances from the Foreign Office that its staff would be evacuated in the same manner as Embassy staff.[77] Jebb's plans, however, involved the British Council carrying out intelligence work ranging from weather reporting, to more direct reporting on the state of mind of the Turkish Government, as well as 'whispering' – the technique of spreading rumours or 'sibs' (outlined in the previous chapter) in neutral countries to influence both neutral opinion and the opinions of enemy personnel within the neutral countries.[78] He was, however, to be disappointed on this occasion – at least in terms of persuading the British Council to act as a conduit for clandestine activity as an organization. G. L. Clutton, of the Foreign Office, stated that

> [t]hough acting as centres of British culture and influence[,] British Council institutions abroad have never indulged in political propaganda. A short while ago we tried to induce them to depart a fraction from this standpoint in Turkey but with no success.[79]

Kenneth Gurney agreed with this and noted on a minute 'I presume that Mr Jebb will be told (ref R. 10854/G) our decision about the B[ritish] Council'.[80] This did not stop the SOE and the Foreign Office trying, however. Nor did it stop the British Council being suspicious that it was being used as a cover for other activities. And its suspicions were not without foundation.

Around this time, Michael Grant noted in his autobiography that he was asked by 'someone in authority' to send a football team 'consisting of service personnel from Cairo with fine football records' to 'assist our relations with the Turks'.[81] The football tour from a cultural propaganda perspective will be discussed in more detail later, but it should be noted that the appointment of a football trainer, seconded from the Royal Air Force to the British Council, caused the Council some concern that it was being used for other purposes. According to a report in a Foreign Office file, the trainer called Mr Prior 'had received instructions from the Air Attaché [at the British Embassy in Ankara] to take photographs and that he had indeed been selected for the post for his qualifications as a photographer'.[82] The Embassy denied this particular case stating that the Council was 'unjustified in alarm. . . . There is no question of political, intelligence or clandestine activities',[83] but a Foreign Office official, in an internal memorandum, noted that, although the Embassy may have denied that the Council had any cause for concern on this occasion, this type of appointment was actually fairly routine:

> [T]he Embassy (with our approval) are giving instructions to all British subjects (a) to furnish them with regular reports on political events, enemy activities etc., (b) to act as sources of dissemination of Allied views among the Turks. A start on these lines has been made with the British Council in Turkey. . . . Though from the British Council's point of view there can be no objection to (b) they may jib at (a) if they were told what has happened.[84]

It would seem, therefore, that *as an organization*, the British Council was not involved in clandestine activity, but the people it sent to the neutral countries were given other jobs to complete by other organizations such as the SOE while they were in those countries. It was an effective cover to get agents in and out of neutral countries and an obvious conduit for the intelligence services to use during wartime. It would seem, however, that the British Council was never told explicitly. Prior, the trainer, was on the British Council's books for some time.[85]

Now that the British Council had expressed its alarm that its activities were being seen as a cover for other purposes, it was dubious about accepting new teachers to be appointed to Turkish Halkevleri (Colleges for which the British Council were supplying lecturers – to be discussed in more detail later).[86] It had suspicions that the teachers would be British agents who could potentially damage the influence that the British Council was building up in cultural circles, by being seen as just another intelligence agency.[87] Nevertheless, there was little the British Council could do to prevent their employees taking on secondary roles except stressing, on every occasion possible, that it objected to such activity. There were reliable reports from Romania and Greece at the outbreak of war that British Council employees were instructed to observe and report troop movements, and conduct naval intelligence, but the British Council did not discover that this activity had taken place until three years after the event.[88] In Yugoslavia too, where the Council operated until early 1941, there is some evidence in Sebastian Ritchie's *Our Man in Yugoslavia* that the Council 'provided one avenue by which SIS [Secret Intelligence Service – MI6] broadened its influence'.[89]

In Turkey, there has been no suggestion that the British Council representative, Michael Grant, was personally involved in any clandestine activity. In Spain, conversely, there has been a suggestion that Professor Walter Starkie, the Council's representative in Madrid, was involved in more-than-cultural activity. It must be stressed that there are only *inferences* that the British intelligence services persuaded Starkie to act under their auspices, and the Starkie family have always denied the claim. On 22 February 1986, the Spanish newspaper *El Pais* published an article that stated the following:

> Some doctors [at the Hospital Hispano-Inglés (later the Anglo-American hospital)] pointed out yesterday the possibility that Walter Starkie, a Hispanist, who was cultural attaché of the British Embassy and member of the intelligence services of that country, was the person responsible for contacting members of the Allied Army passing through Spain [Original Spanish in footnote].[90]

The Starkie family was outraged by such a suggestion. His daughter, Alma Starkie de Herrero stated a week later in a letter to *El Pais* that '[t]his sentence . . . constitutes a serious insult to the honour and good name of my father . . . I categorically reject such an allegation which is absolutely and totally unfounded, and really grotesque . . . [it is] mere slander and contemptible' [Original Spanish in footnote].[91] Another author has claimed that Starkie was one of many 'unofficial collaborators' in Spain who worked for the British secret services to help refugees who escaped to Spain from occupied Europe continue on to Britain.[92] Recently, in a book by Jimmy Burns – the son of Tom Burns, the British Press Attaché in Madrid – it has again been claimed that 'Starkie was a British agent, his eccentric public persona belying a background of discreet service to His Majesty's Government'.[93] Although the word 'agent' appears to imply a 'secret agent', Burns does not provide any evidence that there was anything particularly secret about his work, or what that work might have been. However, according to David Gordon, who became friends with Starkie in the post-war period when Starkie taught in the United States of America, Starkie stated to him that he was involved in clandestine activities during his time in Madrid, but never elaborated on what this activity involved, nor indeed who he was working for.[94] In the absence of other evidence – particular with Starkie's paper being currently held by an unknown individual (and the contents of the 'papers' unclear) – the role that Starkie played continues to be shrouded in some mystery.[95] It may be that it was just because of the 'whispering gallery' nature of Madrid (i.e. that there were many spies from all sides working there spreading rumours as well as undertaking intelligence work) that Starkie's name has been mixed up with the rumours. What is certain is that there was clearly a fine line between being a British official with a duty to spread the British point of view and being an intelligence agent in time of war. In one poignant paragraph in a letter in the autumn of 1941, Starkie stated:

> The best tribute to the growing sympathy for England among all classes in Spain is the ceaseless Gestapo watchfulness against us. We are full of spies and counter-spies and hardly a day passes without the Embassy informing me that I am being followed and tracked. Some tell me that I am regarded as a spy, others that we are fomenting plots in the Institute.[96]

In such circumstances, it is not surprising that some of the accusations that Starkie was a spy have stuck.

In Sweden, before the full-time British Council representative, Ronald Bottrall, was installed in Stockholm, the British Council had asked the British Press Attaché in Sweden, Peter Tennant, to 'hold a watching brief for them'.[97] This is a good example, as mentioned above, of how the Ministry of Information and the British Council worked well together – as they both supplied materials (books, photographs, etc.) to Tennant. What neither the British Council nor the MOI appeared to know, however, was that Tennant was also working for the Special Operations Executive. Tennant was not merely working for the SOE, but he was actually the SOE's top man in Sweden.[98] Ronald Bottrall and Peter Tennant were old friends from Cambridge University, and it is likely that it was through this friendship that the SOE managed to arrange for Sir Kenneth Clark, the National Gallery's Director (and former employee of the Ministry of Information), to travel to Sweden. As Clark reminisced, however, lecturing on art for the British Council was not his only role. He went

> as a sort of advertisement for English culture . . . Sweden was important to us on account of the ball-bearings made in Gothenberg [sic]. But I was told nothing of this: mine was to be purely a cultural visit. . . . My journeys to Gothenberg [sic] were made uneasy by the fact that I had to take with me various secret documents relating to the shipment of ball-bearings. This turned out to be one of the chief justifications of my visit.[99]

Bottrall himself was often perceived as something more than just the British Council's representative. Many Swedes were convinced he was the head of the secret service but that was due more to his appearance than any evidence that he was personally involved in clandestine activity. As Tennant noted: '[t]he Swedes found it difficult to accept this giant who looked more like a retired boxer with his broken nose, than an emissary of British culture'.[100] An interesting anecdote, recalled by Bottrall's son Anthony, relates to this view.

My father used to tell a joke that suggested that he was NOT involved with SOE (unless he was double bluffing!). Apparently he was approached by someone from the US Embassy (presumably secret service) at a cocktail party who said to him: 'Bottrall, I want you to know that we think you're doing a fantastic job. What's more, nobody would even know you were doing it!'[101]

Perhaps, as with Starkie in Madrid, Bottrall's name was merely mixed up with the rumours in the whispering galleries of Stockholm.

A. J. S. White suggested in his personal account of the Council's work on its 25th anniversary that the Council was aware of attempts to use the Council as a cover for other activities and even co-operated where necessary (but did not elaborate on specifics), but it was not happy about doing so and resisted pressure wherever possible. White stated

> Pressure to broaden its [the British Council's] activities, which came from Government and other quarters, would on occasions have involved the Council in assignments that would have stretched the terms of its Charter unduly to include political propaganda or the use of its organisation to provide cover for 'shady' undertakings. But on the whole the F[oreign] O[ffice] supported the Council in its determination to go straight.[102]

This view, and the experience of the SOE's inability to persuade the Council to act as a cover for clandestine activity, is backed up by the conclusion that Keith Jeffery has reached in his new book *MI6: the History of the Secret Intelligence Service 1909–1949*. Jeffery has stated that though MI6 viewed the British Council as a potential cover for its activities 'it was somewhat grumpily noted that the [British] Council had "never been ready in the past to lend the smallest assistance to the SIS"'.[103] Ritchie's description of the work in Yugoslavia appears more the exception rather than the rule and, by and large, the Council was left to concentrate on cultural activity.

The British Council also worked with a number of Government Departments that had a less obvious connection to propaganda. One example of this is its liaison with Sir Stephen Tallents at the Ministry of Town and Country Planning which had models and photographs on various subjects such as the plans to rebuild London after the war, airports, small English villages and coal mines. The British Council wanted to use such models and photographs in exhibitions in its institutes abroad. It had already received requests from Turkey and Spain for displays on town planning, but wanted to use the displays across many of its institutes in Europe and South America.[104] Plans for Turkey were drawn up first, and were encouraged by Michael Grant who stated that 'the Turks were very keen on architectural things'.[105] Negotiations began with London County Council in July 1943 to create a plaster-cast model of the designs for South Bank Project, Bermondsey, Shoreditch and Bethnal Green and find suitable aerial photography.[106] Negotiations also involved a whole range of organizations such as the Air Ministry in order to supply the model of an airport, the Miners Welfare Commission, West Sussex County Council for photographs of a school, Welwyn Garden City housing centre for photographs and drawings of the new town to be built after the war and the Royal Air Force for a mechanized model with moving parts.[107] As the models could be used for a number of different organizations, negotiations started around how the costs could be shared between the British Council, the Ministry of Town and Country Planning and the Council for the Encouragement of Music and the Arts (CEMA), which wanted to use similar models.[108] The British Council hoped to purchase eight models for about £100 each though expected costs to be slightly higher.[109] If insurance had been paid for transportation this would have been on top of this, which was £400–500 per model.[110] In total the cost was potentially equivalent to the annual pay of four to five of the Council's representatives, so it was not an inexpensive venture.

The exhibition was due to be sent to Turkey in the spring of 1944, but negotiations rumbled on for many months for a number of reasons.[111] They involved many different people and organizations who had new ideas on what might be suitable for display in Turkey (something, as will be shown, that was an inherent problem with the Council's relations with non-Governmental organizations); there were difficulties with insurance and transport; time had to be allowed for the photographs to be passed by the censorship; and there were also difficulties in arranging filming of some of the models. In short, the exhibition took a long time to materialize. In fact, the records about the exhibition in the Ministry of Town and Country Planning stop in November 1944 with no further records – there is a suggestion that the exhibition would leave the country to go to Turkey in early 1945, but there is no evidence that it ever materialized.[112] Eighteen months of planning, it appears, had gone to waste. It is inevitable that not all of the ideas and plans for exhibitions would actually be realized – new and better ideas would come along, costs would be deemed too expensive and the changing fortunes in the war would mean that some would be sacrificed. However, it does seem surprising that it took so long for this exhibition to be organized. Perhaps it was certain peculiarities with this exhibition – the fact that models had to be made and were difficult to transport – that made it more difficult than other exhibitions to organize. Nevertheless, it demonstrates how time-consuming it could be to organize cultural propaganda and negotiate with other Government Departments to realize plans and how much effort and money was required. In light of this it is hardly surprising that the Treasury and MOI in particular were always concerned about how much the Council was costing the Government, and there were often calls to close the organization. Ultimately, however, its relations within Government could always find resolution in some way through escalation to the Chairman of the Council and the Foreign Secretary as they were colleagues working in the same machinery of Government. Negotiations with non-Governmental organizations were not so straightforward, and it is these relationships that will be examined next.

Relations with British non-Government organizations and individuals

Relations with British organizations and individuals outside of Government, such as teachers, artists, scientists and musicians, were complicated. It is true that the vast majority of British organizations and individuals were in favour of helping the war effort in some way and if the British Council asked for their co-operation, most of them were very helpful. Requests from the British Council varied from asking for expertize and guidance as well as writing pamphlets on British life and thought, to seeking lecturers or performers for touring, recruiting representatives and teachers to be sent out to neutral countries on a longer-term basis. In contrast to the relative cohesion that existed in Government (and as demonstrated in the previous section that cohesion was not particularly strong even in Government), each external organization had its own view on how the Council's work should be carried out, and this hampered the Council's organization of propaganda. As will be shown, some people who were asked to help the Council only did so out of a sense of duty during the war, rather than being enthusiastic recruits to the Council's cause. The British Council often had to strike a difficult balance between presenting the image of Britain that British organizations and individuals wanted to be presented and the image of Britain that people in the neutral countries wanted presented to them. Sometimes they were the same images, but there were clear tensions here that the Council had to grapple with throughout the war.

In terms of recruiting teachers and university lecturers (to stay in the neutral country for a long period, rather than as touring lecturers), the Council often worked on an 'agency basis' for foreign institutions for recruiting staff in Britain to work abroad. Recruiting teachers for the Halkevleri institutes in Turkey were a good example of where this took place, but the Council also operated as an agent for foreign schools, universities and Anglophile societies.[113] Interest for these posts was generally very good, especially among women teachers for posts in schools. It has been suggested that interest was high because the women saw the roles 'as an opportunity to undertake wartime work of national importance while continuing in the teaching profession rather than going into one of the armed services'.[114] One advert for a Girls' School in Karabuk in Turkey received nearly 400 completed application forms which kept the Registry Clerks busy for a long time – Council employees from the recruitment department continue to remember this particular advert very well. Perhaps this vast number was a little out of the ordinary, but still, interest was also good for other posts which they advertised, though interest in a post did not necessarily mean suitability.[115] The Council's recruitment for posts such as these took one of three approaches. The first approach was to advertise in one of the public newspapers which, owing to the shortage of paper and newsprint, could only, by necessity, be a short advert. The second approach, particularly for university-level posts, was to register the vacancy with scholastic agencies such as Truman & Knightley and Gabbitas Thring and with university appointment boards – mainly Oxford and Cambridge. The third approach was to consider the so-called chance enquiries about employment overseas, of which there were a considerable number.[116] Application forms were filled in and two sets of interviews were conducted: first by the recruitment department alongside a regional representative for the country where the vacancy was; and second, shortlisted candidates were again interviewed by a regional representative and a representative from the Council's education department with a chairperson – often a Deputy Secretary-General. With Lord Lloyd as Chairman until 1941, a third interview would take place with him for particularly important posts. The British Council worked hard to build a good relationship with the scholastic agencies and university appointments boards, and they were well-disposed and helpful towards the Council.[117]

A. J. S. White wrote in his personal account of the Council's work that filling the junior posts within the Council itself was a 'very hard task' because suitable candidates were 'very scarce'.[118] It was also very difficult when interviewing candidates in London to make a good judgement about how candidates would fare overseas. Many good candidates were found, but it was often the case that a candidate was the 'only runner . . . for a post that had been too long unfilled', and the Council had little choice but to employ them if they wanted to expand their work.[119] It was hardly surprisingly then, that a few unsuitable candidates were posted overseas. Though White gives no specific examples, he noted that the trouble was that

> there were many people besides the *Daily Express* who fastened on one of two poor
> specimens as confirming their belief that a new-fangled cultural organisation would
> be bound to recruit the wrong type: men with long hair and purple corduroys.
> Thus the few bad choices that were made stood out and were exaggerated; and
> although most of the criticisms were unfair there is no doubt that the Council's
> public relations were harmed by them.[120]

Sir Stanley Unwin, a publisher who chaired the Council's Books and Periodicals Committee, also recognized this as a major issue in his autobiography, but expressed the view that the publicity surrounding the appointment of a few poor candidates 'was to be expected in pioneer work' and it had to be recognized as inevitable that 'not a word was heard about the painstaking, conscientious and successful work accomplished by the rest of the staff in scores of other places'.[121] As has been mentioned a number of times, Lord Beaverbrook was no fan of the British Council and his newspapers were always looking for ways to attack it in some way. The appointment of candidates who they disliked was a perfect excuse for them to sharpen their knives.[122]

The British Council was constantly under pressure from outside individuals and organizations about what image of Britain they should be projecting to neutral countries. This extended from who they employed in the Council (as mentioned in White's quote above), to who was on the Committees and what type of person should be sent as a cultural representative of the nation as well as how the Council operated abroad more generally. When it was discovered by MPs in late 1944 that J. G. Crowther, Head of the Council's Science Department, was an open communist, there was an uproar in some quarters, particularly in Parliament among Conservative MPs. An anonymous MP's note was sent on to Sir Malcolm Robertson which stated

> [I]t seems very unfortunate that the British Council, which is financed by HM
> Government for the purpose of spreading throughout the world a knowledge of
> the best of British thought and culture, should have appointed as the Head of one
> of its chief departments, the Science Department, a man who is a Communist. . . .
> Mr. Crowther is understood to be the officer of the British Council who is
> responsible for helping foreign scientists of all grades to establish personal contact
> with their counterparts in the British scientific world. . . . It would not be surprising
> if he were found to use extensively for this purpose individual British scientists
> who have a leaning towards Communism. . . .[123]

Robertson, though a Conservative MP himself and perhaps sharing some of the political outlook of his fellow MP, dismissed the call for Crowther to be replaced, arguing that the Council was a non-political body and therefore people could not be hired or sacked for political reasons. He stated

> Crowther's personal integrity is undoubted. He is a man of considerable ability. He has never aired his Communist views to me, nor, to my certain knowledge to anybody else in the office. It would be difficult for the Executive Committee to get rid of him without a stream of undesirable publicity and adverse comment on the Council. . . . Our staff consists of people of diverse political views as is right and natural. Provided that those views are not pressed to the detriment of our non political ideals, I do not feel that we should enquire into them too closely. . . .[124]

Robertson was in a difficult position. He had to steer the course between the Scylla (on this occasion uproar from Conservatives by not dismissing Crowther) and the Charybdis (uproar from the press from dismissing Crowther for political reasons) and it would seem to be an impossible undertaking where he could not win, whatever he did. On this occasion, largely because Crowther had integrity and did not mix his work and politics, the matter died down without much further issue, but the example served to demonstrate the inherent tensions that the Council had to deal with on a day-to-day basis by being a non-political body. It is ironic that a non-political body had to spend so much time defending itself from political interference.

A similar problem occurred a few months later when the Council sent the composer Benjamin Britten to Paris in early 1945 along with the singer Peter Pears, despite both Britten and Pears being conscientious objectors. Astra Desmond, a contralto singer, who had visited Portugal and Spain for the British Council earlier in the war, wrote to Robertson to complain that two men who had done so little to help the war effort (Britten and Pears had gone to neutral America earlier in the war to avoid being called up for National Service), should be sent to the recently liberated French capital as ambassadors of British culture. She believed also that it was an 'insult to France to send them'.[125] Robertson claimed that it was in fact the French Government who had invited Britten and Pears, a request to which the Council had simply acquiesced. Robertson noted in reply to Desmond 'it would hardly have been proper for the Council to stand in the way of a visit on which the French themselves were so keen'.[126] Although this may have been technically the case, the way the Council was perceived to have acted was what was important to observers and critics, and it was consistently scrutinized to ascertain what type of Britain was being projected abroad.

The Council's Music Advisory Committee often had views on which musicians would be the best ambassadors of British music and musical talent, but was not always successful in preventing people that they deemed unsuitable from touring on behalf of the Council. For example, in October 1941 the Committee received a request from the British Institute in Portugal for a grant to be made to Philip Newman, a violinist (about whom most of the Committee confessed they did not know), to enable him to accept an invitation from the Lisbon Conservatoire of Music to become Professor of Violin there. The Committee originally accepted, noting that 'it was so important to have an Englishman on the staff of the Lisbon Conservatoire that they were prepared to recommend that the suggested grant should be made'.[127] However, a year later, Pamela Henn-Collins, the Committee's secretary, reported that 'she had several interviews with Mr. Philip Newman who was now in this country, and she felt he was an unsuitable person to represent British music in Portugal, though doubtless valuable as a professor at the Conservatoire'.[128] The Committee did not think highly enough of Newman's musicianship to allow him to be an ambassador of Britain's musical abilities. By 1943, however, Newman was still promoting the ability of British musicians in Portugal, much to the dismay of Henn-Collins. She noted 'I am afraid Mr [David] Shillan [at the British Institute in Lisbon] has been entirely deluded by Newman and is, I know, a great admirer of his playing'.[129] Shillan wrote of Newman's performance in Lisbon:

> The interest was exceptional for a recital in this series, and the warmth of reception by the audience before a note was played put Newman more at ease than he might have been in that unsuitable hall, and on very good form. . . . There was on all sides a very favourable impression, and talk of 'a great night'.[130]

Henn-Collins, on receipt of Shillan's letter, wrote to George West, the Council's representative in Portugal, to stress her and the Music Committee's views:

> Whether and to what extent Newman should continue to be used by the Council [in Portugal] is, of course, a matter of policy on which you must decide, but in case you are tempted by reports of this concert to alter your view of Newman's *musicianship* I think I ought to let you know that my own opinion remains unchanged [Henn-Collin's emphasis].[131]

It seems the advice of the Committee had been overruled – the Portuguese liked Newman too much, and the propaganda value was too great not to allow Newman to play to Portuguese audiences. The *Diário de Manhã* reported in 1943 after one of Newman's concerts for the Portuguese Red Cross that 'Philip Newman has the exceptional powers of a soloist: amazing handling of the bow, a technically perfect left hand, voluminous sounds and sweet, variety of tone and the effect of surprise attack' [Original Portuguese in footnote].[132] With reports in the Portuguese press such as this it is clear to see why West would not dispose of Newman easily. Newman's violin playing fitted in well with the existing sociological situation in Portugal and its influence penetrated deep into Portuguese society. He played on well into 1944.[133]

Robertson himself made some judgements in favour of preventing certain personalities from touring on the Council's behalf. For example, he was keen to prevent Noël Coward from travelling to Portugal. Coward had personally granted permission for one of his plays, *Private Lives*, to be translated into Spanish and performed in Madrid under the auspices of the Council, but Robertson had apparent reservations as to his suitability for being physically sent to the Iberian peninsula.[134] Robertson stated to Henry Hopkinson at the British Embassy in Lisbon in November 1943

> to be candid we are a little doubtful whether Noël Coward would be altogether suitable in that capacity. I am well aware that he enjoys a world-wide reputation, and that his appearance, particularly if timed to coincide with the release of one

of his films in Portugal, might arouse great enthusiasm. . . . I confess I am not quite satisfied that Noël Coward, for all his great gifts and personal charm, could do that [give lectures], or indeed figure adequately in the category of British Council lecturers.[135]

To be fair to both Coward and Robertson, Robertson was not saying Coward could not go to Portugal at all, but he did not want him going under Council auspices to provide lectures. Part of the reason may have been that Leslie Howard, the world-famous film star who had recently starred in *Gone with the Wind* had visited Portugal earlier that year and had been killed on his return from a visit to Spain and Portugal, when his plane was shot down over the Bay of Biscay. Perhaps Robertson, to some extent, felt the British Council was somewhat responsible for Howard's death and was not willing to take the risk of sending another high-profile actor, such as Coward, to Portugal in 1943. He certainly compared Howard's visit to the prospective visit of Coward in his letter to Hopkinson stating '[w]e went perhaps a little outside our scope in sending you Leslie Howard',[136] indicating perhaps that he wished he had never sent Howard to Portugal. There has often been a suggestion that Howard was a spy who was given the task of communicating a message from Winston Churchill to General Franco, which may also be another reason why Robertson stated Howard was 'a little outside our scope'.[137] The evidence for Howard being a spy and for carrying a message from Churchill to Franco is based largely on speculation, a supposition that the time Howard had spent 'missing' in Madrid had been spent on espionage rather than on philandering (for which he was famous), and an interview that the Spanish actress Conchita Montenegro, a co-star and rumoured lover of Howard, gave shortly before her death in 2007.[138]

When the Council did decide that it wished to send individuals abroad for a short period, usually to tour the country and lecture or perform, the Council often used informal networks to access these people. Requests were raised at one of the Council's advisory committees who were usually made up of people who would know a lecturer or performer personally, and approaches were made on an informal basis to be formalized later. On occasion, a member of a committee may also have made a visit. There were 14 different committees or panels that existed at some point during the war, including a Fine Arts Committee, a Science Committee, a Books and Periodicals Committee and a Films Committee – all of which provided routes to reaching individuals through informal networks.[139]

Many famous personalities agreed to tour for the British Council and whether one is in favour of its work or not, it would have to be agreed that it was a very impressive list. In alphabetical order, the most famous were probably Sir Lawrence Bragg (scientist), Benjamin Britten (composer), Sir Kenneth Clark (art critic), Astra Desmond (contralto singer), T. S. Eliot (poet), Leslie Howard (actor), Sir Malcolm Sargent (conductor) and Harold Spencer-Jones (astronomer). Arranging for all of these people (and many less famous personalities) to tour was a difficult task in terms of persuading them to tour in the first place and then matching their diaries with dates of transport and ensuring that they were suitably entertained in the country that they were to visit. Some were easier than others to work with.

Dr Robert McCance, an expert on nutrition at the University of Cambridge was contacted through the Medical Research Council for a proposed visit to Portugal and Spain. He took some convincing to go by Dr N. Howard Jones of the Medical Department of the British Council. McCance stated:

> I have consented rather unwillingly to go for I don't really feel that I am the right person if the mission is solely one of improving cultural relationships. I hate dagoes and the picture he [Howard Jones] paints to me of being continually fêted by them simply fills me with gloom.[140]

McCance was particularly keen that his assistant, Miss Widdowson, accompanied him to Spain and Portugal. However, the Council had to remain firm that 'only very special circumstances would justify a dual visit. There is a very great pressure on air travel services to and from Portugal and it is difficult enough for us to arrange for accommodation for single lecturers'.[141] To be fair to McCance he wanted Miss Widdowson to accompany him for a good reason – to gather information on the nutritional problems in Spain while he was lecturing there – and it was not just a personal whim, but it took the Council some time to persuade him to agree to go without his assistant.[142] In the end, despite the reservations which he had about going as a cultural representative, and the concerns he had of going alone, his report of his visit gives the impression that he rather enjoyed himself and wrote a 19-page report about the contacts that he met, praising the arrangements made for him by Professors Starkie and West.[143] McCance's visit will be studied in more detail in the following chapter.

T. S. Eliot also wanted to make his visits for the British Council conditional on personal grounds. When he returned to Britain from Stockholm from his visit in 1942, he wrote to Robertson stating that he had discovered on his return that his secretary had been called up into National Service, and that unless this decision was reversed he would never be able to be away from London for such a long period again.[144] John Gielgud, having played Hamlet in Sweden prior to the outbreak of war, was seen as a good candidate to go again to Sweden, but was simply too busy acting in Britain to find the time.[145] And it was the same for many famous people. Visits had to be arranged well in advance. When Professor Walter Starkie wrote to the Council in London in June 1942 seeking to arrange a visit for Sir Malcolm Sargent to Spain in the autumn of the same year, he was told by Robertson that 'a busy man such as he makes his engagements from six to nine months ahead' and 'we have already engaged him to go elsewhere for us then'.[146] Starkie had missed the opportunity of Sargent's visit on this occasion as he was going to Sweden for the British Council.

Even when visits could be arranged, travel issues made visits difficult. Sir Malcolm Sargent was delayed for over a week waiting at Leuchars airfield, near St Andrew's in Fife, in late 1942 on his way to Sweden, along with other passengers including Ronald Bottrall's wife Margaret and son Anthony. Conditions had to be suitably overcast to fly over occupied Norway for security reasons.[147] Returning home was often even more complicated and dangerous and in Sweden, the British Minister in Stockholm Sir Victor Mallet noted, 'nobody ever knew how soon they would be given a passage home again and they sometimes stayed for two or three weeks before this happened'.[148] Leslie Howard's tragic death in 1943 demonstrated just how dangerous it was for people to tour neutral countries in wartime and the event no doubt made people think twice before accepting an invitation from the British Council – there was a notable lack of tours arranged in the months after Howard's death.[149] It is quite astounding, therefore, that the British Council persuaded so many people to go, and that it got the vast majority in and out of neutral countries safely.

The Council was often criticized for how it operated abroad, not just in terms of who the Council sent, but also in day-to-day operations. Unwin gave one example of this in his autobiography about the selling of English language books by the British Council representative after they had been exhibited. The MOI gave away books and was not criticized for doing so. By contrast the Council was 'condemned in Parliament and in a section of the Press for trading at a loss in that they had not covered the cost of air freight, which would have made the price of the books prohibitive'.[150] Unwin dismissed this argument stating 'anyone with the most elementary knowledge of psychology is aware that a book for which money is paid is more effective in its influence than twenty given away and in consequence dismissed as propaganda'.[151] It would seem that the Council, even when it took the most effective measures to extend Britain's influence, could never satisfy its critics at home.

Closer to home, the Advisory Committees were made up of groups of interested parties and experts in their field. They were not always the same people, and the different Advisory Committees varied in the frequency of meetings. For example, the Fine Arts Committee only held 11 meetings throughout the whole war with nearly a year between some of the meetings (though there were sub-committees established for specific exhibitions in the intervening periods).[152] By contrast, the Music Advisory Committee met 26 times (with over a year between two meetings)[153] and the Books and Periodicals Advisory Committee met far more frequently at 54 meetings during the war, usually on a monthly basis.[154] Members were often famous in their particular subject. For example, composers William Walton, Arthur Bliss and Ralph Vaughan Williams attended the Music Committee along with Leslie Boosey (of Boosey and Hawkes) and Sir Adrian Boult (conductor). The difficulty with such a high-brow membership was that members did not always agree with each other or fully support the Council's efforts. Sir Kenneth Clark, who had briefly worked for the MOI early in the war but was Director of the National Gallery for most of the war, resigned from the Fine Arts Committee in late 1943. Clark was seen as perhaps the most active member of the Committee and advocate of the Council's work with regard to art prior to his resignation. His resignation, therefore, as Major Alfred Longden, the Director of Fine Art stated in his reply to Clark's resignation letter:

> . . .is a great and rumbling blow. I did not realise, until you recently spoke on the wireless [on the BBC's *Brains Trust* programme] that you regarded our work as so lacking in importance. Perhaps I am to blame for not keeping the members of the [Fine Arts] committee more fully informed of the far-reaching use of our efforts and in addition I have not given members enough to do and thus they may, possibly, have lost interest.[155]

The relationships that the various Committees had with British cultural figures and organizations demonstrates perfectly the careful juggling act that the British Council played out, keeping them interested in the Council's work on the one hand, and on the other making effective decisions about what types of materials could be distributed abroad to the neutral countries. The artist Paul Nash was often being contacted by Longden to provide copies of his work or permission for it to be displayed abroad. Usually Nash was happy with Longden's suggestions (though on occasion had to be reminded to answer letters addressed to him), but it must have been a logistical challenge for Longden to keep all the artists interested and maintain their goodwill while also trying to find works of art that were suitable for display in Stockholm, Madrid and elsewhere.[156] Longden's letters usually gave the impression that he was trying to cajole the artists that he was writing to and hoping not to let them down. For example, the statement '[w]hile not exactly the type of watercolour we originally had in mind, we are very glad to include this as showing an additional aspect of your work', hardly promotes the notion that the Committee was entirely in the driving seat for what image of Britain they were promoting – they needed to keep the cultural figures that they depended on 'on side'.[157]

On occasion, too, the Advisory Committees – that is, the people closest to, and who had most influence over the Council – were accused of being too out-of-touch with ordinary British life and culture. They were, it was alleged, promoting an image of Britain that may have reflected their own interests, but did not reflect a truthful image of Britain. There is a link here to the sociological propaganda described by Ellul in that those people on the Committees thought they were representing a truthful image of Britain (and not propaganda) but outside of the Committees that image was one not recognized as accurate. The Books and Periodicals Committee, for example, received a number of complaints from Scottish people and organizations that their *British Life and Thought* series of booklets was too Anglocentric.[158] There were booklets promoted in the series called *The Englishman* (by Lord [formerly Prime Minister, Stanley] Baldwin) and *The Englishwoman* (by Cicely Hamilton) but there had been no attempt up until the complaint was received, to write books called 'The Scotsman' or 'The Scotswoman' (or indeed Welsh or Northern Irish counterparts, but there is no record of complaints from these quarters).[159] The Committee did respond quickly to the complaints and commissioned a number of books reflecting life across the United Kingdom within a month of the complaint, unimaginatively called *Wales and the Welsh, Scotland and the Scots* and *Northern Ireland and the Ulsterman* (as well as *England and the English*).[160] Nevertheless, it seems clear that the Committee would not have done so without having been pushed in that direction. It was noted in the agenda for the meeting that 'Home Division is very anxious that this group of brochures [for Scotland, Wales and Northern Ireland] should be completed as quickly as possible'.[161] Even people on the Committees, such as Kenneth Clark, did not necessarily believe that the Council was influenced by the right people. Clark wrote to a confidante (a former colleague in the Ministry of Information) that he was concerned how much the Council was 'influenced by conservative opinion [in terms of art] and fear of protests by the Royal Academy. Its chairman [Sir Malcolm Robertson] therefore feels bound to include a preponderate number of New English Art Club paintings' which Clark believed would not interest audiences as much as other paintings.[162] It would seem that Clark did not agree that the timeless, conservatism of cultural propaganda mentioned earlier was always the best way of attracting elites and some more modern art would go down well. This letter, written just days after resigning from the Fine Art Committee, probably gives a good idea of the real reason why he resigned – Clark was clearly frustrated at presenting an image of Britain that he thought was not showing Britain in its best light, and that he was lacking influence.

One area from which it is perhaps surprising that the Council did not receive obvious complaints was from left-wing political groups. Admittedly previously the Council had Clement Attlee, the leader of the Labour Party, on its Executive Board until 1940 and other Labour members were closely involved with the Council's work, but having Conservative Party members on the Executive Board did not stop complaints from right-wingers like Lord Beaverbrook (Unwin stated '[a]bout 90 per cent of the criticism of the British Council comes from Lord Beaverbrook's papers'[163]). The Council also took the opportunity of mentioning Trade Unions and providing illustrations in its publications,[164] and even worked with the *Arbetarnas Bildningsförbund*, (ABF – Workers' Educational Association), which was affiliated to the Social Democratic Party and the Trade Unions in Sweden.[165] However, elitist culture (such as fine art, literature, classical music) was more prevalent in the Council's propaganda than details about the working classes and ordinary men and women in Britain. Up until the Nazi invasion of the Soviet Union in June 1941, the Nazi-Soviet Pact would have made it difficult for left-wing propaganda to take hold, as the Communists were allied to the enemy. After this time it should have been easier, however, as the Soviets were then Britain's allies. Perhaps left-wing groups realized that however much they believed in their ideals and inherently disliked the elitist nature of the Council's publications and work, the right-wing dictatorships in Spain, Portugal and Turkey were hardly going to be appreciative of Britain pumping their countries full of left-wing propaganda – particularly Franco who had just fought a three year civil war against an alliance of left-wing groups. While these three countries could be pro-British when fighting the Nazis, they were far less likely to be pro-Soviet. Still, the lack of complaints from left-wing groups about the dearth of left-wing propaganda, are conspicuous by their absence.

The British Council had an incredibly difficult role as a non-political body in trying to present an image of a country that was so diverse in many different ways – particularly politically, socially and culturally. The Council could not please everyone in Britain and it knew it. After all, it could not please everyone in Government, so it could not hope to please everyone in the country. All it could do was present an image that enough people in the country would be content with and be accepted by the audience they were aiming at (i.e. the elites) – and fit in with what Kazimierz Musiał and Nikolas Glover would call the interaction between the autostereotype and the xenostereotype[166] – and hope that it had done enough to deflect major criticisms through constant written and verbal communication and negotiation with people interested in its work. Sir Kenneth Clark's relationship with the Council is a good example of how the Council kept him 'on side'. Though he resigned from the Fine Arts Committee in late 1943, he still agreed to lecture for the Council in Sweden just over a year later. He had been frustrated by the Council, but not alienated by it. And it was true for many of the Council's stakeholders – they may not have agreed with everything that it did and the image of

Britain that it was presenting, but Britain was at war and any image of Britain presented in neutral countries was far better than no image at all. When it came to the crunch, people outside of Government largely supported the Council's work.

Relations with the British Embassies

The British Council's relationships within Britain, as has been shown, were often tense and strained. However, the British Council's role was not to maintain good relationships in Britain, but to promote British life and thought abroad. In essence apart from needing to keep enough people in Britain interested in the Council's work to keep propaganda materials being produced and lecturers and performers travelling to the neutral countries of Europe, it did not matter whether the Council's work was popular within Britain. What mattered was the role that it played abroad. There was one obvious group of British organizations abroad that the Council had to maintain good relationships with – the British Embassies, Consulates and Legations. If it did not maintain good relationships here, then its real work – promoting Britain abroad – could be in jeopardy. The stakes could not be higher for the Council's relationship with British Embassies. Ultimately, both the Council and the Embassies were accountable to the Foreign Office, so relations should have been good. However, as has been seen, Robertson's relationship with the Foreign Office was not always smooth within Britain itself and so Council-Embassy relations were not guaranteed to be positive and productive. As will be shown over the remainder of this chapter through an analysis of the relationship in the four main neutral countries in Europe where the Council operated – Spain, Turkey, Portugal and Sweden – the health of those relationships varied from one country to the next.

Spain: Sir Samuel Hoare and Professor Walter Starkie

Sir Samuel John Gurney Hoare (Lord Templewood from 1944) was Conservative MP for Chelsea from 1910 to 1944, and had been in the British Cabinet during the Conservative and National Government administrations since the early 1920s. From his background, therefore, it could be justifiably claimed that he was the personification of 'The Establishment'. The pinnacle of his career came in 1935 when he accepted the office of Foreign Secretary but within months his career was in tatters after press reports about a pact between himself and the French Foreign Minister, Pierre Laval, to offer the Italian dictator, Benito Mussolini, two-thirds of Abyssinia (modern-day Ethiopia), a country Mussolini had recently invaded, in return for stopping the war. The so-called Hoare-Laval Pact, which was never put into action, caused an outcry in Britain and Hoare was compelled to resign. Although he returned to the Cabinet a number of times he would never recover from this humiliation and his name, like that of Chamberlain, became synonymous with 'Appeasement' and the destruction of collective security.[167] With Winston Churchill as Prime Minister he was dispatched to Madrid as a Special Ambassador to Spain – some say into exile; others say the role of Ambassador in Madrid was so crucially important, it required someone of Hoare's stature.[168] Hoare certainly suggested that 'the Spanish Government was flattered at the appointment of a former Foreign Secretary'.[169] Although he recognized the importance of Spain in the war and carried out the role with a huge sense of duty to his country, he coveted the role of Viceroy of India which he believed was more or less guaranteed for him, but a role he would never undertake.[170] Originally he was only due to be in Madrid for short while as an extension to a visit he was to pay to Portugal, but he ended up staying almost five years.

By contrast, the British Council representative, Walter Fitzwilliam Starkie, was an Irish Roman Catholic and Professor of Literature at Trinity College, Dublin and spent much of his time prior to Second World War in Italy, Eastern Europe and Spain mingling with gypsies and wandering minstrels. It might not seem, therefore, that the words 'Starkie' and 'Establishment' would have been heard in the same sentence. However, like Hoare, he had crossed paths with Mussolini and had even been accorded a private audience with the Duce in 1927. Starkie admired Mussolini, later recalling the meeting with some delight: 'I was hypnotized by his large dark eyes which sparkled when his voice became animated'.[171] Throughout the Spanish Civil War he had been a supporter of General Franco, and as late as the autumn of 1939, in correspondence between his two sisters Nancy and Enid, Nancy reported

> Walter looks blooming. Of course he really has great belief in Hitler and Mussolini, and none in the others. . . . Walter and Italia [Starkie's wife] are of course very pro-German – perhaps I am wrong in saying that – but anyway they are anti-English.[172]

One might be forgiven, therefore, for questioning why on earth Starkie was appointed Director of the British Institute in Madrid only a few months later.

Certainly, it is easy to see why Franco would accept him – he was a *persona grata* by virtue of his support for Franco during the Civil War – but it is less clear why he was entrusted with being an emissary of a culture to which apparently he had little fondness. Starkie certainly appeared to have fascist sympathies prior to the war but in the post-war period, Starkie promoted the view that he was a 'West Briton', had always been loyal to the British crown and was more 'rightist' than his background might suggest.[173] He had, after all, been educated at Shrewsbury School. Could it be that his sisters were poor judges of his character (which has been suggested is probably the case by his friends later in life) or is it more probable that after the collapse of the Axis (or perhaps during the war itself) he changed his mind about where his loyalties lay?[174]

Being in debt may be a better explanation for his acceptance of the role which overrode any political sympathies that he may have had, as the Director's salary would provide him with a steady income of £1,000 a year.[175] Plus there is some evidence that he simply forgot to tell his employer, Trinity College in Dublin, where he was in the autumn of 1940 a few months after accepting the role of Director which leads to the suspicion that his acceptance was a rather impulsive and perhaps a desperate move for money.[176] The important point here, however, (particularly for this book) is that once in post in Madrid he never wavered from promoting British culture, and his contacts in Spanish cultural life were his ticket to appointment as Director.

Starkie had previous (though short-lived) experience of establishing a cultural centre in Genoa soon after the end of First World War to improve Anglo-Italian relations and was the only non-Spanish member of the Royal Spanish Academy of the Language, which 'included the most prominent scholars and writers of Spain'.[177] Both of these facts, as well as being a friend of the Duque de Alba (the Spanish Ambassador in London – who was also the Duke of Berwick)[178] made him an attractive candidate for the role of Director of the British Institute in Madrid. He understood Spain better than the vast majority of people from the British Isles and was accepted in Spain – these advantages would enable him to engineer the British Council's cultural propaganda to fit in with the existing sociological situation in Spain and be readily acceptable to the Spanish elites. Starkie recalled that Lloyd gave him 'freedom of action' and stated 'I shall always back you up'.[179] Lloyd clearly thought Starkie was the ideal candidate, and was probably influenced by positive feedback received from Brendan Bracken in the summer of 1939, who had visited Starkie in Dublin. Bracken believed that Starkie was an Irishman who could be trusted to play a role for Britain in the war.[180]

Whatever their backgrounds and the reasons behind their appointments and their acceptance of their respective roles, Hoare and Starkie were both in Madrid to promote a better understanding of Great Britain – Hoare through political and diplomatic means; Starkie through cultural means. Their roles should have complemented each other. By contrast to how it should have been, it is not an exaggeration to state that they detested each other. It was not that they saw each other's role as conflicting with their own – Hoare for example was reported as having 'expressed great interest and belief in the Council's work and seemed anxious to help it forward in Spain'.[181] And Starkie expressed his hope in 1940 that 'it will be possible for Sir Samuel Hoare to initiate the course of lectures [at the institute]'.[182] But there was a personality clash which had significant repercussions for how they both operated. Two private documents – one a letter from Lord Lloyd (on Starkie's behalf) to Lord Halifax, the Foreign Secretary, in November 1940 and the second a telegram a year later from Hoare to Sir Malcolm Robertson illustrate the distrust that permeated the Hoare-Starkie relationship. Both are worth quoting at length:

> *Lord Lloyd to Lord Halifax, 19 November 1940:*
> He [Starkie] has just been home and he tells me privately that the Embassy, far from assisting him and the Institute staff in their work, is actually putting obstacles in their way. He alleges that Sam Hoare takes no interest at all and gives no support. To repeat any of this to Sam would, I am sure, only do harm, but if next time you write you could say what importance you attribute to the work of the British Council and the British Institute in Spain, and what good things you hear of Professor Starkie's work, it would, I am sure, do much good.[183]

> *Sir Samuel Hoare to Sir Malcolm Robertson, 12 November 1941:*
> I fear that the position I have found here on my return does not justify your report in your letter to me of Professor Starkie's contact with Spanish intellectual life. Institute has undoubtedly gone back in Spanish estimate. Staff are discontented and two at least of them should certainly be replaced. Mrs. Starkie seems to make

trouble everywhere. Organisation is from all accounts very bad. As I have no right or wish to interfere in its administration I cannot do more than say that a good inspector should immediately be sent to report to you upon the state of affairs.[184]

It has been said that Hoare wanted Starkie sent home on the grounds that he was a drunkard.[185] As alluded to in his telegram above, Hoare did not care much for Starkie's wife either, and it did not help that Starkie's wife was of Italian descent – Italy, of course, being an enemy country at the time. It should be stated that Starkie was going through a particularly difficult time in the period when Hoare's telegram was written. Correspondence between him and the Council in London give the impression that he was exhausted and frustrated. For example, he spent whole days in bed recovering from illness and no doubt was exasperated from the constant pressure of being followed by German agents and Spanish police (on one occasion during the autumn he was almost arrested inside the Madrid institute in front of some students – but his diplomatic status of 'Cultural Attaché' saved him from arrest[186]). In addition to this, press reports about the Council in London giving a luncheon for the exiled Republican leader during the Spanish Civil War (i.e. Franco's main enemy), Juan Negrín, could not have helped and he complained bitterly about reports 'in the gutter papers such as the Daily Mirror, growing attacks upon me as an Irishman, a Catholic and so-called Right-Winger'.[187] With these issues, the unfortunate situation described in Hoare's telegram to Robertson might be seen as more of a transient phase than a long-term issue. Negrín's presence in London, along with other Spanish Republicans (a significant number of whom seemed to be employed in the Ministry of Information), was also causing a major headache for Hoare in his relations with Franco.[188]

Prior to these events in the autumn of 1941, a number of letters from Starkie to the British Council in London in March and April 1941 show that Starkie and Hoare were getting on rather well and that their differences were perhaps more due to circumstances than fundamental differences of opinion. Again, the letters are worth quoting at some length:

> The Ambassador [Hoare] himself has told members of the Embassy how enthusiastic he is about the work done by our Institute. He likes the surroundings and he wishes to rely upon us to develop the cultural side of things. Furthermore, he is eager for me to start British Council work in other centres in Spain, especially in Barcelona, Bilbao and Seville. He even told me that he would write back to London to back up proposals to start other Institutes. This attitude of the Ambassador is all the more gratifying to me when I look back on my weeks of depression last autumn [1940] when Lord Lloyd and I talked over relations between Embassy and Institute. Those difficult days are now over and though we still have very great anxieties here on account of the political situation, and the intrigues of our enemies, I yet look with confidence to the future.[189]
>
> . . .[W]hereas formerly he [Hoare] was inclined to be critical about the Council and even cold-shouldered me in my work. Now he wants to speed up our work and he asked me whether there was any way in which he could possibly help.[190]

These letters were written before Hoare started to complain to Robertson about Starkie's inability to run the institute, but nonetheless show that Hoare and Starkie could get on well and that the Hoare-Starkie relationship was not one that always resulted in feelings of animosity on both sides. It appears that it was often circumstances outside of Hoare's and Starkie's control that often led to problems. For example, Hoare's reversal of his enthusiasm for opening an institute in Barcelona was directly due to the German invasion of the Soviet Union in June 1941 which led to an Anglo-Soviet alliance. The Franco regime despised the Soviet Union (later sending a 'Blue Division' to fight alongside the Germans on the Eastern Front, despite professing neutrality) and the Communist influence on the Republican side in the Spanish Civil War was never far from the Spanish Government's mind. With Britain now allied to the Soviet Union, Hoare 'thought this was a bad moment to start Institutes in Barcelona, Malaga and Bilbao'.[191] In particular, Hoare was concerned about the opinion of the Spanish Foreign Minister, Ramón Serrano Suñer (who was particularly pro-Axis and anti-Soviet, and brother-in-law of Franco), who 'would refuse to grant permission' and Hoare 'set his mind definitely against opening them'.[192] As will be shown later, Serrano Suñer attempted to block the opening of the institute in Madrid in 1940, so Hoare's opinion of Serrano Suñer's views had significant weight. Starkie no doubt understood Hoare's concerns, but all the same he must have been disappointed that he could not go ahead in Barcelona – his view surely being that this was the time when an expansion of British cultural influence was most needed.

Only after the initial shock of the Anglo-Soviet alliance had passed, and after Serrano Suñer had been replaced as Foreign Minister (in September 1942) by Conde de Jordana (who was more sympathetic to the Allies), did the Hoare-Starkie relationship recover over the Barcelona institute. In March 1943, Hoare was at last 'willing to allow me [Starkie] to go ahead in Barcelona' and 'agreed to let me prospect any other centres'.[193] Hoare even agreed to open the Barcelona institute personally in October 1943.[194] Although the official opening was delayed owing to the lack of English books that had arrived in the institute, Hoare still visited the new institute on 28 October 1943 remarking on 'the importance of cultural work in the Spanish institutes. In his opinion cultural work of this kind is of immense significance now, and will be still more in the post-war world'.[195] Nevertheless, feelings were still delicate. Hoare remarked only 10 days prior to his visit that

> I am surprised Professor Starkie is still absent from Spain [he was in London meeting British Council officials] and seems to have done nothing to arrange for opening of institute in Barcelona about which he talked to me last July.[196]

Any positive moments were often short-lived and differences between Hoare and Starkie kept on cropping up throughout the war. It is clear that they indeed had some very fundamental differences of opinion that went beyond Starkie's alleged drinking habits, his wife's nationality or how he organized the British Institute's work in Madrid. A prime example of this was Starkie's belief that Gibraltar should be returned to Spain.[197] Gibraltar had been a British possession since it was captured in 1704 during the War of the Spanish Succession and had later been ceded to Britain in perpetuity as part of the Treaty of Utrecht of 1713 – it had been a major issue in Anglo-Spanish relations ever since and indeed still remains an issue to this day. During the Franco era, and particularly during the war, Gibraltar became an emotive issue that at times eclipsed the war itself in importance in Anglo-Spanish relations. When Hoare first arrived in Spain, he was greeted with chants of 'Gibraltar Español' – something he said he 'was often to hear in the next two years'.[198] However much the Gibraltar issue was a sensitive one emotionally for relations between Spain and Britain, it was nonetheless strategically imperative to the success of British and Allied operations in the Mediterranean, North Africa and Italy, and there was no way Britain could afford to give it up regardless of the effect on Anglo-Spanish relations. Although the British could have taken the Canary Islands as strategic recompense if the Spanish (with or without Axis help) took Gibraltar, maintaining control of the Rock was clearly a major priority as it has been estimated the Canaries 'would scarcely provide compensation' for Gibraltar.[199] For Hoare, it was bad enough that German propaganda was promulgating that Hoare had arrived in Madrid to offer Spain Gibraltar (a sign of a weakened and desperate nation),[200] but worse still to have Britons in the country stating their belief that the Rock should be returned to Spain, however 'West' their Britishness might be.

Following Hoare's telegram to Robertson in November 1941, Robertson did indeed take up the suggestion that an inspector should be sent out to Madrid. Professor B. Ifor Evans visited the institute in January 1942 (who Starkie disliked and nicknamed 'B' for Evans'[201]) and wrote a report with recommendations on how to improve the work of the institute (and thereby the relationship between the institute and the Embassy). In the report (which for an unknown reason is only available in a somewhat obscure British Council file regarding an art exhibition in Portugal), Evans wrote that there was a ' "domestic" atmosphere' in the institute (a reference to the fact that Starkie and his wife were living inside the institute) which was making the institute appear unprofessional. Once this was removed, he stated, this 'should give us an opportunity of developing a genuine, and perhaps in time a valuable British centre in Madrid'.[202] Quite why Starkie was living in the institute is not entirely clear, but Evans was congratulated on his achievement in persuading Starkie to move out.[203] By living within the institute Starkie was taking up two rooms which Evans believed were needed for the school and the institute generally if they were to develop adequately.[204] Evans wrote to Starkie stating '[i]t was becoming, I think, an impossible position by which you should be housed in such cramped quarters, and with the expansion of the Institute all the accommodation will obviously be required for public purposes'.[205] The timetable for the institute and school had to be revised a number of times during the autumn of 1941 due to an influx of new pupils which the institute didn't have space for with the Starkie family living on site.[206] This on its own was not the only reason for tensions between Starkie and Hoare, however. The report also recommended (and accepted by Starkie) that two members of staff at the institute should be removed and returned to London (as Hoare had suggested in his telegram). The problem with them was not entirely clear other than a statement that said '[t]hey may possibly have had some provocation for the state of restlessness and dissatisfaction which they have reached'.[207] One of the two members of staff had almost been dismissed a few months earlier – again the reason is not clear, though it would seem to be regarding relations between the institute in Madrid and the institute in Lisbon.[208] A member of the Council staff in London, Carmen Wiggin, who had been involved with the Madrid institute from London was sent out to replace the two who were being removed. What is clear, however, is that it was not designed to undermine Starkie to the extent that he might consider resigning but instead it was intended 'most earnestly to strengthen your [Starkie's] position, particularly in official quarters. . . . You have friends everywhere, and even in some quarters of which you are unaware'.[209] Nevertheless, Robertson commented to Hoare '[t]his report has been worded so that it may be suitable for general circulation, but Ifor Evans has reported to me in greater detail on the actual circumstances in the Institute'[210] – that is, Starkie obviously was not told what Evans (and, by proxy, Hoare) really thought about the institute's work but was given a 'watered down' version. The report was keen to stress that the institute had a key role to play as part of the British presence in Madrid but the political circumstances in Spain at the time meant that the institute staff had to play 'as a single team' with the Embassy.[211] Apparently, the Embassy and Council staff made up one-quarter to one-third of all British people in Madrid at the time and therefore any indiscretions by the institute would be noticed.[212]

Evans' visit, however, had few long-term effects. A year after Evans' report, the animosity between Hoare and Starkie was still all too palpable. John Steegman, who was sent to Spain and Portugal in late 1942 to lecture on art, provided another report to the Council in early 1943, and he appeared resigned to the fact that Hoare and Starkie would never get on well:

> In Madrid this [the relation between the Institute and the Embassy] is largely a question of an undoubted personal antipathy between Sir Samuel Hoare and Professor Starkie, which seems to be reflected, on the Embassy side, down through lower levels. . . . Obviously nothing can be done about this, except to warn Council visitors to Madrid that they will have need of all their tact.[213]

Communication difficulties between Britain and Spain may also have been a contributory factor in the continuing rocky relationship between Hoare and Starkie. Both Hoare and Starkie believed it necessary to follow their own course of action in order to maintain British influence without waiting for instructions from London, and they had different ideas on how that maintenance of British influence should be carried out. Hoare's view was that he had been given plenipotentiary powers stating that 'the British Government realized the urgent and critical nature of the situation, and from the first gave me the free hand that was indispensable if I was to succeed'.[214] Starkie, as one former Council employee has described him, was a ' "one-off" character' who 'ran his own show in Spain, where he was very popular. Even had communication been easier, he would not, I think, have ever kept closely in touch with Headquarters!'[215] He too, therefore, considered it necessary to assume a free hand in his work and would not wait for the 'all clear' from London before proceeding with his ideas. Even so, they could have co-ordinated their activities and aligned their objectives without recourse to London if Hoare and Starkie had seen eye-to-eye. Therefore, it was only their irreconcilable ideas on how to extend British influence in Spain that can be really responsible for their differences, rather than the circumstances of Franco's Spain or communication difficulties in wartime.

Whatever the reasons behind the rocky relationship, it is clear that Hoare and Starkie were still unhappy with each other by the time Hoare returned to London in late 1944. For example, Hoare did not mention the British Council or Starkie once in his autobiography of his wartime mission in Spain titled *Ambassador on Special Mission* written shortly after the war. Had Hoare had little to do with the institute this would not seem so surprising. However, he lectured there, visited and practically inaugurated the Barcelona institute, and his wife was the patron of the British Institute School. The omission, therefore, speaks volumes about what Hoare really thought about the role of the Council and Starkie in complementing his work as Ambassador. It was not lost on Starkie or on Reuters – who published a special feature on the book and stated '[i]f ever anyone had a "special mission" in Spain it was that scholar gypsy Professor Walter Starkie'.[216] Whether the fact that the wife of Reuters's Madrid correspondent (though admittedly not the author of this special feature) taught at the British Institute had any influence on the article is unclear.[217]

Turkey: Sir Hughe Knatchbull-Hugessen and Michael Grant

Sir Hughe Montgomery Knatchbull-Hugessen was a career diplomat and had extensive experience throughout Europe and Asia of the complexities of maintaining and extending British influence. He had already served once in Turkey (or as it was then, the Ottoman Empire) in Constantinople (now Istanbul), as well as in the Netherlands, Belgium, France, the Baltic States, Persia and China. In China, he had been seriously injured during the Japanese attack on Shanghai in 1937 with bullets passing through him close to his spine and took a good year to recover. In later life, however, his injuries would increasingly disable him.[218] He was, therefore, someone who had first-hand experience of the horrors of war, and the difficulties of diplomacy in a variety of circumstances. Knatchbull-Hugessen was sent as the British Ambassador to Ankara, the new capital of Turkey after the Turkish revolution and the disintegration of the Ottoman Empire, in February 1939. With such a wealth of experience, it is unfortunate that his career should be overshadowed by the 'Cicero affair'. 'Cicero' was a Yugoslav of Albanian parents called Elyesa Bazna, who had been hired by Knatchbull-Hugessen in 1943 as his valet. Bazna was a spy who photographed up to 150 British top secret documents between September 1943 and March 1944 and passed them onto the Germans, where they found their way to Joseph Goebbels and Joachim von Ribbentrop. Among other important information, the documents gave details of the plans for the D-Day lands and the minutes of the Tehran Conference.[219] The 'Cicero affair', however, does not appear to have made any appreciable difference to the outcome of military operations in the war, and although Michael Grant, the British Council representative in Turkey, knew Cicero, there is no evidence that any British Council documents or activities were ever compromised and can therefore be said to be of only passing interest to this book.[220] Before war broke out and before the British Council had arrived in Turkey, Knatchbull-Hugessen had already negotiated the Anglo-Turkish Declaration on 12 May 1939 in response to the Italian invasion of Albania. Shortly after war had begun he had engineered the Tripartite Treaty between Britain, France and Turkey of October 1939 which was to ensure that should Turkey be attacked, Britain and France would assist her.[221]

Michael Grant, in contrast to Sir Hughe Knatchbull-Hugessen, cannot be said to be experienced in foreign affairs or diplomacy at the time he was sent to Turkey in 1940. The lack of experience was not, however, due to inability. He was just simply too young, having been born in 1914, to have been experienced. After going to Harrow School and Cambridge University, he applied to join the Army soon after war broke out.[222] His Army career did not last long. He 'had offended against army procedure' by going directly to see a General about the prospect of being a witness for a German friend who was going in front of an internment tribunal, rather than through the army hierarchy. Then he lost his temper at the tribunal – 'a security man at the back of the hall reported my behaviour to the War Office, and I was in disgrace' noted Grant in his autobiography.[223] Fortunately for Grant, Lord Lloyd had become interested in him as he was apparently about the only person in the Army who could speak Turkish. He may have been one of the candidates who, in White's view, was the 'only runner' for the post.[224] Lloyd whisked Grant out of the Army before Grant even managed to return to the War Office after an interview with Lloyd, so impressed was Lloyd with Grant's honesty and appropriateness for the role of British Council representative to Turkey.[225] Grant first went to Egypt to be trained in the role of representative by C. A. F. 'Flux' Dundas, the British Council's representative in Cairo, and then travelled onto Ankara, arriving in the autumn of 1940.[226]

Unlike the relationship between Hoare and Starkie, the relationship between Grant and Knatchbull-Hugessen was amiable and productive. Though, like Hoare, Knatchbull-Hugessen did not mention the Council in his autobiography, and barely mentions it in his diaries.[227] However, in Grant's autobiography, he described Knatchbull-Hugessen as 'friendly, displaying the cheerfulness which proved such an asset to us young British during the subsequent black times of the war'.[228] The close working relationship between Knatchbull-Hugessen and Grant was undoubtedly helped by the fact that Sir Malcolm Robertson was an old friend of Knatchbull-Hugessen – evidenced by the beginning of all of Robertson's letters to him starting with 'My dear Snatch' and always cordial in tone, and Knatchbull-Hugessen's replies every so often starting with 'My dear Arnold' (being Robertson's middle name by which no one else, at least in the archives, addressed him).[229] Knatchbull-Hugessen even asked Robertson at one point whether the British Council would employ his daughter somewhere in the Middle East, such was the friendship between them.[230] It was unfortunate then, that the relationship between the Council and Embassy staff in Ankara at lower levels was often not nearly as amiable or productive, and required the strength of the friendship between Knatchbull-Hugessen and Robertson to resolve disputes.

Dundas had already visited Turkey before Grant's arrival and it was clear from his report that any British Council representative would at best have to live with the scepticism of the Embassy employees. Dundas wrote

> The general census [sic] of opinion amongst British officials and the junior Turkish officials whom I have met is that a British Institute such as the Council has sponsored in other countries would be extremely difficult, if not impossible, to open, and, if it were successful, it would most probably be either closed down or taken over by the Turks. This opinion is expressed by [James] Morgan [the Minister at the British Embassy] (forcibly), Baker (at great length), Middleton Edwards (rudely), and Turks (unanimously).[231]

Admittedly, their scepticism here relates to the wisdom of opening an actual institute, rather than having British Council representation in Turkey in some form, but still, it shows that even before Grant's arrival in Turkey there were many in the British Embassy who would need convincing that his role was justified.

Like the Hoare-Starkie relationship, the disquiet in the Embassy-Council relationship in Turkey was a long-term problem. Grant noted 'courteous though Sir Hughe was, the other members of the British Embassy, when I arrived [in 1940], were in some cases dauntingly unhelpful about my job'.[232] The Embassy staff did not appreciate another British Government organization invading territory that it regarded as its own. Worse still, the Embassy staff were often confounded by strict protocol about what they could and could not do – protocol to which the British Council, as a non-Embassy body, did not have to adhere. For example, James Morgan, Minister in the British Embassy, thought it inconceivable that Grant should try to get English teachers into the Turkish Halkevleri institutes and even tried to obstruct Grant from carrying out his work in this regard.[233] The problem can be described as political from two aspects. First, the Halkevleri were run by the Turkish People's Party (Turkey being a One-Party State at the time) and Morgan was concerned that the Embassy may be seen as supporting the *Party* in Turkey, rather than influencing the *Government* of Turkey. Morgan, Grant noted in February 1941, was 'against all forms of international relationship (cultural, commercial, propagandist) other than the purely diplomatic'.[234] Second, though the People's Party in Turkey was undoubtedly more pro-British than pro-Axis, they did not want to incur the wrath of the German or Italian military.[235] Opening up as much contact with Britain in the cultural sphere was their way of being pro-British without being seen to be politically pro-British. Inviting a non-Embassy based British Council to supply teachers allowed them to carry out this policy successfully. Morgan and many of the Embassy staff believed, however, that the Turks would not recognize the difference between the Embassy and Council or at the very least, the German Embassy in Turkey may press the argument that they were essentially two organizations of the same British Government and that the Turks should not be supporting either if they were really claiming to be neutral.[236] An overly successful Council could, therefore, perhaps make Embassy-Turkish Government relations more difficult. Nevertheless, Grant was approached directly by the Director of the Ankara Halkevi to supply him with an English teacher and later provided many more teachers to many more Halkevleri. Grant stated 'the Party could accept our teachers without seeming to take a political line, which it wanted to avoid, especially during the war'.[237] Morgan and other Embassy officials were not so convinced of this.

The trouble between the Embassy and the Council was also an extension of the Ministry of Information-British Council disputes mentioned earlier in this chapter. The MOI worked through the Embassy via the British Press Attaché (or Councillor), while the Council worked through its own representative. This was not necessarily a problem if the agreed delineation line between Sir John Reith and Lord Lloyd was kept to, but when Lloyd died in February 1941, debates in London about the Council's future permeated through to the outposts in neutral countries. At the Embassy in Ankara the Press Councillor, Leigh Ashton, was a very strong advocate of the view that the MOI should take over the British Council. Ashton and Grant were on amiable personal terms throughout the period and travelled to Smyrna (now Izmir) for an exhibition at the Smyrna Fair, lunched together and discussed ancient coins, but they had fierce differences of opinion at a professional level.[238] Also, owing to communications difficulties between London and Ankara during the war, it took some time before Ashton realized that it had been decided in London that the Council would remain in place after Lloyd's death and that Sir Malcolm Robertson would succeed him. He 'continued to express the view that the Council should come under the Ministry of Information – unaware, apparently, that his battle had been lost in London'.[239] Ashton was, however, to cause Grant some more discomfort later in the war.

During 1941, with the fall of Greece and Yugoslavia to Germany and with Bulgaria joining the Axis, it was increasingly feared that Turkey would be the next target for German aggression. Many British Council representatives from these newly occupied countries had already arrived in Turkey and it was clear that a contingency plan was needed to evacuate British Council staff in Turkey to Egypt or elsewhere in the Middle East or Africa, in the event of a German invasion. Istanbul, where many Embassy and Council staff were based, was clearly the highest priority for a plan owing to its strategic location on the Bosphorus and being the closest large city in Turkey to Axis territory. A plan existed on paper for a tug and a barge to take both Embassy and Council staff on the European side of Istanbul across the Bosphorus to rendezvous on the Asiatic side, but there was no fuel for the boats and indeed, one of the boats had been taken away by the Turkish authorities since the plan had been drawn up. Grant remarked

> no meeting-places have been announced and no instructions whatever given to the Council staff or other residents. Nor has any thought been given to transport through Anatolia if anyone succeeded in crossing the Bosphorus. . . .
> I must therefore state with regret but certainty that the Embassy will take no effective measures to evacuate the Council staff from Istanbul in the event of an emergency.[240]

Morgan was again identified as the culprit of many of the Embassy's shortcomings from Grant's point of view. Grant clearly had no faith in relying on the Embassy to help in any evacuation stating that they would 'throw the blame for the loss of staff on the Council' – 'I have time after time begged the Ambassador and Consul-General and their staffs and so-called "wardens" to get something done'.[241] It took Sir Malcolm Robertson's intervention, by writing to Sir Alexander Cadogan in the Foreign Office, to get the situation resolved.[242] Cadogan claimed that

> [w]e have assumed that the British Council staff and their families have been included in the general scheme [for evacuation], but have not been informed of its details. These must necessarily remain as secret as possible, and it is probable that the Embassy has not communicated them to your representative.[243]

Nevertheless Knatchbull-Hugessen was instructed to 'communicate the general outline of the plans to Mr. Grant confidentially'.[244] It was very fortunate that in the meantime no German invasion of Turkey took place, but trust between the Council and the Embassy was severely tested by this incident, however secret the plans may have been.

Two years later, in the late summer and autumn of 1943, relations had not improved between the Embassy and the Council and appeared, in fact, to have hit an all-time low. Grant wrote a note to Knatchbull-Hugessen on 30 August which is worth quoting at some length, as it demonstrates that Grant was venting a lot of pent-up frustration (albeit politely and respectfully) which had clearly been building up over several months:

> With regard to the general question of messages, we shall of course be very glad to fall in with your wishes and show you messages before passing them on. I am writing to Sir Malcolm informing him of your request. As you know I am most anxious not to do or say anything that would conflict with your policies vis-à-vis the Turks; although, owing to the greater indirectness of our methods of trying to strengthen British influence (and the extreme desirability of not compromising these methods), it is not practicable for us to appear in any positive way to be guided by such policies. I submit to you the suggestion that it is in accordance with British interests for us to continue on our way apparently unaffected by the vicissitudes of political and commercial relations. These vicissitudes, and the violent criticism that they are arousing among leading Turks, are not preventing us from continuing to extend our influence at present, and surely it is desirable that they should not do so (providing, of course, that we do and say nothing contrary to Embassy interests), since the concessions that they are giving us in this field will certainly make themselves felt later on. . . .
>
> With regard to the accusation of 'buttering up' which is levelled against me with monotonous frequency, I should like to point out yet again that any individual cases of apparent 'buttering up' that I do are undertaken as a result of deliberate and calculated policy, that is to say to fulfil specific aims (e.g. to secure an appointment) directed solely towards the general purpose of increasing British influence. The assertion that we are 'pro-Turk', meant in a pejorative sense, which is heard from time to time in the lower ranks of the Embassy, is in the light of this rather annoying, but I suppose it is more or less inevitable in view of the unwontedly far-reaching system of personal and educational contacts with Turks that we are trying to achieve. It would be a help to me if critics or enquiries on matters of Council policy or business could pass their criticism either straight to Mr. Covington or myself, or through Mr. Busk, rather than allowing them to reach junior members of my staff who are necessarily imperfectly informed on the details of Council policy.[245]

Clearly Grant's ability to make good contacts with the Turkish authorities, helped by his position of not being connected directly to the Embassy, was causing some of the Embassy staff to become envious, or alternatively wanted, in Grant's words, to 'cash in' on the Council's successes.[246] Ashton, as might be expected in his position as Press Councillor, was the instigator of Grant's troubles in this event – 'the occasion of this note [to Knatchbull-Hugessen]' Grant wrote to Robertson on the same day attaching a copy of his note, 'was an ill-mannered complaint by Ashton about the amount of publicity that the Council received in the Turkish newspapers'.[247] Ashton was not the only complainant, however. Knox Helm, the Commercial Attaché (and later from 1951 to 1954 Ambassador to Turkey), Grant noted, 'often gets angry because our friendly reception from the Turkish Press, which conflicts strangely with the recurrent crises in commercial and other relations'.[248] And Helm was generally pro-Council.[249]

Robertson wrote to Knatchbull-Hugessen on 8 September after he had received a copy of Grant's letter to Knatchbull-Hugessen which he said 'disturb[ed] me very much'.[250] No copy of the 8 September letter appears to have survived but Knatchbull-Hugessen took over a month to reply to it, so that he could 'look all round the question' as, he said, 'there appears to be something in it'.[251] Knatchbull-Hugessen replied on 11 October agreeing to much of what Robertson had raised in his letter of 8 September. However, Knatchbull-Hugessen disagreed that there should be a real separation between the work of the Embassy and the Council which he 'ha[d] been told' was being pursued by the British Council. He said he wanted to 'confine [his] belief in separation to "ostensible separation"', so that both organizations would not be in the position of 'not knowing what the other was doing while the Turks would still believe that we were working together'. Lastly, he stated, '[a]nother cause of the trouble is the consciousness that the British Council people here have more money to spend than have the Embassy staff; and in fact are better paid generally'.[252] When Grant saw the letter he was fuming stating '[t]he whole letter is obviously drafted by Helm, of whose views every paragraph bears the mark. There are only a few interpolations by the Ambassador'.[253] However, the incident faded after a time, and Grant returned to London in late 1943 to meet Robertson and other Council officials – not about this incident but about funding issues and related future policy which was difficult to communicate by letter and telegram.[254] He returned refreshed and no other major flashpoints appear to have occurred between Embassy and Council during the war.

Nonetheless, like the Hoare-Starkie problems, therefore, the difficulties in the Embassy-Council relations were long term and although there were peaks and troughs, the relations were never very positive. The question is whether it really mattered if the Council and Embassy were able to achieve their objectives. Constant irritations could be tolerable if success was being attained. An assessment of the Council's success will take place in later chapters.

Portugal: Sir Ronald Campbell and Professor S. George West

Sir Ronald Hugh Campbell had made his career in the Foreign Office. He did not have the breadth of Ambassadorial experience of Sir Hughe Knatchbull-Hugessen, having worked his way up through the ranks of the civil service in the Foreign Office. He had, nevertheless, travelled widely and had a very good knowledge of foreign affairs. It was only in 1929 that he was first appointed abroad, as envoy-extraordinary and minister-plenipotentiary in Paris. Then, after a few years as Minister in Belgrade in 1935, he returned to be Ambassador in Paris in July 1939. With the German invasion of France the following year, Campbell had joined the French Government's exodus from Paris to Bordeaux and left France for Britain when the Franco-German armistice had been signed.[255] Campbell was an 'unassuming and gently persuasive Scot' though with 'an unflinching purpose at the back of his non-committal manner'.[256] He had perhaps a more congenial manner about him than Hoare and had a 'meticulous' attention to detail which was perhaps lacking in Knatchbull-Hugessen through his apparent aloofness from the quarrels between Grant and members of his Embassy.[257] Both attributes were good omens for his relationship with the British Council in Portugal. Sir Walford Selby, who was replaced by Campbell as British Ambassador to Portugal in 1940, had already actively supported Professor George West, the Council's representative in Portugal, and 'expressed relief that at long last serious steps were being taken to counter German propaganda.'[258] Selby wrote a letter to Charles Bridge, the British Council's Secretary-General until 1940, containing his opinion of the work of the British Institute in Lisbon. Bridge sent it on to the Foreign Office 'to help them in their attack on the Treasury to get authority to spend' – although the letter does not appear to have survived, its content clearly supported the Council's work in Portugal.[259] Campbell was evidently entering a situation in Portugal, where the relationship between the Embassy and the Council was already good.

Professor Sidney George West, known by his second name George, was an expert in Portuguese culture. He had been a lecturer at the University of Coimbra – Portugal's foremost University – since the early 1930s and, according to a friend of his (and later librarian at the British Institute Library) had 'incorporated the spirit of the Coimbra student – he was affable, very sociable'.[260] West had also lectured at King's College, London on the Portuguese language where a collection of his Portuguese images from the 1930s is still available at the College's Archives.[261] Throughout the 1930s, West had attempted to improve Anglo-Portuguese cultural relations, and was perturbed that the Germans, Italians and French all had institutes in Portugal, but the British did not.[262] His advocacy for a British Institute in Portugal was partly responsible for the establishment of the British Council itself in late 1934 (as the British Committee for Relations with Other Countries) together with other advocates for similar institutes around the Mediterranean area.[263] West noted in October 1937 in a lecture at the Royal Institute of International Affairs in London that 'Portugal's confidence in Britain's role as protector of the smaller, defenceless countries against aggression was shaken by our attitude over the Italo-Abyssinian dispute, and she is taking no chances'. Nevertheless, he stated, Portugal was still 'genuinely anxious to retain Great Britain's friendship and interest' despite the fact that '[m]isrepresentations in the British Press' regarding Portugal 'have not passed unnoticed'.[264] It was these misrepresentations in both countries that West was working in Portugal to overcome during the 1930s. In the mid-1930s he had taken a leading part in setting up an English Institute within the University of Coimbra.[265] Though this was not under the aegis of the British Council, the Council later provided grants for lecturers, books and lantern-lectures at the University through the institute.[266] When, in 1938, the British Council decided to establish a British Institute in Portugal (the first in Europe, and second only in the world to the one opened in Cairo), West was the obvious choice for the Director of the institute.

Unlike in Spain, Turkey or Sweden, the British Council had started to operate in Portugal before war broke out, and cannot be seen as a knee-jerk reaction to the immediate threat of German troops entering the country. It was more of a move to extend British influence where German and Italian influence was generally more obvious and forthright. Indeed even during the war Portugal was never bordered by an Axis or Axis-occupied country, unlike the other three countries that are being examined in detail here. The Germans were on the Pyrenees not the Douro. Although it would be wrong to assume that the course of Second World War was not relevant to Anglo-Portuguese relations or that Portugal was unimportant to either side in the war (it clearly had a key strategic position as a refugee transit port), the lack of pressure for *immediate* action allowed the British Council and the British Embassy in Portugal to plan their actions and ways of maintaining and extending British influence in a more thorough and collaborative manner. One former British Council employee, who met West after the war described him as 'fairly approachable' in comparison to other representatives who, by contrast, had 'very alarming' personalities.[267] Another employee described him as 'devoted to Portugal and all things Portuguese and he was popular and well thought of in that country'.[268] There were many reasons for believing that a good relationship between the Embassy and the Council in Portugal were highly likely as both Campbell and West were much more collaborative and tolerant personalities than in some of the other countries studied here and the relationship between the Council and Embassy started before the war on a much firmer basis. Lord Lloyd travelled to Lisbon to open the '*Instituto Britânico*' in November 1938 together with the Portuguese Minister of Education, Dr António Faria Carneiro Pacheco, with both Selby and West attending, showing that the Embassy and Council were united.[269]

However, the Foreign Office and by extension, the Embassy, still wanted to maintain an official separation of duties between the Embassy and the Council, even if logistically it may have seemed more sensible to merge the two. In late 1939, the British Institute was trying to acquire some property and, so as to 'avoid difficulties' with the Portuguese authorities, 'an enquiry was made to the Foreign Office [by the Embassy] as to whether the Institute could in some way be annexed to His Majesty's Embassy' but was met with 'a categorical negative'.[270] There was a clear understanding that

> if the cultural work and propaganda of the British Council is to continue its present undoubted successes it must not become associated with the political propaganda of the Ministry of Information, for if it is every activity of the British Council and the Institutes would be the subject of protests from the German Minister in Lisbon and an embarrassment to the Portuguese Government and to our best friends in Portugal.[271]

Nevertheless, it was noted that the Portuguese Government certainly viewed the 'Instituto Britânico em Portugal as an offshoot of the British Embassy.... Indeed we believe it is proposed to pass a decree to give legal effect to that view'.[272] Lawyers advising on behalf of the institute recommended that the Portuguese Government should be 'allowed (if not invited) to recognize the *Instituto Britânico em Portugal* as being a part or dependency of the British Embassy, and the property as being necessary for the purpose of the Embassy'.[273] Other alternatives suggested creating the institute as a Limited Company, which would have required the word 'Limited' to be inserted into the title which was 'probably not desired', or requesting the Government to recognize the institute as a 'legal entity' separate from the Embassy. However, that too was 'open to misinterpretation' by the Portuguese authorities.[274] The desired official separation was increasingly seen as the solution in an ideal world – but that pragmatism had to be the order of the day, especially in time of war, and some sort of merging would be necessary. It was recognized by the Embassy that until 'normal conditions return' it would be sensible to make the institute an offshoot of the Embassy, though with the requisite caution so that there was not a move to 'mix propaganda with the teaching curriculum of the Institute'.[275] D. Cowan, of the Ministry of Information, who had visited Portugal in early 1940, was very supportive of the Council and had no objection to the ostensible separation of the Council's and MOI's work, even if legally they were in fact joined.[276] It appears, however, that the Foreign Office maintained its opposition to the merger and put pressure on the Council to establish a company titled 'British Council Nominees Limited' to own the property in which the British Institute in Lisbon operated and it was envisaged that this company would own all of the Council's buildings around the world. The Council and the Embassy continued to urge the Foreign Office to change its mind for practical reasons, but it is unclear from the archival records whether they made any progress.[277]

Whatever the legal implications for merging or separating the Embassy and the institute, in the end it did not really matter. The important point here is that they certainly worked closely together. In the organization of the British representation at the centenary celebrations for the Portuguese Youth Movement in 1939, Selby worked closely with West to ensure that there was a single British representation organized by the British Council with the Embassy giving direction.[278] Campbell considered the institute in Lisbon to be a model institute remarking that 'its work is far more valuable than that of any other propaganda in Portugal'.[279] In fact it is difficult, unlike the numerous examples of animosity between Council and Embassy in Spain and Turkey, to find any example of such difficulties in Portugal. Examples of a good working relationship range from the visit of the Oxford University delegation who travelled to Portugal to confer a degree upon Dr Oliveiro Salazar, the Portuguese leader (to which Anthony Haigh, an employee of the Embassy in Lisbon, stated the Council could be proud of 'having contributed to a first-class propaganda achievement'[280]); to the co-operation to support the ailing newspaper *Anglo-Portuguese News* (APN) which had been in financial difficulties since the late 1930s. It was agreed that APN should be kept going 'at whatever cost' as the Germans would have 'made great capital out of a cessation of publication' despite it being viewed by one visitor as 'useless as an organ of propaganda'.[281] (The APN will be discussed in more detail in the next chapter). Whenever lecturers visited from Britain, they usually remarked that Embassy and the institute worked together to provide their hospitality.[282] Whether legally one and the same, or separate organizations, there was a clear high level of co-operation between all the British government bodies in Portugal.

Henry Hopkinson, the British Minister in Lisbon summed up the Embassy support for the Council's work at a talk in March 1944. He showed his support for cultural relations when he opened a book exhibition at the British Institute in Lisbon, by stating

> I think everyone will agree with me when I say that the best way to learn about foreign countries, their people, their lives and their cultures – is to go there and live there. But if, by misfortune, that is not possible as is now the case because of the conditions imposed by the war, the best thing we can do is study the art of those countries and, above all, familiarise ourselves with their literature [Original Portuguese in footnote].[283]

There is one example, however, that delves a little deeper under the surface than all of the examples above, which shows that not everything was quite as rosy as it appeared from the outside. John Steegman, who, as mentioned earlier, visited Spain and Portugal in late 1942 and early 1943 to lecture on art, highlighted a number of problems and improvements that could be made between the Embassy and the institute. True, in comparison to the difficulties between Hoare and Starkie, Steegman stated 'there are no difficulties of that sort. . . . Mr. [S George] West is on good personal terms with the Ambassador, and has constant liberty of access to him whenever he wants it'.[284] However, Steegman noted, 'the Ambassador is not, I think, very much interested in the Council'.[285] That in itself would not be too much of a concern. But, Steegman went on:

> [The] Embassy in Lisbon, and some of the colony, are inclined to criticise Mr. and Mrs. West on merely social grounds. I think it might be better if they played a more distinguished part in social life, but they have no intention of doing so, and are probably right; they have not got, and could not be expected to acquire, the social gifts of the Starkies and, in any case, Lisbon is not Madrid. If it were, the criticism would be valid.[286]

Valid or not, the criticism was still there and relations clearly had some scope for improvement. Steegman also suggested another reason for the lack of interest in the Council's work in Portugal, stating that 'I fancy that the higher levels in the Embassy are not yet sufficiently impressed by the significance of the Council. Possibly they regard the "Anglo-Portuguese News" as typical of the Council's abilities and are discouraged from looking further'.[287] In addition to this, Steegman noted, 'relations between the Institutes and the Embassy Press Sections [in both Madrid and Lisbon] are in drastic need of improvement'.[288] While the 'prominence given by the [Portuguese] Press to the exhibition and lectures' was good '[t]his must, I think, be regarded as a symptom of the goodwill existing between the British Institute and the Press, rather than as being due to any activity on the part of the Embassy Press Section'.[289] There were over 3,000 articles listed in the British Council's Portuguese Historical Archive about the British Institute or Anglo-Portuguese in the Portuguese Press during the war period, which was an average of nearly one and a half each day.[290] This was a vast number and is an excellent example of that goodwill. There was evidently some room to improve aspects of the relationship between the Embassy and the institute, but this should not detract from their good relations overall, which were clearly lacking in Spain and Turkey, or the good relations which the Embassy and the institute collectively forged with the Portuguese authorities, press and people.

Sweden: Sir Victor Mallet and Ronald Bottrall

Sir Victor Alexander Louis Mallet had a similar length and breadth of diplomatic experience as Sir Hughe Knatchbull-Hugessen. After serving in First World War, he held diplomatic posts in Persia, Argentina, Belgium and the United States of America before being appointed Minister in Stockholm in 1940. In fact, he was in Persia at the same time as Knatchbull-Hugessen in the mid-1930s and said that the Knatchbull-Hugessen family 'at once attracted young contemporaries from London society, which added greatly to our gaiety'.[291] In his unpublished autobiography, Mallet always tried to see his work in the context of the bigger picture of world events and looked forward to a chance to work with new people and in new situations.[292] Stockholm was his first chance to head a British mission, and he was very keen to get a good understanding of Sweden, Scandinavia generally, and how to extend British influence at a time when Germany was already at war with Britain and France.[293] He was keen, no doubt, to create a collaborative working environment not only to impress the Swedes, but also to keep the British colony together – they were, after all, practically surrounded by German-occupied territory. For 18 months after the German invasion of Denmark and Norway in April 1940, there were only five courier flights from Britain to Sweden.[294] To try to avoid feelings of isolation, the British colony would have needed to work together.

Francis James Ronald Bottrall, known by his third name Ronald, was a poet who had met the Ministry of Information's man in Stockholm, Peter Tennant, at Cambridge University. Bottrall had already published his *Festivals of Fire* (1934) and *The Turning Path* (1939) before the war, and so was a respected poet when he was in Sweden even before he published his more famous post-war work. Tennant had been asked by the British Council to 'hold a watching brief' for them as Press Attaché in Stockholm, but in the autumn of 1941, because of the lack of time that he had to devote to both the Press Attaché work and British Council representative, he asked the Council if he could be relieved from his Council duties.[295] He suggested that Bottrall be sent to Sweden, as he had some experience as a lecturer in Finland before the war, but was then 'languishing from boredom as a Principal in the Ministry of Aircraft Production'.[296] Within a few weeks Bottrall was flown out to Stockholm with his wife Margaret. Ronald Bottrall and Victor Mallet were clearly good friends. Unlike Knatchbull-Hugessen and Hoare, Mallet mentioned the work of the British Council (and Bottrall's role in particular) in a positive light in his memoirs – this clearly shows that they worked well together in Sweden.[297] The fact that they worked together again after the war in Italy when Mallet was Ambassador there and Bottrall again was British Council representative, is good evidence that their relationship in Sweden was productive and there could have been no irreconcilable differences between them.[298]

Bottrall worked as a Cultural Attaché in all but name. Owing to the war, Bottrall's son Anthony recalled that there was 'a likely reduction in the B[ritish] C[ouncil]'s capacity to operate as independently of the Embassy as in peacetime' and a need to 'sing to the same hymn sheet when dealing with Swedish officials and other influential people'.[299] Bottrall and Tennant collaborated in the production of a weekly newspaper titled *Nyheter från Storbritannien* (News from Great Britain) – which after D-Day had a circulation of 250,000 per issue.[300] Notionally a Ministry of Information publication, it contained all the details of Bottrall's work such as an exhibition of English watercolour paintings in January 1942, summer schools for Swedish teachers of the English language in Sigtuna, Lundsberg and St Sigfrids and adverts for a translation of T. S. Eliot poems by Bottrall and Gunnar Ekelöf.[301] Mallet had only good things to say about both Tennant and Bottrall in his memoirs. Tennant, he stated, was a 'first class Swedish scholar. He did wonderful work throughout the war, having contacts in many directions and putting me in touch with two or three extremely pro-British journalists and professors'.[302] As for Bottrall, he said he was 'a man of imagination' who 'admirably arranged' cultural events and was 'most active and successful' in doing so.[303] The three men clearly had a high regard for each other and worked well together under difficult circumstances and looked after each other's work when they made visits to London.[304]

Sir Malcolm Robertson wrote to Sir Victor Mallet in June 1942 after the visit of T. S. Eliot to Stockholm on behalf of the Council to acknowledge Mallet's support. He wrote:

> I am more than grateful for all that you and Peggy [Victor Mallet's wife] did to help and for the great hospitality that you showed him [Eliot]. . . . The Council at all times appreciate the advice and help which they continually receive from you and your Legation.[305]

Tennant had taken Eliot out on his sailing boat while he was in Sweden where they discussed poetry.[306]

In 1945, from Kenneth Clark's diary of his visit to Sweden, it is clear that the Legation and the Council were still closely co-operating. First, Clark was visiting under Council auspices and his lectures and entertainment were organized by the Council. However, he stayed at the Legation with Sir Victor Mallet.[307] A press conference was organized by the British Council in Mallet's official residence.[308] However, it was not just a matter of Legation-Council co-operation in Stockholm. When Clark visited Gothenburg, Uppsala and Malmö, the local British representatives of many British organizations ensured that he was well entertained through lunches and dinners, and all played their part in arranging meetings to visit local Swedish artists and dignitaries.[309] It no doubt helped that this particular trip was organized at the request of the Crown Prince of Sweden and the Director of Swedish National Museum. Perhaps it would be unthinkable that the two British government bodies would not have co-operated, but nevertheless the level of co-operation was still far higher than occurred in Spain, Turkey or Portugal.[310] Ewan Butler, an SOE member who was in Stockholm during the later war years, noted in his autobiography that Bottrall had

> struggled manfully to keep the flame alight with such unpromising material as lay to hand. Anybody in the British Legation who happened to have an evening, or better still, a day, off, was recruited by Bottrall to travel, often to a remote part of Sweden, and to deliver a lecture to the local branch of the Swedish-British Society.[311]

The Council and the Legation were clearly closely connected and worked well together in Sweden. Partly, this was due to the isolation that the British colony felt in Stockholm. Morale needed to be kept high and constant interaction between the members of the British community would have helped. However, it was largely because Bottrall and Mallet got on so well that this friendship permeated down to lower levels in both organizations.

Unlike Ronald Campbell who was on congenial terms with West in Portugal but was perhaps not particularly interested in the Council's work, or Knatchbull-Hugessen who was friendly but aloof from the Embassy-Council problems in Ankara, or indeed Hoare, who was at times set against the Council's work in Spain, Victor Mallet was not just on friendly terms with Ronald Bottrall, but actively suggested ways in which the Council could extend its work and encouraged the Council at all times. So much so, in fact, that Sir Malcolm Robertson had to politely turn down many of the requests that

Mallet made for visitors to Sweden during the war largely owing to transport difficulties. In September 1942, Mallet was keen to see a visit from a theatrical company, as well as a football team, but Robertson had to decline stating

> I am afraid that we must consider such visits as being impossible for the time being. . . . I should very deeply appreciate it if you would let me know whether you have any further comments to make upon these two suggestions or whether there are any alternative proposals which you may care to make.[312]

Perhaps Mallet did not receive his letter or suggested a way round the difficulties that Robertson had stated, as he asked again on the 20 October for the football team, and Robertson again had to politely turn down his request.[313]

A year later, however, Mallet was becoming disappointed with the Council's performance as they had turned down so many of his proposals for lecturers to be sent to Sweden. He wanted them to push forward with expanding British influence beyond their capacity to deliver. Robertson, in reply, wrote to Mallet on 1 November 1943 stating

> I cannot see that the picture is quite as black as you paint it. Indeed, to be frank with you, we feel here that it was a matter for congratulation that we have been able to do so much for Sweden rather than for complaint because we have failed to do more. . . . I take it a little hard that we should be trounced because our efforts are not always as successful as we could wish.[314]

Mallet perhaps realized that he had pushed his wishes a little too far beyond what was actually possibly during tough wartime conditions. He was later to express his admiration for the British Council for sending out so many visitors and particularly for organizing a watercolour exhibition (having flown all the paintings to Sweden in sixteen different packages).[315] Mallet was also keen to purchase some of the paintings that were sent to Sweden, and therefore showed that he held art exhibitions in great esteem and congratulated Major Alfred A. Longden, the British Council's Fine Art Director, for 'all the efforts you have put into sending out these water-colours which are playing their part in the *most* successful drive which the British Council is making nowadays in Sweden' [Mallet's emphasis].[316]

In his memoirs, Mallet expressed the view that the British Council had played a major part in helping to convince the Swedish Foreign Minister, Christian Günther, by way of a concert of English songs, of the importance of British culture, to the extent that he agreed to send to England the wreckage of a prototype V2 bomb that had landed accidentally in Sweden. Mallet noted:

> Soon after we had started home [from Sigtuna, where the British Council concert took place] Günther said to me that he had been very deeply moved by the beauty of the music and indeed by the whole atmosphere of this Anglo-Swedish school, which had been so admirably arranged by Mr. Bottrall. It had made him reflect on the subject of the bomb and he had decided that it would not be right for him to deprive us of the opportunity of counteracting such a devilish weapon, which might be used to destroy thousands of innocent British civilian lives. . . . When people have abused the British Council to me, I have always answered that there

was one occasion at least upon which the British Council played a very important part in the war. Had it not been for the opportunity they gave me of this drive with the Swedish Foreign Minister and had it not been for the emotion which their concert had aroused in him, we might have spent weeks of wrangling and even possibly never have got the bomb.[317]

Clearly, the Mallet-British Council relationship worked well, and after this incident, he was never to have a bad word to say about the organization.

Conclusion

The British Council had to deal with extraordinary tensions in its relations with British organizations and individuals, at an extraordinary time. Both inside and outside the Government, the Council came under immense pressure with regard to how it should operate, what type of propaganda it should undertake and what image of Britain it should present to neutral Europe. As an officially non-political body representing Britain, the Council had to represent Britain as a whole. This involved the balancing of an array of different interests to ensure it represented both right and left wing political opinions, all four nations of the United Kingdom, a variety of different interpretations of what British culture was and a variety of expert opinions. This was difficult enough in peacetime and it proved impossible to please everybody all the time with regard to the image of Britain which should be presented abroad during the war. Yet it believed it was presenting a truthful image of Britain and not one that could be dismissed as propaganda in a negative sense. On top of this, the Council had to balance the pressures within Britain about what image to present and the image to which the neutral countries would be receptive. Philip Newman may not have been thought of by the Music Committee as a great violinist, but he was popular in Portugal. Benjamin Britten, though a conscientious objector, was arguably Britain's foremost composer at the time and could not just be ignored. On numerous occasions, the Council had to make judgement calls like these in favour of what would work as propaganda abroad in the face of criticism at home.

Once a consideration of the issues regarding the image to be presented had been undertaken, the Council was under other pressures. Aligning its work with that of the Embassies in neutral countries (working much better in Sweden and Portugal than in Spain and Turkey), budget pressures from the Treasury (who maintained that the Council's finances were not under control) and political pressure from the Ministry of Information (in an argument surrounding spheres of influence and what type of propaganda the Council should be conducting, if any at all) were three of the most significant pressures if faced from an administrative point of view. Cultural propaganda was often seen as a long-term strategy with little to offer to the war effort itself. Hoare in Spain was often directly guided by the events in the war, such as the British-Soviet alliance in June 1941 and the Allied invasion of North Africa in 1942. Diplomacy with Franco to keep him out of the war and from disrupting Allied military plans for Africa was a major part of his role. He was reluctant to give much time and effort to cultural questions when his attention was needed elsewhere. In Turkey and in Balkan countries, the SOE and SIS certainly saw the Council as a cover for other activities rather than as conducting an important activity in itself. At certain times – particularly from the autumn of 1939 to early 1940, and again in February 1941 – the British Council's very existence was in doubt largely due to questions about the value of cultural propaganda during wartime. These doubts, of course, focused on the need for an immediate 'return on investment' which missed the point about how cultural propaganda worked on a long-term, but pervasive, basis.

The strength of personality in these relationships was a major factor in whether the British Council succeeded or failed both in balancing the numerous pressures it was under and in conducting successful cultural propaganda. The animosity between Starkie and Hoare, and between Grant and certain Embassy officials in Ankara had implications for how much time both Starkie and Grant had to promote and defend their activities among the British colony as opposed to spending their time concentrating on conducting cultural propaganda. West and Bottrall clearly had far better relationships with Campbell and Mallet respectively, and knowing that they had their support would have undoubtedly improved their efficiency and effectiveness in promoting Britain's image in Portugal and Sweden. Personality and personal networks also played key roles in persuading famous personalities to join Advisory Committees and to travel to neutral countries. Longden's constant engagement with artists and art critics played a major part in keeping them interested in the Council's work. He, and many others, found it difficult to keep in control of such a diverse and opinionated group of people.

There would always be people who did not support the Council and regarded its work as a waste of vital resources in a time of emergency. Lord Beaverbrook and his newspapers were the foremost critics of the Council's work and remained so throughout the war and beyond. However, it is actually remarkable that considering all of the pressures that it was under from other British organizations and individuals that it made so few mistakes and alienated so few of its critics entirely. In a sense, however, it did not matter a great deal what state the relations between the Council and other British organizations were in, as long as any difficulties did not stop the Council from operating effectively abroad. That, after all, was its mission – to promote British life and thought abroad. Its success or failure did not depend on how effective it was in managing its relations within Britain and with the Embassies. Though that undoubtedly influenced its operations, its success or failure can only be based on the effectiveness of its methods of cultural propaganda, which is the subject of the next chapter.

On the Front Line:
Cultural Propaganda in Action

The 'one size fits all' approach versus the bespoke approach to propaganda

In an ideal world, any organization involved in propaganda (cultural or otherwise) would want to work with a 'one size fits all' approach. That is to say that they would ideally like to use common methods of disseminating messages across all of the differing audiences that it wished to influence. This approach, of course, has a lot of attractions particularly resulting in administrative savings both in the design and in the deployment of the propaganda itself, particularly in wartime when resources are stretched and the time available to make an effect is limited. This approach also has many advantages in establishing an overarching framework of complementary themes helping to convey the intended message. However, this approach does not take into account that the world is far from ideal – or more precisely, audiences for the propaganda are rarely similar in outlook, history and values and are unlikely to understand the same message in the same way. This issue was particularly acute for the British Council working, as it did, across a wide geographical area. As was mentioned earlier, each neutral country where the Council operated already had an existing view of Britain, the other combatant countries and the war generally. While Sweden was a democracy, it feared the Soviet Union far more than Nazi Germany as a threat to its liberty and German influence was profound – yet areas of the country such as Gothenburg (which was known as 'little London'¹) were far more pro-British owing to historic trading links. Portugal had an alliance with England dating back to medieval times and had a common sea-faring history. Spain had just emerged from a Civil War where the victorious General Franco had relied on German and Italian support to win and despised the British presence in Gibraltar. Turkey had been a German ally in First World War but since the war had had a revolution, and the new Government had an admiration for British progress which they were keen to emulate in many ways – and they feared the Soviet Union because of Russia's ancient ambition to control the Dardanelles and Bosphorus, and the Italians who were present in the Dodecanese Islands. Also within each country there was a kaleidoscope of differing viewpoints defined by religion, politics, class and separatism to name a few issues. Clearly, a commonality of approach in employing methods of propaganda, let alone the messages conveyed by those methods, would not be appropriate across all of the four European countries in which the Council operated.

Yet, as we have seen from the previous chapter, the operational environments within which the British Council had to function also had a profound effect on the methods that the Council used to disseminate its cultural propaganda. Issues of practicality in transferring people and materials overseas for cultural propaganda purposes in wartime, the money necessarily involved (particularly with challenging and fluctuating exchange rates) and logistical issues of co-ordination were all factors constraining how the Council could adapt its work to the bespoke needs of the variety of audiences it was trying to reach. Relations between the Council representatives and Ambassadors, differing personalities and relations between the Council in London and other British organizations also had an effect on the methods being employed in each country. The methods of propaganda were, therefore, intrinsically linked to the operational environment and could not always be best suited to the needs of the audience.

The Council had to find a balance between the needs of the varying audiences, the issues between British organizations which affected its work, issues of practicality in wartime and the ideal 'one size fits all' approach to devise methods of propaganda that would have the desired effect of promoting British life and thought abroad. There are a surprising number of similarities between how it operated in each of the European neutrals, with a plethora of common themes running through the Council's work wherever it took place. This was partly due to the similarity of the audience that it was aiming for across all of those countries – that is, the elites – but as will be shown in this chapter, this certainly did not mean that the Council was insensitive to local conditions, or simply threw money at producing a certain form of propaganda, just because it had worked successfully elsewhere. The Council was acutely aware of the existing sociological conditions of each country and the differences which needed to be taken into consideration to make its cultural propaganda effective – and attempted to be 'chameleon-like' (in the words of a post-war Swedish Institute director).[2] This chapter also looks at the messages being conveyed through the methods of propaganda because, as we shall see, in cultural propaganda, the message conveyed is often determined by the method of propaganda being employed.

Institutes

British Institutes were established in three of the four countries on which this book focuses. Turkey, as was mentioned in the previous chapter, was the odd one out because the Embassy believed that 'it would most probably be either closed down or taken over by the Turks'.[3] However, even in Turkey there were British Council offices established in Ankara, Istanbul, Izmir (then Smyrna), Mersin and Samsun.[4] Michael Grant, the British Council's representative in Turkey, also established six lending libraries which, taken together, in essence (as offices and libraries were the mainstay of an institute in any of the other three countries) created institutes in all but name.[5] However, Grant concentrated on working with the existing official institutes (the Party-run Halkevleri) instead of attempting to turn the Council offices-cum-libraries into teaching institutes as had been the case in Spain and Portugal. Elsewhere, establishing institutes was still not a straightforward exercise even if the Embassy had given its consent in principle.

In many ways, the establishment of a British Institute in a hostile environment, such as Madrid in 1940, was a great propaganda achievement in itself – it had achieved its first aim of being there, 'flying the flag', for Britain. The difficulties in getting permission to open the institute there, and the views of the Spanish Government in detail, will be examined in the following chapter. The impression that it gave though was immense. Not only was the Spanish Government sympathetic to Germany and Italy, but Starkie's arrival and organization of the housewarming event coincided with the Dunkirk evacuation and the Battle of Britain – defeat for Britain seemed perhaps just weeks away, but yet, here was a British organization spending time in an intimidating land, promoting cultural values which were seemingly under threat. Nevertheless, it was only one of a number of institutes already established in Madrid by other countries and the British Institute's voice was still to be heard above the noise of competing opinions and interests in the whispering gallery that was Madrid. An Italian institute had been established in late February 1940, which by contrast to the opening of the British Institute, received a huge amount of publicity in Spanish newspapers.[6] Despite this, the German Ambassador's attempts to persuade the Spanish Government to ban all British propaganda and seize all methods of distribution during 1941 and 1942 can perhaps be seen as a backhanded compliment to the success of British propaganda in a wider sense, of which the British Institute's efforts were a major factor.[7] Given the circumstances of the war situation at the time, the opening of the institute in Madrid, although ostensibly a non-political cultural institute, has also to be seen as a political statement. Although Lord Lloyd and Sir John Reith had agreed upon a separation of responsibilities along the lines of cultural and political propaganda between their respective organizations, it is clear that it was not possible to separate political and cultural propaganda entirely, as the two concepts cannot be divorced.

In neighbouring Portugal, the institute in Lisbon had opened in November 1938 (prior to the war) with both the Portuguese Minister of Education, Pacheco, and Lord Lloyd present – and so the problem of actually establishing institutes during war conditions was avoided here.[8] Clearly, having a Portuguese Government Minister in attendance at the opening sent a clear signal that the Portuguese Government was likely to be supportive of the institute's activities, and they confirmed this through a formal letter outlining their support for the institute.[9] An *Abertura solene* (solemn opening ceremony) was held on the 23 November in the *Academia das Ciências* (Academy of Sciences) for a wide public audience and a *Copo de agua* (literally 'glass of water', but meaning a drinks reception) the following day in the institute itself for a smaller number of guests.[10] At the *Abertura solene*, Pacheco clearly stated his support:

> I can confidently prophesy [sic] for the 'British Institute in Portugal' the fullest success in its noble task of converting the historic and vital association of interests into a dynamic ideal of co-operation in the present and future: - These are the earnest wishes of our Government.[11]

Unlike in Madrid, the opening of the institute in Lisbon was widely publicized in the Portuguese press. Many articles stressed the old alliance between Britain and

Portugal.[12] 'Portugal and England' wrote the *Diário de Manhã*, are 'countries which are friends and old allies – know each other well and there is nothing more useful than study for obtaining good and perfect knowledge' [Original Portuguese in footnote].[13]

In Portugal, however, once the war had broken out in September 1939, it was not quite as easy as it had been to get support from the Portuguese Government. In Coimbra, although the *Casa d'Ingleterra* (English Room) had existed prior to the war within the University, the newly established institute was accommodated by the Faculty of Letters which meant, as Portugal was adhering strictly to its policy of neutrality, 'its immediate neighbours [were] the German, Italian and French Institutes'.[14] It was clearly an advantage, therefore, to be ahead of the game and avoid such unhelpful situations. The Council was always aware that it was not operating in a vacuum and was in competition with the other combatant countries. It is important to stress that at least in Portugal, unlike in Spain, the authorities were not allowing the German and Italian institutes to open and operate in a disproportionately bombastic way compared to the British institutes. Nevertheless, the British institutes did not seem to have any particular advantage either.

In Sweden, as in Spain, the institute had opened after the outbreak of war – and it took until December 1941 before its doors were finally open.[15] Largely this was due to the practical difficulties in getting enough resources to Sweden in order to make the opening of an institute worthwhile. Peter Tennant, the British press attaché in Stockholm, had been in a caretaker role for the British Council, and it was not until late 1941 that Ronald Bottrall made it to the Swedish capital. As in Portugal, the Education Minister, Gösta Bagge, was in attendance at the opening along with the British Minister Victor Mallet. Bagge's presence at the opening, however, was not as well received as Pacheco's presence had been prior to the war. The Swedish press reported Nazi Germany's condemnation of Bagge's action:

> At today's press conference in Wilhelmstrasse[16] there was an item on Education Minister Bagge's presence at the British Council in Stockholm. This procedure has been described as a tragic-comic charade by the [German] Government who know that the British Council, at least according to German opinion, is merely a layer of the Secret Service [Original Swedish in footnote].[17]

> A spokesman for the German Government called it a 'political somersault' for the Cabinet Minister [statsrådet] Bagge to appear at the opening. The British Council is nothing but an English espionage centre, he further explained ... [Original Swedish in footnote].[18]

The Swedish secret police did not actually take the view that the British Institute in Sweden was a centre for espionage very seriously – they considered that view to be a German rumour.[19] However, the fact that the view was given such prominence in the Swedish press shows that the opening of the institute was certainly not an overwhelming victory in propaganda terms. Again, as in Spain, it was a political statement to open the institute, and the German backlash clearly showed that they, at least, saw the Council as a force to be reckoned with. To survive against the German onslaught, the Council was plainly going to have to fight its corner.

The British Institute in Sweden was also less like the institutes in Spain and Portugal that were the centre of the British Council's activities. Instead, the Council operated in a similar way as in Turkey by way of sending lecturers out to the University of Uppsala (Sweden's foremost University), Sigtuna, Malmö, Gothenburg and even Kiruna in the Arctic north of Sweden.[20] Bottrall also collaborated with Swedish organizations such as the *Arbetarnas Bildningsförbund* (ABF – Workers' Educational Association) rather than teaching 'in-house'.[21] The Stockholm institute itself was therefore much more of a library and an exhibition space than the teaching locations which were more predominant certainly in Madrid and to an extent in Lisbon. All the institutes provided a number of practical functions – libraries, schools, exhibition spaces and places to hold social events. Douglas Coombs, in his assessment in the Council's library work, *Spreading the Word*, noted that libraries

> were a normal feature of these Institutes, and their supply was just one aspect of the massive wartime expansion of the Council 'printed word' activity; but before the war ended, a policy had emerged which greatly enhanced the priority given to library work, as well as significantly altering its pattern.[22]

This new policy was to start to establish libraries outside of institute buildings in an attempt to increase the attendance figures, leaving the institutes more as office-only functions.

Just the fact that institutes existed at all often in difficult, if not hostile, conditions was a propaganda success and, as mentioned previously, a political statement. The institutes had a convening power, a focus for those people who were sympathetic to Britain to congregate (particularly long-term sympathizers), but also those who came over to a more pro-British viewpoint later in the war (largely because they began to see who would win the war). It was noted by John Steegman that the Marqués de Lozoya, the Spanish Minister of Fine Arts, for example, in November 1942

> [u]ntil very recently [was] rather in the hands of the Germans – and never went to the British Institute – but he accepted to-night's invitation [to a dinner party held by Walter Starkie] willingly and promises to come to the Institute on Sunday: perhaps events change opinions?[23]

Once neutral people were ready to be pro-British, the institutes provided an ideal focus for them to show their new-found sympathy. This is also perhaps an example of how a member of the 'hostile elite' group, as shown in the model of influence described earlier, was reached through pro-British and more indifferent elite groups, but the change in the war situation obviously was a key factor in the change in Lozoya's opinions.

However, while it was not always within the Council's control who was attracted to the institute in Spain, Starkie was the master at tapping into a broad Spanish culture and was able to appeal to a wide audience. His *tertulias* (in Starkie's words 'a customary reunion of people for the purpose of discussion on subjects of common interest'[24]) were a key tool in Starkie's adaption of the institute for Spanish needs. Taken straight out of the pages of his pre-war book *Spanish Raggle-Taggle* (where he devoted a whole chapter to them), there was, Starkie believed, nothing 'more characteristically Spanish than the *tertulias*'.[25] They were not held for any particular occasion, but allowed anyone who wished to visit the institute the opportunity to come and talk about anything they wished to anyone. The only rules were that discretion was abandoned and gossip was encouraged.[26] One Council employee noted that individual one-to-one contact was the cornerstone of a representative's work, and Starkie was very adept at creating the right atmosphere for this one-to-one contact to work successfully.[27] Other events such as cocktail parties and dinners were also mainstays of the Council's work in Portugal and Turkey, which, though not so adapted to local conditions as the *tertulia*, provided a similar opportunity for those who were pro-British to show their sympathy.

The events, in particular, gave those attending an opportunity to meet the visitors from Britain who were there on lecture tours and for other similar events. This enabled them to receive uncensored word-of-mouth propaganda about wartime Britain which would not have been available through any other source. To reference one example from a cocktail party held in the British Club in Oporto, about half of the people attending were Portuguese and half British.[28] As these events were usually by invitation only, those invited were usually either member of the British Institute or were 'carefully selected persons, not members, . . . [who were] asked according to the nature of the occasion'.[29] This gives a clear confirmation that the Council's propaganda was carefully aimed at specific people, people with influence in certain areas of Government, professions or in a cultural field. These were undoubtedly pro-British people at first, but people with the ability to influence less sympathetic people in local life to persuade them to a more positive view of Great Britain. As was shown above, the Marqués de Lozoya was persuaded to come to the British Institute even though he had been very much pro-German previously. Though Steegman believed that it was the change in the war situation that had persuaded him to attend the event, Lozoya must have been aware of the institute's work from contact with more pro-British Spaniards, and it is likely they would have informed him of the type of information he might be able to receive there and the benefits of him attending.

Institutes were often used as a space not just for purely social events, as was the case with the *tertulias* and cocktail parties, but also for musical performances and plays. John Skelton's play *Magnificence* was performed at the institute in Lisbon and produced by Charles David Ley, a lecturer at the British Institute in Lisbon (and later Madrid). *Magnificence*, a play dating from the Tudor period (and the only one of Skelton's to survive), about the evils of ambition and how wealth can suddenly disappear (perhaps trying to draw some kind of analogy to the rise and hoped-for fall of Germany), was played by a mixture of Portuguese and British actors including Ley himself.[30] Play-reading circles and poetry societies also needed somewhere to indulge in their cultural interests, and the institutes provided a perfect location for this. William Shakespeare, of course, was the mainstay of play-reading, but other Anglophone authors such as Oscar Wilde, R. B. Sheridan, Daphne du Maurier and George Bernard Shaw were performed in the institutes as well.[31] Music performances also gave the institutes a convening power and a focus for discussion – and these will be examined in more detail a little later in the chapter.

Teaching

The welcoming atmosphere created by the institutes through the variety of functions which they undertook was a key attraction and therefore a key feature in their propaganda role. The warmth of the institute is exemplified by the example of the British Institute School in Madrid. Unlike in Turkey where teachers were provided to English (and, indeed, other specialist) schools in Istanbul and elsewhere, in Spain the teaching of English in a school environment actually took place within the Madrid institute itself, largely because of security reasons.[32] The school was established predominately for Spanish pupils, though British, American and a few other nationalities were also allowed to join – there were 80 pupils in the school itself in January 1942 and 550 older students learning English. The school was established as soon as the institute opened in 1940 but, recalled a former pupil, at first 'very few people knew about it' because of the political situation and censorship in Spain at the time, 'so they started quietly and little by little more people became aware'.[33] Just as the institute was opened without the blaze of publicity and then gradually increased in influence, so did the school housed within it. As with much of the Council's work, the school's success was built on an incremental basis – one small success would be built on top of another small success until cumulatively a large success was achieved.

Starkie established the school because he saw it as the most effective way to win sympathy for the British cause. He believed it was 'imperative to show the Spaniards that England has always been right in the forefront in such work [youth problems, formation of character, child welfare]'. Establishing a school, he stated, would 'draw to our side not only the parents – Spanish and British – but also the educational authorities generally'.[34] '[M]any Spanish friends informed me', Starkie wrote, that 'it was one of the best means of attracting the "simpatía" of Spanish parents'.[35] Starkie was of the view that schools, and certainly good schools, in Spain were scarce and therefore the establishment of the British School, run on approved lines, would be a propaganda coup.[36] Again, Starkie showed that he had an acute understanding of the existing sociological situation in Spain. In view of the general difficulties that occurred between Hoare and Starkie, it was no doubt a bonus for Starkie that Hoare and his wife were very keen on the idea of the school, and Lady Hoare agreed to become its patron.[37] The Council in London organized a collection of materials for the school such as scrap books, coloured paper, finger painting sets, counting and reading aids and so on, all of which helped in giving the impression in Spain that the institute school was well organized and well equipped, though some of the equipment was difficult to send out due to export restrictions during the war, and had to be sourced from Gibraltar and Lisbon.[38] A bus service was also introduced as '[co]mmunications are so difficult here [in Spain], that most parents seem to expect this' wrote George Reavey, who was helping Starkie establish the institute.[39] Of course, complying with this demand increased the school's prestige. The German institute had five buses in operation in 1940 and starting to compete against this was clearly a priority.[40] Making these special efforts to ensure the schools did not just exist but were ground-breaking, new and genuinely attractive to Spanish parents was what really counted when competing with the German schools. By the end of October 1940, there were 30 children of ages 4–10 in the school 'without any advertising', and Reavey believed that '[i]f we did advertise we should be swamped, but for the moment we are not prepared to deal with large numbers'.[41] If true, and there is no reason really to doubt this, then the establishment of the school was clearly an adept move by Starkie who understood his audience to an impressive degree. By January 1945, the numbers had reached 182 pupils, with 143 (nearly 80 per cent) of them Spanish.[42]

The teachers, Mrs Nancy Fernandez-Victorio and Mrs Ruiz de Alda, both English but married to Spaniards, and Miss K. P. Jackson ran their classes on 'modern lines' – according to Froebel and Montessori methods (play-based and child-centred learning techniques devised by educational specialists in Germany and Italy in the nineteenth and early twentieth centuries), which was unusual for Spain at that time.[43] The enlightened nature of the institute's teaching method was recalled by one former pupil, Manuel Balson:

> . . .the atmosphere was the best of it – I can tell as I attended the British [Institute] School in the morning and in the afternoon I went to a [S]panish private school, while at the British we were learning by playing, singing [and] doing gym[,] and in the [S]panish one everything was done by memory and punishments. This way of thinking was generally the same for the other pupils.[44]

There is a striking link to Ellul's example of post-war American cultural propaganda in France where the advantages of new American technology were so obvious to the French that they readily consumed this aspect of the propaganda.[45] Many Spaniards here could just as clearly see the advantages of the methods of teaching that the British Council was employing that they were keen to benefit from the opportunity.

The pupils at the school were taught a range of subjects from geography and history (largely British history but also topics such as Ancient Egypt) to mathematics and religion where pupils could choose between Catholicism and Anglicanism.[46] The pupils adored Starkie because of his storytelling abilities. He addressed them in assemblies and told them about his adventures with gypsies and wandering minstrels – such as those that he had recorded in *Spanish Raggle-Taggle*.[47] Balson was given his first communion at the British Institute by Catholic priests and the ceremony was carried out in the Spanish tradition of dressing up in sailor and admiral outfits – which is another example of Starkie's ability to tap into Spanish culture.[48] In addition to teaching, the school provided a service of monitoring the physical development of the children. Starkie employed a doctor called Dr Martinez de Alonso, a graduate of the University of Liverpool, who, Starkie reported, 'keeps a record of each child, weighs them, points out defects in bodily development and every week gives lessons in hygiene, breathing etc'.[49] Starkie understood that child welfare and health were key issues in Spain following the deprivation and under-nourishment caused by the Spanish Civil War, and providing a service was yet another way that the school earned a good reputation in Madrid.[50] Of course, spaces were limited, and there were entrance fees which would preclude many Spanish families from sending their children to the school. However, the reputation of the school was clearly spreading quickly without any apparent publicity or organization and this was just as important, if not more important than the teaching activities within the school, essential though these teaching activities were.

Although British schools within British institutes were not the norm elsewhere, the teaching of the English language and providing a British education, either through the funding of schools or the provision of teachers, were important parts of the Council's work. A. J. S. White wrote in his account of the period that

[a]s in peacetime the Council's main emphasis was still on English teaching, whether direct in British institutes or indirectly in the subsidisation of English lecturers in universities and schools, in the provision of libraries and in the many other ways which the Council found of stimulating and strengthening the teaching of English in these countries. It had not taken the Council long to become convinced that, as foreseen by its founders, a knowledge of the English language was a major assistance in securing a proper understanding of Britain.[51]

In Portugal, the Council subsidized, though did not control, the St Julian's School in Carcavelos and Queen Elizabeth's School in Lisbon. As in the British Institute School in Madrid, the Council part-funded the schools on the basis that they were conducted on Froebel methods.[52] According to the British Council's Librarian in Lisbon, Carlos Estorinhno, 'the English language had previously been somewhat overlooked for a variety of reasons, including aggressive attempts by German and Italian agents to win over students and a less ideologically driven attitude on the part of the British'.[53] However, as White suggested above, this now changed with the financial support of the two schools in Portugal from 1943. As with much cultural activity, the direct financial benefits of teaching English rarely accrued directly to the institution organizing the teaching. The benefits were usually non-financial particularly in the short term (by creating an atmosphere of sympathy), and when financial benefits did occur they would be on a broader level rather than to institutions specifically. Financial support for schools therefore enabled the schools to operate as part of a broader fabric of cultural activity generating benefits for the British cause as a whole through extending British influence especially through the English language.

Prior to 1940, St Julian's was largely for children of the British and American communities in Portugal, but grew during the war to accommodate Portuguese and other nationalities.[54] Like the British Institute School in Madrid, Queen Elizabeth's attracted a majority of local pupils (i.e. Portuguese in this case) but St Julian's never managed to obtain a majority at any time during the war, though a rise from near zero Portuguese pupils in 1940 to 32 per cent in October 1944 was nevertheless a good achievement.[55] The Headmaster of St Julian's, Geoffrey L. Thorp, applied for a subsidy from the British Council in October 1943 and stated that he believed that there was 'a very strong case for a subsidy out of public moneys [sic]' as 'the School is a valuable engine of propaganda'.[56] The British Council agreed, though George West was perturbed about the 'somewhat casual, haphazard mode of expansion' at the school, which he sought to control.[57] Similarly, Queen Elizabeth's School was set up privately by Miss D. E. Lester in 1935 after she had apparently been impressed by the German school in Madeira and wanted to 'beat them at their own game'. Lester's aim was for the Portuguese children to be given a high enough quality of education 'to pass their Portuguese examination while at the same time taught in the atmosphere of an English background'.[58] British Council financial assistance had actually begun prior to the war in 1938. At St Julian's, the school was divided into two sections – for those who wanted to take the Cambridge School Certificate and those who wanted to take the Portuguese Liceu Examination. The school had large playing fields, gymnastics facilities and, being on the Portuguese coast, had access to a beach.[59]

Generally, it was believed by the Council that the two schools in Portugal were doing an 'admirable' job in Sir Malcolm Robertson's words, and had 'always been regarded as a very important British activity'. However, the numbers of Portuguese pupils generally declined during the war at Queen Elizabeth's School, and there were questions about the appropriateness of the teaching at St Julian's.[60] An intercepted letter from a K. Heron in Exeter to a R. F. Heron in Lisbon (both appear to have been teachers at the school either at that time or earlier) shortly before the British Council started financial assistance strongly suggested that the school was in need of reform:

> Folk like Miss W [presumably Miss Warren] and such are letting down England badly. The school is so important from a propaganda point of view but I can imagine nothing more Un-English. The beastly unfairness and injustice. [Geoffrey L] Thorpe [the Headmaster] doesn't know what goes on. He's too much in the clouds. So I must write later. Can't you tell him that as you are not sure about staying I shan't return to S[t]. Julian's. . . . Really, apart from S[t]. Julian's which I consider desperately important from the point of view of representing England in Portugal, I think I can do more here. You could see the 'boys side' was rotten at the school. As long as Miss W and her type are there it's no good. Punish, punish and punish to save her face and hide her incapabilities as a teacher. She's not the only one, but the worst.[61]

While no action appears to have been taken specifically upon interception of this letter, and it may well be more assertion than fact (though the following year the Council considered to replace Miss Warren, if that is who 'Miss W' refers to[62]), there was certainly concern about the quality of the teaching. The level of anxiety is exemplified by the fact that Ronald Campbell, the British Ambassador, raised his concern (on George West's behalf) to the Foreign Secretary, Anthony Eden about the 'insufficient number of qualified teachers at present at the disposal of Saint Julian's School', and asked him to reinforce the fact that teaching on behalf of the Council was a valuable wartime activity.[63] In addition to the lack of suitable teachers, the availability of good quality text books for the teaching of English to Portuguese speakers for St Julian's and other Council centres in Portugal was highlighted in a report in July 1944 as another area for improvement. A new text book was commissioned for use in 1945.[64] Nevertheless, despite their difficulties it is clear that there was a general policy within the Council to keep schools such as these going, as it would be an own-goal in propaganda terms to close them. The reputation of British run or funded schools was far more important than the actual quality of the teaching as their reputations could reach a far larger audience through indirect influence. It was important to keep the sympathy generated by the schools within the wider community than to carry out reforms (albeit much needed reforms), which could reveal to that wider community the inadequacies of those institutions.

English lessons also took place within the institute itself in Lisbon, though not for school-age children, but as adult education. It is clear from pictures of the English classes at the Lisbon institute in 1940 that the classes attracted a diverse range of Portuguese students – both male and female, young and middle-aged – and all keen to take advantage of the opportunity presented to them by the Council.[65] Again there is a link to Ellul and post-war American propaganda in France – propaganda is readily accepted if the advantages are clear and fit in with the sociological context. The Portuguese could see that learning English would have commercial advantages after the war had finished, and this became more and more the case, as it became more obvious the Allies would be victorious in the war.

In Turkey, as mentioned before, there were no institutes and so English lessons could not take place on Council premises as was the case in Portugal or Spain. However, as in Portugal where St Julian's and the Queen Elizabeth Schools were supported, the Council gave financial support to the English High School for Boys and the English High School for Girls, the 1943–44 financial year deficit being estimated at £2,325 and £5,700, respectively.[66] Both schools had opened in Istanbul during the nineteenth century but required the financial assistance of the Council because 'the trade depression which preceded the outbreak of the present war nearly spelt its doom'.[67] In a policy called 'Turcising', in Michael Grant's words, Turks were offered an English education in English schools, rather than disproportionately supporting Maltese and British children at the schools.[68] Still, by July 1944 only 41 per cent at the Boys' School and 47 per cent at the Girls' School were Muslim Turks which was still a minority, though admittedly was a lot higher than prior to the Council's involvement.[69] As in Portugal, the Council sponsored specific scholars in the Boys' School and monitored their progress which, the Council was glad to note, had 'improved considerably' from prior to the Council's involvement.[70] Though both schools were deemed to be 'doing good work', the High School for Girls was not seen as a good investment financially as '[i]t was a very expensive school from the Council's point of view'; however, the propaganda value of the school was so great that 'it was considered that it would be unwise from the prestige angle that it should be closed', just as with St Julian's School in Carcavelos.[71] However, with regard to sponsoring specific scholars it was decided that it was too difficult at the Girls' School because the 'subsidy to the School is already so large'.[72] It can be seen here that the Council was actually very cautious about overextending its commitments, and cannot be accused of throwing money at the problem for the sake of propaganda, but actually wanted to see a return on its investment in tangible terms. M. H. S. Everett, at the Council's offices in London, wrote to W. H. Covington in Ankara:

> Although we agreed some time ago to the principle of Council scholarships at the Schools, we are obliged when faced with the extra allocation involved to consider carefully to what extent this policy should be followed, and particularly, whether the Schools are being run with sufficient economy for an increase in our allocations to be inevitable if these scholarships or more of them are offered. Nor are we entirely satisfied that Grant's 'Turcising' plans for the Schools cannot be prosecuted by encouraging the attendance at the Schools of children of the right Turks who can pay the fees, thereby keeping the number of Council scholarships to a minimum. . . . [The School is] incurring unnecessary expenditure, owing to the large number of pupils accepted at reduced fees, many of whom were not children of 'pure' Turks.[73]

Despite this policy, the Girls' School had a broad range of activities which the Council funded, such as the nursery section (known by the German name 'kindergarten', as the nursery was also known in the British Institute in Madrid), which was a key part of the educational system and incorporated the teaching of English at an early age. Books by A. A. Milne and Beatrix Potter, beacon readers (for sentence construction), Puffin books on nature subjects, Chad Valley wooden number toys and plasticine were the key ingredients of the kindergarten's learning environment.[74] As in Spain, the introduction of these new, ground-breaking teaching techniques would undoubtedly have increased the reputation of the school in Istanbul society. To some extent, the fear that the Council had of lack of 'sufficient economy' was unfair in this respect, as the greater benefit of reputation building and maintenance was occurring which, in the longer term, would contribute to enhanced opportunities for extensions of British influence, particularly British commercial influence.

Much English teaching also took place through the Halkevleri, Lycées and Universities – eight British professors resided at the University of Istanbul and six at the University of Ankara – the most famous of which was Professor Steven Runciman, an expert on Byzantium. Army officers and Turkish Government Ministers were also provided with lessons, complemented by two weekly periodicals *The English Supplement* and *Do you speak English?* published by the Council.[75] When the Engineering High School in Istanbul was seeking to establish a Ship Design and Marine Construction School, it was noted by J. G. Crowther, Head of the Council's Science Department, that it was 'of great diplomatic importance at present that the new school should be directed and staffed, if possible, by distinguished British marine engineers and naval architects'.[76] The Council had a reputation to maintain among Government and establishment elites that it could and would supply high quality teachers when requested. Already, by November 1941, there were 41 Council teachers in Turkey teaching a variety of subjects to nearly 3,000 Turks, 95 per cent of them Muslim. There were 10 teachers in Ankara (e.g. at the Ankara Halkevi, Ismet Inönü Institute and Türk Maarif Cemiyeti Lycée), 6 in Smyrna (such as at the Dumlupinar Okulu Halkevi, Gazi Ortaokul Halkevi and Bornova Kahlev), 14 in Istanbul (e.g. at the Eminönü Halkevi, Galatasaray Lycée and Robert College) and 11 elsewhere (e.g. in Karabuk, Adana and Samsun).[77] As was shown in the previous chapter, James Morgan, from the British Embassy, was confident that Grant 'would never succeed in getting British teachers of English into the Halkevis'.[78] Clearly from the figures above, and in Grant's words, '[t]his immediately proved one hundred per cent wrong' as there was range of British teachers across a wide selection of institutions across Turkey.[79] It was undoubtedly an objective to get British teachers into as many different institutions as possible, as Michael Grant stated unambiguously

> One of the aims of this expansion has been the *maximum diffusion of our teachers.* That is to say, we have at this stage preferred the difficult task of forcing a way into organisations hitherto untouched to the much easier one of adding a second or third teacher in institutions where a first is already established [Grant's emphasis].[80]

Grant detected a large amount of 'suspicious temperaments' by Turks resulting in a ' "brick-wall" mentality' (which Morgan thought insurmountable), but once this was broken down by the arrival of one teacher, 'the acceptance of a second one, even in adverse political circumstances' was made much easier. The support of the Turkish Minister of Education, Hasan-Ali Yücel, and the ruling Party was invaluable in achieving the first step – it was an 'exceedingly delicate task that can only be achieved by the intervention of connivance of the highest powers in the land'.[81] It was Yücel that had 'asked that it [the School of Ship Design and Marine Construction] should be directed and staffed by British professors', in early 1943, and the Council was clearly keen to oblige, not primarily because they wanted Turkey to be able to build good ships with British support specifically, but because of the need to maintain and extend British influence generally.[82] President İnönü also put pressure on the Council to find candidates for the School of Ship Design and Maritime Construction after six months of delay in finding suitable people, though no suitable candidates were ever found despite exhaustive searches.[83]

Grant made no apology for proceeding to 'pull strings' with his friend Yücel where necessary to get certain teachers in certain posts where he could. For example, he stated

> As a result of certain intrigues, it has been possible to secure the appointment of Mr C. E. Bazell as Docent of Philology in the Department [the Faculty of Letters at Istanbul University]; I am hoping to get him promoted shortly.[84]

From a twenty-first century viewpoint, this looks particularly unfair, but in Grant's view this was necessary to achieve the spreading of British culture in Turkey during the war. It is also true that if the British had not tried to influence the Turks in this way, there was always the danger that the Germans would instead, and could be seen as a standard practice in Turkey at the time anyway. Not that the teaching of English was unpopular – Grant remarked that according to one 'impartial observer', 'the only time at which the Halkevi is crowded is when English classes are being held'.[85] Using this knowledge Grant, at one point, threatened to withdraw the teaching of English at one of the Istanbul Halkevleri until conditions had improved to the satisfaction of the Council. His audacity had the desired effect and shows how much power the Council was beginning to wield in the country.[86] Outside of institutions, the Council also provided English lessons to the staff of the *Ulus* newspaper and to the Anadolu Press Agency.[87] R. F. Lucas, Grant's deputy, personally taught Yücel English for 10 hours per week, and other teachers taught President İnönü's son and daughter, as well as other Government Ministers.[88] The power that the Council wielded was considerable, though had the Turkish Government ever chosen to take a less sympathetic route during the war, it could easily have restricted the Council's activities if necessary – the Council was only as powerful as the Government allowed it to be. Though this was the case, it is undoubtedly true that the Council was aiming its influence at a specific type of Turk – those elites with the power to influence way beyond where the Council could reach on its own with limited resources. No one, it could be argued, held more influence in Turkey than President İnönü. Concentrating on courting his favour would not only open doors into teaching establishments and areas of Turkish life not usually open to foreign influence, but also create that all important secondary influence of the President persuading elites less sympathetic to the British cause to become more sympathetic and then also allow that influence to trickle down to the wider masses.

Nevertheless, this power to increase the audience for English teaching (and for other subjects taught by British teachers) within defined limitations did not necessarily mean, however, that the influence of British culture was increasing at the rate which the Council expected. In Turkey, the average 'falling-off' rate in attendance was actually quite high and considerably higher than that for other countries. Grant, in a moment of frustration, rather unflatteringly blamed this on the

> considerable proportion of pure Turks [who] lack the necessary intelligence, attainment and environment for learning more than the barest minimum of a language so fantastically different from their own as English is. . . . In spite of the tremendous thirst for knowledge which all Turks possess, 30 per cent of 'educated' Turks are physically, and mentally, incapable of completing Eckersley 'Essential English 1', and 100 per cent will have fallen off before the book is half completed unless the teacher 'chivvies' tirelessly, and infinite charm, personality, and, as far as the women pupils are concerned, good looks.[89]

In another report, he wrote 'Turks can only learn English, I have ascertained, one-sixth the speed of Greeks and Rumanians [sic], one-third of the speed of Bulgarians, and half the speed of illiterate Arabs. . . .'.[90]

Clearly, Grant's outbursts had not considered the possibility that the Council's teaching methods might not be as suitable for Turkish students as they might be for students who had a background in Latin-based or Germanic languages, and the last point is a particularly exaggerated comparison. Yet, these statements underline just how difficult it was to teach English in these circumstances before the English language became predominant in the second half of the twentieth century. Around the same time, however, I. E. Jago, who taught English for the Council at a number of Ankara institutions and in Samsun, wrote a report with a more considered view:

> In this country [Turkey], we are obliged to teach in Turkish institutions. In the British Institutes of other countries, it is possible to steep the students in an atmosphere which constitutes a powerful aid to language teaching. The only possible compensation for this would be to cultivate visual instruction such as films and pictures which deal with British life.[91]

Jago also suggested that a 'dual system' should be introduced whereby classes would have both a native English-speaking teacher and a native Turkish-speaking teacher in the same classroom, which Jago believed had 'great advantages':

> The foreign teacher (in this case that is to say the English teacher) has the advantage of being able to speak the language naturally and correctly, but the teacher of the country has the advantage of having learnt the foreign language himself, he is therefore much better able to perceive the students' difficulties.[92]

Another proposal for making English teaching easier, not just in Turkey but around the world, was the idea of 'Basic English'. 'Basic English', a method whereby only a few hundred English words needed to be learned, was discovered by the Prime Minister, Winston Churchill, after a visit to Harvard University in the United States. Basic English was created by Charles Kay Ogden and presented in his book *Basic English: A General Introduction with Rules and Grammar* and published in 1930.[93] Churchill believed there should be a 'great drive to get it [Basic English] widely adopted as an "auxiliary international language"'.[94] Churchill announced in Parliament that he would encourage the British Council and the BBC to introduce it, but the English teachers in Turkey 'almost unanimously refused to teach Basic English, preferring to resign rather than to do so'.[95] A small trial did start but was soon abandoned, and in his report Jago was less than flattering about it. 'Basic English' is regarded as the inspiration for George Orwell's 'Newspeak' in *Nineteen Eighty-Four* where the number of words reduced in each subsequent publication of the Newspeak dictionary. Orwell certainly was involved in its use during the war through BBC broadcasts to India, and later rejected the idea of a simplified language in his essay 'Politics and the English language' (though did not mention 'Basic English' by name).[96]

There is no evidence that Jago's ideas of the 'dual system' or visual instruction were introduced into English teaching in Turkey, and it was probably difficult to do so in wartime with resources stretched. The only response that can be found is in a letter from M. H. S. Everett which stated '[p]lease convey our thanks to Jago for his very interesting paper ... [it] has been of considerable use at the Council's Committee for the teaching of English overseas'.[97] No direct impact of Jago's ideas, however, can be detected. A book written by Clifford and Margaret Leech titled *Ingiliz Ders Kitabi* ('English text-book') was meant to combine a number of methods for use in Turkey, and was ordered by the Turkish Ministry of Education to publish as soon as possible, but copyright issues appear to have prevented its publication (at least there is no evidence it was published).[98] Nevertheless, the statistics of English teaching are impressive even if methods were not changed. During the war, the Council expanded English teaching in Turkey to all levels of education with a large number of staff and a budget of £300,000 by the end of the war, teaching English to over 10,000 pupils.[99] This number is far more than in any of the other three countries focused on here, and demonstrates how effective it could be to maintain friendships at the very top of the political elite – with President Inönü and Education Minister Yücel. One can only imagine how great the Council's influence would have been in other countries if the political elite had been as receptive as in Turkey. Pictures from Michael Grant's personal photograph album demonstrate just how close the friendship between Grant and Yücel was – Grant is shown at Yücel's residence with Yücel's family in a fairly relaxed atmosphere (if perhaps a little stilted in front of the camera). It is unlikely that any of the other Council representatives had managed to become so integrated into the Government elite as Grant had, and even less likely that they had managed to make their working relationship with Government officials work so effectively to achieve the Council's aims.

In Sweden, English language teaching by the British Council was combined with lectures about Britain generally. For example, the Council collaborated with the ABF for a fortnight summer school held in Brunnsvik in 1943 'for the benefit of ABF teachers and group leaders'.[100] The report written by the Council's lecturer Frederick A. L. Charlesworth stated:

> The object of such a Course was to provide tuition in a selection of kindred subjects which would fall within two lines of study, one concentrating on Language and the other on Social, Political, and Trade Union History as well as Literature relating thereto.[101]

The first week of the course spent two hours (before breakfast) on phonetics, intonation, syntactical problems such as prepositional phraseology, and two hours in the afternoon on conversation exercises. During the middle of the day and in the evening, there were lectures on British society and politics (lectures will be considered in more detail later in the chapter). The second week was similar, though pre-breakfast classes were on oral translation and pronunciation.[102]

Overall, it was considered that the Swedish participants on the course were keen to get a higher standard of efficiency in their use of the English language and a greater 'desire to concentrate more on the linguistic in general, rather than on the lecture series'.[103] The lecture series itself covered subjects such as 'Great Democrats', 'The British Social Structure', 'Principles of British Education' and 'The Novelists from 1870 onwards', which were a somewhat eclectic mixture trying to promote British culture (especially emphasizing the fact that it was a democratic country, like Sweden), and the English language, while trying to tailor the lectures towards the left-wing stance of the ABF.[104] The British Council has often been criticized (particularly by the Beaverbrook press[105]) for perceiving 'culture' to only mean 'high culture', that is to say fine art, classical music and other elitist activities, rather than 'popular culture' – this, however, is a clear example of where the Council worked with a socialist organization. Admittedly, teachers could be viewed as a group with certain elitist characteristics, or at least leadership characteristics as they are often society role models within a community and have significant influence over others. Nevertheless, working with the ABF was a significant departure from the image often created of the Council only working with right-wing establishment organizations. Ronald Bottrall, the Council's representative in Sweden, lectured at Brunnsvik on Arnold Bennett, the British novelist (who, incidentally, had been employed by Lord Beaverbrook in First World War as Director of Propaganda for France), which he admitted was 'not quite as well suited as the first [lecture on British education], as most of the people are interested in politics, education and social reform rather than literature'.[106] Aside from the Brunnsvik course specifically, Charlesworth also toured the country for the ABF. These were not only important tours in themselves, but had an ongoing effect on the local populations, who established Anglo-Swedish societies in the wake of his visits.[107] There was concern, however, that Charlesworth's lectures contained 'large numbers of school children and middle-class people' which, although fine from general point of view of reaching interested Swedish people (and increased the numbers in his audience), was not the point of utilizing the ABF as a mechanism for approaching the Swedish working classes specifically. There were other methods and organizations for reaching the middle-classes, such as the *Tjänstemännens Bildningverksamhet* (TBV – roughly translated as 'Jobholders' Educational Activities') which contained clerks and professional people, or

Folkuniversitet ('People's University'), where '[t]he linguistic approach must therefore be and the cultural approach might well be, different [to the ABF]'.[108]

English language teaching, and teaching of other subjects by British Council teachers, therefore was a large part of the British Council's work and took place in a number of guises. These guises ranged from housing schools within the British institutes themselves covering a range of ages – kindergarten to teenage years – to sending teachers into existing British institutions such as the Halkevleri in Turkey, and the St Julian's School and Queen Elizabeth School in Portugal. The Council was pragmatic in driving forward the English language in whatever way was suited to the particular country where it was operating and the circumstances it found itself in. It was not always a straightforward process, however, and whichever method was utilized, a number of common problems arose. The first was in actually making the teaching work – keeping students on the courses was a particular concern in Turkey, and solutions such as Basic English, or use of pictures and films, were not entirely successful during the war period. The second problem was the legacy issue of taking on and funding schools such as the English High Schools for Boys and Girls in Istanbul and the St Julian's and Queen Elizabeth schools in Portugal, where the quality of the teaching and the school environment was not necessarily how the Council would have wanted had it had the opportunity of starting the schools from scratch. Closing these schools down in wartime was viewed as an own goal in propaganda terms and therefore there remained the problem of keeping the schools open and trying to reform them without giving the impression that the quality of teaching was substandard. English teaching still remains one of the British Council's core areas of work and it is clear that this is a key bedrock component of cultural propaganda. Having a knowledge of the English language allows exposure to other media of information – books, periodicals, films and so on – which have a secondary impact. Michael Grant, in his autobiography, noted that on his return to Turkey in 1990, 50 years after his establishment of the first British Council office in Ankara, that '[a]lmost every one of them [the Turks at a British Council party] spoke English fluently, and I believe that this was to a large extent due to the work the British Council had been doing there'.[109] This type of impact takes a significant amount of time to materialize, and it would certainly be unfair to see the Council's wartime English teaching in isolation – it was the start of a long road which has contributed in a large part, alongside other major institutions such as Hollywood, the United States Information Agency and the BBC, to English becoming the lingua franca of the world in the latter half of the twentieth and early twenty-first centuries.

Reaching out to a wider audience

Beyond the activities of the British Institute itself, and beyond the confines of English teaching, the British Council sought to work through existing local bodies and local media, in order to reach a wider audience than it could reach directly. The key partnerships that the Council forged with organizations such as the ABF in Sweden and the Halkevleri in Turkey still had a very direct role of supplying English teachers through a pre-existing network. While this was a very important component of the Council's work, it also sought to work in a more indirect way with other pro-British organizations. Predominant among these organizations were the Anglophile societies. Anglophile societies straddled the sociological divides between Britain and the host country, and they could understand what would work well in both situations. They were obviously part of the pro-British elite but could also understand the point of view of indifferent elites and hostile elite groups and influence them.

The establishment of Anglo-Swedish societies was a very important part of British Council policy in Sweden, and globally there were several hundred Anglophile societies which had a connection to the British Council.[110] The Council's support often existed in the form of supplying Directors and occasionally other British staff in order to get those Societies onto a more solid basis.[111] However, more usually, it existed through supplying materials (films, books, etc.) and services (lectures and music, etc.), which were unobtainable elsewhere, to keep a 'steady supply flowing of British thought in all its manifestations'.[112] The aim here was not to tie the Anglophile societies to the British Council through the Council directing their operations but more to encourage local communities to develop the societies in their own way with the Council supplying the material they needed to make the societies work effectively. Ronald Bottrall regularly distributed British newspapers (both daily and Sunday), and the literary publications *Horizon* and *Scrutiny* to Anglophile Societies, as well as libraries and publishers, throughout Sweden.[113] Though Latin America had many more Anglophile societies than existed in Europe, they were still important in Europe and particularly in Sweden.[114] Indeed, the only way that the Council operated in Switzerland to any great extent during the war was through already existing Anglophile societies – materials were used that had been sent there prior to the Nazi invasion of France and the entry of Italy into the war.[115] It was the Council's policy, recalled Stanley Unwin, 'to encourage and support such societies wherever they are founded by local initiative, but not to attempt to create them where no such initiative exists'.[116] As one would expect if the Council was only supporting societies that were formed by local initiative, the success of the societies, once formed, was fairly certain. It was the establishment in the first place that was always the tricky part. In many ways, this was similar to the way Michael Grant found it easier to get a second lecturer into a Halkevi, once the more difficult task of getting the first one in had been accomplished. Nevertheless, allowing local initiative and a decentralized approach was not without its problems as it meant that the Council had to effectively surrender control over many of the activities conducted by Anglophile societies, and this had a serious risk of damaging reputations which the Council was fighting hard to maintain. Of course, this was just a risk and many societies were run in a way that was perfectly acceptable to the Council. However, in a report dating from just after Second World War, the Foreign Office, while giving the Council the sanction it needed to begin expanding in the post-war period, stressed that it only wished the Council to set up offices which were not large enough to accommodate Anglophile societies: 'the Council had in some European countries given too prominent a place to foreign-British societies, thus entangling itself in local rivalries and jealousies'.[117] It should be noted here that this is a good example of the tension between the 'one size fits all' approach, and the bespoke approach to propaganda that was mentioned at the beginning of the chapter. Clearly, allowing Anglophile societies to be established by local initiative was a bespoke approach to cultural propaganda and enabled the Council to tap into the existing cultural views held by the host countries, as these societies would be inclined to mould into the existing local culture, but this could always be taken too far.

The Anglo-Portuguese Society and the Ministry of Information collaborated with the British Council to produce *Anglo-Portuguese News* (APN). It was mentioned in the previous chapter that the publication was not without its critics within the British colony and was not seen as a good example of what the British were capable of producing.[118] For example, John Steegman stated

> It is a sad fact that almost all the English residents criticise it [the APN] adversely. The chief ground of criticism is that its lay-out is so unattractive and its contents so dull that it is almost useless as an organ of propaganda; it is difficult to see to what kind of reader it is addressed, for it is not a review, nor is it a news-sheet (which, despite its title, it should not be) nor is it a popular weekly. It is apparently addressed to readers of not very high intelligence, but fails to attract even them. It certainly fails to attract critical readers in either language.[119]

As with a number of the less effective methods of propaganda that were utilized by the British Council, it was decided to keep the publication going because it was deemed that the negative publicity that would result from its closure would be greater than any negativity resulting from its continued existence. Only after the end of the war did the Council review its continuing support for the paper.[120] As Sir Malcolm Robertson stated in a note published in APN itself, the APN was 'the only remaining English language paper now published on the continent of Europe' and that he hoped 'that its directors will never forget the times when they had the honour of being the sole representatives, in a journalistic world, of British life and thought in a continent at war'.[121] The view was clearly that the influence of APN's critics was a minor problem which could actually be solved through changes in editorial style – the Council simply could not avoid any news of APN's closure being picked up by the Portuguese press and then repeated by German publications.

The publication, it has to be said, contained some strange articles, and it is difficult to conceive of who would be interested in reading them. For example, although may be not typical of all of the articles in the APN, one article from September 1941, called 'Shine, Sir?', did not appear to be the best example of British propaganda in Portugal. Nowhere did it mention Britain, and it was focused purely on a very discrete aspect of Portuguese life – the Portuguese 'bootblacks' – that is, shoeshine men. Shoeshine men were undoubtedly prevalent in Portugal and Spain, but the relevance to British influence in Portugal is certainly not striking. Perhaps, its only discernible message was that art comes in many forms and audiences should not dismiss it just because it may come in a form they are not expecting.[122] Nevertheless, the APN served as a useful way of advertising events that were taking place in the institute itself, particularly when touring lecturers arrived, that could be picked up by the more mainstream Portuguese press in a similar way to the way press notices are picked up by newspapers. As it was largely published in English (though not entirely), it necessarily relied on Portuguese readers having a knowledge of English and also that they were already interested in activities at the British Institute and in the British community generally.

To try to reach beyond the already converted, the Council looked to get news of British events and reviews of British books published in the local press directly, rather than using intermediary publications like APN. The local newspapers provided a good route to publicizing the British Council's activities in each of the countries, with the Portuguese newspapers in particular closely following the arrival of lecturers and the opening of new exhibitions. Articles in the local press could tantalize the curious, and encourage them to find out more about a particular event, or search out books that were received, or even perhaps giving them the confidence to enter the British Institute building. The model of influence can be applied quite readily in this context. In many ways, this is no different to how any publisher (in peacetime or wartime) would seek to publicize a book by a new author, or on a subject which is not, at first glance, attractive to a reader. The Council simply utilized well-practiced publicity techniques, just in more difficult circumstances. New audiences could be reached by this method. There were generally three types of article that the British Council tried to get published in the local press: first, short articles giving a brief notice that an event was taking place; second, a report on that event itself; and third, but more rarely, an in-depth article perhaps with an interview with the lecturer or musician (such as Sir Malcolm Sargent or Dr Robert McCance) who had just arrived from Britain.[123]

Portugal was not the only example of where the British Council attempted to work with the local press, but it was certainly most active and most successful in Portugal.[124] They were not just directed at one or two friendly newspapers, but across the majority of Portuguese newspapers, to try to reach as many people as possible. There were 12 Portuguese newspapers that regularly (defined as over 100 articles each, during the war) carried articles of British Council events and related Anglo-Portuguese cultural relations.[125]

More specialist publications were also utilized by the British Council. According to Bottrall, the publication *Bonniers Litterära Magasin* (or BLM – translated as 'Bonnier's Literary Magazine'), which contained reviews about British books, was 'on public sale throughout Sweden and reaches a public that the Legation does not always touch'. Bottrall, who was on good terms with the editor, Georg Svensson, was particularly interested in BLM because, he said, it 'also is sold in Finland, Denmark and Norway, where official British lists – cannot punctuate'.[126] Bottrall even asked his friend John Hayward to reference his own poem, 'Farewell and Waterman' (which he considered his best poem), in a letter to BLM which he stated 'might help my position in this country' through reaching beyond the converted audience to which the Council usually preached.[127] It has not been possible to obtain a copy of BLM dating from the time that Bottrall was representative in Sweden, but one dating from the summer of 1940 (when Svensson was editor), can be analysed to give a good idea of the types of articles BLM contained. First, at the end of the publication, there was a section called '*Nya utländska böcker – ett redaktionellt urval*' ('New foreign books – the editor's choice'). It is interesting for a number of reasons – first, the order of the books listed were under country headings with '*England och Amerika*' (England and America) first, followed by '*Frankrike*' (France), then '*Italien*' (Italy) and '*Tyskspråkig litteratur*'

(German-language literature) last. They may have been in alphabetical order but readers had to search over the page for the German-language literature which made it significantly less prominent. Not only that, but the number of books listed under each title is striking – 24 English books (13 from Britain, 11 from the United States), 12 French books, 10 Italian and only 7 German. The only advantage the German language books had, and this was not within the control of the BLM, was that three out of the seven books were actually published in Stockholm, for a Swedish audience (albeit in German), whereas all of the 24 English language books were published in London, New York or Boston and would have required shipping.[128] The main part of this issue of the publication also concentrated heavily on Swedish and English language literature, with German literature hardly receiving a mention.[129] To reference a brief example of BLM's view of the work of Dylan Thomas, the Welsh surrealist writer, an article titled '*Romaner från England*' ('Novels from England'[130]) called it an '*uttryck för en kärnfrisk begåvning*' ('an expression of a core of fresh talent').[131] This praise is not only important because Thomas was British, but it showed that a Swedish audience appreciated his style and genre of writing – fantasy and surrealist literature – which were the complete opposite of a Nazi vision of artistic qualities which were largely based on neo-classical concepts. While this issue of BLM may not be entirely representative of all of BLM's contents throughout the war, it gives a clear indication of where Svensson's sympathies lay even before the British Council became involved with the BLM. Evidently Bottrall was working *with* opinion already in existence in Sweden, and pushing on an open door, with this sympathetic magazine and a sympathetic editor.

The Council, therefore, tried to make much use of existing pro-British sympathy in a variety of forms (such as local newspapers and other publications, and through the establishment of Anglophile societies) to reach audiences that it could not reach directly. By relying on organizations and media which it did not control, it necessarily decentralized the organization of cultural propaganda and the messages which were disseminated. Occasionally this led to problems such as the squabbling between different Anglophile societies and the supporting of publications such as APN which were not entirely aligned to the British Council's ideals. Nevertheless, by and large, the use of pro-British organizations was successful in reaching beyond the usual audience of the British institutes, and would draw them towards a sphere of propaganda influence which became increasingly Council-controlled. It was an incremental process as with much of the Council's work in building on previous successes.

Exhibitions, visitors and word-of-mouth propaganda

The use of secondary media to try to reach a wider audience was not just confined to an overt campaign of press articles and the work of Anglophile societies. Secondary methods of penetration to a wider audience could and did include influencing of individuals who attended British Institute events such as lectures, film presentations and *tertulias*. As was suggested in an earlier chapter, these events were not only cultural propaganda events in themselves, but also a convenient, perhaps covert, way of influencing people by what was said in the 'margins' through propaganda by word-of-mouth. The Council sent out many lecturers on tour from a variety of backgrounds – film stars, singers and other musicians, artists and art critics, poets, scientists and footballers. These tours served a number of roles, first to show that Britain was still willing to send cultural representatives abroad during wartime, second, to conduct a genuine knowledge and cultural exchange (particularly in the case of scientific studies), and third, to provide a channel for word-of-mouth propaganda about the British war effort in the sidelines at social events and in general conversations. As Sir Victor Mallet noted in his unpublished memoirs

> [i]t was most refreshing to get news of how civilisation still existed in wartime England and of new developments in the arts and sciences. The Swedes, who by now were suffering from a kind of isolation complex, took full advantage of these visitors and we were able to make all kinds of interesting contacts in the Swedish cultural world.[132]

Uncensored information could be passed by word-of-mouth at events the Council organized.

The British Council has not been the only organization to see the advantage of word-of-mouth propaganda. As stated in a report on a similar organization in the post-war period (the United States Information Agency – USIA),

> [t]he most effective way to influence people is word-of-mouth. It can accomplish a great deal for a little money. A person is more apt to believe another person. There is a certain warmth of relationship, a certain credibility that you get, more than for a printed piece of material.[133]

It is simply not possible to reach an entire population directly by word-of-mouth, but, as demonstrated earlier, it is possible to start off a chain reaction of word-of-mouth propaganda by talking to the most influential people and expecting them to talk to others who are more difficult to reach directly and eventually through tertiary and further contacts to reach the whole population. Word-of-mouth propaganda is also useful because it is incremental and uncensorable. In a previous study, I concluded that the most predominant form of British propaganda in Eire during Second World War was through word-of-mouth as it circumvented the Irish Censorship so effectively.[134] Little by little the conversations that British people had in Eire (or indeed, Irishmen had in Britain) accumulated into a large information stream which, theoretically, could only be stopped if British people were stopped from going to Eire (or vice versa), which did not happen except just prior to D-Day.[135] Although the British Council itself barely operated in Eire the principle remains the same, and word-of-mouth propaganda was utilized successfully by John Betjeman, the British Press Attaché in Dublin (and later Poet Laureate).[136]

The SOE and the PWE used a 'sib' campaign (from the Latin *sibilare* – 'to hiss'[137]) which was essentially a rumour spreading campaign by whispering rumours in certain key places (primarily in neutral countries) by word-of-mouth, so that they could be spread from one person to the next.[138] In February 1942, it was reported that over 2,000 'sibs' had been disseminated in neutral and occupied Europe during the previous

12 months and 'already in France oral propaganda was the most important medium'. 'Although the enemy may suspect that a certain rumour has been started by the British Government' the report continued, 'they can never prove it'.[139] The Germans, too, had a similar campaign of '*Flüsterpropaganda*' (literally translated from German as 'whisper-propaganda') operating in Spain as well as elsewhere, known to the Spaniards as 'boca a boca' (mouth-to-mouth) propaganda where rumours were spread 'in shop queues, at bus stops, in bars, restaurants etc'. [Original Spanish in footnote].[140]

Indeed, the idea of using a network of personal agitators in this way has antecedents dating back at least to the Bolshevik Revolution, and probably proto-examples can be found long before 1917.[141] It has been estimated that by 1946, there were around three million personal agitators active in the Soviet Union.[142] Further back, as shown by Ranajit Guha, the transmission of rumours by word-of-mouth had a crucial and effective role to play among the peasant insurgency in colonial India.[143]

In a recent study of types of advertising and what forms of media people are most likely to be influenced by when considering to purchase a product, it was found that over 40 per cent of people are likely to be influenced by people that they know personally and had been influenced by word-of-mouth, or some kind of personal communication (e-mail, text message, etc.). While not a majority, it is significantly higher than any other form of influence – magazine articles were the next most influential at around 15 per cent, television adverts were under 5 per cent, as were advertising billboards.[144] These figures clearly suggest that personal influence, and influence by word-of-mouth, has a far more pervasive effect than can be achieved through any single form of mass communication media. In recent years, particularly in relation to the internet, companies selling products have been very keen to utilize 'viral' advertising – that is, to begin a chain reaction of people talking about their product (hopefully in a positive way) which spreads from person to person by word-of-mouth (or word-of-blog) like a virus to increase sales. They are in effect trying to take advantage of the fact that people are more likely to purchase a product based on a report from a fellow customer (someone they think they can trust) rather than on the company's own overt information (perhaps perceived as 'propaganda' in a derogatory sense) about its product. Companies such as Amazon, the online retailer, have long known that positive customer reviews increase sales, and there have been reports in the media recently of how companies trying to sell products through Amazon particularly have posted bogus positive reviews to try to increase sales – so-called shrill reviewing.[145] The historian Orlando Figes has famously been caught out in this way by writing negative reviews of other historians' work and by glorifying reviews of his own books.[146] While it would be difficult to link the British Council's work in Second World War directly with viral advertising on the internet today, the Council would, by targeting its audience in a personal way and by seeking secondary and tertiary effects of that word-of-mouth propaganda to reach a wider mass audience, aim to make use of very similar propaganda techniques to viral advertising. Indeed, it would be at the very forefront of pioneering this technique.

To an extent, the Council would have a loss of control through word-of-mouth propaganda as it would be difficult, if not impossible, to direct the content of the secondary and tertiary (and so on) contacts that are made to wider groups. Mathematical studies have attempted to apply models designed to describe disease outbreaks to the diffusion of information or rumours. One such study, the so-called threshold theorem developed by David G. Kendall in the 1950s, suggested that rumours tended to fall into two categories: those which became 'extinct early' after a few repetitions and those which resembled a 'major outbreak [of disease] affecting a large proportion of the susceptible population'.[147] The model is an interesting theory but based on a series of simplistic assumptions which although have been developed further are difficult to fit into a real-world situation.

One study which has attempted to test rumour spreading in practice using over 40 groups of people in various training courses and schools suggested about 70 per cent of the detail in rumours are lost in just five to six transmissions, but that this amount of content then stabilizes and a core percentage of the original rumour (around 30 per cent) continues to be transmitted many more times.[148] This study has the clear advantage over the mathematical theories above of being tested out on real people, though it should be noted that this was still in an artificial environment and viewing rumour spreading very much in a vacuum – the study was conducted in what could be described as 'laboratory conditions' rather than 'in the field'. While it is arguable that the Council would not be disseminating 'rumours' as such, the rumour effect is still applicable when talking about word-of-mouth propaganda, and it can be assumed, if this study on rumour psychology is correct, that about a third of the content of the word-of-mouth propaganda, that was passed on to other groups, could have been accurately represented. The British Council would have to be constantly coping and dealing with propaganda and rumours being spread by agents of the Axis countries primarily but also by Axis sympathizers in the countries where they were operating. Viral advertisers also have this problem and many negative customer reviews and comments (perhaps placed by rival competitors) which they are unable to counter can have a devastating effect on product sales. Nevertheless, it is perhaps reasonable to state that a certain percentage of the original rumour is likely to have permeated a certain distance down the chain of transmissions, even if that percentage was not as high as 30 per cent. Reports from the PWE during Second World War seem to suggest that in their sib campaign 'comebacks' (i.e. sibs that had been detected as successful by spotting the story in an enemy or neutral newspaper or overhearing it being repeated independently) were relatively high, though an actual percentage is difficult to estimate.[149]

Clearly, it was not a new type of propaganda, but it is a propaganda technique that is often overlooked because of its intangible nature. While it is not out of the question that 'sibs' were disseminated by lecturers and musicians arriving in these neutral countries under British Council auspices (the Ritz Hotel in Madrid was known as a favoured place for starting rumours, because of the large numbers of German spies residing there, and the hotel was close to the British Institute building[150]), there is no actual evidence linking 'sib' dissemination, as a directed and planned campaign, and the British Council. Nevertheless, the word-of-mouth propaganda that the British Council lecturers promulgated was a very similar technique to that used in the 'sib' campaign.

Elites, in particular, in all of the neutral European capitals were keen to learn uncensored news about the status of the war as they could not trust the neutral newspapers and other media to give them an objective account, as Mallet alluded to in the quotation above. Council lecturers relied on a secondary wave of rumour-spreading, or word-of-mouth propaganda, to take place, starting with the relatively few people (with pro-British sympathies) they had spoken to and being transmitted to less sympathetic and even hostile people. All this would happen, of course, without there ever being a direct tangible chain of evidence leading people to discover where the rumour, or word-of-mouth propaganda, actually began. Steegman noted after his visit to Madrid that

> A visitor sent here by the Council has two functions. One, to lecture; the other, to make personal contacts (as long as these are made under the guidance of the Council's Representative). The Institute in Madrid has become, through Starkie's personality, a remarkable centre of intellectual and social life, quite apart from its functions as a teaching organisation and from its charitable work. To lecture, or perform one's purely professional function, is not quite enough by itself. On the other hand, to pay a visit that has no apparent professional reasons, however distinguished the visitor may be at home, carries with it the danger of being falsely interpreted here. Madrid is not a city where simple, innocent motives are likely to be understood.[151]

What Steegman seems to be suggesting here is that Madrid society was *expecting* word-of-mouth propaganda to be disseminated by the British Council lecturers, and to some extent it had to fulfil the needs of its audience by making contacts outside its official reason for existing of organizing and housing cultural events.

Mallet recalled how the various visitors to Sweden went about their cultural activities in their own different ways. It was mentioned earlier that Sir Malcolm Sargent visited Portugal in January 1943, but he also travelled to Sweden a few months earlier to conduct a number of Swedish orchestras in Stockholm and Gothenburg, and also to give lectures to hundreds of Swedish students, which ended 'on a highly emotional and patriotic note which called forth storms of applause'.[152] As the Swedish were actively demonstrating their neutrality, they also invited the German conductor Wilhelm Furtwängler to perform. Though Furtwängler was not a Nazi, it actually helped the British cause that the Swedes had invited both a Briton and a German, as Furtwängler's 'applause was less than Malcolm had got' at least according to Mallet.[153] Clearly, news of Sargent's performance spread quickly – Knatchbull-Hugessen noted in his diary, while on a short trip to London in late 1942 to early 1943, that he met Sargent at the Savoy Theatre noting he was 'fresh from his success in Stockholm'.[154] Sargent returned to Sweden the following year and performed in Gothenburg.[155]

In Portugal, Sargent conducted Edward Elgar's Cello Concerto and Gustav Holst's 'The Planets'. Steegman, who watched one of the rehearsals, noted that 'there's no doubt he [Sargent] has brought the orchestra to a level of discipline no Portuguese conductor has achieved'.[156] At the two concerts that Sargent conducted, Steegman noted that 'Sargent got a tremendous reception' from the 2,000 person audience and was on 'superb form'.[157] The cello was played by the famous Portuguese cellist, Guilhermina Suggia, who had lived in London since the end of First World War.[158] Clearly, skilled and famous musicians, such as Sargent and Suggia, could pull a large and appreciative audience of admirers and were great ambassadors for British music and therefore

British culture. Sargent himself was reported in the Portuguese press as saying that music was a 'language for understanding between peoples' [Original Portuguese in footnote],[159] and it certainly seemed to have that effect. Here again not only were the concerts important but also the whole associated experience of press interviews and publicity which surrounded the concerts broadened and heightened the British influence in Portugal.

Philip Newman, who, as was shown in the previous chapter was at the centre of a conflict between the advice of the Music Advisory Committee and the British Institute in Lisbon, had arrived in Portugal after escaping Belgium at the time of the German invasion and had been promoting British music culture in Portugal by playing the violin. Regardless of the technical musical prowess of Newman, he was certainly able to pull a large audience, much in the same way as Sargent, but over a sustained period of time. Sargent certainly had no qualms about associating himself with Newman while in Portugal, even if the Music Advisory Committee did not want to do so.[160] Newman also ensured he was prominent in British life in Portugal generally, and in his papers at the Royal Northern College of Music there are pictures of him with Leslie Howard in 1943, as well as other British cultural figures who came to Portugal on the Council's behalf.[161] Unlike Sargent's short visit, however, Newman did not keep exclusively to British music in his concerts, and was not afraid to perform works by German and Italian composers such as Ludwig van Beethoven and Antonio Vivaldi at a time when German victory seemed all but settled.[162] It may appear a somewhat strange juxtaposition at this time but it can be better understood if two factors are considered. First, the German Ambassador was trying to persuade the Portuguese authorities to deport Newman to Britain (twice in 1942 he was asked to leave)[163] – by playing German music, Newman successfully scuppered the German Ambassador's main argument that he was using British music as a tool of political propaganda. Second, the propaganda that Newman produced by playing the violin was about British musicians, and how talented they were, and not necessarily about British music. Portuguese audiences were not necessarily ready for British music, and certainly would not have stomached concerts made up of only British music all of the time. It was far better to have British musicians, such as Newman, playing German music with a diverse and interested Portuguese audience than British musicians playing British music with a narrow-minded or uninterested Portuguese audience (or no audience at all).

Only over a longer period of time could British music be played without being interspersed with music from other nations, as the Portuguese audiences were not used to hearing it. Even today it would be odd for a concert to contain the music of only one nation, unless it was commemorating a particular event, and then would be necessarily publicized as such. This was not an unusual approach in Second World War. In Spain, Starkie organized a concert in the autumn of 1940 with the Czechoslovakian pianist Rudolf Firkušný where he played Wolfgang Amadeus Mozart, Antonín Dvořák, Frédéric Chopin, Claude Debussy and Bedřich Smetana. By no means predominately Germanic, it contained two composers from Firkušný's homeland but certainly no British (or Spanish) music.[164] Nevertheless, Starkie was able to draw in some of Spain's foremost composers to the concert, Joaquín Turina and Conrado del Campo, as well as conductors and pianists, which he may not have been able to do if the concert had contained music by British composers unknown in Spain. Starkie certainly took a risk in promoting Czech music and was advised to be very careful by the Spanish authorities. He managed to pull it off by avoiding mention of the Czech music in a speech prior to the concert stressing the importance of Spanish music and the links between Britain and Spain through musicians such as Fernandez Arbós, Manuel de Falla and Ralph Vaughan Williams.[165] Quite how these composers were connected was not made clear in Starkie's report of the concert, but he was able to guide the audience's thinking and achieve the difficult task of promoting British music without the aid of British musicians or British music being played. In Samuel Llano's analysis of the British Council's promotion of music in Spain, he also concluded the Council often resorted to the use of foreign performers so as to draw larger audiences, but also to keep down the expense of sending out British musicians to Spain.[166] Llano noted that the international nature of the music was a way of attracting the Spanish to a British lifestyle and not necessarily British music.[167] By 1943, British music was being performed in Spain by the Orquestra Nacional including Vaughan Williams's *Fantasia on a Theme by Thomas Tallis* with music supplied by the Council, but British music in Spain did not really get going until much later in the war.[168]

In contrast to Sargent's visits to Sweden, T. S. Eliot's visit in the spring of 1942 was not as extroverted – Eliot, noted Sir Victor Mallet, 'pursued his quiet way with the Swedish Pen Club and other intellectual bodies' – but was no less popular with the Swedes. Mallet remarked in his memoirs that '[t]he Swedes were hungry for intellectual contact with the West and showed a remarkable appreciation of Tom Eliot and his poetry'.[169] Eliot's visit showed that cultural propaganda did not have to be widely publicized to be effective (though, as we shall see Eliot received some attention in the Swedish press), and perhaps shows that an understated propaganda offensive was more able to attract curious Swedish minds when they did not have to show where their sympathies lay so openly. Peter Tennant, the British press attaché, also noted that Eliot 'charmed the children with stories' and was a very popular figure particularly on a personal level.[170] Sir Lawrence Bragg also spent a lot of time talking privately with Swedish scientists. Tennant recalled in his autobiography that Bragg was 'kept under wraps' while in Sweden and 'stayed quietly at the Legation for a month', but that is not the impression that is given by his report that he wrote for the Council, or his diary now kept at the Royal Institution archive in London.[171] His report described the lectures that he gave to the Universities of Uppsala and Stockholm and the *Teknolog Förening* (Technology Association) on X-ray optics and Proteins as well as what he called 'popular lectures' with titles such as 'Seeing ever-smaller worlds' about his work with electron microscopes.[172] Science was a particularly strong cultural trait in Sweden and Bragg's lectures went down well.[173] Perhaps in contrast to Sargent's flamboyant visit, Bragg's was rather quiet, but he certainly attempted to reach a variety of audiences, both scientific academics and wider, more populist, audiences. Bragg noted in his diary of his visit that he was taken aback that one of his lectures 'must be *very* popular' because '[i]t is to be followed by a dance, which sets the tone' [Bragg's emphasis].[174] For a respected Cambridge professor and winner of a Nobel Prize this was conceivably rather shocking, but Bragg rose to the occasion and '[m]ade it still more popular and put in a few jokes' – and the Swedish audience laughed in the right places which he was delighted about – he added 'I decided I was making myself understood'.[175] The text of his lecture was translated into Swedish as '*Inblick i allt mindre världar*', and was handed out, which was a great help if at any time the Swedish audience were not clear on what he was saying. After the lecture, Swedish translations appeared in the Swedish press.[176] The dancing, unfortunately, was cancelled because it was deemed inappropriate at a time when many in Sweden were preoccupied with the news that the Swedish submarine, the *Ulven*, had been sunk, which was presumed to be the work of the German Navy.[177]

Dr Robert McCance, a Cambridge scientist, had been sent to Portugal and Spain a few months earlier than Bragg had been sent to Sweden – in February 1943. In the previous chapter, it was noted that McCance was not the most willing of ambassadors of British culture and it took some persuading to convince him to go.[178] McCance was the first visitor to the British Institute in Madrid to be invited to lecture outside of the British Institute building itself, first by Professor Jiménez Díaz, Franco's personal doctor, who invited him to lecture at the Faculty of Medicine and the Institute for Puericultura, and then later by Dr Carlos Blanco Soler, who invited him to lecture at the Academia Medico-Quirúrgica Española.[179] McCance spoke in Spanish at most of his lectures, and he stated he was 'certain that the trouble I had taken to learn enough Spanish to be able to lecture in that language was well repaid, for by doing so I commanded much larger audiences, and I think my efforts were appreciated'.[180] McCance also tried to lecture in Spanish in Portugal as he did not speak Portuguese – although the Portuguese audiences understood him they 'suggested that I should lecture in French' because of 'their pride' and 'tendency to have no associations with Spain'.[181] Taking account of political and cultural sensitivities such as these could make all the difference for a successful lecture tour. McCance noted that during one lecture in the University of Coimbra 'the audience was less interested and attentive than in any of the other places where I spoke, and a number of students went out when I was showing slides'.[182] Although McCance does not suggest a reason for this, it could well be that speaking Spanish in Portugal's foremost University did not endear him to his audience.[183] In the Portuguese newspapers, however, there is no hint that he was unpopular and certainly no mention that he spoke in Spanish, let alone that it caused people to leave the lecture theatre – they all instead stressed the applause that he received.[184] Nevertheless, in Spain, McCance believed he was given a much more 'favourable reception' than in Portugal and gave two reasons for this, other than the fact that he lectured in Spanish. First, the change in the war situation which by early 1943 had resulted in Operation Torch in Algeria and the advance on El Alamein, and an ensuing change in the Spanish mindset. 'The Spaniards', McCance stated, 'have decided in their own (individual) minds that the Allies are likely to win the war and are making provision accordingly'.[185] It was noted earlier that with the changing war situation there was increased interest in the British Institute in Madrid from those who had been earlier indifferent or even hostile to its presence in the Spanish capital. It was also clearly the case that British Council lecturers were becoming more popular and were being invited to venture outside of the institute building itself. The second reason was that his work in particular 'was well known to Professor Jiménez Díaz and the people of his Institute'.[186] Choosing a good subject which the audiences were interested in, from a practical point of view, was evidently a wise move. McCance was particularly impressed with Díaz who 'demonstrated a number of most interesting medical cases, including some six of lathyrism which had been specially collected for my [McCance's] benefit'.[187]

In Turkey, there were relatively few visitors because of the length of time it took to get there from Britain during the war. However, the visitors who did arrive tended to meet all of the key people in Turkey and stay for an extended period of time. For example, a picture from Michael Grant's personal photograph album from his time in Turkey shows John Steegman, who lectured in Turkey on art during late 1943 and early 1944, meeting Halide Edip.[188] Edip was an associate of the late founder of modern Turkey, Kemal Ataturk, and still remained an influential figure – she was 'more or less the leading woman in Turkey', noted Steegman in his diary.[189] Edip attended a number of British Council events, including one of Steegman's lectures, and spoke at length to Steegman about her time in London, English literature and her views on the reform of the Turkish language that had been ongoing since the revolution.[190]

As well as giving lectures, Steegman also organized an exhibition on English Graphic Art in Istanbul. He noted that it was very similar to ones that he had helped organize in Spain, Portugal and Iceland and shows that where possible the British Council did seek to conduct a 'one size fits all' propaganda role in this respect. Nevertheless, it was not necessarily the art on display that was so important, but that the exhibition itself created a talking point and was an excuse for socializing and networking across political boundaries. For example, Steegman noted the number of 'gate-crashers' and 'political doubtfuls' that attended the exhibition.[191] From correspondence in the British Council papers, Steegman had evidently known Starkie prior to the war which made the organization of his lectures on art while he was in Spain easier than with some other visitors.[192] His relationship with Grant, however, was not so smooth and there are a number of references to friction between the two men while Steegman was in Turkey.[193]

The art that was displayed by the Council was generally an eclectic mix of modern artists which did not appear to have much of a general theme, apart from the fact that it was the work of British artists. However, some discerning reviewers in Sweden detected a twofold approach including the Impressionists and Abstract artists.[194] A British graphic art exhibition in Spain in 1941 and Portugal in 1942 showed a variety of artists, materials and techniques being utilized such as etchings, wood engravings and lithographs.[195] The artworks were not obviously propagandistic especially in a political sense, but instead show images of Britain and a British way of life in a number of different guises – industrial, at home and out in the British countryside. What was important, however, with all of the art exhibitions was that the art was not blatant propaganda with war subjects as their theme, but were far more subtle and incremental in approach, producing a cumulative impression of the British way of life and achievements and to maintain and inculcate sympathy for the British cause in the war.

However, John Steegman's art exhibitions in Spain and Portugal in the autumn of 1942 and early 1943 were less eclectic than usual. They were specifically prints and portrait engravings in the period from Queen Elizabeth to Queen Victoria, so although there was a theme in terms of type of materials used, there was still a large sweep of history covered by the content of its art itself.[196] Steegman, in his plan of his exhibition, stated that

> [t]he exhibits in each main section would be predominantly portraits, but would include a few contemporary engravings of historic events or of topographical interest. The portraits would be selected from certain categories: Sovereigns and the Court; statesmen; soldiers and sailors; churchmen and lawyers; scientists; founders of the Empire; writers, artists, musicians and actors.
>
> In general, only portraits of the very famous will be included; on the other hand, since it is an exhibition of engravings, we should include a number that are fine examples of the art while not representing an historic figure, e.g. a McArdell print of a Reynolds' female portrait.[197]

Clearly, therefore, while Steegman was conscious of the fact that it was an art exhibition that he was organizing and therefore the actual focus on the artists' techniques and talents should not be lost, it was primarily designed to show the people of Madrid a positive view of high British society – those who were either aristocrats or people who had achieved recognition for a particular reason. Robert Burns, Josiah Wedgwood, the Duke of Wellington and Sir Robert Peel were all represented as were George IV and William IV.[198] This was not an exhibition to show the more ordinary side of Britain. Steegman accompanied his exhibition with three lectures on 19, 21 and 22 November 1942 in Madrid on 'The Engraved Portrait', 'The Earlier Portrait Painters' and 'The Golden Age of Portrait Painting', respectively.[199] He believed these were well received and was pleased with the number of Spanish students that attended his lectures. After each lecture, there was either a cocktail party or sherry party which enabled the word-of-mouth propaganda mentioned earlier to flow in a less formalized setting.[200]

At an English watercolour exhibition in Sweden in 1943, Bottrall regarded the total number of visitors, 12,610, across all of the exhibition locations (in Stockholm, Gothenburg, Malmö, etc.) as 'quite satisfactory', but that there was a 'disappointing attendance at Stockholm, as compared with Gothenburg and Malmö, [which] was in part due to the fact that [Erik] Wettergren [the Director of the National Museum in Stockholm] made no attempt to advertise the Exhibition and little effort to publicize it'.[201] Nevertheless, he stated, '[t]here is no doubt that the Exhibition did a great deal to awaken interest here in contemporary British Art'.[202]

The cost of 1523.96 Swedish Krona (about £91) for the whole exhibition was also deemed 'very reasonable indeed'.[203] 'In view of the very small expenses incurred at this end', noted Bottrall, 'I think we can agree that it was a really great success'.[204] However, in a review of Swedish newspaper coverage of the exhibition, there was a variety of views as to whether the 'modesty of our show' was too evident and that there should have been more of an attempt to provide blatant political propaganda, as that was what the Swedish audiences were expecting.[205] There was clearly some disquiet in London

Table 2 Attendance figures for the English Watercolour Exhibition in Sweden, 1943, organized by the British Council

Dates	Location	Population	Visitors	Catalogues Sold	Visitors per Population (%)
19 Jan–6 Feb 1943	Gothenburg	283,550	3,452	402	1.217
9–28 Feb 1943	Stockholm	605,575	2,150	336	0.355
4–19 Mar 1943	Uppsala	38,926	599	139	1.539
23–30 Mar 1943	Linköping	41,100	482	19	1.173
4–11 Apr 1943	Lund	28,345	500	257	1.764
13–26 Apr 1943	Malmö	157,527	5,427	95	3.445
Total		1,154,973	12,610	1,248	1.092

Source: TNA BW 57/4, 'Exhibition of British Water Colours in Sweden, 1943' attached to Bottrall to Longden, 26 May 1943.

when news was received of the attendance figures – the Chairman of the Fine Arts Committee, Sir Eric Maclagen stated

> I must say I am rather disappointed with the attendance figures. Malmo is all right; but if the average figures at the other five Exhibitions only amounted to under 1500 in each place I think it is extremely difficult to justify all the trouble and expense of sending out such a collection, let alone the risk involved.[206]

It did not help that Wettergren, who had helped to organize the exhibition, wrote an unfavourable review in a Swedish newspaper of the British art – Major Alfred Longden, the Director of Fine Art at the British Council, sent a strongly worded letter to him via Bottrall. '[W]e are exceedingly busy' wrote Longden, 'and do not need to send work where it is not really wanted'.[207] However, it was probably an overreaction to the situation, as Bottrall pointed out to Longden, that if a Swedish watercolour exhibition had been held in England, would 88,270 people (a comparable number for the difference in population between Britain and Sweden), have attended it? Bottrall thought not, but forwarded on Longden's letter nevertheless.[208] Maclagen was still not persuaded by Bottrall's argument stating 'I still feel that the members of the [Fine] Art Committee were hoping for more result in organizing that particular exhibition'.[209] Whether the attendance figures are impressive or not in terms of population must not, however, disguise the fact that it must have struck the population who read about the exhibition as rather audacious to send over 50 pieces of art to Sweden during the war, even if the art was not to their taste or they did not feel confident in attending the exhibitions themselves for fear of being seen as too pro-British. In Sweden in particular, the secret police were constantly monitoring who visited the British Legation and the British Council's exhibitions.[210] A secret police agent attended the opening of the English watercolour exhibition at the Stockholm National Museum to monitor who was there.[211] It was very difficult, therefore, for the Council to predict the suitability of each art exhibition and the willingness of the local citizens to be active consumers of the Council's efforts. It very much depended on local conditions, local historical preferences and memory in order for the exhibitions to be a success. A particularly good example of this was the postage stamp exhibition that was first tried in Stockholm, which was deemed by Longden to be 'such a failure', was then repeated in Spain, and was 'a startling success in Madrid, and practically all [stamps] have been sold'. 'I think you', Longden went on in his description of the Madrid exhibition to Bottrall, 'got the collection too soon after your arrival and did not have a very fitting place in which to exhibit it'.[212] Bottrall in reply (and perhaps slightly perturbed by Longden's remark) stated, however, '[t]he failure here was nothing to do with way in which it was exhibited or the place of exhibition. Obviously the Swedes are not interested in specialised collections'.[213] Another report noted that 'Madrid is a great centre for stamp collecting, and nearly all the stamps were sold on the opening day'.[214] It seems clear then that success of exhibitions rested very much on the existing local sociological conditions and preferences, and it was not always easy to 'sell' an exhibition to people where they were not already familiar with its contents.

Selling an exhibition to people was often made easier when the Council knew it had the official backing of the Government or other influential elites in the country where they were operating. Usually, the Council simply organized exhibitions independently and then invited Government officials and elites along at the opening of the exhibition. Rarely, however, did the Head of State turn up at the opening ceremony to demonstrate their support as happened with the Exhibition of Photographs of British Universities, which was held in the Ankara Halkevi in Turkey. Not only did Hasan-Ali Yücel arrive as might be more expected given the closeness of his friendship with Grant, but so did President İnönü.[215] This was unlikely to have happened in any of the other three European countries analysed in this book, as the closeness of the British Council to the Government elite was not nearly as striking – Grant, himself, believed this was evidence that 'the Council played a part in Turkey's eventual line-up with the Allies'.[216] The President was able to openly show where his sympathies lay and would give others within the Turkish elites the confidence not only to attend the Exhibition of Photographs but also to support the Allied cause.

It would be difficult to contemplate General Franco ever taking the same action that President İnönü had at this exhibition, but the Crown Prince of Sweden (who was more pro-British than the King) also attended exhibitions that the British Council had organized, and Dr Oliveira Salazar in Portugal was happy to have a degree conferred upon him by an Oxford University delegation who travelled to Coimbra with the help of the Council.[217] Nonetheless, the effect of İnönü's presence appeared far more profound, and effective, than any of these other events in persuading the elites to become more receptive and sympathetic to the British cause.

There are, of course, other examples of where the Council knew an exhibition or event had been a success in one country, and thought it could be successful elsewhere, but the wartime practicalities of getting that exhibition or event established elsewhere were too difficult to overcome. The sending of a football team to Turkey, as mentioned earlier, had been possible because the close proximity of British troops in Egypt meant that fit young men were available to play the game and hopefully win.[218] Although Michael Grant described the arrival of the football team as 'my most alarming experience in Turkey', largely because he had to step in to manage the football team personally, and had also been instructed by the Council to get a percentage of the gate money royalties from the Turkish authorities (finding out later that the crowds had been let in for free), exhibiting the game of football itself was a success with the British team playing in Ankara, Istanbul and Adana in November and December 1941.[219] When Victor Mallet requested a similar team should be sent to Sweden later that year, the request had to be refused because of the impossibility first of all of getting 11 men to Sweden to play football, and also because all the fit young men were in the armed forces and were not in close enough proximity to be spared to play.[220] Grant's experience perhaps may also have clouded the view of the Council when thinking about the possibility of sending a second team to Sweden. .

By sending lecturers to its overseas institutes and by organizing exhibitions and concerts, the British Council was able to keep a level of interest in the British way of life and culture that would not have been possible if the institutes had only been libraries or teaching establishments, as these would have been perhaps rather static and uninteresting. The events were important in their own right, in demonstrating to local populations the breadth and depth of British contributions to culture, particularly from a scientific understanding and artistic point of view. Success here depended on choosing the right person to talk on the right topic. Perhaps more importantly, however, the events provided excuses for people to meet and talk. Having the benefit of new arrivals from Britain by way of lecturers catalysed a flow of information that was not possible, or at least not to the same extent, by any other method. As with much of the British Council's work, its effect was felt on a cumulative basis and was naturally incremental – one lecture on its own would have little effect, but over time the success of each lecture would build on the success of previous lectures until a more pervasive effect had been achieved.

Films

In many ways, films produced by the British Council were the epitome of the 'one size fits all' approach to cultural propaganda. They were, first of all, produced in Britain centrally and, second, they were designed to meet the needs of the wide range of audiences from various different countries as well as for British audiences. That did not mean, however, that the types of films were necessarily restricted. The Council produced a relatively wide selection of films including newsreels (which were largely outsourced and in collaboration with the Ministry of Information – and therefore not a uniquely British Council venture, nor really cultural propaganda), theatrical productions, films about the geography, history and scenery of Britain designed to be enjoyed by audiences, as well as instructional films on technical subjects designed to aid education. The British Council has recently released a number of its films on websites such as YouTube and Vimeo which show a broad cross section of the material that the British Council produced during the war. As these are easily available, I have decided to focus on those films released recently, so that readers can follow the films themselves and get a better understanding of the analysis here.

Through much of this chapter it has been highlighted how the British Council aimed to keep talk of the ongoing war out of its conversations in neutral countries. In the films it produced, this aim was also apparent particularly in the technical, instructional, films – but it was also clear that the British Council found it impossible to keep the war out of its films entirely. The war was often a running background theme (there were many references, for example, to the men overseas in the forces, and how life and economics had changed through increased Government control – fixing prices, 'show allotments' to encourage people to grow their own vegetables, etc.) or there have been conscious decisions that the films should be about Britain in wartime rather than in a nostalgic past age – though the films remained about life in Britain rather about than military topics. Some of the films such as *Morning Paper* specifically examined how a newspaper was produced in wartime, and *London 1942*[221] dealt with life in London after three years of war – it seems clear that these were designed not to gloss over the fact that Britain was at war but to show that British life was continuing positively *despite* the war.

The films were also not shy in taking the opportunity to imply messages about the war itself metaphorically, if those opportunities arose. For example, in the film *History of the English Language*[222] it would have been very difficult to examine the roots of the English language without mentioning Germany, given the Anglo-Saxon heritage of the English. This was mentioned without much comment early in the film (often referring to 'these parts of Europe' with a map highlighting Germany), but later the narrator stated that English inherited words from Germany to do with metals and mining – like quartz – and war words like 'plunder'. When the word 'plunder' was mentioned, there was a picture of someone rifling through a box, which then morphed into a drawn outline of a Nazi figure also rifling through a box – identified easily owing to the swastika armband. However, this reference only existed for about two seconds out of the whole film, which lasted just over 14 minutes. Most references were more subtle, however, such as in *Country Town*[223], where the newspaper editor, Mr Johnson, described how the marketplace no longer adhered to market principles, and government officials assessed the quality of the animals before assigning them to a fixed-price class. *Country Town* also described how the guild hall, usually used for exhibitions, had been turned into a communal restaurant where everyone could get a meal for a shilling. In *Steel goes to sea*[224] – which was a film about how a ship was built and launched from the shipyard – there was a sub-plot regarding a boy called David, who was the son of one of the shipbuilders, and soon to be an apprentice, and who graffitied some letters onto the steel sheets. At first only the letters H and I were written, which could be mistaken just for a boy who wanted to write 'Hi' – and a very innocent phrase – but this later transformed into a longer phrase during the course of the film into 'Hitler is a B' before he was stopped by one of the workers. Later David did finish the text, but it was difficult to read on the film. Before the graffiti was painted over, the sheet of steel with the text on was lifted into place on the side of the ship for all to see. The main point of the film, however, was to show the great engineering capability of Britain and to demonstrate the effectiveness of the British workforce in delivering ship after ship efficiently.

Like much of the British Council's cultural propaganda, however, the war was not a feature of many of the films but they instead focused on the way of life of many different communities across Britain. For example, *We of the West Riding*[225], produced at the end of the war, followed the Sykes family and their work in the mills of Yorkshire. It covered in detail the work of the mill itself, but also expanded into broader context of where the cloth would be exported to (across the Empire and to the United States). It was also a window into broader Yorkshire life with a cycle ride through the moors and dales of Yorkshire, with the cyclists singing *On Ilkla Moor Baht'at*, references to the stories of the Brontë sisters – *Jane Eyre* and *Wuthering Heights* – football, pigeon-fancying, brass bands and choir singing and so on. *Country Town* charted the life of a Lincolnshire town, which, though not mentioned explicitly in the film, was Boston – as it was the last place the pilgrims saw before heading to the Americas. The film surveyed Boston – its picturesque windmill contrasting with new homes; its industries of fruit and vegetable canning; its connection to London via the railway; and lastly (though Johnson pretended to forget temporarily) how the people of Boston played – in the park, at the cinema, at the inn, with indoor bowls and dancing. Many of the films emphasized the leisure side of British life, and particularly the English pub – in *Island People*, *Lowland Village* and *Market Town*.[226]

One element, however, stood out as being missing from British life – and that was religion. For example, in *Island People*, the film examined the five-and-a-half days that the British people worked in a number of different professions and roles, and then it went on to state that 12 noon on Saturday was the start of the weekend holiday which was typified by sport – bowls, tennis, skating and particularly football – and by staying at home with children and families. Sunday was not mentioned at all, nor in any of the films that the British Council has released online was churchgoing shown as a major element of British life. Only in the *History of the English Language* were religious words seen as significant – such as minster, alms and altar; and in the *Development of an English Town* the fact that towns were built around churches in Anglo-Saxon times was mentioned, but it went onto say that this was weak militarily and was superseded by the feudal system introduced by the Normans. It seems odd that such an important element of British life at the time would be ignored – and surely many of the audiences that the British Council was aiming at would have regarded either Britain as being atheist or agnostic, and perhaps this could have backfired. An explanation probably comes from the fact that the British Council was aiming at so many different types of audience, that a 'one size fits all' approach to presenting British religious activities would have been impossible – with Catholic Spain and Portugal, Protestant Sweden and Muslim Turkey all being catered for – all of which had quite different approaches to religion. It was probably much easier to concentrate on the non-religious, industrial and leisure-time activities of the British people. Also, it is important to remember that films were not a major element of the British Council's activities at this time and the films – especially the instructional ones – were shown for specific purposes. The fact that religion was missing was probably not as obvious as it is now viewing them out of the context in which they were shown at the time.

Language issues

The language barrier was a common theme in all of the British Council's work, partly as it took time for English publications to be translated into the local languages but also because if works were translated then it could be argued that there was no need for the local people to learn English to understand British culture. They would then miss out on the wider range of publications in English that the British Council was not able to translate, because it did not have the time and resources required. Ifor Evans, in his inspection report on the British Institute in Madrid noted that

> if we can interest young Spaniards in this way [by teaching them English], they will become more ready to conduct their own special studies through the medium of English books; they will be able to read our bulletins and newspapers, and generally develop a more friendly attitude towards us.[227]

In other words, a knowledge of the English language would make them reachable through a wider range of cultural propaganda. The Council did translate some English language works into the local language, however, and worked with (and informally encouraged some) commercial publishers such as José Janés in Spain to publish translated British works. Jacqueline Hurtley, in one of her books studying the publishing practices of José Janés (*José Janés: editor de literatura inglesa*) noted that the publisher had adopted 'a Machiavellian strategy in certain circumstances' to ensure its survival under the Franco regime [Original Spanish in footnote].[228] Hurtley stated that Walter Starkie was much more enthusiastic about working with Spanish publishers such as Ortega and Janés than British Council staff in London which was often the cause of some tension. The reason, primarily, was one of lack of money for supporting the publication of books rather than an ideological problem.[229] The Council staff in London much preferred the Book Export Scheme (explained in detail below) which was much less of a risky financial enterprise than funding the publications themselves, but Starkie was frustrated at seeing a wealth of German and Italian books for sale in Spain but relatively few English ones.[230] Nevertheless, William Shakespeare, G. K. Chesterton, Charles Dickens, Oscar Wilde, P. G. Wodehouse and Winston Churchill all had their works translated and published by the Council, or with the Council's backing, and Starkie maintained an informal relationship with Janés from 1942 onwards to encourage the publication of English literature in translation.[231] However, Janés never appears to have received financial support for publishing English literature in Spain, but support was nevertheless there at a non-financial and informal level.[232] Wilde's *La importància d'ésser fidel* was perhaps the most inspired title translation into Spanish, while Dickens's *Documentos póstumos del club Pickwick* was perhaps less inspired.[233] Churchill was presented with a specially bound Spanish translation of his book *Thoughts and Adventures* as *Pensamientos y aventuras* which was arranged through Starkie – Churchill expressed his gratitude to José Janés through the Council stating

> The good work done by publishers in other countries during the war in translating the work of contemporary English writers is worthy of great praise, and it is gratifying to know that English books in Spain have such a good friend in Señor Janes [sic].[234]

A good friend indeed in light of the lack of financial support that Janés received. The Council produced a series of booklets in a *British Life and Thought* collection covering a range of themes. These were originally only in English language versions but were eventually translated into a variety of languages. A few examples of the titles for the four countries explored in this book were *El Hombre Inglés* (Spanish – 'The Englishman') by Stanley Baldwin,[235] *La Mujer Inglesa* (Spanish – 'The Englishwoman') by Cicely Hamilton,[236] *O Sistema Governativo da Grã-Bretanha* (Portuguese – 'The British System of Government') by W. A. Robson[237] and *Det brittiska samväldet* (Swedish – 'The British Commonwealth') by A. Berriedale Keith.[238] These booklets were fairly straightforward and often relatively dry accounts of British life. For example, in *The British Commonwealth* Berriedale Keith began in a very matter-of-fact way, setting out the different statuses of the territories of the Commonwealth and then a table covering four pages outlined the names, geographical area and population (with the date that the population figure represented):

> In the following lists are included all territories which are British possessions, or are under the protection of, or have been allotted in mandate to, the British Crown, or are held in condominium by the Crown with a foreign State. British possessions include all parts of His Majesty's dominions outside the United Kingdom; they make up therefore with the United Kingdom all the territories over which the King has complete sovereignty, as contrasted with a protectorate, a mandate, or a condominium or share in control.[239]

The booklet continued in a similar vein for 56 pages in the English version (and was translated largely word-for-word into other language versions), though it was interspersed with a collection of photographs from around the Commonwealth which helped to lighten the dryness of the text. To be fair, occasionally there was an element of emotion, particularly when Keith talked about the American war of independence, but these occasions were short lived.[240] Perhaps, the Council was deliberately trying to make its booklets dry and non-propagandistic. It did not want to attract adverse criticism that it was trying to glorify the Commonwealth, but was simply trying to educate the readers as to the scale and structure and allow them to imagine the achievements of the Commonwealth in their own way, similar to the way that the Empire had always spoken for itself. It is interesting that the pictures in the English and Swedish versions were different, with only one – a picture of the King and Queen meeting native Amerindian tribes ('Red Indians') in Alberta, Canada – being the same, though there was a similar picture in both of Mount Cook in New Zealand. The English version tended to show landscapes and cityscapes from within the Commonwealth which perhaps would have existed anyway without British influence, such as a Chinese street in Singapore, and Johannesburg from a distance. The Swedish version, although having similar landscape scenes, had a larger collection of pictures showing British influence in the Commonwealth and how the Commonwealth was directly helping the war effort – such as Governors' residences, a bomb factory in Canada for the war effort and Australians in army uniform aboard a ship steaming through the Suez Canal.[241] Two years separate the publication of the two booklets, and it is clear that there had been a reassessment of the types of pictures that were appropriate, and it is arguable that pictures of the war effort in these booklets were stepping outside of the remit of cultural propaganda and into the political sphere. It is interesting that the title of the booklet was 'The British Commonwealth' rather than 'The British Empire'. 'Commonwealth' was still a very new phrase in this context and more commonly linked to the post-war period (being formerly inaugurated in 1949) but had been slowly growing in usage since the 1920s. Churchill had mentioned the word in his famous speech of 18 June 1940: 'Let us therefore brace ourselves to our duties and so bear ourselves that, if the British Empire and its Commonwealth last for a thousand years, men will still say, "This was their finest hour." '[242] Even then, however, he still mentioned 'Empire' and Churchill's use of the word 'Commonwealth' appears to mean something subtlety different to its post-war definition. The British Council was conscious of the need to be forward-thinking, modern and not sounding imperialistic, and Keith met this issue head-on, noting the newness of the phrase:

> Of late years the term 'British Commonwealth of Nations' has come into both official and private use as a synonym for 'British Empire'. The choice of name is not arbitrary; it is felt to be more appropriate to describe a grouping of peoples, which now rests essentially on a voluntary basis, than the older name with its suggestion of the rule of Britain over subject races. Even in its earliest days the Empire had closer affinities to the Empire of Athens in the fifth century B.C. than to that of Rome.[243]

Whether this statement is true is not as important for this book as the impression the Council was trying to give. It wanted to present the 'Commonwealth' as a warm, friendly and likeable group of nations who chose to be together, with which it wanted the foreign people to have fondness and sympathy. Nevertheless, it still had to ensure that the Commonwealth was presented as a force to be reckoned with, so that people did not conclude that Britain was a weaker nation than it had previously been (when it had headed an Empire as opposed to a Commonwealth), and therefore was not able to defeat Germany in the war. A similar change can be noted in the terminology of other British organizations such as the BBC and the Ministry of Information and can be seen partly as a reaction to the growing strength particularly of the Dominions – such as Australia and Canada – and that Britain was no longer the supremely dominant force in the 'Empire', but was becoming more the first among equals.

Other booklets in the series, at least those not written by lawyers (and others certainly were – e.g. W. A. Robson's *The British System of Government*), were far more interesting in their style of writing. For example, Dudley Stamp's *The Face of Britain* started as follows – and its full first paragraph is worth quoting:

It would be difficult to find an area of comparable size anywhere in the world which exhibits quite such marked contrasts as may be found within the very limited area of the British Isles. A journey of twenty-five miles in Britain will often afford as much variety of scenery as one can find in two hundred and fifty miles in many of the newer lands, and within her hundred thousand square miles may be found an epitome, sometimes beautifully modelled by Nature in miniature, of most of the scenery of Europe. Too often the visitor, with but a few days to spare, sees only Lowland Britain – it may be Liverpool and London with perhaps a side trip to Edinburgh – and so fails to appreciate the contrasts between the wild, almost inaccessible fjords or sea lochs of the north-west Highlands of Scotland, the Dutch-like scenery of the drained fens of the Holland division of Lincolnshire, the rolling downland of Salisbury Plain, the secluded, heather-covered glades of the New Forest, the rugged crags of North Wales, the smiling orchardland of Kent, the grimy, narrow, congested valleys of South Wales, and the desolate almost uninhabited moorland of Sutherland. These scenic contrasts are often within easy reach of the great centres, so that a Londoner born and bred can still thrill at the discovery of new bypaths within twenty-five miles of the city, whilst the Glasgow slumdweller has the finest combination of sea and highland scenery within the same radius.[244]

With perhaps the exception of the word 'slumdweller', the whole opening paragraph exuded a passion that was likely to grip any reader and make them want to visit the wondrous land which Stamp described. Though visiting Britain was probably out of the question for most foreign people during the conditions of war, Stamp's articulate description certainly marked a strong contrast to Keith's monograph. Stamp proceeded to describe every corner of Great Britain (he excluded Northern Ireland) with the same fervent infatuation which was sure to enthral. The pictures, of which there are only eight, show a contrast in the scenery of Britain which helped to illuminate Stamp's points even further. Keith's use of the word 'Commonwealth' when the word 'Empire' was still in common use was perhaps unlikely to have won over people in the way that Stamp's writing style might have done.

The series of booklets did not shy away from difficult but obvious questions about Britain and its role in the world. Sometimes a conversational style of writing was used to present these questions, not dissimilar to the way in which organizations today use 'frequently asked questions' (or FAQs) on press releases to address tricky issues. For example, in Michael Lewis's *British Ships and British Seamen* he asks:

'Now why', it may be asked, 'does Great Britain play this troublesome and expensive rôle [of patrolling the world's seas]? We are not, surely, going to be asked to believe that she is altogether altruistic in this important matter, and that it is just for the love of her fellow men that she thus polices the seas?'[245]

'But', once more it may be urged, 'it is all very well to generalise on the subject and to affirm that Britain has benefited others besides herself. How exactly, during the last century, has she kept the seas free and safe for all? And in what ways has she used her outstanding sea power to help her fellow men, not necessarily seafarers, and to promote the freedom of all?[']²⁴⁶

Self-posed questions such as the one above, if chosen carefully and answered well, have the potential to make the reader believe that any concerns that they may have had are being allayed. More often, however, self-posed questions, like FAQs, tend to only address issues which the author thinks the reader wants answers to or thinks they need answers to, but does not actually address the real issues the reader is concerned about. This can lead to a certain amount of despondency on the part of the reader. It is difficult to assess the importance of the conversational style of writing in Lewis's booklet specifically as there are no records of readers' views on the way the booklets were written. Nevertheless, Lewis's style of writing was attractive and the questions that he posed were generally well chosen which would lead to the conclusion that people reading the booklets would have some sympathy with the points he was trying to make.

The problem with Lewis's booklet, and indeed all of the booklets in the *British Life and Thought* series, as well as other English books, was that readers had to physically pick up the book in the first place before reading it. Of course, the content of books and the ways in which they were written were important, but getting over the first hurdle of actually persuading people in neutral countries to pick up the book was far more difficult. Just as Michael Grant had shown it was far easier getting the second and third teacher into the Halkevleri, than the first, and that it was far easier for the Council to support pre-existing Anglophile Societies than establish them from scratch, it was also far easier to write a convincing argument in a book than persuading someone to pick the book up and get past the front cover. Essentially therefore, these books were designed to maintain existing sympathy and tap into unconvinced yet curious thoughts of the neutral mindset, and not to try to win over the non-sympathetic and hostile elites. To try to nurture the unconvinced, yet curious, a number of techniques were employed. When books arrived (and many were sent – the 3,000 flown to Sweden are testament to the large numbers involved²⁴⁷), the Council established exhibitions where anyone could come and view the books – and the 'public poured in' according to Stanley Unwin.²⁴⁸ The libraries with the British institutes were, of course, an opportunity for those with curiosity to view the books at their leisure without having to attend an exhibition, but they still had to enter the premises of a British organization which was always going to be an issue for some, especially as the police in many of the neutral countries monitored who entered the institutes.²⁴⁹ However, given the critical shortage of paper during the war (by 1941, the paper shortage was 'reckoned to be the biggest obstacle to the 'functional work' of the Council'²⁵⁰) and the efforts needed in physically getting the books to these countries, these efforts would have surely have been impressive to the local populations. The fact that the Council had flown 3,000 books to Sweden was reported in the Swedish press – so it did not even require people to view the books to make the political statement that the British commitment to cultural exchange was strong enough to keep it going even in what appeared to be the throes of defeat.²⁵¹ Similarly, on a small group of islands such as Malta, word would have quickly spread that, during the intense air raids of 1940 and 1941, the Council was stocking its library from books arriving by submarine.[252] The Council ran a Book Export Scheme from 1940 to 1947 which greatly increased the availability of British books abroad as the Council offered a 'sale or return' policy for overseas booksellers which publishers in Britain were either unable or unwilling to offer. What this basically meant was that booksellers were offered books to sell to their customers without having to fear having excess stock which they had already purchased and could not sell – they could return them to the British Council without any financial liability being incurred if they could not sell the books. While it did run successfully and was sound economically, some staff found the complexities of fluctuating currency exchanges and customs problems difficult to work around, particularly when they had plenty of other duties to attend to. How widespread this view was is unclear, but the policy was certainly effective enough to increase sales of British books abroad during the war period.[253]

Conclusion

It can be seen from this chapter that the Council used a variety of techniques and methods of cultural propaganda to reach audiences in neutral Europe. The methods ranged from sending out lecturers, teaching English, subsiding schools and arranging art exhibitions and music concerts, to the provision of both English language and translated books. In a number of cases, it was possible to conduct a 'one size fits all' approach through the *British Life and Thought* series and to send lecturers to more than one country – particularly Spain and Portugal as they were geographical neighbours. A surprising amount of time, however, was given to tailoring the cultural propaganda to local audiences. Surprising in the sense that in the context of the time it was incredible that so much effort was put into organizing a specific art exhibition of Sweden, for example, when Britain was preparing for the invasion of Italy in 1943 or organizing a piano recital in the autumn of 1940 when Britain's survival was under threat and London was under the heaviest bombardment in its history. Tailoring propaganda to the needs of the audience, however, was very important. It was often the element that made the Council's message heard above the whispering galleries of the neutral capitals of Europe and above the more highly resourced campaigns of Germany and Italy. Starkie's *tertulias* were a prime example of how the Council tapped into the local culture and produced impressive results. Understanding the sociological context and utilizing word-of-mouth propaganda made it appear that the British Council's work was not propaganda – it did not stand out as being something alien imposed on an indifferent audience.

Establishing institutes and offices in neutral Europe at this time was a major political statement and could not be divorced from the reality that there was a war going on. Britain could not escape the impression that its establishment of overseas institutions was a knee-jerk reaction to the war situation. Throughout the period of the war, the Council was necessarily playing catch-up with other countries who had had institutions established for some years. The institutions provided a convenient meeting place for neutral peoples to show their British sympathies (often new-found) once they were ready to do so. Equally the art exhibitions, music concerts, though interesting and important from a cultural point of view, perhaps played a larger role in providing a focus for people to attend an event that would allow them to show their sympathy. Yet, it would be cynical to take this so far as to say that the content of art exhibitions, lectures and the like were not important as long as they contained a British element. Clearly, McCance's visit to Spain forged new and important links with Spanish scientists who were grateful for the access to British science and information. Great musicians such as Sir Malcolm Sargent and poets such as T. S. Eliot would clearly also have drawn audiences because of their artistic abilities rather than simply because they were British. Nevertheless, the fact that Britain sent 3,000 books to Sweden along with 50 original watercolour paintings (as well as similar numbers elsewhere) and were keen to send lecturers hundreds of miles in dangerous conditions were political statements that Britain was a country that wanted to engage on a serious scale with the neutral peoples of Europe. The Council's work was naturally incremental. Despite the original political statements that were made by way of setting up the institutes and flying in thousands of books, the Council's work was long-term and would take years to accomplish. Each lecturer that arrived in Spain, Portugal or Sweden built on the work of the previous lecturer that had visited. To look at one particular lecturer's achievements in isolation would miss the wider cumulative effect of achievements created by the continual stream of lecturers. It was constantly laying the ground for more propaganda in the future – particularly political propaganda that would help drive people to more direct action than was possible initially.

The cultural propaganda of the British Council was carefully directed at sympathetic elites in the countries where it operated. The aim was to cultivate that sympathy and generate a secondary influence through those elites to other less sympathetic elites and beyond to the wider masses, just as in the model of influence described earlier. To an extent the work of the Council was all about reputation maintenance – keeping open schools and maintaining publications which were perhaps not particularly useful in themselves (and even detrimental in some cases), but were useful in continuing to 'fly the flag' in often hostile territories. These sympathetic elites were often willing participants in the influence and reputation maintenance as they genuinely believed in the righteousness of the British cause. Its work had to penetrate the sociological conditions that were already in place by not appearing to be propaganda by successfully meeting the needs of its audience. Less sympathetic elites and the wider masses would of course be less aware that the secondary influence that they were experiencing was a result of a plan by a British organization to influence them. It is also very difficult to assess the cultural propaganda's effectiveness at this level as a variety of different influences would be operating, not least from Nazi-inspired sources. Some of it helped to create a cumulative effect if it was pro-British (but not as a result of the British Council's activities) and some of it obviously worked against the Council's efforts. Nevertheless, while this chapter has touched on a number of reactions to the Council's work – attendance figures at exhibitions, for example, or the occasional reference in local newspapers about lecturers, the next chapter will examine the reaction of the audiences in more detail. What was the effect of the Council's work? Were the methods mentioned in this chapter successful? Is it ever possible to determine success in such an information battle as takes place in neutral countries during wartime?

The View from the Other Side

Issues in assessing the view from the other side

Determining how the British Council and its work were viewed in neutral Europe during the Second World War is fraught with difficulty. It would be very easy to take references to the Council's work from documents in the archives of foreign governments, from articles in foreign newspapers, and from personal accounts of people who interacted with the Council on a regular basis and build up an exaggerated image of success. Focusing solely on how the Council was perceived without considering the work of the German and Italian institutes would create the illusion that the British Council worked in a vacuum when interacting with foreign peoples – an impression that would clearly be unhelpful in determining the level of success that the Council attained. Yet, trying to pin down what foreign peoples actually thought about the Council in comparison to the Council's rival counterparts from enemy countries is not straightforward – censorship issues render newspapers difficult to assess; political considerations and the effect of the course of the war itself make archive material equally complex terrain. Genuine thoughts and Machiavellian antics are certainly intertwined, and the capital cities of all of European countries that remained neutral during the war were riddled with propaganda and were hotbeds of rumour in the extreme. Although it is difficult to assess the view from the 'other side', it would be clearly unacceptable to conduct no assessment at all. After all, making a success of cultural propaganda was what the British Council was all about. It can be readily recognized that difficulties of this kind must be accepted as widespread and therefore each piece of evidence must be carefully evaluated to take account of its context.

The view from the 'other side' clearly does not amount to a single perception of the British Council's work. As stated in previous chapters, each of the four neutral European countries where the British Council operated had a range of differing opinions about the war situation and about geopolitics more generally, even within the 'official' elites. The difference in the view of city-dwellers compared to the view from the countryside is just as notable as variances owing to broad geographical differences. The Council's influence was naturally directed through institution buildings, Universities and other places of learning such as the Halkevleri in Turkey, where lecturers and teachers could draw significant numbers of people to make their work and tours worthwhile. This meant, to a large degree, that the Council's influence was directed at the people of the main cities where these institution buildings were located – Madrid and Barcelona in Spain (and later on in the war Bilbao, Valencia and Seville); Lisbon, Oporto and

Coimbra in Portugal; Ankara and Istanbul in Turkey; and Stockholm, Malmö, Lund, Gothenburg and Uppsala in Sweden. Although the Council did attempt to reach out beyond the main cities through connecting particularly with Anglophile Societies and sending lecturers on tours (Ronald Bottrall, e.g. frequently travelled within Sweden to try to reach out to smaller communities) these attempts were still more of an 'add-on' to the core business of trying to influence people in the cities.[1] Naturally, therefore, the people in the cities were more likely to have had an opinion about the Council's work than those people in small towns and villages.

The type of person that the British Council aimed to influence in the cities, of course, affected how it was seen by different people within those cities. It was shown earlier that the aim of the British Council was to focus more on the elites rather than on the masses. Pro-British elites were the first line of contact for the Council, which it then hoped would indirectly influence indifferent and hostile elites and eventually the masses (thereby following the model of influence outlined in Figure 1). Except in a few cases, it is very difficult to actually delineate the Council's influence upon the masses as opposed to other influences directed at them. The Council also had misgivings about working directly towards influencing the masses for fear of being seen as a political rather than a cultural organization. For example, Frederick Charlesworth's work with the Swedish ABF examined previously was carefully scrutinized by Council officials in London, who stated that the 'the proposed lecture on "The Labour Party's Foreign Policy" might well be postponed till a more suitable period . . . [w]e think it to be outside the Council's fixed rules regarding political propaganda.'[2] Instead, the Council generally hoped to influence the masses indirectly. The elites, in this chapter, will be split into two main groups to understand the views of the 'official' elites (i.e. Government Ministers and officials) and second, the 'non-official elites', covering the artists, musicians and scientists. It is logical to assume that the elites, therefore, had more of an opinion about the Council than the masses, simply because, as with the city-rural divide mentioned above, the elites had actually heard of the Council's work and could see its day-to-day operations.

Focusing initially on the elites who were already pro-British would also help to reinforce pre-existing views within all of the elites, that the Council was there to give succour to those who were pro-British. The pro-British elites were, of course, quite happy that the British Council was there to support them. Those in Spain against the Franco regime or the Axis such as the Basque writer Pío Baroja were clearly in this category. As will be shown, by attending the institute every Sunday, Baroja overtly showed that he viewed the Council as a haven for anti-regime or anti-Axis Spanish elites. Baroja was 'Anglophile from the beginning, in contrast with the fascist, Germanophile atmosphere prevailing in Spain' [original Spanish in footnote].[3] Ley noted that Baroja's presence was a 'decisive victory' [original Spanish in footnote] because Baroja rarely visited other such cultural centres.[4] The institute was described by Tom Burns, the British press attaché based at the British Embassy in Madrid, as

> an embassy to the survivors of Spain's intellectual eclipse. Any evening one could count on finding there a great novelist such as Pío Baroja, a rising star like José Camilo Cela (since then a Nobel prize-winner), that prince of essayists, Azorin [the pseudonym of José Martinez Ruiz], composers like [Joaquín] Rodrigo.[5]

Simply by attending the institute, these artists and writers showed that they appreciated the institute for being a kind of safe house that they needed in time of war or because they distrusted the Franco regime. Where the Council fulfilled a particular need such as this it was bound to be popular. It was no surprise that the Council was able to be viewed highly in the eyes of these people – indeed, it would be more surprising if it had failed to do so given the conditions in Madrid at the time. It was largely slotting into the view that was ready made for it by providence of circumstance. If the Council was to be viewed as anything other than an organization existing to reinforce the status quo, then at least one of two events had to occur. The Council could expand its influence beyond its 'natural' audience of pro-British elites (particularly beyond those cities which had a tradition of being pro-British) – this was within the Council's control but perhaps would also involve some abandonment of its principles depending on how this was carried out. The second event would be through its 'natural' audience expanding beyond the initial grouping that were originally attracted to the Council's work – in other words, by those indifferent and hostile groups in the model of influence becoming smaller in number and the pro-British group expanding to contain a complex mixture of overt ideologues, covert ideologues and 'barometer elites'. The term 'barometer elite' covers those elites who reflected the changing times either because of pragmatism or because of genuine changes in sympathy.

The enlarging of the pro-British elite group could happen in three general ways: first by those indifferent and hostile groups becoming aware through their contacts with pre-existing pro-British elites that the Council was worth visiting; second, by other external influences such as the state of the war affecting the overall environment in the neutral country which either allowed their opinion of the Council and Britain to be more favourable or allowed their latent favourable opinion to be more publicly acceptable; or lastly, by being alienated by the Axis institutes (or Axis influence generally) and looking for a new social and cultural and pseudo-political outlet which the British Institute represented. Realistically, it was likely to be a mixture of all three of these ways in which the indifferent and hostile elites could change their opinion of the Council.

Individuals who held particular and important roles either in Government or among the 'non-official' elites could also have a significant influence on how the British Council was viewed by the wider elite. A lot depended on the views of certain individuals – not least the individuals occupying the roles of Head of State, Foreign Minister and other Ministerial roles (particularly those for Education and Culture) – as in the course of the war these roles could have been held by different people of contrasting opinions. However, it was also true that the same individuals could stay in place (the Head of State for all four countries focused on here remained in place throughout the Second World War), but instead their sympathy could change with the times, and as suggested above those could happen for a number of reasons. The 'non-official' view of scientists, artists and musicians could be just as flexible. The number of people who did not hold strong opinions or have strong sympathies either pro- or anti-British Council during the war should not be underestimated. Unlike politicians, most neutral scientists were primarily interested in science, and not in the war situation and they were wise enough, therefore, to understand that they had to be careful with whom they associated for their longer-term career prospects. As will be shown, many scientists only associated with British Council lecturers once they knew that doing so would be beneficial to them in the long-term.[6] 'Backing the wrong horse' was a risk they were not, unlike the Government elites, prepared to take.

The Council may well have felt uncomfortable about formerly pro-German elites becoming more involved with the British Council but that was, after all, its longer term objective. To capture the minds of those beyond its natural audience and fight Britain's corner on the cultural battlefield was a key part of the war effort in neutral Europe and key to whether the Council's work was to be seen as a success. To only shore up the existing pro-British elites, though undoubtedly an important task, would always be seen as preaching to the converted. It is essential to understand the view from the other side, therefore, particularly those initially hostile to the British Council, if the success of the Council is to be determined.

Official views of the British Council

In order to gain an understanding of the 'official' view of the Council within the four long-term neutral European countries where the Council operated, there are notable roles, and individuals who held them, that are of course essential to examine in detail. Clearly, the Head of State played some kind of role in the Council's operation in each country. This role was more important and active in some countries than others – the Turkish President Ismet Inönü, for example, attended some Council events and his family had English lessons provided by the Council, whereas in Sweden there is no evidence that King Gustav V, who was notably pro-German, was ever particularly interested in the Council's work.[7] Nevertheless without their blessing, at least in a tacit sense, the Council's operation would have stalled at the first hurdle.

General Franco had given his personal permission to Lord Lloyd in 1939 for the establishment of a British Institute in Madrid (Franco 'would unreservedly welcome the establishment of British Council activities in Spain in as full measure as we cared to develop them' noted Lloyd after a meeting between Franco and Lloyd on 23 October 1939), but dealing with the Spanish Government bureaucracy was a different matter.[8] In the absence of Lord Lloyd's meeting with General Franco in October 1939, it seems unlikely that an institute would have opened in 1940 in Madrid. Lloyd travelled to Madrid on behalf of the British Government in order to stress to Franco the importance of Spain to Britain. Indeed, the Council's arguments for opening an institute during 1940 very much hinged on the Lloyd-Franco meeting the previous year even though, in reality, discussion of the Council was a relatively minor aspect of the meeting itself, concentrating on other aspects of Anglo-Spanish relations and the outbreak of war the previous month.[9] Lloyd's report of his meeting with Franco on this point is worth quoting in some detail:

> I [Lloyd] described the world-wide activities of the British Council in some detail, and told him [General Franco] how anxious the Council was to obtain permission for the prosecution of the same activities in Spain now the [Civil] war was over. He seemed already well acquainted with the nature of that work, about which

he had clearly made enquiries, and asked me questions about certain aspects of the Council's work in other countries. He said that he respected and admired the British cultural standards more than those of any other country, and would unreservedly welcome the establishment of British Council activities in Spain in as full a measure as we cared to develop them. He begged to be excused from going into further detail on British Council affairs as he particularly wished to use the occasion to talk to me on other matters. He had already given instructions to the Minister of Foreign Affairs [Juan Beigbeder], under whom Spain's Cultural Department existed, that all facilities were to be given to the inception of our work. He would be glad if I would, therefore, discuss all our plans with Señor Beigbedir [sic].[10]

It is worth quoting in some detail because it perhaps shows Lloyd's skill for embellishing his report with more enthusiasm by Franco than was perhaps the case, or that Franco was apt at flattering his guest and passing responsibility for action onto his staff. Nevertheless, Franco's endorsement, though briefly made, was critical in levering the Spanish Government into accepting a British Institute in Madrid. The Head of State of any of the four countries may not have been a great supporter of the British Council, or indeed Britain, at this time, but would be wise enough to recognize that in order for their neutrality to be credible they had to operate an official policy of fairness between the belligerents. If Germany or Italy had been granted the right to open institutes, then the same had to be the case for Britain, even if it was grudgingly. Actually getting the machinery of neutral Government to carry out this official policy of fairness was a different matter, however. As will be shown, even with Franco's endorsement of a British Institute in Madrid, the route to actually opening the institute was scattered with obstacles.

Foreign Ministers and Education Ministers, as well as the Ministries for which they were responsible, also had key roles to play in formulating the 'official' view of the Council. Unlike the Heads of State who had to take more the role of a statesman – by understanding what was in the interest of the country as a whole – individuals at Cabinet level were able to take a more political view of the Council. While they were in post individual personalities could make or break, at least temporarily, the success of the Council's work. This was partly because of the practical power that they wielded in actually approving which directors or lecturers could come to that country, but more importantly, were a leading voice in the official opinion of the Council in the Government, and in the country more widely. Juan Beigbeder, the Spanish Foreign Minister for the first year of the war, may have been described as 'rather a tiresome windbag' by Lloyd when they met just prior to Lloyd's meeting with Franco, but at least he had a certain understanding and growing friendship for Britain.[11] Beigbeder was one of the few Spanish Ministers in early 1940 who was not overtly pro-Nazi and was seen as a potential ally of the British colony in general, and particularly by Sir Samuel Hoare when he arrived in June of that year.[12] Without Beigbeder's position as Foreign Minister, it is unlikely that Hoare would have successfully negotiated the extension of the April 1939 Anglo-Spanish trade accord (which played a major part in keeping Spain out of the war in July 1940), nor would the British Council have managed to get Walter Starkie to Madrid.[13]

Tom Burns believed the Spanish Government could not have refused the request to send Starkie to Spain as the British Council's representative,

> [f]or how could official Spain ever say that Starkie was *persona non grata*? He knew more about the country, its literature and folklore than most Spaniards, its politics had never concerned him and he could hardly be suspected of being a British agent.[14]

As the analysis earlier showed, Starkie's politics were not as straightforward as Burns suggests. Nor was it correct to say that Starkie was never regarded as a British spy. But it was true that he knew a lot more about Spanish culture than many in Spain itself and on this standing could be regarded as an inspired choice for a representative. An inspired choice perhaps, but it was not so straightforward from a bureaucratic point of view and it was fortunate that Beigbeder was Foreign Minister at the time to ensure his appointment was approved.

When the British Embassy asked for permission to bring Starkie to Madrid as Director of the proposed institute, on 9 May 1940, Beigbeder ordered his staff to complete an internal check of their archives to ensure there were no records to suggest that Starkie would be a poor candidate from a Spanish point of view. This was completed just 10 days after Starkie's name was proposed. Enrique Valera, of the Spanish Foreign Ministry, noted that 'as Mr Starkie is Catholic and is arguably qualified in principle, we can consider him to be a *persona grata* to the Spanish state' [original Spanish in footnote].[15] However, Valera went on to note cautiously that

> even though in this department we cannot find any unfavourable precedent on the behaviour and attitude of Mr Starkie during the National Movement . . . [I] deem it advisable that before responding to the British Embassy, we should hear the views of our Ambassador in London [original Spanish in footnote].[16]

Beigbeder therefore sent a telegram on 24 May 1940 to Alba in London, to see 'if, in his view, he would raise any objections against the candidate [Starkie]' [original Spanish in footnote].[17] The inference from Beigbeder and Valera was that in their view Starkie was acceptable but that neither of them, however, wanted to be responsible for allowing him into Spain without the approval of Alba. The Spanish Consulate in Dublin also provided information to Beigbeder (particularly on reports in the *Irish Independent* of Starkie's appointment), given that Starkie was from that city, but it seems Alba's opinion was the one that counted in Madrid.[18] A strong underlying fear that both Beigbeder and Valera had at that time for their positions (and perhaps ultimately their lives) can clearly be detected given the military situation in May 1940 in the Low Countries and neighbouring France.

The Duque de Alba, Jacobo FitzJames Stuart, was descended, illegitimately, from James II of England (VII of Scotland) and still retained the British title of the Duke of Berwick. He played a crucial role as Spanish Ambassador in London in smoothing relations between Britain and Spain on a number of occasions during the war.[19] In recently released files at the National Archives, it appears that MI5 were concerned about how much influence Alba had among the British political elite and the information he was seemingly able to obtain. However, they also saw the opportunity of feeding 'misinformation through Alba's high-up political and social contacts' back to the Franco Government as he was so highly respected in both London and Madrid.[20] It is not clear whether, in the end, MI5 used him in this way, but it is the principle that they considered it would be possible that is important here. Prior to the end of the Spanish Civil War, Alba had already located himself in London as 'El Agente de España' for the 'Estado Español' – in effect the Ambassador in London for the Nationalist side of the Civil War.[21] And he was already making contact with the British Council at this stage particularly through his friendship with Lord Lloyd. In June 1938, one of Alba's staff wrote to the Nationalist Ministry of Foreign Affairs in Spain to seek permission to accept Lord Lloyd's offer to renew cultural ties with Nationalist Spain.[22] It is clear that Lloyd and Alba were keen to improve cultural relations between London and the Franco regime even before the British Government had officially recognized Franco as the legitimate ruler of Spain – and this keenness to improve relations continued until Lloyd's death in February 1941. Alba was eager to help establish a British Institute in Madrid and was instrumental in persuading Franco's Government to support the British Council's cause. Following the delay after the Franco-Lloyd meeting in October 1939 in getting the institute open and before Starkie's name had been suggested as a candidate for being the British Council's representative, Alba had written to Beigbeder in February 1940 to state:

[T]he way this [the Spanish] Government has refused to grant permission for the opening of the British Institute [is not helpful], I have tried to reflect the impression this has made during my conversation with Lord Lloyd, who told me that this refusal would be regarded here [in London] as a very unfriendly gesture on our part. No one understands the reason why England [sic] is not authorised, but Germany and France are permitted, especially considering their past attitude to the glorious National Uprising, which was no more favourable to that observed by Great Britain [original Spanish in footnote].[23]

With this knowledge of previous correspondence, asking Alba for a view on Walter Starkie was clearly something that Beigbeder was pretty confident he knew the answer to already, but it was no doubt very important to have in writing; such were the conditions in Madrid at that time. Beigbeder was fully aware that his job was in a precarious position and the Interior Minister Ramón Serrano Suñer, Franco's brother-in-law, was seeking a more pro-Nazi Spanish foreign policy with himself vying for the role of Foreign Minister. Beigbeder did not want to give his rival, or Franco, cause for relinquishing him of his duties and taking Spain into the war against Britain and France. Fortunately for Beigbeder, Alba replied promptly on 27 May to his 24 May telegram:

I consider it a very wise appointment of Professor Starkie, who is Catholic and has been a great defender of our cause in the press from the first moment. Very knowledgeable of the Spanish language and an excellent author on Spain and academic correspondent of the language [original Spanish in footnote].[24]

As with Alba's influence in persuading the Spanish Government to open the institute at all, Alba's role was again critical to Beigbeder's acceptance of Starkie as the British Council's candidate in Madrid. Interestingly, Alba was also working behind the scenes in London at the same time to ensure Starkie's reputation remained positive in Britain, so that no negative publicity arose about the British Council's proposed representative in Madrid. He wrote to the editor of *The Observer* newspaper J. L. Garvin, to complain about a critical review of Starkie's book *Grand Inquisitor*:

> Referring to the Epilogue of Professor Starkie's book, your reviewer dismisses it with the words 'The Epilogue is an unworthy piece of irrelevant propaganda'. The Epilogue of Professor Starkie's book consists of a tribute to the Spanish Nationalist front in Madrid and a description of the glorious defence of the Alcazar, an epic which will live for ever in History and in the hearts of all true Spaniards. To dismiss this Epilogue in the words I have quoted above is nothing short of insulting, especially at this moment when this country is anxious to extend friendly relations with Spain. If our firends [sic] are to publish such things, how can it be expected that those who are working in this country for more firendly [sic] relations should meet with the success that they desire [original in English].[25]

Garvin replied very apologetically and promised it would not happen again, but the important point was how much of Alba's reputation and judgement was on the line with regard to Starkie's appointment. He was keen to identify and suppress any information that might undermine his position, and shows that the fear of being sacked in Franco's Spain for making a wrong decision, stretched all the way to London. Fortunately, following Alba's telegram, on 5 June 1940 the British Embassy received a letter, at last, informing them that Starkie would be an acceptable representative.[26]

Even after this success, on 14 June 1940, the Spanish Interior Ministry (headed by Serrano Suñer) tried to thwart Starkie's journey to the Spanish capital, and 'published a decree forbidding all forms of propaganda by belligerents', which shows the innate tensions between Beigbeder and Serrano Suñer.[27] All authorities were ordered to close 'premises in which, under name of reading-rooms, libraries and the like, propaganda is done for belligerent countries by oral or written means, by supplying books, notes, pamphlets, broadsheets, documents etc.'[28] This description of activities appears to reflect exactly what the Council intended to do in Spain, as indeed it intended to do in all of its institutes. The Council and the Foreign Office were in two minds about what to do. Starkie already had his bags packed for his journey to Spain and his Directorship of the institute had been approved by the Spanish Foreign Ministry – but there was a real chance that the British Institute would never be established for the duration of the war because of this decree. On the other hand, Lloyd believed that unless the German and Italian institutes were closed down, the Council should push ahead with their plans and make representations to the Spanish Government to this effect if it objected.[29] The Foreign Office in London was in concurrence with his views, though Starkie was asked to postpone his departure until things were a little clearer.[30]

Lloyd contacted Alba on 27 June for his help and the Spanish Ambassador agreed to do his 'very utmost in a private way' to resolve the situation.[31] Lloyd seemed unaware of the work Alba had already done to secure Starkie's appointment in Madrid, and Alba appeared to have not felt it necessary to tell him. Nevertheless, Starkie was eventually allowed to go to Madrid in July 1940, and agreed in his first letter to London that, although he did not believe that the decree itself was directed at the establishment of a British Institute (which seems doubtful),

> I think it would be a mistake to open an Institute at the present moment with the full blare of publicity, for incidents would then occur of an unpleasant character which might injure our cause at this delicate moment. But most of my Spanish friends agree that it would be a good thing to open in a small, unofficial way, and give classes during the Summer to those left in Madrid who are willing to learn English, and to organise social gatherings of those friendly to us, etc. In the Autumn, when the situation has clarified, it would be possible to engage upon more ambitious schemes and open the Institute formally.[32]

The Council had to agree to strict conditions with the Spanish Foreign Ministry before the institute could open including that all staff in the institute had to be Catholic.[33] However, soon the institute would be open.

As was the case with Alba, the Portuguese Ambassador in London, Armindo Monteiro, was well respected in London and in his home capital. He was also formally a member of the British Institute in Lisbon, which demonstrates the importance that the Council had in the Anglo-Portuguese relationship generally. Sir Malcolm Robertson was listed as a frequent associate of Monteiro on that same MI5 file mentioned above, and Monteiro was also seen by MI5 as a potential candidate for feeding misinformation to Portugal if necessary.[34] Monteiro was also in frequent contact with Salazar and reported his meetings with Robertson to Salazar directly as he did regarding meetings with a whole range of individuals from the British elite. By influencing Monteiro's opinion in London, the Council would have an indirect lever to influence the 'official view' of the Council back in Portugal as this was highly dependent on Monteiro's thinking. This was just as the view from Spain was highly dependent on Alba's opinion.

As has been described in previous chapters, the British Council opened its institute in Lisbon prior to the outbreak of war and the Portuguese Government had given it an enthusiastic response, and the Portuguese Minister of Education, Pacheco, had attended its opening. The Portuguese historian, António José Telo noted that, at that time 'the initiative [in Portugal] was welcomed and it found a large audience' [original Portuguese in footnote].[35] The atmosphere, however, had changed significantly since its opening in 1938 and during the war itself the Portuguese Government relied heavily on the reports from Monteiro in London for how they should respond to the Council in Lisbon. It is true that Salazar had accepted an honorary degree conferred upon him by Oxford University at Coimbra in the early years of the war, but generally he had been careful not to show his hand too readily when the outcome of the war remained uncertain. His speech at Coimbra at the Oxford degree ceremony focused on the role of academics generally and morality in society, rather than any aspect of Anglo-Portuguese relations.[36] A short reference to the 'cultural bonds uniting Western civilisation' was seen by the Ambassador Ronald Campbell as enough of anti-German statement to rile German opinion, but it was hardly an overtly pro-British stance.[37] Salazar had also held a dinner party for the Oxford delegation where apparently the conversation was free and frank, but the official report also noted how unusual it was for Salazar to do this and it was certainly not an everyday occurrence.[38] Newspaper reports, though very positive and more numerous than the usual coverage of British Council events, were perhaps designed more to flatter the Portuguese leader than to benefit British cultural propaganda.[39] The benefit to the British Council was just a useful side effect.

It was noted previously that the Foreign Office was concerned about the Portuguese authorities withdrawing support for the British Institute in Lisbon because of protests from the German Minister in 1940. It is clear, therefore, that the congenial backing of the Portuguese authorities that had existed before the outbreak of war was no longer guaranteed, at least publicly.[40] In a letter to Pacheco marking the first anniversary of the institute's opening in November 1939, George West, the Council's representative, wrote

> We enter on our second year of activity in the hope that the good offices of Your Excellency will be extended, as hitherto, towards the maintenance and promotion of Anglo-Portuguese intellectual relations, which as we profoundly believe, is one of the greatest services which our two nations can render to each other.[41]

The tone of the paragraph above does not give an overwhelming feeling of expectation that the Portuguese Education Minister would oblige. Apparently the Minister did not see it as important enough for replying to West personally but asked one of his colleagues to quote a memorandum on his thoughts. Nevertheless, it was positive, if short:

> The Director of the British Institute is to be informed of the fullest appreciation with which we regard its cultural activity, in the interests of science and for the greater reciprocal understanding to the two great and Friendly Nations. Co-operation will be continued in the same spirit.[42]

Certainly, there was no suggestion that the Portuguese Government was unsupportive of the Council's efforts, but the length and tone was hardly a repetition of the warmth that Pacheco had conveyed the year before. However, West noted that he had received numerous letters and telegrams congratulating the Council on its first anniversary from various organizations and individuals within Portugal, even if the Government could no longer be as openly pro-British as it had been prior to the war.[43] Nevertheless, Pacheco did not break off relations and still attended lectures given by the Council during the war.[44] In comparison to the British Council's efforts in Portugal, the Germans had originally only pursued cultural relations through a relatively small *Gesellschaft* (association) but were later allowed to open a *Deutsche Kulturinstitut* in new and larger premises.[45] The successful expansion of the Council's work, especially in Oporto and Coimbra, must therefore be seen in the context that the German cultural mission was also successfully expanding until at least 1944.

In the papers of Philip Newman, the violinist mentioned in the previous chapter, there is an anonymous account of Newman's time in Portugal that claims that concerts organized by the British Council were to 'counter to the best of his [Newman's] ability the lavish propaganda concerts organized by the German official circles in Lisbon with military and government support'.[46] This claim that the German concerts were supported by the Portuguese Government, but the British concerts were not, does not appear to be entirely supported by other evidence however. The Portuguese Government attempted to be neutral by supporting both the British and German cultural events, or not supporting either of them. There is no doubt that it may have felt like the Portuguese were favouring one side rather than the other when they supported an enemy's event, but it may have been more of a perception than a reality. For example, one of Philip Newman's concerts was forbidden by the Portuguese police just two hours before the performance was due to begin, and it was instead performed on Portuguese radio.[47] When this type of control was used, it is not difficult to understand how such a perception of one-sided victimization was formed. However, most of his concerts were in fact authorized and performed in person.

Though Monteiro and Robertson were frequent associates, Monteiro-Robertson meetings were not always amicable. Ironically, however, this may have indirectly helped the British Council in Portugal, rather than hindered it. One meeting in October 1942 resulted in a heated discussion on the 'Mocidade Portuguesa' (literally 'Portuguese Youth' founded in 1936 and modelled on the Hitler Youth) to which the British Council had supplied a boxing instructor, George Gogay. Gogay had been in the service of the *Mocidade* for a number of years and had been very successful in integrating into the organization, but suddenly Gogay was dismissed by the *Mocidade* at around the same time as this Monteiro-Robertson meeting. Gogay's dismissal was viewed by the Council in London as being for political reasons, as Gogay's conduct had been exemplary, which probably explains Robertson's frustration at the meeting.[48] Monteiro reported his meeting with Robertson to Salazar, noting that Robertson was

> visibly agitated [and replied that he] could not conceive how the official organisation 'Mocidade' could be an ally of England, as it was at the moment accepting invitations to visit Berlin, after making a pilgrimage to Vichy Morocco [original Portuguese in footnote].[49]

The heated conversation went on to cover Anglo-Portuguese relations more generally, with Robertson making an 'attack of rage' [original Portuguese in footnote] on how Portugal needed to decide whether it was a British ally (from the long-standing Anglo-Portuguese alliance) or a neutral country.[50] Although Monteiro thought Robertson's attitude to be unacceptable and noted that he had reported the incident to Brendan Bracken, the Minister of Information, (as he regarded Robertson, incorrectly, to be 'in some ways his subordinate' [original Portuguese in footnote] – words which would have riled Robertson even more), it seems clear that by reporting the incident to Salazar that he expected it to have some effect in Lisbon.[51] Monteiro regarded Robertson's attitude to be just the tip of the iceberg in British frustration on the Portuguese position in the war generally and was not just an issue relating to the British Council. He noted that the *Mocidade* was 'on the verge of entering a Black List' [original Portuguese in footnote] in the Foreign Office and if Portugal were to keep Britain as a friendly country, it needed to work harder to maintain its sympathy.[52] The Portuguese view of the British Council, therefore, cannot be divorced from the view of Britain as a whole. The Council here appeared to be one of a number of barometers used by Portuguese officials to test their relationship with the British Government and help guide their overall policy towards Britain. Just days after the Monteiro-Robertson meeting, the British and US armed forces invaded North Africa at Algiers and quickly became the unassailable military force in the western Mediterranean and the straits of Gibraltar. This certainly gave Portugal good reason to reconsider how it wished to carry out its policy of neutrality. It will be examined a little later how the events of late 1942 changed Portugal's view of the British Council.

Overtly supporting the British Council's activities, particularly early on in the war, was a potentially dangerous activity for a Foreign Minister, or an Education Minister, even if they also supported equivalent activities by the German or Italian Governments. When the British Council opened its institute in Stockholm in December 1941, as was noted earlier, the German Government made it clear that it was not happy with the Swedish Government's position nor the fact that Gösta Bagge, the Swedish Education Minister, had attended the opening ceremony.[53] Reports in the Swedish press reported the German Government's view, although the detail varied from one newspaper to the next. For example, the column space given to the German reaction was actually significantly smaller (103 words) in *Dagens Nyheter* than the space given to the report about the opening of the institute (395 words).[54] The *Aftonbladet* appears far more sympathetic to the German point of view with the headline 'German attack on Cabinet Minister Bagge. Endgame for the opening of the British Council office: political somersault' [original Swedish in footnote].[55] It caused enough of stir in the Nazi capital that Christian Günther, the Swedish Foreign Minister, clearly believed that it was something worth responding to in order to assert the Swedish right, as a neutral power, to associate with whoever they wished. Günther sent a telegram of protest to the Swedish Ambassador in Berlin, Avrid Richert, to hand to the German Government. It stated:

1. The Swedish Education Minister [Gösta Bagge] will, as a self-evident measure of civility, attend various foreign cultural events in Stockholm. His presence at the German Book Exhibition and at the inauguration of the German School is well known.
2. The message from Berlin had stated that the British Council would be a centre of espionage. Until the contrary is proved or is done, the Swedish Government has no good reason to suspect that foreign cultural institutions are being used for illegal activities in neutral Sweden.
3. Sweden's relations with the British Council are older than our relationship with the *Akademischer Austauschdienst* and will address questions about student and lecture activities. The Swedish Government has received official assurances regarding the British Council – that the agency's activities here will be conducted along these lines [original Swedish in footnote].[56]

There does not appear to have been any further response from the German Government on this issue and the Germans probably decided that in the grand scheme of the war it was better to allow the Swedes to choose a pro-British Council policy than to risk the ending of the that country's benevolent neutrality in terms of supplying raw materials essential for the German war effort.

Günther and Bagge had similar views to each other on foreign policy and both have been described as Machiavellian or 'players' (in Swedish *'spelaren'*) when it came to preserving Swedish neutrality against interference from the belligerent countries.[57] Günther was described by Henrik Arnstad, in his book *Spelaren Christian Günther*, as a politician who could move seamlessly between conservative views, then liberal views; becoming anti-Semitic at times (not uncommon among Swedes at the time), then moving in Jewish circles.[58] Günther was someone who did not seem to have particularly set views on any subject, but had a sole aim of keeping his country out of the war and not to become overly influenced by any viewpoint. He did admit to Mallet at one point that 'we Swedes have a certain feeling of shame when we look at our neighbours and brethren living under German oppression' [original Swedish in footnote], but this one statement, argues Arnstad, is in stark contrast to other comments made by him on the war situation.[59] At the time of the Nazi invasion of the Soviet Union in June 1941, Bagge and Günther agreed that a declaration of war by Sweden against Germany would be a disaster, but that they would also have to work hard to ensure public opinion in Sweden did not favour Sweden joining the Nazis against the Soviets – the Swedes historically were far more concerned about Russian expansion, than German influence.[60] Günther was very keen to maintain Swedish neutrality, but at the same time, avoid making substantive concessions to any of the belligerents.[61] Günther's flexible ability was noted by Sir Victor Mallet, the British Minister in Stockholm, who stated that he had 'admirable qualities, not least his ability to turn a blind eye on occasion'.[62] Peter Tennant had a less flattering view of Günther, remarking that he was usually defeatist and did not have the qualities he regarded as necessary for a Foreign Minister, leaving much of the delicate work of diplomacy to his officials.[63] What this meant, though, for the British Council was that as long as Günther, and his ally Bagge, were in charge of foreign policy, Ronald Bottrall would, by and large, be left alone to receive the same favourable treatment that the Germans were receiving. Günther and Bagge continued to attend British Council events throughout the war, and it was noted earlier that the Council's summer school in Sigtuna in 1944, which Günther attended, persuaded him to hand over the wreckage of a prototype V2 bomb that had landed in Sweden to the British.[64] At least in the Swedish newspaper *Dagens Nyheter*, the British Council seems to have received very fair treatment with regard to coverage of its events and particularly visiting lecturers and could not have done so without the tacit support of Günther and Bagge. There were numerous articles, as we shall see later, on visits to Sweden by T. S. Eliot, William Holford and Sir Lawrence Bragg to name a few, as well as some prominent front page pictures of Eliot and the English watercolour exhibition in early 1943.[65]

Hasan-Ali Yücel, the Turkish Education Minister, was, by contrast to Ministers in similar positions in other countries, far more overtly pro-British and pro-British Council. It was shown earlier that Michael Grant and Yücel were good friends throughout the war and this access to the high political elite was essential for the Council's success. Grant noted that Yücel was 'the only member of the neutral Turkish Cabinet who was a hundred per cent in favour of ourselves and our allies (except Russia), and believed that we would win the war'.[66] It was not just Grant's impression either – it was clear to visitors, such as John Steegman who in December 1943 noted that '[c]learly he [Yücel] is extremely well-disposed to the Council, which is as well since he is the supreme head of all education in Turkey'.[67] Evidently, Yücel's position was not then typical of the Turkish Cabinet, but he also commanded enough respect for his position to remain in post throughout this period which must have meant that being pro-British was not a career destroying move. Many officials within the Turkish Civil Service – Grant mentioned one particularly notorious official called Feridun Cemal Erkin, at the Foreign Ministry – 'plugged away at the theme that the British Council was illegal' but their work does not appear to have much success.[68] It certainly helped Yücel to be able to show to others in the Turkish elite that he was able to get worthwhile support from the British Council for Turkish activities in education and culture and it was not simply a matter of Turkey allowing the Council in to do whatever they liked. Drawing English and technical teachers into the Halkevleri was clearly something that Yücel could show as a benefit to the Turkish economy and development generally. The fact that not only had Yücel been successful in getting long-term teachers and short-term lecturers all the way from Britain (which was not an easy journey during the war), he also had the added benefit of a visit from Robertson in 1943. Robertson did not visit any of the other countries in Europe where the Council operated, except for a brief stopover in Lisbon on his way to the Middle East and Turkey and shows the importance that this area of the world had to Robertson personally. Yücel noted to Robertson after his visit that

> For a man who loves his country, it has given a great happiness to see that such an eminent and esteemed man as you should love it too. I shall treasure the fotograph [sic], which you have been so kind to give, as a present from a friend, and shall keep it in my own house which you honoured by your visit [original in English].[69]

Grant, in a covering letter for this note to Robertson, remarked that Robertson's visit had 'created an excellent impression' in Turkey and was widely reported in the newspapers – clearly events that boosted Yücel's position as Minister of Education.[70] The opening of a Halkevi in London in February 1942 which Anthony Eden and Robertson attended together with '400 distinguished guests', [original Turkish: '*400 seçkin davetlinin*'] also created a great impression in Ankara particularly in the newspaper *Halkın Sesi* as it was the only Halkevi outside of Turkey.[71] Robertson returned to lecture there after his visit to Turkey in July 1943, which was also well received in both London and Ankara, with copies in Turkish being distributed to President İnönü and 'other friends among the head of [the Turkish] Government'.[72] The reception that the British Council received in the Turkish newspapers has not been examined in detail due to the lack of access to Turkish newspapers from the wartime period. However, as was discussed previously, Grant reported that 'our friendly reception from the Turkish Press' caused friction between him and Embassy staff as it 'conflict[ed] strangely with the recurrent crises in commercial and other relations'.[73] It can safely be assumed therefore that the reporting of the Council's work was generally positive, even if reporting of Britain as a whole was less positive. The success of Grant, and his Council colleagues in Turkey, was obvious, and their work provided reciprocal benefits for those in the Turkish Government, like Hasan-Ali Yücel, who associated with Council. It is interesting that there is evidence that this method of reaching out to the Turks made an impression on the US Ambassador Laurence A. Steinhardt, after the USA joined the war in December 1941. He wanted to collaborate with Grant to reap similar benefits. It is unclear, however, how far collaboration between the United States and British cultural agencies went during the war and it is not something that Grant elaborated on in his memoirs or is apparent in the British Council files.[74]

Unlike Turkey where the benefit of associating with the British Council to Yücel was clear, it was not such a straightforward story in Spain. The British Institute had been established without Starkie or the Council asking the Franco Government whether the decree of 14 June 1940 applied to the Council. Though inviting over 70 people to a housewarming party in late August perhaps was not everyone's idea of what the phrase 'to open in a small, unofficial way' actually meant, it was, however, small enough and discreet enough for the Spanish Government not to object.[75] This was confirmed a few weeks later by Beigbeder, who invited Starkie for an interview with him. Starkie reported that Beigbeder 'said that he would put no restrictions on my work and would not press too strictly the conditions laid down at the beginning.'[76] However, though Beigbeder was fortunate to secure Alba's blessing for Starkie's appointment and had successfully allowed the British Institute to open, ultimately Beigbeder had failed to secure his own position more generally and had shown his hand too readily in associating with Hoare to be able to stay in his post. The appointment of Starkie was one of many contributory factors leading to his downfall on 16 October 1940. Sir Samuel Hoare noted in his memoirs that Beigbeder was

> a doomed man. The completeness of his conversion [to the Allied side] and the panache that he waved over it had delivered him into the German hands. Serrano Suñer's opportunity had come. Franco, who habitually suppressed all independent ministers except his brother-in-law, could not permit his Minister for Foreign Affairs [Beigbeder] to proclaim his confidence in a corrupt and decadent England.[77]

Beigbeder's rival and successor as Foreign Minister could not have been more different in his policy towards Britain generally and the British Council specifically. Serrano Suñer was pro-Nazi and anti-British, and held a great deal of influence over the Spanish press, which made communicating information about events happening at the institute very difficult. Even before he became Foreign Minister, Serrano Suñer had visited Berlin and Rome in the late summer of 1940 to show his support for the Axis cause.[78] Hoare again noted

> I was now faced with a grim prospect. Hitherto, the Foreign Minister with whom I had been dealing had been a convinced friend of the Allies. Now his place had been taken by the man who was not only his irreconcilable enemy, but was at the same time the moving spirit of the Falange and the leader of the Axis party in Spain. To make matters worse, the well-known intimacy between Beigbeder and myself made it very unlikely that I should be able to exercise any influence over his vindictive and hostile successor.[79]

Serrano Suñer's opinion of Beigbeder (written in his memoirs published in 1977) was that he was 'capable of a thousand follies' [original Spanish in footnote], and though originally pro-German at the beginning of the war, he became pro-British within a year having being 'seduced' by Hoare [original Spanish in footnote].[80] For as long as

Serrano Suñer was Foreign Minister, the omens did not bode well for the success of the Council. Even Serrano Suñer, though, understood that although he could isolate and restrict the activities of the Council, he could not close down the institute without causing a diplomatic crisis with Britain. Franco was not prepared to precipitate such an event in 1940.

Serrano Suñer's views on the British Council specifically are not recorded either in his memoirs, or in the archives of the Spanish Foreign Ministry, but his views generally about Britain were clear enough for his staff to expect that the Council's activities would be heavily restricted, at least in terms of publicity. If Serrano Suñer's control over the Spanish press had been extensive prior to becoming Foreign Minister, it was now near absolute, thereby thwarting the small amount of publicity that the Council may have received, had Beigbeder remained in office. Behind the scenes, though, it was a different story. Either Serrano Suñer's influence was not as great as he would have liked among the Spanish elites, or he turned a blind eye to the activities of the British Institute, but he was seemingly unable, or unwilling, to stop the Spanish elites from attending the Council's events. For example, under Serrano Suñer's tenure as Foreign Minister the British Institute even attracted members of the Falange (the movement of which Hoare described Serrano Suñer as being the 'moving spirit') as students and attendees of its events.[81] Starkie also reported that the first major lecture series conducted in the British Institute by a touring lecturer – that of Sir James Purves-Stewart in January 1941 – was attended by Government officials and the scientific elite of Madrid in clear defiance of Serrano Suñer's public wishes. Starkie wrote

> His [Sir James Purves-Stewart's] visit has been a great boon to the Institute for it has brought into our orbit all the principal men of science and doctors in Madrid. I made a special point of entertaining them and getting them into personal touch with Sir James. Everyone was delighted and I was told by members of the Government that Great Britain was very wise in sending abroad men of great prestige and technical ability. It was significant that Sir James in his lectures did not play down to his audience but kept them at the highest level of his profession, in this way he won over the sympathies of the Spanish doctors. The lecturers we need from England in Spain are those who will talk as masters of their subject; in this way there is no fear of political propaganda creeping in.[82]

Commenting specifically on the pro-German propaganda in the Spanish newspapers, Starkie noted

> [T]hose of us who know Spain through and through after many years of experience did not feel dismayed at the sight of this anti-Britain façade, for we were conscious that behind it there is always throughout the whole country an innate sympathy for England – a sympathy which no amount of foreign propaganda can destroy.[83]

It appears that the bombastic and overt political propaganda in Spanish newspapers was so out of touch with what the Spanish elite actually wanted to read, according to Starkie at least, it had little effect. Although Serrano Suñer's policy of anti-British propaganda pervaded the operation of his Foreign Ministry machine through what resembled a 'go slow' principle wherever possible, he never developed a policy of destroying the British Council's work. He allowed the Council to do what it wanted, by and large, as he knew significant sections of the Spanish elites wanted the British Institute to exist and succeed, but instead he decided not to react quickly to its needs. Examples of this range from the relatively small scale but essential help that the Foreign Ministry gave to the Council in arranging for material sent from London (designated as being for diplomatic purposes) that got caught up in customs disputes, to the approval being given for lecturers to be able to attend the institute.[84] In one approval for lecturers Hugh Ruttledge and Laurence Binyon to travel to Madrid, the Spanish Foreign Ministry wrote:

> [The Ministry] has the honour to signify that at the moment and in principle we have no objection to the holding of conference on mountaineering and British poetry respectively by Mr Hugh Ruttledge and Mr Laurence Binyon, with the understanding, of course, that appropriate time be requested by the British Institute in the capital for the relevant regulatory approvals to be obtained for each of these conferences [original Spanish in footnote].[85]

It seems that Ruttledge and Binyon never made it to Madrid (as least no mention of them can be found in the British Council files at the National Archives in London with regard to Spain). Perhaps, the undertone of the Foreign Ministry's note to the British Embassy that approval was conditional may have led to a reconsideration as to whether the lectures were worth the trouble of organizing. That is what Serrano Suñer's policy seemed to be aiming at – making things difficult where possible but nothing more proactive because Serrano Suñer did not have the control over the elites that he needed in order to stop the activities. Starkie commented to Robertson in September 1941 that he felt that it was solely down to himself being a *persona grata* of the Spanish state that Serrano Suñer had not felt able to do anything more active against the Council. Starkie wrote:

> I do not think that it is fully realised in London how heavy has been my task in starting our work here and how ruthless and indefatigable our adversaries have been against us. Zuloaga, the painter, who is a personal friend of Sr. Serrano Suñer, told me that greater difficulties would have been put in my way as Director of this Institute had I not been persona grata here owing to my writings and my connection with Spain over many years. For this reason I made as full use as possible of my personal connections with the cultural and musical and artistic life of the Spanish capital. . . . I have made the acquaintance of the Jesuit Padre Otaño, the Director of the Conservatoire here, and a great personal friend and confidant of General Franco and Sr. Serrano Suñer. . . . Padre Otaño has promised to do his best to secure me an interview with Sr. Suñer and to support our claim for expansion.[86]

There does not appear to be any record of a Starkie-Serrano Suñer meeting but it seems clear that Serrano Suñer's opinion of Starkie personally was good enough (or at least not bad enough) for his close friends to believe that a meeting would be possible. His dislike of Britain was more a mixture of his political beliefs against the British way of life and domination of the world rather than being a vendetta against specific individuals.

In Stockholm, Swedish Government officials also seem to have been far more interested in the individual of the British Council's representative, Ronald Bottrall, than the British Council's work in the country generally. The secret police followed Bottrall regularly and examined his motives for various meetings. The secret police reports on him are rather revealing about the official view of Bottrall. 'From newspaper photographs Bottrall appears to be Jewish' [original Swedish in footnote] wrote Otto Danielson, who had been following Bottrall's movements, which speaks volumes of the ingrained anti-Semitism of the time in Sweden.[87] Another description by an agent known as 'Cassel', wrote a very unflattering portrait of how Bottrall appeared to the Swedes:

> Around 190 cm tall, slim, poor posture, with a long stride, short neck and round head, the nose is long and thin and seems segmented, (see illustration), eyes protruding with thin eyelids and slightly melancholic, large mouth when talking. Bare crown. He behaves carelessly at the table, sitting crooked, talking with food in his mouth, is loud etc., (observed at lunch) [original Swedish in footnote].[88]

Throughout Bottrall's file held at the *Riksarkivet* in Stockholm, there is little interest shown actually in the cultural side of the British Council's work. Bottrall was followed largely for political and security reasons. A number of the intercepted telephone conversations reported in the file, soon after Bottrall's arrival in Sweden, were picked up because the word 'political' was mentioned.[89] This approach perhaps had the disadvantage of a lack of official interest in the cultural work of the Council, but had a greater advantage in the fact that as long as Bottrall and the other Council staff kept to cultural events and made only cultural contacts, they would be, by and large, left alone to make progress in any way they saw fit with the Swedish elites (outside of Government) and beyond. Take, for example, the report of the agent who attended the opening of the British Council's watercolour exhibition in February 1943:

> Among the first to appear was Mr and Mrs [Victor] Mallet. Later there was Mr [Ronald] Bottrall and a lady, who was probably his wife, and Mr Urquhart and Mr [Roger] Hinks. Through an acquaintance, I had heard that Mr. Hinks was 'Director Roger', as she called him, who knew the art well and had an art dealer trade or similar in London. Eventually there gathered a whole lot of people, both Swedish and English, but I did not know any of them and did not get to know any further names successfully. In all probability, it can be determined that the Head of the British Council in London, who was expected to be in Stockholm, was not present. He would have been there for the arrival of the Crown Prince and Crown Princess, and he would have been presented to them. However, it was mainly Minister Mallet himself, who showed them around [the exhibition] [original Swedish in footnote].[90]

The agent was clearly not particularly interested in the exhibition from an artistic point of view, but more interested in who might be attending and the conversations they may have been having. Some members of the official Swedish elite were interested in the visitors who arrived from Britain from a cultural point of view, however. Sven Grafström, a Head of Division in the Swedish Foreign Ministry, was particularly interested in the arrival of Harold Nicolson, whom he met on a number of occasions during his visit to Sweden in October 1943. Nicolson, he remarked

> is as fascinating a human in society and as a lecturer, as he is in his books, which I read a lot. When he talks about the tradition of English life – which he does with intense expertise and restrained pathos – one seems to understand better the properties which make the British such skilled imperialists [original Swedish in footnote].[91]

Grafström was not the only person who was delighted that Nicolson had made the journey to Stockholm. There were numerous reports in the Swedish press about his arrival and his lectures. They considered him to be the most 'distinguished' of the guests that the British Council had sent over the North Sea and were pleasantly surprised that Nicolson was open and frank about the state of Britain after years of war, the role of food rationing, and how the reconstruction of Europe would take many years.[92] Nicolson was taken aback by the reception that he received in Sweden. He noted in a letter to his sons, Benedict and Nigel that:

> At first I could not understand the fuss that was made of me. I thought they must imagine that I was far more important than I really am. But I think that it was merely that they hate the Germans and like welcoming Englishmen. Moreover, they were flattered that an elderly M[ember of] P[arliament] should trouble to undertake so hazardous a journey on their behalf.[93]

Nicolson's supposition was a common one among British visitors to Sweden – the Swedes of both official and non-official opinion, it seems, were so surprised that Britain bothered sending lecturers to a country that was neutral and difficult to get to in wartime that they were very keen to show their appreciation. This sentiment matches well with the theories mentioned near the beginning of this book regarding the *Handicap Principle*, by Amotz and Avishag Zahavi, as well as Robin Wight's *Peacock's Tail and the Reputation Reflex*. Going beyond what is expected or necessary for survival – being able to show that resources can be 'wasted' through the sending of lecturers to neutral countries, instead of on military equipment and the armed forces – can pay dividends in terms of increasing and reinforcing the reputation and status. Only the successful can be seen to 'waste' resources in this way.[94]

The alignment between official and non-official opinion in Spain was not so apparent. For despite the anti-British propaganda supported through the Serrano Suñer-sanctioned press in Spain, there was a rapid increase in student numbers and popularity of the institute in early 1942 to the extent that invitations had to be restricted due to lack of space in the building.[95] The lectures of Purves-Stewart were also only the start of a successful number of events taking place within the institute including talks by Arnold Lunn, an Olympic athlete, and a series of concerts by the soprano Astra Desmond during late 1941 followed by Thomas Bodkin and Professor Cairns in 1942.[96] Having said that, however, the activities of the British Council in Spain were still restricted to taking place inside the institute building itself. To an extent, therefore, perhaps Serrano Suñer considered that it was better to allow this outlet of pro-Britishness to flourish in Madrid and freely allow the elites to attend if they wanted to and not to force it underground. By keeping it alive, but only in the institute building, he could control its movements and influence beyond the institute. This certainly appears to be plausible explanation of his policy. The tide was turning against Serrano Suñer – Starkie reported in May 1942 that the Spanish newspapers were keen to start reporting the events of the institute in detail and reporters started to attend the events. They were prevented from reporting the events by Serrano Suñer, but it was only a matter of time before the pressure building up on Serrano Suñer would begin to have an effect.[97] On 3 September 1942, Franco sacked Serrano Suñer and replaced him with Conde de Jordana, who had been Foreign Minister previously, just prior to the war, and had been driven out of office due to his opposition to the Axis.[98] Serrano Suñer's downfall was precipitated by an incident in Valladolid where the Spanish War Minister, General Varela, who was a foe of Serrano Suñer, narrowly escaped being assassinated by the Falange. Franco had to act to placate the Spanish Army. In reality, this incident was only the final act in a growing concern among the Spanish Government of the power of the Falange, and its leading light, Serrano Suñer.[99] Franco's appointment of Jordana was a clear signal that he had decided to be far less anti-British from then on. Jordana ensured that Spain remained firmly neutral in the autumn of 1942 while the British armed forces amassed in Gibraltar for the invasion of French North Africa – Operation Torch – on 8 November. 'What' Hoare remarked, 'would have happened in these weeks if Serrano Suñer had still been in office?'[100]

The events in Spain in the late summer and early autumn of 1942 with Serrano Suñer's dismissal, also affected Portugal and the British Council's involvement there. Monteiro noted an 'unexpected change' [original Portuguese in footnote] in the attitude within the British Council in the relative importance between Portugal and Spain.[101] Monteiro reported to Salazar that he had been told that the Council's position had changed because

> Spain is a country that, having started from an enemy position, day-by-day moves towards us, their interest in England *is rising. Portugal, however, despite the treaties of alliance, tends to move away from us* [original Portuguese in footnote – emphasis as original in Rosas et al., 1996].[102]

Due to 'interventions of higher stations' [original Portuguese in footnote] within the British Government, the Council was now to send lecturers who were originally bound for Portugal, onto Spain, in order to try to capitalize on the new situation resulting from the change of Foreign Minister in Madrid.[103] By reporting this to Salazar, Monteiro clearly regarded it as an important development and could have implications beyond the role of the British Council. Portugal was still sulking from the arrival of Australian troops in neutral Portuguese East Timor in late 1941 and early 1942 to try to pre-empt a Japanese invasion of the island. Although there was a pragmatic reason for the arrival of the troops, to try to prevent the island of Timor becoming a base for an invasion of Australia by Japan, the Portuguese took it as an insult to their sovereignty. Gogay, the British Council's boxing instructor at the *Mocidade Portuguesa* certainly believed that the Timor effect had had significant bearing on his dismissal, in a letter to Robertson.[104] Now that Portugal's foremost rival, Spain, was being seen as more important than Portugal by the British Council, there was yet another reason for Portuguese pride to feel bruised. Earlier on in the war, when the Oxford University delegation visited Portugal to confer the honorary degree on Salazar, they were careful not to venture over the border (though it was considered and Spanish visas were requested from the Spanish consulate in London).[105] Professor William Entwistle, one of the delegation, noted that there was a concern that 'it would weaken the impression in Portugal if the Oxford mission were to go on to Spain. It would seem as if we could not find enough to interest us in the country we had come to visit'.[106] Not anymore. The Council saw the opportunity of cashing in on a more benevolent Spain, and it seemed prepared to accept the consequences of how this might be viewed in Portugal. A culmination of Spanish-Portuguese rivalry, which the British Council played a part through Monteiro's feedback to Salazar about the *Mocidade* and Portugal's position generally towards the Council's work, was perhaps one reason for the Portuguese agreement to allow Britain and the United States to use air bases in the Azores in August 1943.[107] Although Spanish approval for the British to use bases in the Canary Islands was a remote possibility, it may be that Salazar was keen to show Britain that its relationship with Portugal was more beneficial than anything that could be gleaned from Franco's regime.

For the British Council in Spain, nothing actually changed overnight with Jordana as Foreign Minister, but with time the restrictions placed on the British Institute by Serrano Suñer were lifted and the Council was, at last, able to reach out more publicly to a wider Spanish audience. The Marqués de Lozoya, the Spanish Minister for Fine Arts, as was noted in the previous chapter, was described by John Steegman as 'rather in the hands of the Germans' but attended an art exhibition at the British Institute on 13 November 1942 for the first time – five days after the Allied invasion of North Africa.[108] But he was clearly not someone who had changed his opinion of Britain so much so quickly as to no longer attend the German institute's events. In the Spanish newspaper *ABC*, it was reported that he had helped organize a concert at the German institute – the *Instituto Alemán de Cultura* – and he attended it 'along with prominent personalities of Spanish cultural life' [original Spanish in footnote].[109] *ABC*'s report was dated 13 February 1943, exactly three months after Steegman's note. Steegman's observation of the fact that Lozoya had 'accepted tonight's invitation [in November 1942] willingly and promises to come to the Institute on Sunday; perhaps events change opinions?' was either naïve, premature or perhaps more accurately a reflection of the start of a long road that Lozoya was on to start to infiltrate himself into pro-British circles.[110] Ironically, in the case of Baroja, when formerly pro-German Spaniards, like Lozoya, started visiting the institute, he actually started visiting less often, stating '[i]t has all changed with the circumstances and I will end up not coming here' [original Spanish in footnote].[111] The British Council had to strike a balance, of course, between maintaining its core audience and reaching out beyond to indifferent and hostile elites and manage the inevitable conflicts which would result by doing so. The changing of sympathies in Sweden was recalled by Anthony Bottrall, Ronald's son, who stated that 'I recall my mother saying how uncomfortable she felt about previously pro-German Swedes becoming ever more ingratiating [towards the British Council] as the war went on'.[112]

In Spain, this difficulty was even more acute because not only was there a World War in progress with people sympathetic to either side but also the recent Civil War had torn the country apart. As Steegman noted:

> The Civil War ended 3½ years ago, and there has been no political amnesty. Since about half Spain was on the 'other' side, I suppose it follows (the Spaniards having an almost Irish memory for grievances) that all those people regard themselves as opposed to the regime.[113]

In February 1944, there were still famous English language books such as *Gone with the Wind* (despite Leslie Howard's role in the film of the book, and his subsequent visit to Spain), *Rebecca* and *Wuthering Heights* that continued to be banned in Spain, which shows just how far the British Council had to come to overturn the ingrained anti-British views in many areas of the Spanish Government. It was noted on the list, however, that 'in England, this may cause a very bad effect' [original Spanish in footnote] which was a recognition that views of Britain could no longer be ignored.[114]

Until 1943, the British Institute in Madrid was the only British Institute in Spain largely for fear of being seen to be promoting Catalan (in Barcelona) and Basque (in Bilbao) separatism. In addition to this, while Sir Samuel Hoare had given his consent to a Barcelona institute in 1941, he changed his mind with the German invasion of the Soviet Union in June of that year, fearing an extension of the Council's work would be inappropriate, now that Britain and the Soviets were allies, as the Communist influence on the Republican side in the Spanish Civil War was still a fresh memory.[115] Later in the war when Germany was on the back foot militarily, institutes started to be opened in Barcelona and Bilbao as well as Seville, but even then those institutes were deliberately publicized as branches of the institute in Madrid, rather than as autonomous institutes. Conde de Jordana had informally given Starkie his backing on this basis.[116] Starkie was very aware of the difficulties and in his official report of the situation wrote:

> Barcelona today presents many difficulties to our mission in Spain, owing to the separatist elements which are so general there. If one had only to think of Barcelona, or indeed Catalonia, it would be very easy to push right ahead and play up to the Catalan intellectuals, many of whom are brilliant writers and charming personalities, especially as those Catalan separatists are 100% pro-British. If we did this it would be not only to destroy our work, but the Institute in Barcelona would have a very short life indeed. In Barcelona we must be careful not to play too public a game. We have to go slowly because of the present Government in Spain. Any of us who play up to the separatist elements in this country whether the the [sic] Catalan, the Basque of the Galician type, injures the British mission at present, for the Spanish authorities are doing all in their power to preserve a unified Spain. . . . It is for this reason that I intend to keep a close watch on the work of [Christopher] Howard [the Director of the British Institute in Barcelona] and his staff in Barcelona. There is no reason why we should not be on good terms with all the Catalans without mixing up in their internal politics.[117]

The official letter from the Embassy to Jordana again stressed the subsidiary nature of the Barcelona institute to Madrid, though the reply appeared to suggest that the Spanish Government was not as concerned about the independence of the Barcelona institute as Hoare or Starkie had feared.[118] Indeed, during the spring and summer of 1943, records in the *Archivo General de la Administración* show that the Spanish Government was looking to substantially improve cultural relations with Britain and was undertaking an assessment of the feasibility of a British Institute-style Spanish institute in London. This would exist, it was hoped, alongside the funding scholarships, encouraging Anglo-Hispanic Societies and working through the Spanish Department at the University of London. The British Council's work was being seen as a model for reciprocating its work in London, and it seems clear that Jordana was keen to learn as much as possible from the activities of the Council in Spain.[119] Interestingly, the Swedish historian Nikolas Glover, in his book *National Relations*, has also noted that the post-war Swedish Institute (which opened an office in London in 1945) was largely based on the British Council model – so it is clear that the Swedish Government too was keeping a keen eye on what it could learn from the British Council during the war for its post-war operations.[120]

To conclude this section regarding the official 'other side' view of the British Council's work in neutral European countries, it seems clear that the war going on outside had a significant effect on that view in a number of different ways. In Spain, the changing of the Foreign Minister along with changes in the war situation over time benefited the Council's work by allowing it more freedom to publicize its work. Later, it will be shown how the non-official Spanish elite took advantage of this situation by being increasingly bold in their interaction with the Council. In Sweden, Christian Günther, by and large, allowed the Council to do as it wished as long as the Swedish Government was not asked to give more concessions to the Council than those being given to the Germans. In Turkey, the support of Hasan-Ali Yücel was crucial to Michael Grant in the British Council's success, but it was also crucial to Yücel that he could show real benefits by allowing the Council to be so influential. In Portugal, there was a fear that the Council would start to concentrate on Spain in preference to Portugal and began to try to show the worthiness to the Council of its work in Portugal to the Portuguese. Overall, however, the most significant conclusion appears to be that the official elite tended to see the Council as an opportunity or a threat to their own influence in their home country, and, particularly for Portugal, their country's position in the wider world. As a general rule, when the war was going badly for Britain, they saw it as a threat; when the war was going well for Britain, they saw it as an opportunity. A more detailed examination shows that it was not always quite that straightforward – Starkie, for example, was seen as such a *persona grata* in Spain that even Serrano Suñer did not go as far as he perhaps wished in restricting the Council's work. But as a general rule it worked.

There are two interesting references showing the views of Salazar and Franco at the end or soon after the end of the war, which show their renewed personal interest in the Council's work, now that the Council did not pose a threat, but only an opportunity for their own countries. First, after a visit to Portugal in May 1945, W. H. Montagu-Pollock and George Hall, from the Foreign Office, reported a conversation that they had had with Salazar, which stated:

> Dr. Salazar expressed his satisfaction with the Council's work in Portugal, drawing attention to its importance for the furtherance of Anglo-Portuguese relations, and added that he shortly hoped to make English the first foreign language in the Portuguese education system.[121]

Second, Franco sent Starkie a message on 8 January 1946 telling him that he wished to see him the following day, and Starkie readily complied and reported his interview to the new British Ambassador to Spain, Sir Victor Mallet, who had moved from his post in Sweden.

> He [Franco] started off by informing me that he had followed very closely the work of the British Institute in Madrid and the branches in other parts of Spain, ever since the beginning. I was able to prove that he was exceedingly well informed about all that we have tried to do in Spain ever since 1940. . . . [H]e welcomed the possibility of strengthening the cultural bond between nations: 'we need to know one another', he said, 'not just to speak one another's languages but to know how we live, what our general masses think, what each of us has to offer the other in the way of science, technical equipment, literature, art, ideas'. He then questioned me upon the methods I had adopted in the early difficult days of 1940. I told him about the methods we had adopted and how we had tried to make the Institutes real centres so that the Spaniards who came to us would find themselves in an English atmosphere. . . . He gave me the impression of being extremely friendly to Great Britain and he was certainly most complimentary about the work that we had achieved.[122]

Both reports could be viewed with a cynical eye and the conclusion drawn that this was a sign of two quasi-fascist dictators trying to integrate themselves into a post-fascist world and trying their level best to flatter Britain and the work of the British Council in particular. Although there is a strong element of truth in this, both reports also show that the Council's work was known in some detail at the highest level in both Spain and Portugal and seen as an important element in relationships with Britain. Franco even recognized that the conditions in Spain for the British Council during 1940 had not been easy. Although no apology is apparent, he showed an admiration for the dogged determination that Starkie had shown in the early years. The Council, it is clear, had achieved recognition from the official elites that cultural relations were important, and the way that the Council had carried out its cultural propaganda had a large amount of respect from those official elites. Those official elites now hoped to benefit further from associating themselves with the work of the Council in the post-war world.

Non-official views of the British Council

The second part of this chapter will focus on the views on the 'non-official' elites – that is, the elites outside of the Government. Among the non-official elites, the actual cultural work of the Council was usually more important than the potential political, and security implications that were a higher priority in official circles. Non-official elites saw the Council naturally as a source of information about a world that neutral people were otherwise temporarily severed. This was particularly the case for Sweden which, prior to the war, had been fairly well integrated with the British and American worlds of scientific research – and the Swedes were particularly proud of their scientific cultural heritage.[123] For example, Sir Lawrence Bragg, in his diary about his trip to Sweden in April and May 1943, recorded that '[t]he scientists said how much they were cut off from England and begged me to get for them the Proceedings of the Royal Society and Science Abstracts. They get Nature at the [Stockholm] Hogskola, but nothing else'.[124]

As with Nicolson's visit, mentioned earlier, reports in Swedish newspapers of other British Council lecturers such as Bragg, William Holford – a leading British architect – and T. S. Eliot, also gave an impression that the Swedish elites were genuinely interested in the cultural aspects of the British Council's work because they had been isolated for so long from British cultural events. In the *Dagens Nyheter*'s report of Bragg's arrival in April 1943 it noted that there had been 'poor contact during the war' between Britain and Sweden, and that Bragg was there to improve it.[125] Bragg noted later in his diary that

> [b]eing the first physicist to be sent out by the Council I was warmly welcomed by all the Swedish physicists and chemists, and made very valuable contacts. I have brought back with me numerous commissions to execute on their behalf. They are very keen to get closer contacts with our people; in fact it is impossible to exaggerate their eagerness to work with us. I got the impression that now that our fortunes are brightening, many Swedish scientists who did not like to express their sympathy with us openly are feeling bolder.[126]

Clearly the view of Swedish scientists was in flux during the war. The pro-British scientists were keen to re-establish the links that they had had prior to the war, but there were indifferent (or perhaps more accurately described as 'pro-British but not wishing to show it while the Germans were in the ascendancy militarily') scientists who were keen to develop links with Britain through the British Council either because of a latent pro-Britishness or because they could see where the war was heading. At a macro level, therefore, the way the British Council was viewed, and the way in which people in foreign countries responded to its work, could not be divorced from the course of war. In this way, they were no different to the official elites. However, it would be a mistake to see how the Council was viewed at a day-to-day level as being linked directly to the war – there was a genuine need for the scientific communities in particular to interact with a wider world and the British Council provided that method of interaction. It was just that that wider cultural world which they wanted to interact with was no longer German, but British.

Even before Bragg had arrived in Sweden, he received numerous invites from Swedish scientists to lecture at their institutions. One such invitation came from Professor Percy Quensel of the *Mineralogiska Institutionen* in the *Stockholms Högskola*, who wrote to Bragg stating:

> We got to hear through the British Council that you might be exspected [sic] to come over about the middle of April. On mentioning this at a faculty meeting, the

Faculty resolved to formally invite you to lecture at the university. I need not say
how pleased we will be to see you here again [original in English].[127]

Bragg and Quensel had met prior to the war in 1922 when Bragg had collected his
Nobel Prize, but had not kept in touch. Quensel was now keen to make up for lost time
and even offered Bragg the use of his flat during his stay, such was the eagerness for
creating a warm welcome. 'Quensel and [Dr Arne] Westgren [of the Swedish Academy
of Science] could not have been more hospitable or anxious to show their complete
sympathy with the Allies', noted Bragg in his diary.[128] Similar invitations to lecture
and to visit laboratories came from J. A. Hedvall of the *Chalmers Tekniska Högskola*
in Gothenburg and Hans Petterson of the *Ozeanografiska Institutet* in Gothenburg.[129]
Bragg gave a number of lectures and attended dinner parties and other events during
his stay in Sweden. Following Bragg's return to Britain, he kept up a correspondence
with Quensel and Hedvall in particular and sent them copies of books and reprints
of articles to maintain an Anglo-Swedish scientific dialogue during the latter part of
the war.[130]

It was a similar story in Turkey. Turkish artists were keen to engage with the British
Council because they saw the benefit of reaching a wider audience, and a wider respect
than could be achieved in one country, particularly a country that was effectively
severed from the rest of the world at that time of war. In his diary, John Steegman
noted the response he received at a reception in Turkey

[A]ttended a reunion given for me at the Eminonu Halkevi over in Stamboul
by the Turkish Artists' and Sculptors' Union. An extremely successful party,
friendly, informal and talkative. There was nothing of the uncomfortable political
arrierepensee atmosphere that I rather feel at the Beaux-Arts tea-parties, and that
was present even at the big cocktail-party on the 15th [February 1944]. They were
simple artists, wistfully pining for information about what artists were doing in
England. I'm afraid that what I was able to tell them about the War Artists and
[the] C[ouncil for the] E[ncouragement of the] M[usic and the] A[rts] and the
Carnegie Trust made them sick with envy: there is almost no patronage or practical
encouragement of any kind for artists in Turkey, neither State, nor private, nor
industrial nor municipal.[131]

The Nicolson effect (that of neutral country being surprised and flattered that the
Council made the effort of sending lecturers to their country), which was evident in
Sweden, was also plain to see in Turkey as it took even longer for British lecturers to
arrive there. Robertson's own visit must have made a great impression on the Turkish
non-official elites, as did the visits of others who made the effort like Steegman.
Steegman noted his reception in Turkey in his travel diary and the number of people
who turned up to hear him talk. At first he seemed to suggest that his lectures were
increasingly well received and well attended – for example, on 16 February 1944, he
wrote '[g]ave my second lecture at the Faculty [of Letters], at 5 p.m. About 140 people,
roughly twice the number at the first lecture. The room was quite full'.[132] The following
day he seemed to have a similar story to tell: '[g]ave my second lecture at the Academy
[of Fine Arts]. About two hundred and seventy-five people, hall being full and side-

galleries half-full'.[133] But over the time of his stay, the novelty and the effect of his visit appears to have worn off a bit, even though the weather may have been a factor in lower attendance figures: '[m]y third lecture at the Faculty. The attendance was not as good as last week. Halideh [sic Halide Edip] charitably explained this on the ground of the atrocious weather: snow and sleet and N[orth] E[ast] wind'.[134] The word 'charitably' seems to suggest that Steegman was not convinced that the weather had anything to do with the lower attendance figures, and one of his last reports suggests a reason why: '[g]ave my fourth lecture at the Faculty. In conversation with Halideh [sic Halide Edip] afterwards, I found that her view is that the anti-British element in the Faculty is active and is not being discouraged by the Dean'.[135]

Clearly, the British Council's success in getting lecturers placed all over Turkey, in the Halkevleri particularly but also in other institutions, though impressive was not all-pervasive. There were evidently elements within the Turkish intellectual elite who were either becoming tired of the British Council's efforts, or who had never been convinced that the Council's efforts were a benefit to them. Despite this negative effect, it also showed that the Turkish intellectual elite were keen to show their independence of the political, official elite. It also showed that the Council had done relatively well, more generally, in placing British lecturers and in a general sense demonstrates that the intellectual elite by and large agreed with what Yücel and his colleagues were doing to bring in outside lecturers from Britain and saw the benefit to them of doing so and were keen to interact with a British cultural world that the Council represented.

In Spain, as the political situation was more delicate, the position of the non-official elites in their relationship with the British Council tended to appear far more dependent on the signals coming from the Government than in other countries but as has been shown this appearance was not always the reality. Nevertheless, soon after the sacking of Serrano Suñer and the Marqués de Lozoya's move to attend British Council events, Dr Robert McCance became the first British Council visitor to be invited to lecture outside of the British Institute itself – and the invitation came from leading scientists. As was explained in the previous chapter, McCance was actually invited to lecture by two different Spanish scientists – first by Franco's doctor, Jimenez Diaz, to talk at the Faculty of Medicine and then by Diaz's rival Dr Carlos Blanco Soler, to speak at the *Academia Medico-Quirúrgica Española*.[136] These two invitations certainly gave the impression that, now that the war looked as though it was turning in the Allies' favour, and that the influence of Serrano Suñer had retreated, rivals within the Spanish elite were starting to fight out among themselves who could best curry favour with the British Institute. There was clearly a parallel here between the rivalry between Spain and Portugal where both parties were keen to show that they were the best friend of Britain, for their own interest. McCance, in his report of his visit to Spain, noted the differences between Diaz and Soler – Diaz, he wrote, ran an institute which 'struck me as being quite outside politics, and I felt they [the institute workers] were working on an international basis and deserved all our respect'.[137] Soler, on the other hand, was 'an important political counter . . . everything he did was for effect and for the glorification of Blanco Soler'.[138] Clearly, politics was a significant force in Spain even outside of Government. In the Spanish newspapers, though McCance's visit was reported (which was rare for a British Council event at this time), Diaz's name was not mentioned at all but instead his rival Carlos Blanco Soler took all the credit. Though this may have been against what the British Council was aiming to do in the sense that it shied away from being seen as an institution designed for political propaganda purposes, it could benefit from the increased publicity from those within the elites, who wished to use the Council as an object from which to obtain political prestige. The fact that McCance also spoke in Spanish, and on a topic that had a real significance in Spain since the Civil War – that of nutrition and health – (there had been outbreaks of typhus in Madrid in 1941 and 1942 resulting in many deaths), made McCance's visit something even more valuable to Diaz and Soler for purposes of increasing their own influence and status.[139] It should be noted that McCance's visit was still shown as a minor article in *ABC* compared to the events of the *Instituto Alemán de Cultura* (the German Cultural Institute) and the *Instituto de Cultura Italiana* (the Institute of Italian Culture) described on the same page. The page from *ABC* on 13 February 1943 demonstrates the strange juxtaposition of *ABC*'s report of the British Council event, and the events of the German and Italian institutes: the British Institute was not mentioned by name at all and the differing sizes of the headlines were poignant (the reports about the German and Italian institutes, of course, being in larger font).[140] And it was not just *ABC* – a similar situation existed for other Spanish newspapers such as *Arriba* and *Ya*.[141]

The British Council clearly still had a long way to go before it would be recognized by Spanish newspapers as being at the same level or higher than the German and Italian institutes. But it was a start. The newspapers, of course, were still heavily censored and controlled by the Government, and McCance's visit had a much greater effect on the scientists of Spain than was evident from *ABC*, *Arriba* and *Ya*. McCance noted that people like himself

> can pass right across the barriers of politics and make intimate contacts with their fellow experts. . . . Any good man who has got something original to say (and can say it preferably in Spanish) would make his own contacts out there and would, I have no doubt, be a successful medical emissary.[142]

Nevertheless, he noted,

> There are critical men in Madrid, and it would be far better not to send anyone than to send a man who was not on top of his subject. I can picture such a person being ruthlessly exposed round the tea table at the Instituto de Investigationes Médicas. Such visitors could only do harm.[143]

To consider the Spanish newspapers to be reporting the real effect of visits like McCance's would be a mistake. Of course, they had a large amount of influence in publicizing visits and making them well known, but in terms of communicating to and between elite audiences, there were plenty of discreet, unrecorded and word-of-mouth methods of communication which were far more important. Newspaper reports should therefore be seen more as a lagging indicator of elite opinion rather than having a significant effect on elite opinion.

Previously in the war, the Spanish newspapers were full of reports about activities taking place in the *Instituto de Cultura Italiana* and also the *Instituto Alemán de Cultura*, from short notifications about the inauguration of the new academic year to reports on book exhibitions and to more detailed reports on Professor Francesco Severi's lectures on Galileo Galilei in April 1942.[144] After McCance's visit there was a subtle difference with more and more obvious reports of British Council activities which included coverage of Leslie Howard's visit to Madrid, as well as his tragic death, and a positive review of a translated publication of British Catholic G. K. Chesterton's *Life of Dickens* in October 1943. The review noted its 'originality and quality', 'his understanding of Dickens is perfect' and 'needless to say that the book is important and worth reading' [original Spanish in footnote].[145] Quotes such as these would have been just a dream earlier in the war and were a godsend now. Late on in the war, in 1945, the visits of Frank Wallace and the Douglas Woodruff, the editor of the Catholic *The Tablet*, caused great interest in the Spanish press – Woodruff's speech was reported as being 'greatly applauded by the audience' [original Spanish in footnote].[146] Being an editor of a Catholic newspaper clearly gave Woodruff a ready audience in Spain, and he was keen to stress that there was a growing interest in Catholicism in Britain, and that the Pope's messages had 'created an overall conducive environment' in Britain [original Spanish in footnote].[147] Changes in how newspapers reported the events of the British Council from a wider perspective will be examined in more detail later in the chapter, but it seems clear that reports tended to follow the course of the war, and follow the opinion of the elites, rather than having a particular effect on the elites in themselves.

In Sweden, the newspaper coverage of the arrival of lecturers was more obvious than coverage afforded in Spain. Coverage of T. S. Eliot's visit in local newspapers is significant for a number of reasons. First, the British Council did not really begin work in Sweden until the arrival of Bottrall in December 1941, and T. S. Eliot's visit was just a few months after the institute's inauguration. As we have seen, the institute's opening was received in the Swedish press in less than welcoming terms. When Eliot arrived, however, in April 1942 he was an immediate hit in the press with his picture appearing on the front page of the *Dagens Nyheter* on 21 April with the title 'English poet to lecture here' [original Swedish in footnote].[148] Over the following weeks, the *Dagens Nyheter* followed his progress with interviews and adverts highlighting the publication of Eliot's poems in translation. He was described as 'probably the greatest English critic since Coleridge' [original Swedish in footnote].[149] In the press conference that Eliot gave, he was quite frank about how the war had affected book publishing in Britain stating that 'the editors are quite difficult, the paper is scarce, and there are few workers [in publishing]' [original Swedish in footnote].[150] This openness to talk about the conditions in wartime seemed to go down well with the Swedish people and contrasted dramatically with the approach taken in Spain, where talk of the war was avoided at the institute. Eliot was perhaps unconsciously satisfying the need of the Swedish people to hear news, real news, which they had not been able to receive for so long.

The Swedish newspaper reports on William Holford, a leading British architect, who visited in October 1942 also noted his openness and frankness about the need to reconstruct London after the war, following the extensive bombing raids. One report noted his comments that

> There are streets where only a few houses are destroyed, and here it is important to build the new houses so that they completely blend in with the old street scene.

Then there are districts where there has been a lot of destruction, and here we must tear down the old and make entirely new neighbourhoods in a modern style. We have areas [of London] which were almost half-bombed, and there we proceed with caution to make the new construction not too ultra-modern. We are not lovers of skyscrapers . . . [original Swedish in footnote].[151]

Open and frank it was, but also in hindsight rather audacious given that the war still had two-and half-years to run, and there was no sign yet of the 'second front' in Western Europe. A little too audacious perhaps, and although impressive there is a hint in Robertson's letter to Mallet on Holford's return from Sweden that the Swedes were either blown away by Holford's optimism, or sceptical of how realistic it was: '[t]he Swedes were very much astonished to learn how much progress was being made here in the work of architectural planning and reconstruction'.[152]

Nevertheless, the fact that both Eliot's and Holford's visits were publicized in Swedish newspapers lends weight to the view, if the Spanish model of newspapers being a lagging indicator of elite opinion is applicable to Sweden, that the Swedish elites were already significantly pro-British and overtly so by the time of Eliot's visit. It certainly seems that by the time of Bragg's visit in April 1943, from the reception that he received from Swedish scientists and his post-visit correspondence with them, that there was a general lack of fear of associating with the Council lecturers, and the Swedes were flattered that such eminent cultural figures were being sent over the North Sea to visit them. This, now, was being reflected quite clearly in the Swedish press, and there was an increasing and significant lack of articles about German cultural events during this period.

In Portugal, the newspapers had always been far more pro-British Council than in any of the other three neutral countries where the Council operated in Europe. As mentioned earlier, and will be analysed in more detail later in this chapter, over 3,000 articles in the Portuguese press were printed during the war period on the British Council and related Anglo-Portuguese cultural relations. Nearly 70 articles were published in February and March 1940 reporting Lord Harlech's visit with remarks such as 'when he finished his beautiful session, he was much applauded' and that he was a 'recognised authority on the monuments in England having written a guide on important monuments, in 3 volumes, and rightly considered one of the best works in the genre' [original Portuguese in footnote].[153] No such positive comments were published in Spanish or Swedish newspapers this early in the war. Nearly 80 articles were published on the Oxford University Delegation conferring their degree on Dr Salazar in April 1941 and nearly 30 on McCance's visit – significantly higher in number than articles published in Spain on McCance's visit. It is clear that the response in Portuguese newspapers was far greater that elsewhere and probably reflects a greater freedom of thought about the war generally among the elites than was possible elsewhere – Portugal was the only one of the four countries which did not border an Axis country or a country occupied by the Axis. The risks of showing sympathy towards Britain and showing the British Council in a positive light were significantly less.

It was not just the newspapers and scientists that had to follow the lead of the official elite in Spain. *La Real Academia de la Historia* (the Royal Academy of History) had expressed its wish in May 1942 to appoint Walter Starkie as one of their *Académicos Correspondientes*, along with Don Enrique Leite Pereira de Paiva (the Conde de Campo Bello) from Portugal.[154] Although there does not appear to be a reply to their letter on record, they recognized that the appointment could be inconvenient at that time, and, given that the letter was sent to Serrano Suñer, it would be no surprise if the request was refused immediately, or just ignored. In December 1943, a second request was made, but again it was rebuffed, this time by Conde de Jordana.[155] Jordana's statement on the matter was conveyed to the *Real Academia*:

> As for Mr Walter Fitzwilliam Starkie and Mr François Piétri, given that the first is the Cultural Attaché from the British Embassy and the second Ambassador of France, and, moreover in view of present circumstances, it seems appropriate to postpone the processing of their appointments given their official positions, or at least until their current circumstances cease [original Spanish in footnote].[156]

It was not until after the war, in July 1945, that the request was at last granted, along with a whole host of requests for Starkie to talk at various Universities – such as at Oviedo and Salamanca – which had been awaiting approval for some time.[157] It seems clear that academic and non-official elites were keen some time before the end of the war (as early in many cases as mid-1942) to engage seriously with the British Council and did so quietly. But where official approval was needed, this was nearly always postponed because of the political risks involved in the approval. Even for Jordana, who was far more sympathetic to Britain than Serrano Suñer, postponement was often his preferred tool in his dealings with the Council. Only the ideologically pro-British non-official elites, those who had no choice but to associate with the Council to receive protection against the current regime, were openly prepared to take the risk of association when the war situation seemed still unfavourable to Britain.

The effect of the war outside was always going to colour the thinking of the neutral peoples, and the Council's successes and failures cannot be seen outside this overall context. However, in Spain to a significant extent the Council tried to avoid mention of the war itself and only referred to difficulties in how the Council operated logistically – such as of getting lecturers and materials out to the neutral countries safely. They wanted, and tried to all possible extent, to concentrate on cultural propaganda only. Perhaps this could be easier said than done, but in many ways not mentioning the war was probably a significant factor in ensuring the institute was not accused of being a political institution. In the British Institute School, at least, this approach had some success, as the children were educated in a war-free environment. Manuel Balson, a pupil at the school recalled that

> [T]here was no feeling of a war outside. Spain was not in the war and at the school there was never mention of the fact. I don't think it was relevant to the way the school was operated. I have to say that even when the [U]nion [J]ack I was carrying on my bicycle was torn out by somebody in the street, my teacher did not pay any attention and it was only my father when I got home that mentioned the fact that most probably it had been done by [F]alangists or pro-[G]erman individuals.[158]

This non-partisan atmosphere in the school was attractive to many Spanish parents, but the school also fulfilled the need of providing sought-after methods (the Froebel and Montessori methods mentioned in previous chapters) and a standard of education that was difficult to find elsewhere in Spain. The school was clearly going to be over-subscribed, even if it was not publicized. Balson, noted that students were

> children from the pro-Anglo aristocracy in Madrid, from well known established merchant (Bourguignon, the florists; Brooking, the jewellers; Lecock, the Belgian Company with big forest properties in the Madrid Sierra etc.) Also of high middle class [S]panish families, who like my father realized the importance of the English Language despite the war.[159]

In stark contrast to how the British Council was perceived through reports in the Spanish newspapers, the number of students attending the British Institute School increased from 160 in the first quarter of 1941 to 762 in the third quarter of 1942 – an increase of nearly fivefold, which was still while Serrano Suñer was at the helm of the Foreign Ministry. The membership of the British Institute also increased from 60 members to 420 in the same period – a sevenfold increase.[160] These may be relatively small numbers in terms of the overall population of Madrid or Spain, or even the elites themselves, but it is important not to forget the amount of influence that these 420 members of the institute had among their peers. Following the model of influence, it was important to start small and allow the power of the Council to spread through influential circles. By the end of the war, the Council would have 1,213 members in Spain, 2,153 students in Madrid, 1,374 students in Barcelona and 763 students in Bilbao – numbers which could only have been dreamt of at the start of the war.[161]

It was always going to be difficult, however, to gear a teaching course to the needs of all those in the class as the numbers increased and the expectations of those being taught (and their families) widened. Charles David Ley, who joined the British Institute in Madrid in 1943 recalled how one particular course had not been well received in 1945:

> Most of the attendees did not agree with my methods of teaching, and claimed they were very slow given that after two or three classes, had not come to have a thorough knowledge of the [English] language. 'I am not interested in the essence of the English language', noted Victor Ruiz Iriarte [one of the attendees], 'I just want to learn some fairly easy-to-read Shakespeare in the original' [original Spanish in footnote].[162]

Perhaps, as this was 1945 and the war was drawing to a close, the attendees of courses at the British Institute were no longer satisfied that the institute was providing them with the haven that they needed during the war. They wanted more focus on the teaching itself though as was shown in the previous chapter, the teaching in Turkey was often difficult throughout the war period. As we have seen, with Salazar and Franco in particular now openly interested in the work of the Council and seemingly ready to support its development, attendees no longer needed the protection status that the Council had provided. Instead, they wanted to be provided with courses which prepared them for the post-war world, whatever that post-war world might bring.

To conclude this section of the chapter, it seems clear that the non-official elites were keenly aware of the general war situation and this affected their relationship with the Council, and in this way they were no different from the official elites. In the 'indifferent' camp, the non-official elites tended to follow the lead of the official elites to make sure that they were not taking too many risks if and when associating with the Council. To an extent they can be seen as 'barometer' individuals and groups, reflecting the current state of thought in the neutral elites. However, to see them only following the official elites and to see the newspapers as a reflection of elite opinion would be a mistake. The British Council in Spain particularly attracted a lot of the intellectual and academic elite at the same time as Serrano Suñer, the arch enemy of all things British, was at the height of his power. It seems they simply ignored him and Serrano Suñer was unable or unwilling to stop them associating with the Council. In other countries such as Sweden, the signals from the official elite were less clear – Günther in particular, kept a firm non-committal policy throughout his tenure at the Foreign Ministry – and so found their own way to interact with the Council. In all of the four countries, but Sweden and Turkey in particular, the non-official elites seemed flattered by the Council spending the time and effort to send eminent British cultural figures to their countries and this had a tremendous effect. To use the Zahavi and Wight analogy, by sending artists and scientists abroad in time of war Britain was showing that it able to 'waste' resources when that money could be seemingly better spent elsewhere. It was signalling its reputation as a great power that could afford to 'waste' resources in this way, while fighting the most resource intensive war that had ever been fought.[163]

Statistical analysis of newspaper reports about British Council activities

Examining how the British Council was portrayed in foreign newspapers gives interesting insights into both the official view, as well as the wider elite view, of the Council. Most of the newspapers, though designed for the elites and literate masses (depending on the newspaper) were either controlled by those foreign Governments directly, or were subject to censorship restrictions to help maintain neutrality or a certain sympathy to one belligerent or another in the war. They, therefore, say more about the Government view of the Council than the view of the masses, and as has been argued earlier, tended to lag behind their views. Previously in this chapter, there has been an examination of particular articles focusing on specific lecturers and events held by the British Council, but it is important to also examine the overall picture to see how coverage changed over the course of the war. By examining the variations in frequency of articles about the British Council and comparing this to the frequency of articles about other countries' institutions, a number of important observations can be made which are not at all obvious from examining specific articles on a case-by-case basis. Fortunately for the modern-day historian, a number of these newspapers have been digitized and placed online with search functionality for no charge. Notable among these are the Spanish newspapers *ABC* (Madrid and Seville editions) and *La Vanguardia Española* (based in Barcelona).[164] Although the search function is not perfect due to inherent limitations in optical character recognition (OCR) technology and misspelling in the original newspaper articles, analysing the results of searches gives a good idea of the frequency of articles about the British Council and this can be compared against the results for the equivalent German and Italian institutions.

For *ABC* (in both the Madrid and Seville editions), there were 76 articles which mentioned either 'Instituto Britanico' (translation of the British Institute), 'Consejo Britanico' (the British Council) or 'Starkie' during the course of the Second World War. In comparison, there were 141 articles which mentioned the equivalent German institution or personnel (either 'Instituto Aleman de Cultura', 'Petersen' (for Wilhelm Petersen, the German cultural attaché to Spain), 'Beinert' (for Berthold Beinert, the Secretary-General of the *Instituto Alemán de Cultura*) or 'Heinermann' (for Theodore Heinermann, the Director of the *Instituto Alemán de Cultura*)) and 205 articles which mentioned the equivalent Italian institution or personnel (either 'Instituto de Cultura Italiana' or 'Zuani' (for Ettore De Zuani, the Director of the *Instituto de Cultura Italiana*)). Clearly, overall the Spanish press and, by proxy, the Spanish Government favoured the publicity of the Axis institutions at the expense of the British institution. What is more interesting, however, is the distribution of the articles, which the overall numbers do not show. A more detailed examination of the figures shows that 72 per cent of the articles about the British Council were from October 1943 onwards, 50 per cent of the articles were from October 1944 onwards.[165] In comparison, 77 per cent of the articles about the *Instituto Alemán de Cultura* and 84 per cent of the articles about the *Instituto de Cultura Italiana* were *before* October 1943. The graph in Figure 3 (articles mentioning foreign cultural institutions in *ABC*) helps to illustrate the point, using moving averages to take account of seasonal variations (there were always less articles in the summer months – the third quarter – for all institutions) and any

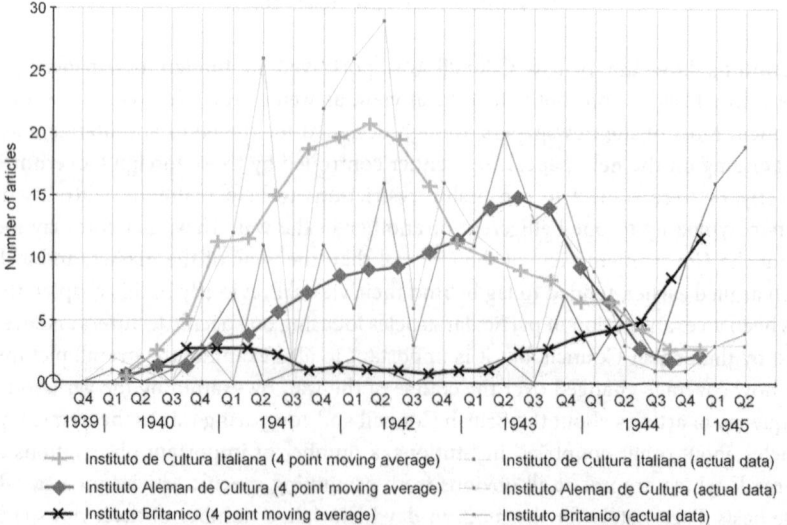

Figure 3 Articles mentioning foreign cultural institutions in *ABC* (Madrid and Seville editions).

possible data errors resulting from OCR limitations and articles being detected about people with the same name as employees of the institutions but unrelated to them.

The result is striking. There were three clear waves of popularity, starting first with the Italian Institute, peaking in the middle of 1942, then second, with the German Institute, peaking in late 1943, and lastly with the British Institute, which was on an upward trend during 1944 and early 1945. In part, this reflects the overall state of the war from which newspaper coverage of the institutes was clearly influenced, as well as the activities of the institutes themselves. The clearest example of this is the 'tipping point' date in the graph – where the popularity of the British Institute overtook the popularity of both the German and Italian institutes – which is in the second quarter of 1944. This is the same period as D-Day, perhaps the most obvious reversal in fortunes in the war militarily in which the British were involved. The increase in popularity of the German Institute after the second quarter of 1941 (at the time of the Nazi invasion of the Soviet Union), and its rapid decline after the third quarter of 1943 (after the reversal of fortunes on the eastern front following the Battle of Stalingrad, as well as the end of the African campaign and the subsequent invasion of Italy by Allied forces) are probably largely influenced by events in the war itself. However, one must not see the war situation as the only reason for the changes in popularity. The preference for Italy as opposed to Germany earlier on in the war stems largely from a Spanish preference for a Catholic and Latin culture to be promoted in their country rather than a Germanic culture. Indeed an average of over 20 articles per quarter in early 1942 on the Italian Institute compared with less than 10 articles on the German Institute was hardly a reflection of the relative military strength of the two Axis powers at that time. To a large extent, therefore, it can be assumed that the British culture being promoted at the British Institute was less welcome than if Britain had been a Catholic country. The British Institute's lack of popularity in *ABC* for much of the war must partly have been due to the relative cultural preferences of the Spaniards rather than being solely a reflection of the war situation. What is also perhaps surprising is that given Italy's change of sides in the war, the new Italy (on the British side) was a lot less popular late on in the war than the old Italy (on the German side) had been. The military situation clearly does not tell the whole story. It is interesting as well that although Serrano Suñer had been replaced by Conde de Jordana in September 1942, the popularity of the German institution actually peaked sometime after this date, which suggests that the change of Foreign Minister did not result in a profound change in overt propaganda on this issue overnight, and that the newspaper lagged behind the official elite opinion by a significant time period.

Just showing the results from *ABC*, does not prove there were three waves of popularity in Spain of these institutions – first *ABC* is only one newspaper, and second, as already stated, what was printed in *ABC* said a lot more about the preferences of the Spanish Government than it did about the views of the Spanish people. The first point can be partly solved by examining the results from *La Vanguardia Española*. Using the same search criteria as above, the British Institute was mentioned in 103 articles during the war period, the *Instituto Alemán de Cultura* was mentioned 184 times, and the *Instituto de Cultura Italiana* 99 times.[166] A similar overall distribution, in three waves, can be detected reflecting the overall state of the war, though the popularity of the Italian Institute was barely above the popularity of the German Institute in the first 'wave' which may reflect a regional preference between the Axis countries by the editorship of the newspaper – see Figure 4 (articles mentioning foreign cultural institutions in *La Vanguardia Española*). The second (German) and third (British) waves are much clearer, however, and the 'tipping points' where the British Institute first became more popular than the Italian Institute (late 1943), then the German Institute (third quarter of 1944) can be seen to reflect the Allied invasion of Italy and D-Day, respectively. What is interesting when comparing *La Vanguardia Española* and *ABC* is the particularly strong increase in the popularity of the British Institute in 1943 in the Barcelona-based newspaper, and the rapid increase thereafter, which is not so marked in *ABC*. This is due to the opening of a branch of the British Institute in Barcelona in October 1943 and clearly reflects the interest that the regional newspaper (though not Catalan separatist) had in the Institute opening on its doorstep. Prior to the opening of this branch in Barcelona, *La Vanguardia Española* took less interest than *ABC* in the British Institute largely because it was based in Madrid. There is a noticeable policy change that can be detected in the winter of 1942–43 which allowed a greater freedom in the Spanish press of reporting events happening at the British Institute and those associated with it. In February 1943, the first British Council sponsored event – the lecture of Professor Robert McCance – to take place outside of the institute building was a clear indication from the Spanish authorities that their view of the institute's work had changed significantly.[167] This fact is clearly reflected in the increase in articles in both *ABC* and *La Vanguardia Española* after this date.

In both *ABC* and *La Vanguardia Española* there is also a noticeable lack of articles on any of the institutes early on in the war – in late 1939 and during the whole of 1940 particularly – but more generally there were still a relative lack of articles until 1942

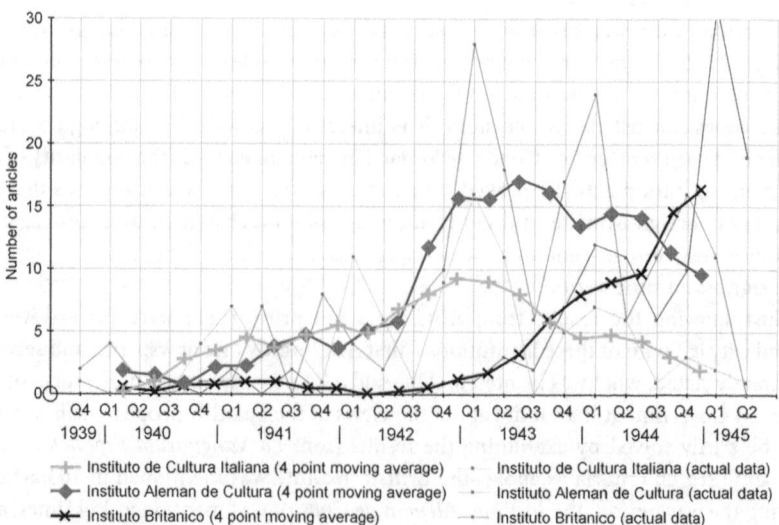

Figure 4 Articles mentioning foreign cultural institutions in *La Vanguardia Española* (Barcelona).

and 1943. Admittedly, the *Instituto Alemán de Cultura* did not open until the spring of 1941, but the *Instituto de Cultura Italiana* opened in early 1940 and the British Institute opening in the late summer of 1940. Cultural events, it appears, were not high on the newspapers' list of priorities of topics to cover in the first year or so of the war but became more important later in the war for both sides. The military battles, of course, had become less decisive and numerous since the years of blitzkrieg warfare in 1939, 1940 and to an extent in 1941, and so the newspapers actually had a chance to focus more on longer term cultural issues which had not been possible earlier.

In contrast to Spain, and on a data set covering a larger number of newspapers (from the British Council's Portugal Historical Archive), it has been evident throughout this book that the Portuguese Press was far more interested in the work of the British Council, with up to 33 articles per newspaper per quarter a number of times dedicated to British Council events or Anglo-Portuguese relations, with over 3,000 articles in total. Also in contrast to Spain, was the apparent slow decline in reporting of British Council events during the course of the war from late 1942 onwards, rather than the gradual increase that is evident in Spanish newspapers. This was certainly not evident from examining the articles on a case-by-case basis and shows the benefit of viewing the newspapers from a broader perspective. There was an increase towards the very end of the war post-D-Day, as there was in Spain, but the decline was quite evident and is perhaps surprising. The contrast is even more apparent when the average number of articles per quarter for Spain and Portugal are compared on the same graph (see Figure 5 (articles in the Portuguese and Spanish press about the work of the British Council)). Admittedly, the average number of articles in the Portuguese Press never declined below the average number of articles in the Spanish Press, although they get relatively close during 1945.[168]

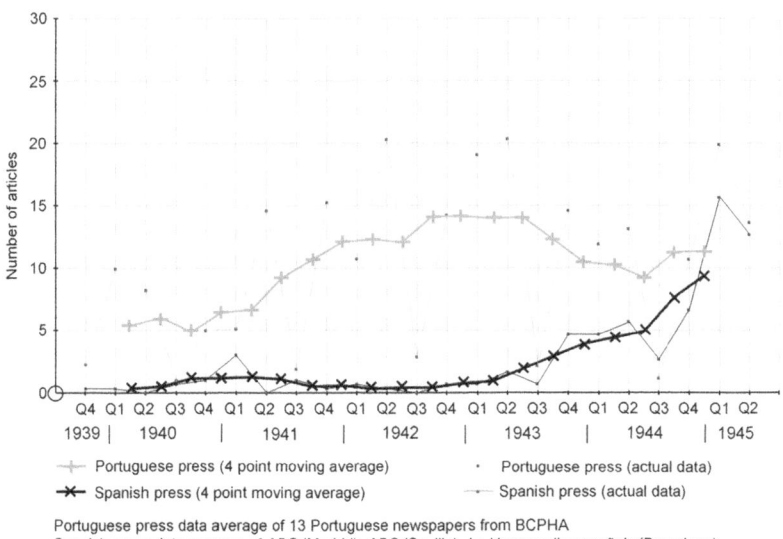

Figure 5 Articles in the Portuguese and Spanish press about the work of the British Council.

Perhaps this decline in the Portuguese Press's interest in the British Council was due not because of a changing view of the Council and Britain generally – for example, there was no apparent slide in popularity directly after the arrival of Australian troops in Portuguese East Timor in late 1941 and early 1942. Instead, perhaps it was as a result of there being less to report, due to a relative decline in British Council events in Portugal during the period late 1942 to mid-1944. As has been shown during this chapter, there was a fear in Portugal that the British Council would start to concentrate on Spain in the post-Serrano Suñer climate, and focus less on Portugal. As the British Council's work in Spain began to take off around the time of Operation Torch less resource and fewer events were focused on Portugal. This is not obvious from examining the newspapers on an article-by-article basis but from the graphs it is clear that there was a subtle decline from this time onwards, in the Council's work in Portugal.

Conclusion

As a conclusion to this chapter, there are a number of points that are important to note when considering the view of the British Council from the 'other side'. Five points in particular should be highlighted. First, the view of the British Council's work could not be divorced from its context. Primarily, of course, this meant the wider picture of the Second World War – the course of the war affected its ability to get its message across and the amount of publicity it was able to achieve in the neutral press, the confidence of its audience to associate with it when the consequences of doing so were unclear. The context, however, should also cover the pre-existing views of Britain and the other belligerents in all four countries ranging from the Anglo-Portuguese alliance, Spanish upset over the British enclave of Gibraltar and Swedish and Turkish fears of the Soviet Union.

The second point to highlight is that official and non-official views were highly dependent on individuals and personalities. Beigbeder, Serrano Suñer and Jordana, and their differing views changed the course of British Council success in Spain and Yücel's support was highly significant in Turkey, to name just a few of the important personalities. Official and non-official views were often analogous as the non-official elites waited with baited breath for signals from the official elites about what was acceptable. But it was not always the case. Serrano Suñer was simply ignored by many of the non-official elite in Spain, showing his apparent underlying weakness to control them. Official elites tended to be more interested in political consequences of the British Council's work and the security implications; whereas the non-official elites tended to be more interested in the cultural subject itself, and their own influence within that cultural sphere than the political dimension.

The third point to make is that newspapers in the neutral countries (owing to censorship restrictions, political interference and, like the non-official elites, waiting to find out what was acceptable to print) tended to be symptomatic of the views of the official elite rather than formative of their views. The newspapers also tended to lag some time behind the changes in opinion within the elite themselves. However, in Spain at least it is clear that there was a rapid increase in articles about the British Council in the final stages of the war.

Fourth, the expansion of the British Council's audience, reflecting changes in the war and in the official elite opinion, was more apparent than an expansion in the British Council's appeal. The model of influence suggested that the British Council interacted primarily with pro-British elites, and this seems to be reflected in reality. It relied on those pro-British elites talking to indifferent and hostile elites and allowing them to join the ranks of the pro-British when they were ready. To a large extent, they only did so when they had assessed that the opportunities presented by associating with the British Council were clearer than the risks and threats of doing so. The barometer elites who reflected the general atmosphere appear more numerous that the ideologues and joined the ranks of being pro-British when they could see it was in their interest to do so.

Lastly, cultural propaganda was viewed as a handicap to the British use of resources while fighting a major war. By apparently 'wasting' resources in this way, the British Council purported that it was an important and resource-rich country in the ascendancy that did not have to use all of the resources at its disposal in order to win the war militarily. Lord Beaverbrook's complaints against the Council throughout the war period that it was spending money on 'useless' enterprises instead of on the armed forces, and was therefore a liability to Britain, were ill-judged. On the contrary, this 'liability' was, in fact, an important and significant British asset.

Lessons for the Future: Towards a Model of Cultural Propaganda

The British Council's vital role

The British Council's wartime activities are one of the forgotten stories of the Second World War. Being less obvious and direct than military battles and more subtle and incremental than political propaganda, it has become hidden away as if it were merely a footnote to history. Even at the time, its cultural propaganda was seen by some as an intangible and ineffectual waste of resources, when Britain needed all the resources it could lay its hands on. Yet, as has been outlined in the preceding chapters, its role was vital in many ways and the Beaverbrook-inspired attacks of the war period were ill-judged and ignorant of the huge benefits that it provided to Britain and the war effort. It provided support to pro-British elites in difficult territory, made genuine connections between cultural communities and provided a conduit for word-of-mouth propaganda to neutral people who were unable to receive uncensored news in any other effective way. It also crucially showed Britain to be a successful country by going beyond what was seemingly essential for Britain's survival, through supporting cultural initiatives and thereby tapping into the Reputation Reflex of the neutral people. In this way, it provided a magnetic attraction to the influential and opinion-forming elites and allowed its influence to percolate through the various strands of elite (pro-British, indifferent and hostile groups) and maintain, and incrementally expand, a backdrop of sympathy among those groups which was crucial part of winning the war.

The British Council was not unique, however, and had precedents in the form of foreign cultural organizations such as the *Alliance Française*, as well as the British Government's First World War organization, Wellington House. The Council's work clearly fitted into a growing realization in the world, generally, that cultural exchanges and global communication were necessary for creating and maintaining influence and for promoting understanding between nations. This was particularly acute for Britain as it began to realize that its reddish-pink colouring-in of the British Empire on a world map was no longer enough to show the world Britain's 'greatness', and an explanation of its culture was necessary to understanding Britain, particularly in an increasingly post-colonial world. The fact that organizations such as the USIA continued this type work in the post-war era, and the British Council survives to this day, is good evidence that the British Council's work during Second World War was part of a broader shift in the history of communications and propaganda – and indeed in British history – and not a footnote to the history of a specific period with specific circumstances.

This chapter will attempt to draw together an array of different themes present in the earlier chapters to outline conclusions on a number of aspects of the Council's work. The first section will conclude and summarize the main ways in which the British Council operated as an organization and how this affected its cultural propaganda work. Second, there will be a conclusion on what the success of the Council was dependent upon, how that success can be measured, and a judgement on how successful it was in achieving its aims. Third, there will be an outline of a model of cultural propaganda to provide a considered definition of cultural propaganda based on the British Council case study and its applicability elsewhere. Lastly, there will be final conclusion on how this book, and particularly this model of cultural propaganda, contributes to the existing literature on the British Council and propaganda more generally.

How the British Council operated and how this affected its cultural propaganda work

It has been shown throughout this book that the British Council did not operate in a vacuum. Whether it was other British Government organizations, British Embassies, the context of the Second World War, or indeed its audience in the neutral countries, the British Council would always be constrained by a various number of other organizations and circumstances outside of its control, however much wanted to have independence of action. In Britain, a number of clear constraints arose which restricted the freedom of the Council. Some, like funding constraints, were nothing extraordinary for any organization and, perhaps ironically, funding was the least of its problems – its budget rose from £353,233 in the 1939/40 financial year to £2,237,060 in 1944/45, which, even allowing for inflation, was a large rise particularly given that the Council's field of operation naturally shrank as the German Army made many of the countries the Council had opened offices in, out of bounds.[1] With only four countries to concentrate on in Europe (though admittedly a growing number in Latin America and the Middle East), it had enough funding to make sure that the cultural propaganda created in those four countries was of a high quality. However, the amount of high quality work it could carry out was physically constrained given the logistical difficulties of the war situation.

Far more important from an internal Government point of view were the constraints resulting from the political haggling between the Foreign Office, the British Council and the Ministry of Information. There was a fierce conflict between Lord Lloyd, the Chairman of the British Council, and Sir John Reith, the Minister of Information, over the delineation of responsibilities which resulted in the political-cultural split between the MOI and the British Council.[2] But arguments about who should control the British Council's work and how much freedom it should have continued in one form or another throughout the wartime period. The death of Lord Lloyd in February 1941 put the British Council's role under the spotlight once again, with various arguments between Alfred Duff Cooper, the new Minister of Information and Anthony Eden, the

Foreign Secretary, on its purpose and whether it still had a contribution to make as part of the British wartime propaganda armoury.[3] On that occasion, the Foreign Office was successful not only in maintaining the Council in existence, but also in maintaining its control over the organization instead of its line of reporting being transferred to the MOI. Under its new Chairman, Sir Malcolm Robertson, the Council continued to grow, but still there were conflicts in which it became embroiled – often due to interference, perceived or real, from the Foreign Office itself. At one point, in July 1943, Robertson threatened to resign due to interdepartmental conflicts and constraints – 'No Chairman that I know of' he stated 'would retain his position in such circumstances.'[4] Clearly, his frustration had been building up for some time. His furious outbursts in front of the Portuguese Ambassador, Armindo Monteiro, in the previous November, regarding the seemingly anti-British nature of the *Mocidade Portuguesa*, could perhaps show that Robertson was easily frustrated. It was more likely, however, that a variety of different constraints on his ability to lead the British Council was making his role seemingly impossible.[5] In addition to his freedom of action being constrained by others, there is an interesting passage in the notes of his Secretary-General, A. J. S. White, which also shows that, though Robertson cared deeply about the Council, he was trying to do too much elsewhere.

> He tried hard, perhaps too hard, to infect his Parliamentary colleagues with his enthusiasm: but he could not, or did not, spare enough time from the House of Commons to carry out the day-to-day direction of the Council's work and his constant failures to keep important appointments in Hanover Street [the British Council's headquarters] led to difficulty.[6]

Clearly Robertson had a vision for the British Council but was personally constrained by a variety of factors within Government and beyond, which were largely outside of his control. This led to constant irritation both for him and for certain other elements of the British Council. Robertson, and the Council generally, had to deal with a barrage of criticism and lobbying from a variety of individuals and non-Governmental organizations, ranging from the likes of external voices such as Lord Beaverbrook to those with a more integral cultural role such as Astra Desmond and Kenneth Clark.[7] All these relationships made for a large array of checks on its freedom of movement, just within a British political context.

On the front line, the Council also had a variety of constraints it had to deal with – many of which were contradictory and resulted in a complex collection of methods of propaganda that the Council employed. Logistical issues meant that the Council was constrained in what it could physically do, particularly in terms of transporting people and cultural freight over to neutral countries because of security concerns for flights, and resource limitations (the lack of paper being a particularly major problem[8]). Communication constraints more generally resulted in a lack of direct central control from London and a pragmatic decentralized approach to the way the Council operated. With a decentralization of control from an organizational point of view, on the one hand, coupled with varied situations and audiences on the ground in each of the four neutral countries, on the other, the Council's work varied significantly. Though it may have wanted to have a 'one size fits all' approach to its propaganda, it found that the political situation in each country and the attitude of the authorities (and certain personalities in those authorities), as well as their historical memory and pre-existing view of Britain clearly varied to a large degree. However, the Council also relied on a decentralized approach for its activities to work on the ground. This actually worked well from a practical point of view and enabled the local British Council representatives to understand their audiences thoroughly and craft their cultural propaganda to suit local conditions. Nevertheless, it led to such a heterogeneous situation that the work of the Council in one neutral country was unrecognizable in the next, by the end of the war. For example, the British Council did not open its own institutes in Turkey for teaching purposes because of the amount of time that it took to get to Turkey (via South Africa for much of the war) and the local preference of Hasan-Ali Yücel for placing British Council lecturers within Turkish institutions (the Halkevleri primarily, but also Universities and schools). There was also a real fear that opening a British Institute would be unwelcome by the wider Turkish community.[9] By contrast, the British Council in Spain, until relatively late in the war, did not conduct any activities outside of the British Institute building, and, therefore, conducted not only teaching activities there (through the establishment of the kindergarten and the British Institute School) but also its art exhibitions, music concerts and lectures. In Sweden, the Council aimed to reach out to as many Swedes as possible across the country but were severely restricted by the difficulties in getting people and bulky materials there, because of limited flights and limited load capacity of those few flights.[10] Therefore, the Council worked primarily through Anglophile Societies in Sweden and thereby encouraged pre-existing pro-British sympathies. This inevitably carried a level of risk for the Council due to being unable to control those Societies, but it seems to have worked well enough during the war period. When the relatively few lecturers such as T. S. Eliot, Sir Lawrence Bragg and Sir Harold Nicolson did touch down on Swedish soil, the Council ensured that they received as much publicity as possible and met as many influential people as possible emphasizing implicitly that these lecturers had risked their lives in travelling there, which created a great impression. In Portugal, the Council had relatively few restrictions and could be more easily served from London through the regular flight services to Lisbon (though clearly still not safe, given the tragic death of Leslie Howard). There was also a more congenial atmosphere created by the Portuguese Press and Government, partly created, of course, by the fact that Nazi troops were not on the borders of the country.

On the other hand, and because of economic and resource constraints (despite the growing budget), the Council also tried to find ways in pooling its activities together. This ranged from a number of publications, like the *British Life and Thought* series of booklets and *Britain To-day*, being centrally authored and distributed for a number of different countries, to the same lecturers and art exhibitions being moved from one country to the next – particularly between geographical neighbours Spain and Portugal, but also elsewhere.[11] There was, to an extent, an attempt to create a corporate identity through these publications and events. Though by doing so there was always a risk that the corporate identity would not be suitable across the range of different audiences at which the Council was aiming its propaganda. Some exhibitions, such as a postage stamp exhibition organized first in Stockholm and then in Madrid, were failures in some places (in this instance, Stockholm) and large successes in others (Madrid) – yet, it was essentially the same exhibition presented in the same way in both Stockholm and Madrid. Though direct feedback is less apparent, the Council was often criticized for creating publications that were the same 'for a businessman in Toronto and a businessman in Damascus' (in the words of a post-war review of the Council by M. R. K. Burge), and clearly the focus for the Council had always to be a bespoke approach wherever possible for each of its audiences.[12] Yet, it was important for the Council to try to show it was one organization presenting a single image of Britain to a range of foreign peoples. Although perhaps unlikely during the war period because of communication difficulties, there was always a risk that each of the countries where the Council operated would start to detect differences in approach by the Council and question why they were not receiving the same treatment as another country. Already during the war, the Portuguese were beginning to fear that a more sympathetic Spain from late 1942 onwards would make the British Council concentrate its efforts on Madrid rather than Lisbon, and this fear could be exacerbated if the approach taken across the board was not sufficiently homogenous.[13]

Owing to existing resource limitations, the British Council needed to focus on a relatively small audience. However, focusing on a relatively small audience also fitted well with the British Council's intended aim of targeting the elites, rather than the masses, and the towns and cities instead of rural areas. This focus clearly affected the way the British Council was organized, the way it operated and the content of its cultural propaganda. The Council concentrated on cultural propaganda that was going to interest the elites and provide events that they would want to attend. The aim was not to directly influence those who were indifferent or hostile to Britain, but to influence those who were already pro-British but had a certain influence among the elites so that the message of the British Council could spread through a secondary influence. Focusing on a small group of people meant also that a very effective form of influencing, but one which is often overlooked, could be utilized – that of word-of-mouth propaganda. The message of the Council could spread in a similar way to a rumour and have a relatively high level of fidelity even after being passed on by a number of people. Clearly, it is very difficult to measure this effect in any meaningful way. Anecdotal evidence has suggested that the British Council, particularly in areas like Spain where it was starved of publicity, was still able to attract many pupils to its school and members to its institute, and the only conceivable way that it could have done so was by its reputation being passed on from one impressed elite member to the next.[14] The only other way of doing so would be by the staff of the British Council actually going around talking to hundreds of people across Madrid to persuade them to enrol onto the membership list, without them hearing anything from other people in the meantime. This is clearly an impractical and unreasonable assumption to make. Word-of-mouth propaganda worked well and was a mainstay of the way the British Council extended its influence among the elites who then influenced others.

The constraints outlined above about its relationship with other British organizations and individuals as well as its work on the front line are a particular factor in determining the content and method of the British Council's propaganda work and its overall success. However, it must be stressed that a constraint does not necessarily equal a barrier to success. The constraints that the British Council had to deal with could just as easily be drivers for efficiency and for focusing on a particular audience such as the elites or a particular way of operating. This could enable the Council to be successful in its constrained field while leaving other areas of propaganda and other audiences to other organizations. Nevertheless, there is a certain link between how the Council dealt with its constraints and whether it was successful, which will be explored in the next section as well as examining the range of other factors on which its success depended.

Factors critical for the success of the British Council

The British Council's success in neutral Europe was dependent on a variety of different variable factors, some of which were within the Council's control and some were not. The first factor critical for its success was an agreement among interdependent organizations on its remit – that it should exist at all, and then once that was secure, what it should be doing to achieve its aims. For the Council, this agreement took some time to come to fruition, but after the Lloyd-Reith agreement on the political-cultural split, and the subsequent Royal Charter enshrining the Council's objectives, it is clear, nonetheless, that there was a broad agreement within the British Government that some kind of promotion of British culture abroad was worthwhile and that the British Council was the best placed organization to provide it. Despite Lloyd's death and the constant irritations that Robertson felt were eroding his ability to run the organization, the British Council was strong enough and had enough friends in Government to continue its operation throughout the war period and, indeed, still thrives in the present day despite recent Government cuts to public services. There may well have been disagreement on the detail of what kind of image of British culture to present abroad, but the important point here is that there was enough general agreement on the issue that an image of British culture should be presented abroad at all – and this was critical to its success. Achieving a general agreement depended heavily on the personalities involved. Pro-British Council individuals (such as Lloyd, Halifax, Robertson, Eden and the British Council representatives on the ground) had an ability to persuade others of the benefits of the British Council. The British Council sceptics (such as Beaverbrook, Reith, Duff Cooper and even Hoare and the British Embassy staff in Ankara to an extent) were unable, or unwilling, to make effective counterarguments.[15] Fortunately, the Council had a mixture of forceful personalities in its favour and a general lack of people with vested interests who were prepared to undermine the Council.

The second factor on which success of the Council depended was the broad context in which it operated. By this, it is not meant the day-to-day operations or the general internal agreement on its role mentioned above but more the context of the war itself and the views of the people and the Government in the countries where it operated. As stressed throughout this book, the British Council was not working in a vacuum, and in extreme cases in Italy, the Low Countries, France, Yugoslavia, Greece, Romania and Bulgaria, when those countries either joined the Axis or were invaded by the Axis, the British Council staff had to be evacuated and its work stopped. Any successes achieved prior to evacuations, such as creation of general pro-British sympathy, or more specific English language skills, were either lost or went underground. Where the Council continued to operate, the course of the war was clearly something of acute importance to those countries, even though they may not have been directly involved in the war itself. When the war was going badly for Britain (in reality or in perception only), then the British Council would clearly suffer the consequences and struggle to make its voice heard; equally, when the war was going well for Britain, then the British Council would reap the benefits. The overall context of the war was then crucial, and the Council could not be successful in a non-conducive context. Yet, has been shown previously, it was not always as simple as a direct correlation between success in the war and success for the British Council. The Council often created a focus for pro-British elites in neutral countries who, regardless of the war situation, were ideologically against the values of the Axis systems, or who could see through the context to the benefits of what the British Council was offering. Under the tenure of the pro-Nazi Serrano Suñer as Spanish Foreign Minister, the British Council's influence actually grew considerably in terms of membership and student numbers, and this was mirrored in other contexts. For example, Hasan-Ali Yücel was always a pro-British Turkish Education Minister regardless of how the war was going for Britain, and the spread of British Council lecturers around the Halkevleri was similarly unhindered by the general context of the war. Nevertheless, although at the detailed level it was complex, there was always going to be a general link to the war situation that the Council would never be able to get away from – as it became more and more obvious that Germany could not win Second World War, less and less neutral people felt hindered in engaging with the Council. Perhaps more important than the war situation for the Council, was the general feeling among the neutral elites about whether the war situation was important or not to how the Council should be treated. It was this assessment of the importance of the war to the Council's operations on which, in reality, the Council relied. Tacit approval was vital if overt approval was not forthcoming, because of the war situation. It is important to consider that if the Handicap Principle, which was outlined earlier, is applied here, it actually follows that the Council could demonstrate (albeit unwittingly) that the war situation was a handicap with which it could cope, instead of the unhelpful war situation being a hindrance to the success of the Council. By showing it could operate quite well enough with the constraints that the war presented and by giving the impression that the culture that it was portraying was so inherently positive, then the constraints of war would become unimportant. This concept, of course, only goes so far. It seems clear that the elites were not going to be overwhelmed by this principle if they were pro-Nazi, or worried about showing any sign of pro-British sympathy, but for many, the Handicap Principle may have been an important factor that should not be forgotten.

The third factor on which the Council's success depended was the overall approach that it took on the ground. This, of course, had many facets that this book has examined in detail but there are some broad themes which can be highlighted. The first point to make is that the Council had to provide something that was actually wanted by the neutral peoples that it was trying to engage with and influence rather than trying to impose propaganda that was not needed, wanted or necessary. The most obvious example of this approach was explained by Stanley Unwin, the Chairman of the Books and Periodicals Committee, in his memoirs where he remarked that the Council only ever established Anglophile Societies where there was local interest in establishing them.[16] Unwin also applied commercially sound incentives for bookstores in neutral Europe, to encourage them to stock English language books or English books in translation, through the Book Export Scheme and the sale or return policy.[17] This approach, to a large extent, though perhaps less obviously elsewhere, was a major part of the Council's approach. Supplies of British Council teachers to the Halkevleri was clearly something that Michael Grant pushed considerably in Turkey, but he could not have had his great success in the Halkevleri unless there had been a need among those Turkish institutions for those teachers.[18] In Spain, the British Council did not even attempt to teach outside of its institute building until it was invited to do so, and in Portugal the Council could not have received such favourable press coverage for its activities had the Government and non-official elites not wanted to read about the Council's activities.

The second point on the approach the Council took was that it was an incremental approach. No one particular event made the British Council's work a success, but instead it was the culmination of many events building on the successes of previous events that made the Council such a force. Over time, it constructed strong foundations, working on the creation of long-term sympathy rather than short-term superficial successes. It may have been slower, therefore, to produce results (which was always going to cause a problem at a financial level when trying to defend a return on investment), but its effect was more profound. There is another important point to make on its incremental approach which is that the Council relied on the maintaining and servicing of the foundations on which each of its incremental steps was based. The Council could not forget about maintaining its old foundations when new activities and events came onto the horizon, even if those new activities were building on the success of previous visits. What is meant by that is best provided by the example of Sir Lawrence Bragg's continued correspondence and connections with the Swedish scientific community long after his visit to Stockholm in April-May 1943. In his archive at the Royal Institution, there are letters going back and forth across the North Sea until late 1944, and they were still referencing his visit nearly two years beforehand and the direct consequences of it on subjects such as facilitating the publishing of articles by Swedish scientists in British journals.[19] Though subsequent visits to Sweden by other important figures, such as Harold Nicolson, built on the success of Bragg, it was imperative to ensure that Bragg himself continued to secure his long-term success through maintaining the contacts that he had made personally. Incremental propaganda also affected the themes of the propaganda by making it more timeless, old-fashioned and conservative – which made it ideal for the (largely) conservative elites who were the target of the propaganda. The image of Britain in the *British Life and Thought* series, for example, focused more on a very comfortable, nostalgic picture of pre-war Britain, rather than wartime ammunitions factories, and the slums of the inner cities where the workers lived.[20]

A third point on the approach was that it had to ensure that when opportunities arose through changes in the war situation, or changes in sympathy by people in neutral countries, it took advantage of those opportunities. Those opportunities could arise from a change in who held the position of Foreign Minister (such as the change from Serrano Suñer to Jordana in September 1942), the arrival of new elites at a British Council event (such as the Marqués de Lozoya in November 1942[21]), the interest aroused in Britain among Swedish scientists that was detected by Bragg (in May 1943[22]) because of the realization that Germany could not win the war and also things which did not change but were relatively rare – such as Hasan-Ali Yücel's pro-British sympathies.[23] These examples clearly link with the earlier point made about the broad context in which the Council operated, but there is a difference here in that it was one thing for the broad context to be conducive to the British Council's success and quite another for the British Council to cash in on that conduciveness effectively. The two had to work in tandem and as that conduciveness was fragile and uncertain, owing to the nature of the war situation, the Council had to ensure it took opportunities when they arose. Lozoya's apparent change of heart, commented upon by John Steegman, was clearly not a profound one (he often visited the *Instituto Alemán de Cultura* after November 1942[24]), but the British Council had to, and did, make every effort to seize upon glimmers of pro-Britishness among the neutral elites.

A final important point to make on the approach that the Council took is that just as it had to cash in on the opportunities that came along, it also had to ensure that its enemies – both the equivalent German and Italian Institutes as well as those among the people of the neutral countries where it operated – did not take advantage of any mistakes, gaps or reversals in its own propaganda. This often meant continuing to spend money on institutions and events which were not in themselves particularly effective in terms of cultural propaganda. Not spending money on them, and closing them down, would have been very costly to British reputation – an own-goal in propaganda terms. The non-financial cost of acting to close down schools and newspapers outweighed the financial cost of keeping them going. With finite resources this was always going to be difficult to justify, but there were plenty of examples where it happened. These include maintaining *Anglo-Portuguese News* when it had a declining readership and keeping open two schools in particular – the St Julian's School in Carcavelos and the English High School for Girls in Istanbul – which were considered to be very costly for what they achieved.[25] It could also be argued that, to an extent, the reason for the British Council's survival at the beginning of Second World War (in September 1939) and at the time of Lord Lloyd's death (in February 1941) rested on a similar argument. To close down the Council's institutions across neutral Europe, or to subsume them into the overtly propagandistic Ministry of Information, would have been costly in propaganda terms. Many considered that the Council was ineffective (misguidedly as argued by this book), but it simply was not worth the backlash that would have been received from the Axis, by closing it down.

The fourth and final main factor on which the Council's success depended was its ability to work through others and the extent to which others were prepared to extol the virtues of the British Council. This clearly has links to the points above, but was so critical to the Council's success that it deserves to be a factor in its own right. The model of influence showed that influencing the pro-British elites could have a chain reaction effect to influence other groups; first the indifferent and hostile elites and then the wider masses. The primary audience of pro-British elites could be seen as being a channel to reach a wider audience rather than solely as a receptacle in themselves.[26] This book has shown that this model evidently has a lot of merit and enabled the British Council's influence to expand. Perhaps, however, it is a little simplistic to group the elites into pro-British, indifferent and anti-British in opinion, as the elites were more complex than this suggests, and the model does not take into account the confidence of each group in demonstrating their opinion. For example, some elites were proudly pro-British and keen to show it (overt ideologues), and other elites were more cautious until the war outcome was more certain but were pro-British from the outset (covert ideologues). The model also does not cover the extent to which the groups were made up of ideologues and 'barometer elites' (their barometric behaviour being either due to pragmatism or genuine changes in sympathy), which makes the picture far more complicated. Nevertheless, the important point here is that the British Council, by working with others who had influence elsewhere, was able to reach out beyond its natural audience of overt pro-British elites to these complex groups of individuals to incrementally change sympathy. The Halkevleri, Anglophile Societies, and the favourable Portuguese Press are perhaps the most obvious of these routes from spreading influence beyond the pro-British enclaves to a wider audience. It was also true for non-newspaper publications, such as *Bonniers Litterära Magasin* in Sweden, which Ronald Bottrall noted 'reaches a public that the Legation does not always touch' and was even distributed in occupied Scandinavia which was clearly out of bounds for the usual British Council branded publication.[27] This was something the British Council utilized and influenced wherever possible, though this is a more extreme example. The use, and encouragement, of other non-official, but more mainstream, publications like *Nature* and *The Economist* was widespread, and such publications were perhaps more effective because of their non-official nature. British-Council-published books such as the *British Life and Thought* series had great examples of literary creativity particularly the Dudley Stamp booklet *The Face of Britain*. However, these booklets could not directly penetrate beyond those who were likely to read the booklets because they were always going to be seen as official. They could be extremely well written but remain unread because of their branding and title. Getting covert ideologues and barometric elites to read British Council books, or step inside the British Council buildings, and attend events such as book exhibitions, was always going to be difficult particularly when the general course of the war was not going in Britain's favour. The influence of such events and the *British Life and Thought* series, as well as other British books displayed at book exhibitions, was always going to be limited in a direct sense but they could, however, be significant (if incremental) through word-of-mouth from pro-British elite (who attended the events or read the books) to not-so-pro-British elite. Well-presented facts about Britain (or 'soundbites' as they might be called today) could be quoted in general conversation without reference to the booklets themselves.[28] The SOE 'sib' campaign worked on a similar basis, providing easily remembered rumours for spreading – the British Council technique may have been more subtle in approach, but it worked on very similar foundations.[29] The potentially unread books could also have an indirect effect of showing 'evidence of . . . intellectual achievements' which have 'value even if it deals with an esoteric subject of relatively little interest to the target audience' – words of an observer of the cultural propaganda work of the USIA, but just as applicable here.[30] Just by showing that it could produce books covering what could be seen as 'intellectual' subjects, even if they remained unread, had an important propaganda value, which should not be underestimated. One final barrier, that could be overcome through working through others in this way, was the ever-present language barrier which always caused a dilemma for the Council – should it work in English only to spread the influence of the English language and wider access to English language material, or should it translate its work for non-English speakers who it wished to influence directly? By working through others it could do more in English, as the pro-British elites were very likely to speak fluent English (which saved time and effort), and then allow the messages of the Council to spread in the local language among the elites, reaching a far more extensive audience.

Assessing the success of the British Council

The previous section has shown that the British Council's success was dependent on a range of different variables, some of which were in its control but many of which were not and relied instead on the goodwill of pro-British elites and British organizations in order to make its work successful in time of war. Having favourable conditions did not mean, of course, that the British Council was automatically successful, merely that a number of conditions had to be satisfied to make that success possible. It is far more difficult to measure the success of the Council for a number of different reasons, such as determining what success would look like in the first place, whether the indicators for measuring success are reliable indicators or whether they are really a measure of other influences (such as the general state of the war), and whether it is possible to determine success in the absence of an unknowable counterfactual situation (i.e. what would have been the outcome had the British Council not acted in the way that it did). However, the previous chapter explored a number of different ways to determine the view from the other side, which attempted to assess the success of the Council in getting an audience reaction. Key among these ways of determining success is assessing the views of people in specific roles – the Heads of State, Foreign Ministers and Education Ministers – particularly if the views of the individual changed over time or the specific post changed hands. Clearly, this will only give an indication of individuals' views of the British Council, as they would have been exposed to a variety of other influences in those positions. What can be determined, however, is to what extent the British Council became more able to deliver its objectives with official support or the frequency of visits made by the official elites to the British Council's institutes. The most striking example of this is perhaps the invitation of Jimenez Díaz and Carlos Blanco Soler to Dr Robert McCance to lecture outside of the British Council building in February 1943 – the first time that that had been sanctioned in Spain.[31] Also in this category could be placed the attendance of Gösta Bagge at the opening of the British Institute in Stockholm despite the barrage of complaints from the Nazi Government, the attendance of the Marqués de Lozoya at a dinner party at the British Institute in Madrid in November 1942, and the attendance of President Ismet Inönü of Turkey at an exhibition of photographs of British Universities.[32] The correspondence between Alba and Beigbeder, Monteiro and Salazar and the views of Serrano Suñer and Jordana, are good examples of a general trend of increasing engagement and freedom for the British Council and its work. It will always be difficult, however, to separate the success of the Council's work itself from the wider, more conducive, context when it comes to official views and attendance at events. The views of Franco and Salazar at the end of the war show that, though they talked about the British Council specifically, it would be a brave historian who concluded that their views were not affected by the general post-war climate and their need to keep on the right side of the victorious Allies.[33]

What the previous chapter showed is that a better indicator for the Council's success was the level to which the non-official elites followed the official lead – in effect, how far was the Council successful in going beyond what was officially acceptable and reaching out to the non-official elites. A numerical way of measuring this is through membership numbers and the number of students who attended British Council courses and through the number of newspaper articles reporting British Council events. As was stated in that same chapter, the local newspaper coverage of the British Council's work, and tracking the frequency of articles during the war period, cannot give such a good indicator as the membership and student numbers. This is because the newspapers were largely influenced by the official elite (or censored by them), and therefore were more symptomatic of the official elite view (which as stated above is difficult to separate from the wider context) rather than having an opinion-forming role. Looking at the membership and student figures for the institutes and how independent those figures were from newspaper article frequency, and the views of the official elites, gives a better indicator of the level of success attained by the Council. Assessing this independence is potentially a good indicator of whether the Council was successful in achieving support and interest among the wider elite population. There are a number of examples of this. First, when Serrano Suñer issued a decree in June 1940 effectively banning the work of the British Council, he was seemingly unable to stop the institute opening and building up its work with the support of the Madrid population.[34] Even when Serrano Suñer became Foreign Minister later that year, he still was unable to thwart the work of the Council, despite being openly pro-Nazi. Membership of the British Institute increased from 60 in the first quarter of 1941, to 420 in the third quarter of 1942, and student figures rose from 160 to 762 over the same period – all while Serrano Suñer was Foreign Minister.[35] As a comparison, the number of articles per quarter in *ABC*, over which he had a strong influence, steadily declined in this period from around three articles in the fourth quarter of 1940 (on a four-point moving average) to around one article (again, on a four-point moving average) in the third quarter of 1943, only rising after Serrano Suñer had left office.[36] Clearly, the Council was successful at attracting a large increase in new members and students in spite of Serrano Suñer's efforts to choke the publicity that the Council could receive and an implementation of his 'go slow' policy whenever the Council needed assistance. Even more surprisingly, a significant proportion of the new members were observed as being from the Falange movement, which Serrano Suñer was meant to be the central player.[37]

In contrast, the situation in Portugal was somewhat different. The membership numbers of the British Institute in Lisbon were recorded as 1,717 in the first quarter of

1942 (a higher number than the Madrid institute ever achieved during the war), which rose slightly over the next year then dropped to 1,664 in the third quarter of 1943, then dropped again to 1,024 (a figure less than 60 per cent of the peak figure) in the second quarter of 1944 before rising slightly towards the end of the war.[38] The articles in the Portuguese press about the Council and Anglo-Portuguese cultural relations generally seem to almost mirror this trend with around 12 articles in the first quarter of 1942 (on a four-point moving average), rising to around 14 in early 1943, dropping back to 12 again in the latter half of 1943, then dropping again to around 9 articles in the second quarter of 1944, before rising again to around 11 before the end of the war.[39] There is an apparent linkage between the success of the Council (or lack of success) in attracting members to the Lisbon institute and the number of articles about the British Council in the Portuguese Press, and it could have a number of explanations.

First, there could be a direct causal link between the two in either direction. This could be through the number of articles in the press directly influencing who knew about the Council's work and creating interest – and therefore driving up or down the membership figures for the Council; or by the number of interesting events taking place in the Lisbon institute being reflected by the number of members anyway, the events being merely recorded in the press; or a mixture of the two.

The second possible explanation could be that both the membership figures and the number of articles in the Portuguese Press reflected the general mood among the Portuguese elite with regard to their views about the Anglo-Portuguese relationship and were only connected indirectly through this general feeling. This general mood reflected the wider events of the war (including the effect of the East Timor landings and Allied use of bases in the Azores) and the fact, mentioned in the previous chapter, that Britain appeared to be focusing more on wooing Portugal's great rival Spain, than on Portugal itself from late 1942 onwards, with Portuguese interest in Britain only recovering after D-Day. The general mood may well have been affected by war fatigue meaning that as the war dragged on, the Portuguese people saw less urgent need to show their sympathy for Britain as they had done earlier in the war.

The third possible explanation could be that the mirroring was just coincidental, but it does seem too striking for this to be likely. It was most probably a combination of the first two possible explanations – that there was a definitive causal link (from press to membership) because the press in Portugal seemed to have a significant impact for the Council particularly in attracting new members. For example, unlike in Spain, it dared to report British Council events in some detail (being symptomatic of the official line rather than formative of it) and a lower number of articles would have directly created less interest in the Council from those who had not attended its events before. However, it is also true that it suffered a net decline in membership figures of 693 from early 1942 to early 1944, meaning that at least that number of members cancelled their membership or did not renew their membership. It seems, therefore, that it can be concluded there was also a definitive causal link (from membership to press), as the declining numbers of those interested in the Council's work would have given the newspaper journalists less cause to write articles. It seems sensible to assume that these lapsed members were unlikely to have been directly influenced by articles in the Portuguese Press about the Council, as they would have known the details already as members. Despite those causal links, however, the press and the membership figures were also significantly reflecting the state of the war. This is because both new and existing members' relationships with the Council did not exist in a vacuum and would have been influenced by the general mood of the country. It is a highly complex and interdependent set of relationships which do not give rise to a simple explanation.

What does this mean for the overall measurement of success of the Council's work? In Spain, it seems clear that the membership figures and numbers of students were increasing despite the lack of articles in the Spanish press and the implementation of Serrano Suñer's 'go slow' policy – that is, the British Council was increasingly successful in reaching out to a wider audience despite those constraints. In Portugal, the picture is more complex. The membership figures did not rise in spite of a lack of articles and official support as they did in Spain, and in fact the two sets of data appear to track each other in a downward direction from 1942 to 1944. If the numbers of articles had risen, while the membership decreased, it would have been tempting to conclude first that the two sets of data in both Spain and Portugal were independent, and second, that the Council was not very successful in Portugal even though it had increasing publicity and failed to convert that publicity into support and success for its work. But that was not the case, and instead it is difficult to conclude whether the decreasing membership of the Lisbon institute was a sign of the Council's poor performance, or merely a reflection of the wider context in which it operated. This wider context included knowledge of the official Portuguese view of the Council's work and war fatigue among the Portuguese population.

In Sweden and Turkey, it is less easy to measure the success of the Council in the same way as Spain and Portugal because of the lack of data on press articles that can be compared against membership or student numbers. Nevertheless, there are some proxy indicators that can be used in both cases. For example, the number of students that the British Council taught in Turkey increased from zero in 1940 to over 10,000 in 1945, teaching in 42 Turkish institutions in early 1942, 123 in late 1943 and 150 in 1945.[40] While it has been argued above that using one set of figures, like student numbers, cannot in itself show how successful the Council was, it is also reasonable to argue that such a rapid increase in student numbers and a proliferation in the number of Turkish institutions being utilized, are reasonable indicators that the Council was more successful than not. It must also mean, by deduction, that the activities it was carrying out were wanted by the Turkish authorities and it was doing them in a way which the Turkish authorities approved, otherwise it would not have been allowed to continue expanding particularly in the Government-controlled Halkevleri. Similarly, in Sweden, the number of Anglophile Societies increased from 37 in late 1943 to 51 in 1945 which, though in a democratic country, shows that the Council must have been continuing its work in a way which was acceptable and welcomed by the Swedish people and Government.[41] The Council's work in Sweden came under pressure when the English watercolour exhibition in a number of cities in the country attracted, what was viewed in London as, a small number of visitors – 12,610. Bottrall was keen to point out that in a population of just one-seventh of the size of Britain, this was actually quite high, and proportionally would have produced an audience of 88,270, if it was held in Britain. Nevertheless, the criticism from London showed that the British Council was keen to concentrate on events which were successful, and known in advance to be successful, rather than taking a gamble on success.[42]

To conclude this section, the success of the Council in the four countries where it operated is difficult to determine. What can be said is that in all four countries the work of the Council expanded during the war and in a number of cases this expansion was independent of direct support from the host country's authorities, though it always needed their tacit approval. Some events like its stamp exhibition in Stockholm were considered outright failures. Others, like its English watercolour exhibition in Sweden, were events which were regarded as disappointments, even if not an outright failures. More generally some events did not make the wider impact that could have been the case in different circumstances (such as touring lecturers to Spain, because of the lack of publicity). The Council learnt from these failures and disappointments, recognized its limitations and constraints, and therefore focused on events which were more likely to give it success. The Council understood, therefore, that the Turkish authorities were keen for the Council to place lecturers in the Halkevleri and therefore focused resource on this, which they knew would be a success. The same occurred in Sweden where the Council understood that supporting home-grown Anglophile Societies was always going to give them a good return for their money. In Spain, the Council focused on lecturers who were at the forefront of their profession, and spoke about subjects of keen interest to the Spanish authorities (nutrition, child health, British Catholicism). In Portugal they focused on touring visitors that they knew would be publicized widely in the largely pro-British press. Success, therefore, was something that the resource constraints actually made more likely, as the British Council understood that it had to get as much payback from its expenditure as possible in this time of war, in order to ensure its existence remained justified.

Towards a model of cultural propaganda

Near the beginning of this book I considered what cultural propaganda actually was from a theoretical point of view, how it differed from political propaganda, and how the different propaganda and related theories of Nicholas Cull, Joseph Nye, Jacques Ellul and Leonard Doob might be applied to the Council's work, as well as the more interdisciplinary theories of memetics and the Handicap Principle. Later chapters of this book have considered the British Council's work of cultural propaganda in practice: first, by seeing how it operated within a British context; second, how it operated on the ground; and lastly, how it was received by the local populations. In other words, those chapters attempted to see how applicable those propaganda theories were to the reality of operation. This chapter has so far summarized how the Council operated and has concluded the factors on which the success of the Council was dependent, how its success can be measured, and to what extent it was successful. The coming section is designed to draw all of those elements together into a model that will help to define the concept of cultural propaganda. This will not be a 'dictionary definition' as such, but more of a transferable framework template that can be applied to other eras and situations. This model will be divided into three key elements, which will be termed

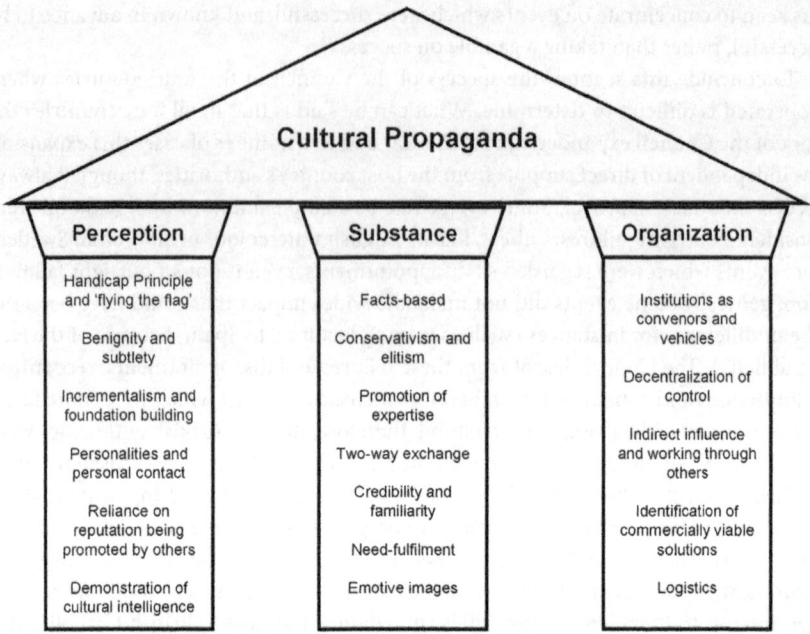

Figure 6 A model of cultural propaganda.

'pillars' to emphasize the argument that all three pillars are equally important and the edifice of cultural propaganda which they support cannot work without all three being in existence. The three pillars will be termed 'Perception', 'Substance' and 'Organization' – and are visually represented in Figure 6 (a model of cultural propaganda). Each of those pillars, it will be shown, have a number of important sub-elements.

Perception pillar

The 'Perception' pillar contains all of the elements relating to how cultural propaganda is presented and in the case of the British Council, how it presented itself and British life and thought to the people of neutral Europe.

The Handicap Principle and 'flying the flag'

It has been emphasized throughout this book that it was remarkable that the British Council actually managed to exist at all in the countries in which it operated. That it did so and kept its presence felt throughout the war (except in those countries that it had to evacuate because of military reasons) was an essential part of the cultural propaganda of the Council. This is before the actual substance of the Council's work is considered. To spend time and resources on art, music and lecture tours at a time when Britain was fighting for its survival may have raised criticism at home from the likes of Lord Beaverbrook, but doing so gave out an audacious signal to those who were the target audience for its work. Not only was it an opportunity to 'fly the flag', as was the case with the Embassies and other British organizations, but also the Zahavi Handicap Principle can be applied here. To show it could afford to 'waste' resources on cultural adventures at this time (however well targeted) demonstrated that the Council had the ability to impress, and unlock the Reputation Reflex recently proposed by Robin Wight. Harold Nicolson's remarks that he was surprised at the great reception that he received in Sweden and that he considered the reason for that reception to be that he, as an elderly MP (in his words), had made the effort to make the dangerous journey there is an obvious example of this.

What made the British Council's work even more remarkable, compared with other types of propaganda used in Second World War, was that it required a significant amount of intensive resource to make it worthwhile. Of course, other types of propaganda such as influencing the press through a press attaché at an Embassy, the production and distribution of posters and the dropping of leaflets over occupied Europe, all required resource in some form. However, the way the British Council operated from an institute, involving the organization of one event after another, with numerous staff on its books, was particularly resource intensive. Its work was not obviously propagandistic in the sense of having an obvious immediate audience reaction and return on investment that it was aiming for, unlike other forms of propaganda. Nevertheless, it targeted its resources at specific activities which it knew were more likely to bring it success. The Council was seen by the target audience as strangely, and intriguingly, benign and seemingly directionless. All that resource intensive effort for art exhibitions and music concerts was spent at a time when its audience surely thought that Britain needed all the resources it could lay its hands on to shore up the last line of defence against military attack. Britain demonstrated that it could spend significant resources on cultural propaganda, and by doing so, sent out the signal that it was in a healthy enough state to do so and definitely not a country on its last throes.

Benignity and subtlety

Creating a perception through style of operation is something that is a key feature in the success of cultural propaganda. The British Council's propaganda work was not focused on the war situation, and at times blithely ignored that there was a war on at all. Instead, it took a long-term, positive image of the British way of life and presented it in a way that was attractive to its audience and not in a way that appeared to impose a way of life or a way of thinking onto its audience. The Council merely presented its propaganda in a way the audience could take or leave (in Joseph Nye's view this would definitely be 'soft power' as no coercion or payments were necessary – the Council's propaganda was genuinely attractive because of its benignity). Admittedly, the Council focused on those areas of the British way of life which were more impressive – scientific achievements, impressive art and music – than on the mundane and potentially uninteresting (which, of course, fits under the 'Substance' pillar below). But nevertheless that more impressive image of Britain was not in itself enough – it is probably fair to say that most propaganda is going to deliberately focus on impressive issues when representing a way of life – so the difference in terms of taking a subtle approach, instead of a patronizing and imposing one, was crucial in getting a more profound response from the audience. Benignity and subtlety therefore may not have such an immediate impact, but their impacts are more likely to last longer.

Incrementalism and foundation building

Connected with the benignity point above, cultural propaganda must be a slow, incremental process, with one event building on the success of the previous event. No one particular event is important enough on its own, but the cumulative effect of a constant stream of events (as much as is practical) is very important. Indeed, too great a focus given to one particular event could invoke censorship restrictions, or a counter propaganda campaign, whereas an incremental approach, just below the radar of the censor's view, can continue successfully without disruption.

Creating a perception and presence through cultural propaganda, also provides a foundation upon which other propaganda can build. Without it political propaganda would often have little effect because the latent need for it, created by the advanced guard of cultural propaganda among the audience, would not exist. This links very well with the ideas of Ellul and Doob in their proposed 'pre' or 'sub' propaganda paving the way for the main propaganda. While it has been argued that cultural propaganda is actually far more than just 'pre' or 'sub' propaganda, and should be seen as central to general propaganda efforts, it can also provide the basis for other 'main' forms of propaganda as well.

Personalities and personal contact

'Personalities and personal contact' has a number of different facets. First, it is important to ensure that the individuals representing a culture are accepted both by the country they are being sent to and by others in the culture they are representing, as being good and true representatives of that culture. As has been shown in this book, this is not always easy to achieve. Walter Starkie, for example, was not even British formally, and this fact played a part in a certain suspicion among the British establishment as to whether he was a reliable and accurate representative for British culture. However, the Spanish Government accepted him as a *persona grata* and found it very difficult not to accept his presence in Madrid, given that he was an expert on many aspects of Spanish culture and highly respected in Madrid society. Many have commented that, had the Council been represented by anyone else in Madrid, the successes it would have made would have been severely limited and perhaps the Council's very existence in the Spanish capital would have been short-lived. These are counterfactual arguments, the details of which clearly cannot be known, but the overall point remains that choosing the right personalities is a key factor in cultural propaganda.

The second point to make here is the personal contact made by cultural representatives is crucial for the spread of cultural propaganda, because most people are likely to be influenced by the arguments of people they know personally and trust – and who can spread propaganda by word-of-mouth. Word-of-mouth propaganda spreads effectively, is uncensorable and has a certain level of fidelity of message even after a number of transmissions from one person to the next. Historians and other commentators have often overlooked word-of-mouth propaganda because it is intangible, a 'writ in water', and its effects are difficult to assess, but it is most definitely effective in getting a message through to those who it is directed at, and then passed on again.

Reliance on reputation being promoted by others

Linked with word-of-mouth propaganda, because of the way reputation spreads, cultural propaganda relies on the secondary and tertiary effects of its influence (as defined in the model of influence) for its message to be disseminated. Cultural organizations, like the British Council, cannot expect to have the resources to do all of the work they need to do themselves, and even if they do, any messages promoted would not necessarily be effective. As stated above, most people are likely to be influenced by the arguments of people they know personally and trust. The British Council could rely on a lot of the hard work of reputation building being done for it by its friends, and this would actually be a lot more appealing to those who it could not reach directly than if it tried to make the efforts itself.

Demonstration of cultural intelligence

The last point to make under the 'Perception' pillar is that a cultural organization needs to show that the country, or way of life, it is representing has cultural intelligence (i.e. ground-breaking science, pioneering art and music etc.), without its audience actually having to engage with that science, art and music directly. This is where a lot of the critics of the British Council – Beaverbrook particularly – missed the point of how the British Council was successful and was worth investing in. The cultural events were not necessarily important in themselves for all of the people the British Council was aiming to influence, but they had a further level of importance by demonstrating the cultural intelligence of Britain – and the implication being that Britain was a 'civilized' country that had interests that were worth defending. Many of the people the British Council influenced in this way may have read about the British Council's latest exhibition, or the arrival of an eminent cultural representative in the newspapers, but that was about as far as they would personally get involved with the cultural element of the British Council's work. All that was needed for them was to know that the Council was operating in this way, and that one eminent cultural person after another was visiting their country. The distance from the cultural aspect of the British Council's work may not have been quite as extreme for others. Elites may have visited exhibitions that the Council was showing, but they did not necessarily have to understand the cultural significance of the exhibition in any detail.

Substance pillar

The 'Substance' pillar contains the genuine connections and benefits that are made as part of cultural propaganda. In the British Council's case this included the links between scientific communities, the teaching of the English language and the advancement of British art and music to those elites who appreciated the art and music for its own sake, and not as part of a wider propaganda war. It is true that political propaganda can have substance, but it has been argued in this book that it is not as essential in political propaganda as it is in cultural propaganda, simply because of the timescales involved and the mode of operation – that being one of slow, incremental but profound maintenance and extension of influence.

Facts-based

Cultural propaganda has to be based on facts. It is not there as a deception tool, or as a way of creating an image of the country that is not based on the truth. It can, as mentioned in the 'benignity and subtlety' section under the Perception pillar, focus on the elements of that country and culture which are the most impressive, and thereby provide a joined up story of constant cultural success, rather than a mundane story of everyday life, but those cultural successes have to be real. If there was any way in which the work of the British Council could have been shown as being false by its opponents in the German and Italian institutions, its whole credibility would have been damaged. Unlike the 'sib' campaign of the Special Operations Executive, where the rumours sent out could not be traced back to an official source (i.e. the SOE), the work of the British Council could very easily be traced back to the British Council. The SOE could afford to be deceptive and mix truth with falsehood, but it was not something the British Council could afford to do. It was an overt, long-term operation that needed to be based on facts.

Conservativism and elitism

Being long-term in nature, cultural propaganda has to be able to stand the test of time and often this means a conservative and old-fashioned substance that is known already to be robust and worth investing time and effort to promote. It also tends to dictate who the audience is likely to be in the short-term – for the British Council these were people who were going to be receptive to conservative and old-fashioned pro-British 'substance' (the pro-British elites). Their support can be more easily entrenched before the process of spreading influence to other audiences can commence. Focusing on ideas and individuals that have stood the test of time – such as William Shakespeare and his famous plays – is a very safe form of propaganda. To put it rather flippantly, there was no danger for the British Council of Shakespeare turning into a Communist and threatening to undermine the Council's success in promoting his plays in Falangist Spain. The British Council did mention the war occasionally, but for the main part steered clear of it, and presented an image of Britain that was a pre-war and nostalgic one – very comfortable for the audience that it was being presented to. In wartime, it was quite safe to do this as well because the likelihood of any visitor coming to Britain during the war from a neutral country, to see what Britain was 'really' like, was highly unlikely because of the travel and visa restrictions imposed during the war period.

Conservativism also fits well with the Universal Tradition Meme idea promoted by Michael Drout. The Universal Tradition Meme essentially justifies the reason for doing something because it appears has always been done in that way. By promoting nostalgic and old-fashioned substance, the British Council was helping to harbour the Universal

Tradition Meme, and was not only safe, but could be shown to be long-standing – and should, by extension, be continued. There is no need for explaining the reasons for the conservative traditions existing, as all that is needed for the Universal Tradition Meme to work is the perception that something has been done for a very long time.

Promotion of expertize

The British Council was advised on many occasions to make sure it sent only experts abroad as touring lecturers. Robert McCance noted that someone could be 'ruthlessly exposed' if they were put in front of a panel of local experts on a particular subject, and did not know their subject well enough.[43] Cultural propaganda relies on only the crème-de-la-crème of the cultural world being sent abroad, as it is only natural that the true local experts of a particular subject are the ones that will want to meet the touring lecturers, and exchange views and knowledge with them. If those local experts are not impressed, then the visit will have failed to achieve its objectives, and the reputation of the organizing body will be damaged as that view will filter through to other areas of the elite and wider masses.

For the British Council this fear of failure was acute – it simply could not afford to make mistakes in sending someone who did not know their subject well enough. It was better to send a smaller number of people who were experts, than a lot of people who were not at the forefront of their subjects. Its reputation depended on being seen to be the pinnacle of excellence in cultural terms and if damaged by sending someone who was not an expert, its whole reputation for excellence would have been very hard to rebuild.

Two-way exchange

Linked with the promotion of expertize above, is the point that cultural propaganda is often very much about showing a real sense of wanting a cultural exchange. Opinions are far more likely to be accepted by one party, if their opinions are considered and accepted by those who are trying to influence them. A clear example of the two-way exchange promoted by the British Council was the visit of Bragg to Sweden, where he not only gave a number of lectures about his work on X-rays and related subjects, but he also spoke with Swedish scientists to get their work published in British scientific journals and recognized by a wider Anglo-American scientific community.[44] The two way exchange was not always quite so obvious as in the Bragg example but could cover the talks given by Starkie in Spain on comparing the work and lives of Shakespeare and Cervantes or Vaughan Williams and de Falla. It could also include the way in which Turkish artists were given information about how artists were patronized by the state in Britain, and started to think about how that model of patronization might be applicable in Turkey.

This clearly also links with the benign and subtle approach mentioned under the 'Perception' pillar where the two-way exchange, though genuine, also plays a part in the general approach taken by the cultural propaganda organization. Two-way exchange requires an invitation to the audience to be recognized as equal cultural partners, and an invitation of this sort is clearly going to be friendly and benign. Cull clearly recognized that two-way exchange is a crucial element of public diplomacy through exchange of students particularly – although the opportunities for student exchanges during wartime were limited.

Credibility and familiarity

Mentioned earlier was the point about the need to make the British Council's cultural propaganda facts-based. This was very true, but it was not just important to make it facts-based but also to make it credible and familiar. Credibility was a key part of the British Council's work and is important for cultural propaganda generally. True, but seemingly unrealistic facts, have no place in cultural propaganda. This often means that evidence has to be provided to support the facts and this can be supplied through photographs, books, art and music – the things which make a culture tangible – to avoid any sense that the propaganda is all just assertion. In the British Council example this was one good reason to hold exhibitions where people did not just have to hear British officials talk about cultural successes (though this was extremely important for word-of-mouth transmission) but they could see, hear, touch and perhaps even smell British culture 'as it really was'.

This point has particular resonance with Drout's 'Word-to-World Fit' concept – that it is crucial for all memes to fit well into their context so that they are acceptable to the audience. This therefore makes credibility and familiarity an especially important section of the Substance pillar.[45]

Need-fulfilment

The fulfilment of a need among an audience, and perhaps a latent need, is not just something important for cultural propaganda but also for other types of propaganda, including, in particular, advertising. The British Council went out of its way to ensure it did not force something upon its audience. It either allowed its audience to choose what it wanted from the British Council (such as help in establishing Anglophile Societies in Sweden) or analysed its audience to ensure it provided what it wanted. An example of the second point is where Starkie set up the British Institute School in Madrid teaching Froebel and Montessori style education, which was unusual, but preferred by many Spanish parents. An interesting example of where the British Council did not get this right was the organization of a stamp exhibition in Stockholm which was poorly attended, but when it was re-constituted in Madrid, it was a great success. The needs of the different audiences had to be analysed carefully to ensure that the right exhibitions went to the right places. In some of the activities the British Council had the official backing of the local Government – the work in the Halkevleri, for example, was very much supported by the Minister of Education in Turkey – and its success there was much more certain than if it had gone ahead with setting up its own institutions offering English courses – something that was not needed or wanted in Turkey. To an extent this goes back to the 'one-size-fits-all' and bespoke approach argument outlined earlier where there was always going to be a tension between the preferred economy of scale advantages of the 'one-size-fits-all' approach and the preferred way of working to make the propaganda as appropriate for the audience as possible, through a bespoke approach.

Emotive images

Lastly under the 'Substance' pillar, and something that has been touched upon by the other points above, is the need to make that the substance of cultural propaganda attractive and emotive. For the British Council, the everyday British way of life may be more representative of Britain, but it was not something that was going to be appealing to the audiences it was aiming at. It needed, instead, to focus on the achievements (albeit facts-based, credible and familiar) of Britain and give people a real reason for showing sympathy with the country. However, it was not in itself enough to focus on achievements, but it had to make those positive achievements attractive through a set of propaganda tools – the art exhibitions, music concerts, publications and touring lecturers – and make those events engaging for the audience. An example of this was Dudley Stamp's description of Britain in the *Face of Britain* booklet produced by the Council.[46] He used emotive imagery to engage his readers and draw them into an emotive sympathy with Britain.

Organization pillar

The 'Organization' pillar is in the model of cultural propaganda to emphasize the fact that cultural propaganda is not something which just happens in the way of Jacques Ellul's 'sociological propaganda' (which is naturally self-perpetuating) but needs to be directed and encouraged. Of course, many types of propaganda need an organizing body and so organization in itself is not unique for cultural propaganda. The sub-sections below will demonstrate what type of organization is necessary – the institutions, the physical logistics of transportation of materials and people, etc. – to make cultural propaganda different from those other forms of propaganda.

Institutions as convenors and vehicles

Earlier it was mentioned that the theory of memetics, which proposes that culture can be viewed as replicating units passing from one person to the next, mutating slowly over time, had also suggested the existence of 'meme vehicles'. Vehicles are used by memes to get them into a situation, or preserve them in a situation they would not be able to arrive at on their own. Vehicles are used, therefore, for the preservation and propagation of those memes.[47] This book then suggested that the need for a 'vehicle' – in other words the Council itself as an organizing body and more specifically the institute buildings – is the element that distinguishes cultural propaganda from sociological propaganda.

Theoretically, memetics conceivably works in both situations – with or without a vehicle – but in the British Council case study the vehicle was needed to perpetuate the units of culture because those units of culture were being injected into an alien and often hostile society and could easily have been crowded out. The institutions provided a focal point for the British Council activities, and though the Council operated through other organizations and placed British Council lecturers in schools and universities it tended to have a central location as its headquarters in a particular country. This had a benefit of drawing people together into a safe haven if they felt the local society was alien and hostile to them, or simply providing a convenient place where people could talk and exchange ideas and thoughts about a range of issues. This was regardless of whether the society outside the institute building was hostile to them or not. Word-of-mouth propaganda, as stated previously, could easily spread in these situations in the margins of cultural events and it was not the culture element of the cultural events that was necessarily important, but more the fact that people were drawn together.

Decentralization of control

The war situation meant that communication difficulties were rife in the British Council's operation and though the British Council may have wanted to direct all of its work from London, it simply could not do so for practical reasons. Often the representatives out in Madrid, Lisbon, Stockholm and Ankara were left for days, weeks or even months without any, or any meaningful contact, with London. Telegrams could be used instead of transporting correspondence to and from Britain, but were costly and use of the telegraph lines were restricted on a regular basis for the more immediate need of the Embassies. Materials and people took even longer to arrive, and were even more costly to transport. What this meant was that the British Council relied on its local representatives to make their own pragmatic decisions depending on the local situation and was forced to operate a decentralized policy.

Even if the war situation had not been so restrictive for British Council operations, the decentralized model worked well for its cultural propaganda as the British Council concentrated on fulfilling the needs of the local population rather than determining it centrally. At the end of the war, the way the Council operated in each of the four countries focused on in this book was very different. In Turkey, there was a concentration on placing English and other subject teachers in Turkish institutions, primarily the Halkevleri and Universities. In Sweden, there was a concentration of working through Anglophile Societies. In Spain there was a concentration on working from the institute buildings themselves and providing a variety of cultural events from those premises. In Portugal, there was a concentration of touring lecturers speaking at Portuguese institutions with a great deal of publicity in the Portuguese Press. Taking this decentralized approach was not only necessary, therefore, but also sensible and effective from a propaganda point of view to match the needs of the local situation.

Indirect influence and working through others

As has been stated, the institutes needed to work as vehicles for cultural propaganda and centres which drew people together. An element stressed throughout this book was the importance of working through other institutions which the organizing body does not control directly. This has a number of benefits for the cultural propaganda organization by being able to reach out beyond its natural audience (such as with the example of *Bonniers Litterära Magasin* being distributed in occupied Norway and Denmark) and having a far greater influence if its virtues are being extolled by an influential local figure rather than directly. There was actually very little that the British Council could do to reach indifferent and hostile elites directly – it tended to be more of a case of waiting for circumstances to change for those elites to be interested in the British Council's work, or of reaching them indirectly through the pro-British elites in the manner outlined in the model of influence. The Anglophile Societies established in Sweden and the placing of British Council lecturers in Turkish institutions are particularly good examples of how the Council worked through others. By being able to show that it had official backing in Turkey, and had the support of the local community in Sweden, the British Council was able to have far greater influence than if it had only set up its own institutions and worked from a degree of isolation. Circumstances were different, of course, in Madrid where the Council was not allowed to work outside of the institute building for many years, but the Council was still able to influence the pro-British elites who arrived there through Spanish-style receptions (i.e. the *tertulias*) who would then proceed to relay the message of the Council outside of the institute building walls.

Identification of commercially viable solutions

To an extent the 'need fulfilment' section under the 'Substance' pillar (which covered the actual propaganda needs of the audience) has to be coupled with an understanding of the economic and commercial needs of the audience in order to work successfully. Of course, a large part of the Council's work was done on a 'free at the point of use' basis and was funded by the grant provided by the Treasury. Examples include the cocktail parties, book exhibitions, the talks of the touring lecturers – but it could not rely on the grant for all of its work. During the post-war period, the Council became more and more dependent on the fees it was able to extract from its audience (in particular charges for English language courses). Audiences tend to be suspicious of activities that are totally without a financial charge and expect to pay some kind of fee for something that will benefit them, otherwise they fear they will be subjected to propaganda, in the dreaded derogatory sense, rather than education. Therefore cultural organizations like the Council need to find commercially viable solutions that enable the audience to purchase the cultural propaganda. The Book Export Scheme, devised by Stanley Unwin, is clearly a good example of this where local booksellers were not made liable for excess stock.[48]

Logistics

Logistics is the key component of cultural propaganda as the events, and in particular the touring lecturers (the element that often made the British Council's work appear in the local press), would not happen without careful and proactive organization. This extended to visa applications, organization of transport, managing diaries, paying fees, organizing of venues for exhibitions, liaison with the local press, printing and distribution of invitation cards and seeking and carrying out interviews with Government Ministers to help make events happen. There are many more examples, and all of which are absolutely essential for supporting the work of the cultural propaganda itself. The British Council did not get it all right – a number of famous personalities, such as John Gielgud, did not travel abroad under its auspices and space in the diary could not be found for everything the Council wished certain personalities to do. For example, Sir Malcolm Sargent did not travel to Spain, despite the wishes and organization of Starkie. At a more mundane level, the Council's materials and equipment were often delayed in transit, being held up by transport difficulties and customs restrictions, and did not always arrive intact after the journey. However, the fact that the Council managed to do so much, and managed to convince so many famous personalities to travel abroad in its name, is testament to the logistical organization that the Council carried out behind the scenes and should not be underestimated. The logistical skill of the Council employees in organizing all of the events in a time of extreme constraints was a crucial foundation necessary for the Council's success. Although cultural propaganda may not always work in such extreme circumstances, the logistical skills of a cultural propaganda organization are perhaps one of the most essential parts of its work.

Contribution to existing literature

This book has offered a great deal to the existing historiography on the British Council and on cultural propaganda. Many books written about the Council itself have either been the 'official version' (such as Frances Donaldson's *The British Council: the first fifty years*) covering a large chronological sweep of the Council's work, have focused on periods other than Second World War (such as Philip Taylor's *The Projection of Britain* which examined the Council's work during the 1930s), or have considered only certain aspects of the Council's work during the war itself (such as the work in Spain and Walter Starkie (Jacqueline Hurtley and Jean François Berdah) or Portugal and George West (Alison Roberts)).[49] No book to date has attempted to tell the story of the Council's work across Europe during Second World War and compare and contrast its work in the four countries in which it operated and analyse its successes and failures during this period. A previous PhD thesis from 1982 at the University of Leeds by Diana Eastment, titled *The policies and position of the British Council from the outbreak of war to 1950* and a study undertaken by D. W. Ellwood, published in the same year, did not focus on the propaganda aspects of the British Council's work (the work of Starkie in Spain covered just a few pages), but its changing relationship within the British Government.[50] Until now, no examination has taken place of non-British sources which are essential to understanding the view from the other side.

Many of the contributions this book has made were summarized in the introductory chapter, but one last and very important contribution is the construction in this chapter of a model of cultural propaganda bringing together all of the elements of the British Council's work. Construction of a model of cultural propaganda has not been attempted before and has been designed to show the equal importance of Perception, Substance and Organization in the British Council's cultural propaganda work. It has not been the purpose or aim of this book to examine how well the model fits with other examples of cultural propaganda, but merely to construct it from the British Council case study examined here. However, there are clear links that can be seen with the work of the other institutions operating in neutral Europe alongside the British

Council – those of the German and Italian Governments in particular. Reports in the Spanish newspapers of the work of Ettore de Zuani, at the *Instituto de Cultura Italiana* in Madrid, demonstrates that the Italians too invited touring lecturers from Italy, and organized similar types of exhibitions to the British Council focusing on art and music. Examples include lectures in Madrid of Professor Tamberlini on 'Spanish authors and Italian actors in the 16th century' [Original Spanish in footnote], and the numerous references to music concerts at the *Instituto Alemán de Cultura* sponsoring German music.[51] Similarities can also be spotted with the work of the USIA, examined by Leo Bogart and Nicholas Cull, which operated on a very similar basis to the British Council in the post-war period and broadened the work of cultural propaganda (or 'diplomacy') into public diplomacy – although I believe that the model presented here fits very well with Cull's analysis. Its work was conducted through institutions, through other organizations, targeting elites, and demonstrating the cultural intelligence of the American people.[52] The Spanish and Swedish Governments clearly saw the British Council as an example they wished to emulate as demonstrated by Nikolas Glover and the files in the *Archivo General de la Administración*.[53] The *Alliance Française* and *Goethe Institut* are other clear examples where this model could be applied in different time periods.

For the British Council itself, it is still very much in existence today as its appearance in the news recently shows. It remains controversial in many places in the world, particularly in countries where its presence is either not wanted by the local Government (e.g. Iran), the local Government is suspicious of its true aims (e.g. Russia), or local interest groups or terrorists wish to disrupt British activity (e.g. Afghanistan).[54] Its purpose and role are often confused by those who have less antagonistic aims as well. As numerous authors have pointed out its name has often been confused by non-English-speakers with 'British consul', which has an entirely different purpose, but more importantly in many countries its promotion of British culture is seen as an official extension of the work of the British Government, when in reality it is politically non-partisan.[55] The British Council is often viewed in a similar way to how the BBC is often framed – as the 'mouthpiece' of the British Government – because both receive funds from the British taxpayer or licence-fee payer despite being editorially independent (though the percentage of public sector funding has fallen significantly for the British Council since the war period). These issues are clearly as acute now as they were when Michael Grant and the British Embassy staff in Turkey had a difference of opinion about how the Council's work would be viewed by the Turks. And yet, the Council is often also recognized as the best place to find out about Britain, opportunities to visit and study, and to receive the best English-language courses available. It is, in short, far more important abroad for people wanting to engage with Britain than many in Britain realize. Its promotion of British culture is extraordinarily profound for the relatively small amount of money that is needed from the British taxpayer to maintain it and for that reason has often been regarded, in the words of Cull, as one of the 'great bargains on the Treasury's list'.[56] These are, of course, issues which were as present during Second World War as they were during the whole of the post-war period. There is no reason, therefore, why the model of cultural propaganda that has been outlined cannot be applied to its existence today. It is, and remains, an important cultural propaganda institution and has had far greater influence and success in gaining long-term sympathy for British culture and its way of life – and has allowed much more immediate propaganda to flourish on the foundations that it has created and nurtured than its greatest critic, Lord Beaverbrook, would have ever appreciated.

Notes

Chapter 1

1 'Russia to limit British Council', *BBC News Website*, 12 December 2007. http://
news.bbc.co.uk/1/hi/world/europe/7139959.stm; 'British Council in Russian
test', BBC News Website, 3 January 2008. http://news.bbc.co.uk/go/pr/fr/-/1/
hi/world/europe/7169940.stm.;'In full: British Council statement', *BBC
News Website*, 17 January 2008. http://news.bbc.co.uk/go/pr/fr/-/1/hi/uk_
politics/7193954.stm; 'Russia row offices "to stay shut"', *BBC News Website*, 17
January 2008. http://news.bbc.co.uk/go/pr/fr/-/1/hi/uk_politics/7193186.stm.
2 'British Council in Iran "illegal"', *BBC News Website*, 5 February 2009. http://
news.bbc.co.uk/1/hi/world/middle_east/7872525.stm.
3 'Attack on British Council compound in Kabul kills 12', *BBC News Website*, 19
August 2011. www.bbc.co.uk/news/world-south-asia-14585563.
4 Donaldson, 1984, pp. 1–2.
5 Taylor, 1981.
6 Ellwood, 1982; Eastment, 1982; and Donaldson, 1984.
7 Hurtley, 1992; Berdah, 1993; Llano, 2002.
8 McLaine, 1979.
9 Ellwood, 1982, p. 61.
10 Ellul, 1973; Doob, 1950; Blackmore, 1999; Zahavi and Zahavi, 1997; Wight,
2007; Conte, 2000; Nye, 2004.

Chapter 2

1 Jowett and O' Donnell, 1999, pp. 2–3.
2 CAC BRCO 1/2, Robertson to Law, 15 July 1943.
3 CAC BRCO 1/1, Robertson to Game, 17 July 1942.
4 See, for example, TNA FO 800/322, Lloyd to Halifax, 13 September 1939.
5 Forbes Adam, 1948, pp. 284–5.
6 Mackenzie, 2002, p. 142.
7 Taylor, 1981, pp. 125–6.

8 Cull, Culbert, Welch, 2003, p. 101.

9 Cull, 2008, p. xv.

10 *Ibid.*, p. 497.

11 *Ibid.*, p. xv.

12 Nye, 2004, p. 7.

13 *Ibid.*, pp. 100–5.

14 *Ibid.*, pp. 44–68.

15 *Ibid.*, pp. 107–9.

16 See Ellul, 1973, pp. 32n5, 70–1.

17 Doob, 1950, pp. 399 and 403.

18 Ellul, 1973, p. 64.

19 *Ibid.*, p. 15.

20 Blackmore, 1999, p. 19.

21 Ellul, 1973, p. 69.

22 *Ibid.*, p. 70.

23 Dawkins, 2006, pp. 190–201; also see Blackmore, 1999, and Williams, 2002, pp. 29–30.

24 Blackmore, 1999, p. 63; Dawkins, 1976.

25 Blackmore, 1999, p. 7.

26 *Ibid.*, pp. 42–3.

27 *Ibid.*, pp. 65–6.

28 Williams, 2002, pp. 29–30. Bribiesca, 2001, pp. 29–31.

29 Drout, 2006, pp. 48–58.

30 Conte, 2000, pp. 98–109.

31 Zahavi and Zahavi, 1997, pp. xiv–xv and 223–5; Wight, 2007, pp. 10–11 and 14–15.

Chapter 3

1 Taylor, 1981, p. 127.

2 Sanders, 1975, p. 119.

3 Taylor, 2003, p. 177.

4 *Ibid.*

5 Sanders, 1975, p. 144.

6 *Ibid.*, p. 120.

7 *Ibid.*

8 Reeves, 1986, p. 14.

9 Sanders, 1975, p. 139.

10 *Ibid.*, pp. 141–2.

11 Messinger, 1992, p. 40.

12 Kenneth Clark, the art historian, also saw the parallels between the work of Wellington House and the British Council in November 1939. See Foss, 2007, p. 160.

13 Sanders, 1975, p. 131.

14 *Ibid.*, p. 126.

15 *Ibid.*, p. 143.

16 Taylor, 1980, pp. 896–7.

17 TNA INF 4/5, Report of committee of Department of Information, 9 April 1918.

18 Taylor, 1981, pp. 131–2.

19 Taylor, 2003, pp. 196–7.

20 Taylor, 1981, pp. 132–3.

21 *Ibid.*, pp. 138–9.

22 TNA FO 371/14178, 'Report of the British Economic Mission to South America' 18 January 1930, p. 6. Also see Donaldson, 1984, p. 18; and Taylor, 1981, p. 139.

23 Donaldson, 1984, pp. 18, 21.

24 D'Abernon, 1929, pp. 570–1.

25 Donaldson, 1984, pp. 23–4; Roberts, 2008, pp. 9–10.

26 Taylor, 1981, pp. 139–40.

27 *Ibid.*, pp. 145.

28 *Ibid.*, pp. 149–50.

29 *Ibid.*, pp. 125–6.

30 See *Ibid.*, pp. 127, 136 and 143.

31 Michels, 2004, p. 207.

32 *Ibid.*, p. 224.

33 *Ibid.*, p. 212.

34 The words 'English' and 'British' were often interchangeable in the German language at this time.

35 Thierfelder, 1940, pp. 64–5.

36 Michels, 2004, p. 222. Interestingly, Thierfelder managed to reassert his influence on German cultural policy after the Second World War by demonstrating that the Deutsche Akademie was not a Nazi institution. Thierfelder was the driving force behind the reformation of the Deutsche Akademie, renamed the Goethe-Institut, in 1951.

37 *Ibid.*, pp. 223–4.

38 Forbes Adam, 1948, p. 285.

39 Nicolson, 1955, pp. 4–5.

40 Donaldson, 1984, p. 2.

41 'Our vision, purpose and values', *British Council website* www.britishcouncil.org/new/freedom-of-information/information-guide/who-we-are-and-what-we-do/vision-purpose-and-values/.

42 Donaldson, 1984, pp. 377–81 (Appendix 4); Taylor, 1981, pp. 154–60.

43 White, 1965, pp. 19–20.

44 See Corse, 2011, Appendix A.

45 Taylor, 1981, p. 162.

46 *Ibid.*, pp. 165, 168.

47 *Ibid.*, pp. 167–8.

48 *Ibid.*, p. 165; TNA FO 370/634, Eden to Churchill, 20 May 1941.

49 Donaldson, 1984, p. 1.

50 *Ibid.*, pp. 377–8 (Appendix 4).

51 See British Film Institute, Film & TV Database at www.bfi.org.uk/filmtvinfo/ftvdb/.

52 Donaldson, 1984, p. 368 (Appendix 2).

53 Taylor, 2003, p. 178; Also see Malvern, 2004, pp. 21–2.

54 See Bogart, 1995, p. 56.

55 Greig, 1944.

56 Bogart, 1995, p. 104.

57 See White, 1965, pp. 26–9.

58 There is often an argument about whether Turkey should be regarded as a European or Asian nation – for the purposes of this book, I have defined it as European.

59 TNA BW 82/9, 'The British Council: Report for Fourth Quarter, 1940', January 1941, p. 17.

60 See Stone, 2005, pp. 127–47.

61 Knatchbull-Hugessen, 1949, pp. 146–7; Hale, 2000, p. 79.

62 See Tennant, 1992, pp. 14–15, 20–2, 25–9.

63 See, for example, Roberts, 2008, p. 29.

64 Bogart, 1995, p. 62.

65 Roberts, 2008, p. 29.

66 See notes on Bolshevik agitators in Inkeles, 1964, pp. 404–13; For notes on Goebbels's 'rumour-mongers' see Doob, 1964, pp. 516–17; Richards, 2005.

Chapter 4

1 CAC BRCO 2/2, Robertson to Eden, 14 August 1942.

2 There were four Foreign Office staff with responsibility for overseeing the Council's affairs: Charles Peake (to December 1939), Reginald Leeper (December 1939 to early 1940), Stephen Gaselee (early 1940 to May 1941) and Kenneth T. Gurney (May 1941 onwards).

3 For further references on the establishment of the Ministry of Information, see McLaine, 1979, pp. 12–33.

4 TNA FO 800/322, Lloyd to Halifax, 13 June 1939.

5 White, 1965, p. 30.

6 TNA INF 1/443, Hale to Welch, 13 September 1939.

7 TNA INF 1/443, Hale to Bamford, 29 September 1939.

8 White, 1965, p. 30.

9 TNA INF 1/443, Lloyd to Macmillan, 20 September 1939.

10 TNA INF 1/443, Note by Bamford dated 7 October 1939 on a minute by Waterford to Hodson, 3 October 1939.

11 White, 1965, p. 31.

12 TNA INF 1/443, Halifax to Simon, 12 January 1940.

13 White, 1965, p. 31.

14 Bruce Lockhart. Diary entry for 11 March 1940 in Young, 1980, p. 48.

15 TNA INF 1/444 and TNA T 161/1104, Barlow to Waterford, 12 April 1940. The 'would' and 'had' in parentheses replace 'will' and 'has' in the original to make the sentence flow.

16 White, 1965, p. 32.

17 Bruce Lockhart. Diary entry for 9 July 1940 in Young, 1980, p. 66.

18 *Daily Express*, 4 August 1939; Donaldson, 1984, p. 65.

19 Donaldson, 1984, p. 67.

20 *Ibid.*, pp. 63–7, 142–5, 306, 329 for an outline of the Beaverbrook campaign covering both wartime and the post-war periods.

21 See, for example, Greig, 1944.

22 'London Day', *Daily Telegraph*, 8 March 1940.

23 TNA INF 1/443, Hodson to Waterford, 4 October 1939.

24 White, 1965, pp. 32–3.

25 TNA PREM 4/20/3, Churchill to Bridges, 15 February 1941.

26 TNA FO 370/634, Churchill to Eden, 18 May 1941.

27 TNA FO 370/634, Eden to Churchill, 20 May 1941.

28 TNA PREM 4/20/3, Butler, 'Enclosure B. Note by the Foreign Office on Demarcation of functions between British Council and the Ministry of Information'. Attached to Bridges to Churchill, 19 February 1941.

29 TNA INF 1/444, Hodson to Waterfield, 11 March 1940.

30 See TNA HO 215/344, for details of the British Council and the organization of lectures for Prisoners of War, and TNA MAF 223/90, for details of lectures at the Carlton Hotel in Haymarket, London in May-June 1944 on 'The Administration of Food Control, Rationing and Distribution'.

31 TNA INF 1/444, Hodson to Waterfield, 11 March 1940.

32 TNA DO 35/1011/3, Bridge-Adams to Pugh, 13 August 1941. See Corse, 2008, p. 12.

33 TNA DO 35/1011/3, Pugh to Bridge-Adams, 2 August 1941. See Corse, 2008, pp. 11–12. My emphasis.

34 Ó Drisceoil, 1996, p. 149; Corse, 2008, p. 12.

35 See Corse, 2008.

36 TNA INF 1/444, Eden to Reith, 4 May 1940.

37 TNA PREM 4/20/3, Duff Cooper to Churchill, 7 February 1941.

38 *Ibid.*

39 TNA FO 370/634, Eden to Churchill, 20 May 1941.

40 'Min. of Inf. is angry', *Daily Express*, 12 June 1941; 'Cassandra', *The Daily Mirror*, 14 June 1941.

41 CAC BRCO 2/5, Robertson to Riverdale, 14 July 1943.

42 CAC BRCO 1/2, Robertson to Law, 15 July 1943.

43 CAC BRCO 1/2, Robertson to Grant, 7 September 1943.

44 CAC BRCO 1/2, Robertson to Law, 15 July 1943.

45 TNA FO 370/782, Robertson to Eden, 23 December 1943.

46 TNA FO 370/782, [Author's name illegible] to Cadogan, no date - attached to Robertson to Eden, 23 December 1943.

47 CAC RBTN 1, Robertson, draft autobiography. Chapter titled 'The British Council 1941–1945: A Plea', pp. 15–16 and 18.

48 Lysaght, 1979, pp. 202–3; McLaine, 1979, pp. 189, 242–9.

49 Lysaght, 1979, pp. 163–4.

50 Eastment, 1982, p. 36.

51 Tennant, 1992, p. 109.

52 TNA INF 1/444, Hodson to the Deputy Secretary of the Ministry of Information, 15 October 1940.

53 CAC MALT 1, Mallet, unpublished memoir, p. 75 (Note: There are two different page numbers on each page of the unpublished memoir – one for the whole work, and one for the particular chapter. Page numbers used here are for the whole work).

54 Eastment, 1982, p. 36.

55 *Ibid.*, p. 39.

56 Webb, 2006; Corse, 2011, Appendix A.

57 British Council, 2007a, p. 88.

58 Eastment, 1982, p. 39.

59 White, 1965, p. 123 (Appendix C).

60 TNA INF 1/444 and TNA T 161/1104, Barlow to Waterford, 12 April 1940.

61 TNA T 161/1104, Syers, untitled note about a meeting between Syers and Lloyd on 4 March 1940. Note undated.

62 Eastment, 1982, p. 39.

63 Tennant, 1992, p. 263.

64 TNA T 161/1104, Syers to Barlow, 12 February 1940.

65 *Ibid.*

66 TNA T 161/1104, Barlow, note appended to Syers' untitled note about a meeting between Syers and Lloyd on 4 March 1940. Barlow's comments dated 5 March 1940.

67 TNA T 161/1104, Syers, note of a meeting with Leeper, 18 April 1940.

68 *Ibid.*; also see Cole, 1990, pp. 39–40 for relations between the British Council and the Treasury.

69 Eastment, 1982, p. 40.

70 *Ibid.*, p. 42.

71 CAC BRCO 1/2, Robertson to Law, 15 July 1943.

72 Eastment, 1982, pp. 44–5 citing minutes of evidence taken before the Committee of Public Accounts, 13 July 1944, paragraphs 4810 and 4816.

73 CAC BRCO 1/3, Robertson to Grant, 5 October 1943. My emphasis.

74 Eastment, 1982, pp. 45–9.

75 TNA INF 1/443, Hodson to Waterford, 4 October 1939.

76 TNA FO 371/33880, Clutton, minute titled 'The British Council in Turkey', 26 January 1942.

77 TNA BW 61/12, Cadogan to Robertson, 6 November 1941, which states the main areas of concern.

78 Richards, 2005.

79 TNA FO 371/33880, Clutton, minute titled 'The British Council in Turkey', 26 January 1942.

80 TNA FO 371/33880, Gurney, note on Clutton's minute titled 'The British Council in Turkey'. Gurney's comments dated 28 January 1942.

81 Grant, 1994, p. 79.

82 TNA FO 371/33880, Clutton, minute titled 'The British Council in Turkey', 26 January 1942.

83 TNA FO 371/33880, Knatchbull-Hugessen to Foreign Office, 14 February 1942.

84 TNA FO 371/33880, Clutton, minute titled 'The British Council in Turkey', 26 January 1942.

85 See TNA BW 61/13, File on British Council staff in Turkey, 1942.

86 Singular Halkevi, Plural Halkevleri. However, many English texts will use Halkevis as the plural.

87 TNA FO 371/33880, Clutton, minute titled 'The British Council in Turkey', 26 January 1942.

88 Eastment, 1982, p. 10.

89 Ritchie, 2004, pp. 42–3.

90 Gardner, Loren and Heston, 1986. Original Spanish: 'Algunos doctores apuntaron ayer la posibilidad de que Walter Starquie [sic – Starkie], un hispanista que fue agregado cultural de la Embajada británica y miembro del servicio de espionaje de su país, fuera la persona encargada de contactar con los miembros del Ejército aliado que pasaban por España'.

91 Starkie de Herrero, 1986. Original Spanish: 'Esta frase . . . contituye una grave ofensa para el honor y el buem nombre de mi padre . . . , y rechazo de forma categórica y absoluta tal alegación, totalmente infundada y realmente grotesca . . . una mera y ruin difamación'.

92 Martinez de Vicente, 2005.

93 Burns, 2009, p. 252.

94 Gordon, email to author, 20 May 2008.

95 Starkie's papers were sold at auction in January 1987 without the family's knowledge by an unknown buyer from an unknown seller. See Cañas, 1987; Balson, e-mail to author, 27 October 2008. Manuel Balson and David Butler (both residents of Madrid) believe the 'archive' was a reference to books as opposed to correspondence and other documents.

96 TNA BW 56/3. Starkie to Wiggin, 10 October 1941.

97 Tennant, 1992, p. 109.

98 Foot, 'Preface', in Tennant, 1992, p. xi; Also see Mackenzie, 2002, p. 200.

99 Clark, 1977, pp. 48–9 and 51.

100 Tennant, 1992, p. 262.

101 Bottrall, e-mail to author, 29 September 2008.

102 White, 1965, pp. 34–5.

103 Jeffery, 2010, p. 603.

104 TNA HLG 52/1174, Note on a meeting between Longden and Tallents, 20 July 1943; Minutes of a meeting between Longden, Tallents and Holford titled 'British Council – Turkey Exhibition', 22 October 1943.

105 TNA HLG 52/1174, Tallents, note of meeting with Grant and Longden on 30 November 1943. Note dated 1 December 1943.

106 TNA HLG 52/1174, Note on a meeting between Longden and Tallents, 20 July 1943; and Tallents, 'L.C.C. Exhibition', 29 July 1943.

107 TNA HLG 52/1174, Tallents, minute dated 16 August 1943; Holford, minute dated 28 August 1943; Note by Tallents, 22 October 1943.

108 TNA HLG 52/1174, Longden to Tallents, 29 December 1943.

109 TNA HLG 52/1174, Longden to Tallents, 2 December 1943.

110 TNA HLG 52/1174, Tallents to Kendrew, 2 November 1944.

111 TNA HLG 52/1174, Tallents, minute titled 'Planning Exhibition for Turkey', 3 September 1943.

112 TNA HLG 52/1174, Holt to Tallents, 30 October 1944.

113 Thirsk, letter to author, 16 September 2008.

114 *Ibid.*

115 *Ibid.*

116 *Ibid.*

117 *Ibid.*

118 White, 1965, p. 46.

119 *Ibid.*

120 *Ibid.*

121 Unwin, 1960, pp. 417–18.

122 See Bruce Lockhart, diary entry for 9 July 1940 in Young, 1980, p. 66.

123 CAC BRCO 1/4, Anonymous MP, note about Crowther. Attached to letter from Ramsden to Robertson, 16 December 1944.

124 CAC BRCO 1/4, Robertson to Ramsden, 20 December 1944.

125 CAC BRCO 1/4, Desmond to Robertson, 2 April 1945.

126 CAC BRCO 1/4, Robertson to Desmond, 10 April 1945.

127 TNA BW 80/1, Minutes of the 26th Meeting of the Music Committee, 24 October 1941.

128 TNA BW 80/1, Minutes of the 33rd Meeting of the Music Committee, 27 October 1942.

129 TNA BW 52/9, Henn-Collins, minute dated 3 June 1943.

130 TNA BW 52/9, Shillan to Henn-Collins, 28 May 1943.

131 TNA BW 52/9, Henn-Collins to West, 7 June 1943. Henn-Collins's emphasis.

132 Liborio, 1943. Original Portuguese: 'Philippe Newman possue excepcionais faculdades de solista: assombroso manejo do arco, técnica perfeita da mão esquerdo, sonoridade volumosa e doce, variedade de timbres e de efeitos de ataque surpreendente'.

133 'O violinista Philippe Newman no Instituto Britânico', *Jornal do Comércio*, 19 March 1944.

134 TNA BW 56/9, Coward to Bridge-Adams, 23 May 1942.

135 CAC BRCO 1/3, Robertson to Hopkinson, 5 November 1943.

136 *Ibid.*

137 Rey-Ximena, 2008.

138 Rey-Ximena, 2009. pp. 10–11, 130, 158–9, 178–9; Burns, 2009, pp. 256–64.

139 British Council, 1955, pp. 47–52 (Appendices A, B and C).

140 TNA FD 1/6665, McCance to Mellanby, 12 November 1942.

141 TNA FD 1/6665, Jones to Mellanby, 28 October 1942.

142 *Ibid*; also see TNA FD 1/6665, 'Extract from Dr. N. Howard Jones's letter to Sir Edward Mellanby', 4 November 1942.

143 TNA FD 1/6665, McCance, 'Report of Dr. R. A. McCance on his visit to the Iberian Peninsula', received 17 June 1943. Reference to Starkie and West p. 1.

144 CAC BRCO 2/2, Eliot to Robertson, 9 June 1942.

145 CAC BRCO 1/2, Robertson to Gielgud, 23 December 1942.

146 CAC BRCO 1/1, Robertson to Starkie, 2 July 1942.

147 Bottrall, email to author, 29 September 2008.

148 CAC MALT 1, Mallet, unpublished memoir, p. 142.

149 See the differences between the Quarterly Reports on Lectures and Music Tours in early 1943 and later 1943 in TNA BW 82/9. Some of the difference may be due to seasonal changes – there were generally less tours in the summer.

150 Unwin, 1960, pp. 421–2.

151 *Ibid*, p. 422.

152 TNA BW 78/1, Minutes from Fine Arts Committee Meetings 15 to 25.

153 TNA BW 80/1, Minutes from Music Committee Meetings 24 to 49.

154 TNA BW 70/1 and 70/2, Minutes from Books and Periodicals Committee Meetings 14 to 67.

155 HKRC TGA 8812/1/1/17, Longden to Clark, undated but between two related letters dated 6 and 20 December 1943 in the file.

156 See HKRC TGA 7050/163, Longden to Nash, 11 August 1938; HKRC TGA 7050/172, Somerville to Nash, 7 May 1941; HKRC TGA 7050/173, Somerville to Nash, 3 July 1941; HKRC TGA 7050/176, Lindsay, to Nash, 13 February 1942; HKRC TGA 7050/178, Longden to Nash, 30 November 1942; HKRC TGA 7050/181, Longden to Nash, 10 May 1943; HKRC TGA 7050/184, Longden to Nash, 18 September 1944; HKRC TGA 7050/185, Longden to Nash, 17 October 1944; HKRC TGA 7050/187, Longden to Nash, 15 November 1944.

157 HKRC TGA 7050/187, Longden to Nash, 15 November 1944.

158 TNA BW 70/2, Minutes of the 56th Meeting of the Books and Periodicals Committee, 13 January 1944.

159 Baldwin, 1940; Hamilton, 1940b.

160 TNA BW 70/2, Minutes of the 57th Meeting of the Books and Periodicals Committee, 10 February 1944.

161 *Ibid.*

162 HKRC TGA 8812/1/1/17, Clark to Beddington, 24 December 1943. Clark's reference was actually with regard to American audiences but can be read as his opinion for neutral countries as well.

163 Unwin, 1960, p. 437.

164 Baldwin, 1941, pictures between pages 16 and 17, titled 'Obreros de una fábrica de municiones rodeando a Ernest Bevin' and 'Un congreso sindical. Las "Trade Unions" nacieron en un pueblecito inglés'.

165 TNA BW 57/1, King, remarks dated February 1943 attached to a letter from Bottrall to Blake, 2 March 1943.

166 Glover, 2011, pp. 18–19.

167 Cross, 1977, p. 311.

168 *Ibid*, p. 322.

169 Hoare, 1946, p. 17; Also see Hurtley, 1992, p. 39.

170 Hoare, 1946, p. 16; Cross, 1977, p. 324.

171 Starkie, 1940, p. 392.

172 Hurtley, 2005, p. 61.

173 Gordon, e-mail to author, 20 May 2008.

174 Gordon, e-mail to author, 11 September 2009.

175 Hurtley, 2005, p. 61.

176 TNA BW 56/8, White to Starkie, 4 October 1940. The telegraph states 'Have telegraphed Dublin University explaining your absence'.

177 Starkie, 1963, pp. 199, 203–4; TNA BW 56/3. Starkie to White, 24 October 1941.

178 Starkie dedicated his book *Spanish Raggle-Taggle* 'to His Grace the Duke of Berwick and Alba' – Starkie, 1934, p. 5.

179 Starkie, 1953, p. 7; Hurtley, 1992, p. 72.

180 Lysaght, 1979, pp. 163–4; Burns, 2009, p. 252 and endnote p. 370.

181 TNA BW 56/3, White to Starkie, 3 November 1941.

182 TNA BW 82/14, Starkie to Lloyd, 11 December 1940.

183 TNA BW 56/11, Lloyd to Halifax, 19 November 1940.

184 TNA FO 954/23A, Hoare, telegram titled 'Personal for Sir Malcolm Robertson from Sir S. Hoare', 12 November 1941.

185 Gordon, email to author, 20 May 2008.

186 TNA BW 56/3, Starkie to White, 2 December 1941. Starkie was unique among the British Council representatives in Europe in actually being officially affiliated to the Embassy as 'Cultural Attaché' so that he could receive protection from political inference by the Spanish authorities. See CAC BRCO 1/4 Robertson to Palairet, 2 January 1945.

187 TNA BW 56/3, Starkie to Wiggin, 10 October 1941; Howard to Wiggin, 31 October 1941.

188 Hurtley, 1992, pp. 40–41, 46–7.

189 TNA BW 56/6, Starkie to Wiggin, 25 March 1941.

190 TNA BW 56/6, Starkie to Wiggin, 1 April 1941.

191 TNA BW 56/6, Starkie to Robertson, 2 July 1941.

192 TNA BW 56/6, Starkie to Blake, 5 July 1941.

193 TNA BW 56/6, Starkie to White, 29 March 1943.

194 TNA BW 56/6, Starkie, 'Professor Starkie's official report on the arrangements made for starting the new Institute in Barcelona', 25 August 1943.

195 TNA BW 56/6, Starkie to Robertson, 4 November 1943.

196 TNA BW 56/6, Hoare, telegram to Foreign Office with a message for Starkie in London, 18 October 1943.

197 Gordon, e-mail to author, 20 May 2008.

198 Hoare, 1946, p. 21.

199 Kershaw, 2008, p. 77.

200 Hoare, 1946, p. 30.

201 Gordon, e-mail to author, 11 September 2009.

202 TNA BW 56/4, Evans to Yencken, 30 January 1942; TNA BW 52/12, 'Report by Professor B Ifor Evans on the British Institute, Madrid, January 1942', 28 January 1942; Also see TNA BW 56/4,Ramsden to Evans, 30 January 1942; Evans to Starkie, 2 February 1942; Robertson to Hoare, 2 February 1942.

203 TNA BW 56/4, Ramsden to Evans, 30 January 1942.

204 TNA BW 52/12, 'Report by Professor B Ifor Evans on the British Institute, Madrid, January 1942', 28 January 1942.

205 TNA BW 56/4, Evans to Starkie, 2 February 1942.

206 TNA BW 56/3, Howard to Wiggin, 31 October 1941.

207 TNA BW 56/4, Evans to Starkie, 2 February 1942; BW 52/12, 'Report by Professor B Ifor Evans on the British Institute, Madrid, January 1942', 28 January 1942.

208 TNA BW 56/3, Evans to Blake, 10 November 1941.

209 TNA BW 56/4, Evans to Starkie, 2 February 1942.

210 TNA BW 56/4, Robertson to Hoare, 2 February 1942.

211 TNA BW 52/12, 'Report by Professor B Ifor Evans on the British Institute, Madrid, January 1942', 28 January 1942.

212 *Ibid.*

213 TNA BW 56/10, Steegman, 'Visit to Spain and Portugal: Final Report', 3 March 1943.

214 Hoare, 1946, p. 31.

215 Thirsk, letter to author, 17 August 2008.

216 TNA BW 56/7, Starkie to White, 1 November 1946; TNA BW 56/7, Brown, 'Reuter-Feature No. 3835/D. Should an Ambassador Tell?', 1946; Also see Berdah, 1993, pp. 285–6.

217 Note about the wife of Reuters's Madrid correspondent (Mrs Wells) working for the British Institute is available in TNA BW 52/12, 'Report by Professor B. Ifor Evans on the British Institute, Madrid, January 1942', 28 January 1942.

218 Langhorne, 2004.

219 Denniston, 2004.

220 Grant, 1994, p. 65; Grant, A., telephone conversation with author, 2 July 2008.

221 Knatchbull-Hugessen, 1949, p. 147.

222 Grant, 1994, p. 51.

223 *Ibid*, pp. 58–9.

224 White, 1965, p. 46.

225 Grant, 1994, p. 59.

226 *Ibid*, pp. 60–4.

227 See Knatchbull-Hugessen, 1949; and CAC KNAT 1/13, Knatchbull-Hugessen, diary 1939–40 and KNAT 1/14, Knatchbull-Hugessen, diary 1943–4 (the diary for 1941–2 either was not written or is not the archive). Sir Hughe's handwriting is not the easiest to read, but I could only find three references to Grant or the British Council in the year 1943 – 5 January, 6 January and 13 March.

228 Grant, 1994, p. 65.

229 For example CAC BRCO 1/3, Robertson to Knatchbull-Hugessen, 1 November 1943; and CAC BRCO 2/3, Knatchbull-Hugessen to Robertson, 4 October 1943.

230 CAC BRCO 2/3, Robertson to Knatchbull-Hugessen, 30 August 1943, and Knatchbull-Hugessen to Sir Malcolm Robertson, 4 October 1943.

231 TNA BW 61/4, 'Mr. C.A.F. Dundas's Report on his tour of Turkey, August, 1940'.

232 Grant, 1994, p. 65.

233 *Ibid*, pp. 65–7.

234 TNA BW 61/12. Grant to Blake, 19 February 1941.

235 Knatchbull-Hugessen, 1949, p. 204.

236 Grant, 1994, pp. 65–7.

237 *Ibid*.

238 *Ibid*, p. 77; CAC BRCO 1/2, Grant to Robertson, 30 August 1943; and
     CAC BRCO 1/2, Grant, 'Secret and Confidential: H[is] E[xcellency] (to see
     personally)' to Knatchbull-Hugessen, 30 August 1943.

239 Grant, 1994, p. 77.

240 TNA BW 61/12, 'Mr. M. Grant's Report on the Evacuation of Council staff from
     Turkey in the event of an emergency', 22 September 1941.

241 *Ibid*.

242 TNA BW 61/12, Robertson to Cadogan, 16 October 1941.

243 TNA BW 61/12, Cadogan to Robertson, 6 November 1941.

244 TNA BW 61/12, Gurney to Knatchbull-Hugessen, 31 October 1941.

245 CAC BRCO 1/2, Grant, 'Secret and Confidential: H[is] E[xcellency] (to see
     personally)' to Knatchbull-Hugessen, 30 August 1943.

246 CAC BRCO 1/3, Grant to Robertson titled 'Reference Sir Hughe Knatchbull-
     Hugessen's personal letter of 11th October to the Chairman', 27 October 1943.

247 CAC BRCO 1/2, Grant to Robertson, 30 August 1943.

248 *Ibid*.

249 CAC BRCO 1/3, Grant to Robertson titled 'Reference Sir Hughe Knatchbull-
     Hugessen's personal letter of 11th October to the Chairman', 27 October 1943.

250 CAC BRCO 1/2, Robertson to Grant, 7 September 1943.

251 CAC BRCO 2/3, Knatchbull-Hugessen, handwritten note at the end of his letter
     to Robertson, 4 October 1943.

252 CAC BRCO 1/3, Knatchbull-Hugessen to Robertson, 11 October 1943.

253 CAC BRCO 1/3, Grant to Robertson titled 'Reference Sir Hughe Knatchbull-
     Hugessen's personal letter of 11th October to the Chairman', 27 October 1943.

254 CAC BRCO 1/3, Robertson to Grant, 5 October 1943.

255 Balfour, 2004.

256 *Ibid*; also see Spears, 1956, p. 180.

257 'Meticulous' from Balfour, 2004.

258 Roberts, 2008, p. 56.

259 TNA BW 52/3, Bridge to Selby, 29 December 1939.

260 Estorninho, interview by Smith, 2005. My thanks to Alison Roberts for sending
     me a copy of the interview transcript.

261 King's College London College Archives: West, Sidney George (1909–1987). Slide collection of Portuguese images 1934–7, 13 September 1934–6 December 1937. GB 0100 KCLCA K/PP109.

262 Roberts, 2008, p. 9.

263 *Ibid*, p. 10.

264 West, 1938, pp. 215, 221 and 222–3.

265 Roberts, 2008, pp. 29–30.

266 *Ibid*, p. 32.

267 Collins, letter to author, 24 May 2008.

268 Thirsk, letter to author, 17 August 2008.

269 'Instituto Britânico', *Diário de Notícias*, 19 November 1938.

270 TNA BW 52/3, Cowan to Pearce, 22 November 1939.

271 TNA BW 52/3, Harlech to Bridge, 10 March 1940.

272 TNA BW 52/3, Stoneham & Sons to West, 26 February 1940.

273 *Ibid*.

274 *Ibid*.

275 TNA BW 52/3, Scott to Bridge, 14 March 1940.

276 TNA BW 52/3, Cowan, 'Memorandum for the British Council on Mr. Cowan's visit to Lisbon and Oporto' enclosed in Carr to Lloyd, 26 March 1940.

277 TNA BW 56/3, McNeill-Moss to Speaight and Campkin, 3 April 1940.

278 TNA BW 52/3, [Author unclear – possibly West] to Johnstone, 4 August 1939.

279 TNA BW 52/3, White to Evans, 21 November 1940.

280 TNA BW 52/3, Haigh to White, 10 May 1941.

281 Roberts, 2008, p. 64; Also see TNA BW 56/10, Steegman, 'Visit to Spain and Portugal: Final Report', 3 March 1943.

282 For example, TNA BW 56/7, 'Report of Dr. R. A. McCance on his visit to the Iberian Peninsula' received 17 June 1943, p. 8.

283 'No Instituto Britânico: Inaugurou-se ontem a exposição de traduções portuguesas de livros Britanicos' *Jornal do Comércio*, 14 March 1944. Original Portuguese: 'Creio que todos estarão de acôrdo comigo, quando digo que a melhor maneira de conhecer um pais estranjeiro, o seu povo, a sua vida e a sua cultura – é ir até lá e ali viver. Mas quando, por infelicidade, isso não é possivel tal como sucede agora, devido ãs condições impostas pela guerra, a melhor cousa que temos a fazer é estudar a arte désse pais e, sobretudo, familiarisarmo-nos com a sua literatura'.

284 TNA BW 56/10, Steegman, 'Visit to Spain and Portugal: Final Report', 3 March 1943.

285 *Ibid*.

286 *Ibid.*

287 TNA BW 56/10, Steegman to Longden titled 'Exhibition of Engraved Portraits, and Lectures on English Portrait-Painting: Lisbon', 10 February 1943.

288 TNA BW 56/10, Steegman, 'Visit to Spain and Portugal: Final Report', 3 March 1943.

289 TNA BW 56/10, Steegman to Longden titled 'Exhibition of Engraved Portraits, and Lectures on English Portrait-Painting: Lisbon', 10 February 1943.

290 See Corse, 2011, Appendix D.

291 CAC MALT 1, Mallet, unpublished memoir, p. 40.

292 *Ibid.* See for example p. 61 where he was looking forward to working with Lord Lothian in the United States 'this entirely different type of chief'.

293 *Ibid*, p. 63.

294 *Ibid*, p. 75.

295 Tennant, 1992, pp. 8 and 262.

296 *Ibid*, p. 262.

297 CAC MALT 1, Mallet, unpublished memoir, pp. 101, 142–4, 153, 157–8.

298 Bottrall, A., email to author, 29 September 2008.

299 *Ibid.*

300 Cole, 1990, p. 153.

301 Tennant, 1992, pp. 123–4.

302 CAC MALT 1, Mallet, unpublished memoir, p. 100.

303 *Ibid*, pp. 101, 144 and 157.

304 CAC BRCO 1/2, Robertson to Mallet, 4 December 1942.

305 CAC BRCO 1/1, Robertson to Mallet, 24 June 1942.

306 Tennant, 1992, pp. 39–40.

307 HKRC TGA 8812/1/4/58, Elton to Clark, undated but early 1945.

308 HKRC TGA 9712/5/16, 'Sir Kenneth Clark's diary during his visit to Sweden, 1945', undated but probably April 1945.

309 *Ibid.*

310 HKRC TGA 8812/1/4/58, Robertson to Clark, 24 May 1945.

311 Butler, 1963, p. 221.

312 CAC BRCO 1/1, Robertson to Mallet, 21 September 1942.

313 CAC BRCO 1/1, Robertson to Mallet, 2 November 1942.

314 CAC BRCO 1/3, Robertson to Mallet, 1 November 1943.

315 TNA BW 57/4, Note titled 'Parcel No. 16: Exhibition of Modern British Water-Colours, Sweden' with covering note dated 11 January 1943.

316 TNA BW 57/4, Mallet to Longden, 10 February 1943.

317 CAC MALT 1, Mallet, unpublished memoir, pp. 157–8.

Chapter 5

1 CAC MALT 1, Mallet, unpublished memoir, p. 72.

2 Glover, 2011, p. 128.

3 TNA BW 61/4, 'Mr. C. A. F. Dundas's Report on his tour of Turkey, August, 1940'.

4 Grant, 1994, p. 81.

5 Coombs, 1988, p. 14.

6 TNA BW 56/2, Reavey to British Council, 1 March 1940.

7 See Schneider, 1994, p. 373.

8 TNA BW 52/1, West to Bridge, 21 October 1938.

9 TNA BW 52/1, 'Translation: Ministry of Foreign Affairs, Directorate General of Political and Economic Affairs Proc. 38 No. 45', 4 November 1938.

10 TNA BW 52/1, West to Bridge, 21 October 1938.

11 TNA BW 52/1, 'Translation of speech of Minister of Education at Inauguration of B. Institute', undated, but speech given on 23 November 1938.

12 For example, 'A fundação do Instituo Britânico em Portugal vem preencher uma falta que há muito se fazia sentir nas relações culturais entre os dois países aliados', *República*, 22 November 1938; and 'O Instituto Britanico em Portugal: A Inglaterra deseja tornar ainda mais solida a antiga aliança luso-britanica declarou-nos hoje lord Lloyd of Dolobran', *Diário de Manhã*, 24 November 1938.

13 'A visita de "Lord" Lloyd', *Diário de Manhã*, 23 November 1938. Original Portuguese: 'Portugal e Inglaterra – países amigos e velhos aliados – devem conhecer-se cada vez melhor e nada mais util do que o estudo para um bom e perfeito conhecimento'.

14 KCA STE 2/2/2, Steegman, travel diary for Spain and Portugal, entry for 14 December 1942.

15 'Brittiskt kulturinstitut öppnat i Stockholm'. Unclear which Swedish newspaper the cutting is from, but dated 18 December 1941. Newspaper cutting in RAS P3206.

16 'Wilhelmstrasse' was used as a shorthand for the German Government, similar to the way 'Whitehall' is used as shorthand for the British Government.

17 'Berlin vädrar Secret Service bakom teaparty'. Unclear which Swedish newspaper the cutting is from, but dated 17 December 1941. Newspaper cutting in RAS P3206. Original Swedish: 'Vid dagens presskonferens i Wilhelmstrasse förekom som enda punkt på dagordningen ecklesiastikminister Bagges tedrickning hos British Council i Stockholm. Denna procedur sages ha kastat ett traikomiskt skimmer över statsrådet som bort veta att British Council åtminstone enligt tysk uppfattning endast är en avläggare till Secret Service'.

18 'Tyskt angrepp på statsrådet Bagge', *Aftonbladet*, 18 December 1941. Newspaper cutting in RAS P3206 'Bottrall, Francis James Ronald'. Original Swedish: 'En talesman för den tyska rigsregeringen kallade det för en "politisk kullerbytta" av statsrådet Bagge att närvara vid öppnandet. British Council är ingenting annat än en engelsk spionericentral, förklarade han vidare. . . .'.

19 RAS P3206, Danielsson to von Döbeln, 12 February 1942.

20 TNA BW 57/1, King, remarks on extending British Council work in Sweden, February 1943; and TNA BW 57/1, Read, 'Report from Norrland: Autumn 1943'.

21 TNA BW 57/1, 'The British Council – Arbetarnas Bildningsförbund, Stockholm, Sweden: for the session January-April 1944'.

22 Coombs, 1988, p. 11.

23 KCA STE 2/2/2, Steegman, travel diary entry for 13 November 1942.

24 Starkie, 1934, p. 287.

25 *Ibid.*, p. 287.

26 *Ibid.*, p. 289.

27 Hurtley, 1992, p. 70.

28 KCA STE 2/2/2, Steegman, travel diary for 3 February 1943; it was similar in Istanbul – see KCA STE 2/2/4, Steegman, travel diary for Turkey and Palestine, entry for 29 February 1944.

29 TNA BW 52/12, 'Report by Professor B. Ifor Evans on the British Institute, Madrid, January, 1942', 28 January 1942.

30 TNA BW 52/3, Programme titled: 'Instituto Britânico em Portugal: Poetry Society: 17th December 1939 'Magnificence' by John Skelton'.

31 TNA BW 56/9, Starkie to Fernald, 29 July 1941; Starkie to Bridge-Adams, 21 November 1941; Traversi to Fernald, 27 January 1942.

32 TNA BW 52/12, 'Report by Professor B. Ifor Evans on the British Institute, Madrid, January, 1942', 28 January 1942.

33 Balson, email to author, 20 June 2008.

34 TNA BW 56/8, Starkie to White, 27 August 1940.

35 TNA BW 56/8, Starkie, report on the British Institute in Madrid, 3 December 1940.

36 TNA BW 56/8, Starkie to Lloyd, 28 August 1940.

37 TNA BW 56/8, Reavey to Wiggin, 30 August 1940.

38 TNA BW 56/8, Wiggin to Henn-Collins, 6 September 1940; Wiggin to Reavey, 19 September 1940; Starkie to Wiggin, 31 October 1940.

39 TNA BW 56/9, Reavey to Wiggin, 17 September 1940.

40 TNA BW 56/8, [Unclear author, but presumably Starkie] to Lloyd, 17 September 1940.

41 TNA BW 56/8, Reavey to Wiggin, 28 October 1940.

42 TNA BW 56/8, Barker to Wiggin, 17 January 1945; Corse, 2011, Appendix E.

43 TNA BW 56/8, Starkie, report on the British Institute in Madrid, 3 December 1940.

44 Balson, e-mail to author, 27 May 2008.

45 Ellul, 1973, p. 70.

46 Balson, e-mail to author, 27 May 2008; and Balson, e-mail to author, 20 June 2008.

47 Balson, e-mail to author, 27 May 2008.

48 *Ibid.*; and Balson e-mail to author, 20 June 2008.

49 TNA BW 56/8, Starkie, report on the British Institute in Madrid, 3 December 1940.

50 *Ibid.*

51 White, 1965, p. 37.

52 TNA BW 52/10, West to Shillan, 23 June 1944.

53 Roberts, 2008, pp. 57–8.

54 TNA BW 52/10, Graham to Shillan, 17 November 1944.

55 TNA BW 52/10, Thorp, 'St. Julian's School', 5 October 1944; Corse, 2011, Appendix F.

56 TNA BW 52/10, 'Memorandum: Prepared by Mr. G. L. Thorp, Headmaster of St. Julian's School, Carcavelos, and adopted by the Board of Governors on October, 22nd, 1943'.

57 TNA BW 52/10, West to Shillan, 13 January 1944.

58 TNA BW 52/10, Barkworth to Bottrall and Hutton, 21 February 1945.

59 TNA BW 52/10, Graham to Shillan, 17 November 1944.

60 TNA BW 52/10, Barkworth to Bottrall and Hutton, 21 February 1945; and Barkworth to Bottrall and Hutton, 22 February 1945.

61 TNA BW 52/10, Heron, K. to Heron, R. F., 14 July 1943. Intercepted by postal and telegraph censorship.

62 TNA BW 52/10, West to Shillan, 13 January 1944.

63 TNA BW 52/10, Campbell to Eden, 22 February 1945.

64 TNA BW 52/10, 'Report of the Committee on "Text-books for use in British Council Centres in Portugal"', 21 July 1944.

65 BCPHA: Reference c4002011. Also pictured in Roberts, 2008, between pp. 64–5.

66 TNA BW 61/6, Everett to Blake, Rose and Orton, 17 January 1945.

67 TNA BW 61/7, Thompson, 'Ingiliz Kiz Tali Mektebi – English High School for Girls, Istanbul – Beyoğlu', 15 April 1944.

68 TNA BW 61/7, Everett, 'Mr Covington's letter of March 22nd: English High School for Girls' to Blake, Evans and the Finance Division, 12 April 1944.

69 TNA BW 61/7, McNab, 'English High Schools, Istanbul (Extract from Major McNab's report, July 1944)', July 1944.

70 TNA BW 61/6, Sandrey, 'Report on the Council Scholars in the High School', 11 January 1945.

71 TNA BW 61/7, Extract from the Draft Minutes of the 99th Meeting of the Finance and Agenda Committee held on 8 February 1944. Comments by Blake on agenda item 'Turkey: High School for Girls, Istanbul'.

72 TNA BW 61/7, Everett, 'Mr Covington's letter of March 22nd: English High School for Girls' to Blake, Evans and the Finance Division, 12 April 1944.

73 TNA BW 61/7, Everett to Covington, 24 April 1944.

74 TNA BW 61/7, Note titled 'Kindergarten Equipment for the English High School for Girls, Istanbul', undated but around May 1944.

75 White, 1965, pp. 37–8.

76 TNA BW 61/8, Larke to Preece, 18 January 1943.

77 TNA BW 61/2, 'Mr. Michael Grant's Report on Turkey for the Quarter Beginning September 1st and Ending December 31st, 1941'; TNA BW 61/2, Grant to Everett, 26 November 1941 attaching a summary of teaching operations.

78 Grant, 1994, p. 65.

79 *Ibid.*

80 TNA BW 61/2, 'Mr. Michael Grant's Report on Turkey for the Quarter Beginning September 1st and Ending December 31st, 1941'. Grant's emphasis.

81 *Ibid.*

82 TNA BW 61/8, Larke to Preece, 18 January 1943.

83 TNA BW 61/8, Grant to British Council, 16 July 1943.

84 TNA BW 61/2, 'Mr. Michael Grant's Report on Turkey for the Quarter Beginning September 1st and Ending December 31st, 1941'.

85 *Ibid.*

86 *Ibid.*

87 *Ibid.*

88 TNA BW 61/2, 'Teaching Statistics: Private Lessons' – annex to Grant, 'British Council in Turkey – Quarterly Teaching Report April-June 1942', 10 July 1942.

89   TNA BW 61/2, Grant, 'British Council in Turkey – Quarterly Teaching Report April-June 1942', 10 July 1942.

90   TNA BW 62/2, Grant, report on Crews, received by British Council on 29 June 1942.

91   TNA BW 61/2, Jago, 'Notes on Section B of Memorandum on Teaching Methods', received 10 July 1942.

92   *Ibid.*

93   Ogden, 1930.

94   White, 1965, p. 47.

95   'Govt. accept Basic English: B.B.C. to try it out', *Daily Mirror*, 10 March 1944, pp. 4–5; Grant, 1994, p. 68.

96   Orwell, 1949 – see, particularly, 'Appendix: the Principles of Newspeak' pp. 312–26; Illich and Sanders, 1988, p. 109; Orwell, 1946.

97   TNA BW 61/2, Everett to Covington, 18 September 1942.

98   TNA BW 61/2, Grant to Orton, 16 February 1943; TNA BW 61/2, Cover page and contents of Leech, C. and Leech, M., *Ingiliz Ders Kitabi*, 28 January 1943; TNA BW 61/2, Price to Grant, 30 March 1943.

99   White, 1965, pp. 37–8.

100   TNA BW 57/1, 'Mr Frederick A L Charlesworth's Report of the First British Council-Arbetarnas Bildningsförbundets Summer School, Brunnsvik, 1943'.

101   *Ibid.*

102   *Ibid.*

103   *Ibid.*

104   TNA BW 57/1, Timetable titled 'The Brunnsvik A. B. F. Course, from the 1st to the 13th of August 1943'.

105   See Donaldson, 1984, pp. 63–7.

106   TNA BW 57/1, Bottrall to Blake, 5 August 1943.

107   TNA BW 57/1, 'The British Council – Arbetarnas Bildningsförbund, Sweden: Mr F. A. L. Charlesworth's Report for the Session January–April 1943'.

108   TNA BW 57/1, King, remarks on extending British Council work in Sweden. Enclosed with letter from Bottrall to Blake, 2 March 1943.

109   Grant, 1994, p. 81, also see pp. 99–105.

110   Unwin, 1960, p. 419.

111   White, 1965, p. 39.

112   HKRC TGA 9712, Note titled 'The British Council' attached to letter from Fine Arts Department to Wall with a request to 'include it in this issue of your bulletin [the *Fine Art Trade Guild Bulletin*]', 9 November 1943.

113   KCA JDH 26/9, Bottrall to Hayward, 26 December 1942.

114   White, 1965, pp. 38–9.

115   *Ibid*, p. 39; TNA BW 82/9, 'The British Council: Report for Fourth Quarter, 1940', January 1941 p. 17.

116   Unwin, 1960, p. 419.

117   Coombs, 1988, p. 21.

118   Roberts, 2008, p. 64; Also see TNA BW 56/10, Steegman, 'Visit to Spain and Portugal: Final Report', 3 March 1943; TNA BW 56/10, Steegman to Longden titled 'Exhibition of Engraved Portraits, and Lectures on English Portrait-Painting: Lisbon', 10 February 1943.

119   TNA BW 56/10, Steegman, 'Visit to Spain and Portugal: Final Report', 3 March 1943.

120   Roberts, 2008, p. 64.

121   'Kind Wishes from The Rt. Hon. Sir Malcolm Robertson, G. C. M. G., K. B. E., M. P., Chairman of the British Council', *Anglo-Portuguese News*, 17 June 1941.

122   Brass, 1941.

123   There are a few illustrative examples of the three types of article that appeared in the Portuguese press when reporting the visits of a number of lecturers and musicians to Portugal in January and February 1943, which are useful to examine. First, there were short articles announcing the arrival of Dr Robert McCance, an expert on nutrition at Cambridge University (see 'Chegou hoje a Lisboa o sábio inglês dr. McCance', *Diário de Lisboa*, 16 February 1943). This very short press notice was followed by more detailed articles once the event had actually taken place (see 'O prof. dr. McCance falou, ontem, no Hospital de Santo António sôbre a «Fisiologia da infância e a sua relação com a medicina preventiva', *O Comércio do Porto*, 26 February 1943) which was accompanied by pictures showing McCance lecturing at the Hospital of Santo António. For the third type of article, an interview, a good example comes from *Diário Popular* where Sir Malcolm Sargent, who arrived in Portugal just prior to McCance, was interviewed by a journalist from the newspaper (see 'O Dr. Malcolm Sargent chefe de orquestra ingles a quem se deve o desenvolvimento das massas corais nos últimos anos, está em Lisboa onde vem dirigir a Orquestra da Emissora em três concertos em São Carlos', *Diário Popular*, 11 January 1943).

124   'Kultursändebud och känd skald lämnar Sverige' and 'Bibliotek på 3.000 band Kom med Englandsflyget', *Dagens nyheter*, 1 September 1944. Newspaper cutting in RAS P3206.

125   Corse, 2011, Appendix D.

126 KCA JDH 26/9, Bottrall to Hayward, 26 December 1942.

127 *Ibid.*

128 'Nya utländska böcker', *Bonniers Litterära Magasin*, årg IX, Nr. 6, June–August 1940, pp. 502–4.

129 For example, G. Greene's *The Power and the Glory*, R. Heppenstall's *The Blaze of Noon*, J. Rhys's *Good Morning, Midnight* and D. Thomas's *Portrait of the Artist as a Young Dog* were reviewed in Lundkvist, 1940.

130 As was noted earlier for the German language, 'English' and 'British' or 'England' and 'Britain' were interchangeable in the Swedish language as well at this time. The fact that Thomas was Welsh was lost in translation.

131 Lundkvist, 1940, p. 460.

132 CAC MALT 1, Mallet, unpublished memoir, p. 143.

133 Bogart, 1995, p. 185.

134 Corse, 2008 – see particularly the conclusion – pp. 175–6.

135 Ó Drisceoil, 1996, p. 89.

136 Corse, 2008.

137 Richards, 2005.

138 *Ibid.*

139 TNA FO 898/69, 'Political Warfare Executive – Rumours' (author unclear), 7 February 1942.

140 Schneider, 1994, p. 376. Original Spanish: 'Buscar en el mismo ámbito confidentes para la diffusion de consignas por el sistema "boca a boca" (*Flüsterpropaganda*), en las colas en tiendas y paradas de autobuses, en bares, restaurantes, etc'.

141 See Inkeles, 1964, pp. 404–13; also see Doob, 1964, pp. 516–17 for an example of how Joseph Goebbels used the technique within Germany itself.

142 Inkeles, 1964, p. 405.

143 Guha, 1999, pp. 220–77.

144 Ewen, 2008. Graph shown at 8 minutes 11 seconds into Part 1 after research by Euro RSCG.

145 Rohrer, 2009.

146 '"I penned negative Amazon reviews" – Historian Figes', *BBC News website*, 24 April 2010. http://news.bbc.co.uk/1/hi/uk/8641515.stm.

147 Daley and Kendall, 1965, pp. 42–55; Brady, 2008; Hayes, 2005, p. 207.

148 Allport and Postman, 1964, pp. 398–9.

149 See TNA FO 898/71, 'PWE-Sibs (Rumours & Whispers) campaign – comebacks 1940–3'.

150 Baker White, 1955, pp. 18, 78; The British Institute in Madrid (at 17 Calle Mendez Nunez) and the Ritz Hotel in Madrid were about 0.2 miles apart by the quickest walking route, even less distance 'as the crow flies'.

151 TNA BW 56/10, Steegman to Blake, 12 December 1942.

152 CAC MALT 1, Mallet, unpublished memoir, p. 143.

153 *Ibid.*

154 CAC KNAT 1/14, Knatchbull-Hugessen, diary entry for 1 January 1943.

155 TNA BW 82/9, British Council's Quarterly Report for October-December 1943, p. 4.

156 KCA STE 2/2/2, Steegman, travel diary entry for 27 January 1943.

157 *Ibid*, diary entries for 27 and 28 January 1943.

158 Mercier, 2008, pp. ix and 111.

159 'Está em Lisboa o maestro inglês Malcolm Sargent', *Diário de Lisboa*, 11 January 1943. Original Portuguese: 'lingua primordial para a compreensão de todos os povos'.

160 KCA STE 2/2/2, Steegman, travel diary for 20 January 1943.

161 RNCM PN/224, Picture of Newman and Howard, 1943.

162 RNCM PN/91, Concert Programme titled 'Teatro Nacional de S. Carlos 30 de Junho de 1941 Concêrto Sinfónico a favor da Casa dos Intelectuais sob a direcção do maestro Frederico de Freitas com a colaboração do violinista Philippe Newman e a Orquestra Sinfónica da Emissora Nacional', 30 June 1941.

163 RNCM PN/154, 'Philip Newman in Portugal' undated, author unknown.

164 TNA BW 56/2, Concert Programme titled 'The British Institute: Recital by Ruda Firkušny, the celebrated Czechoslovakian Pianist', 13 October 1940.

165 TNA BW 56/2, Starkie, 'The British Institute, Madrid: Report of a Pianoforte recital given by the celebrated pianist Rudolph Firkusny at the British Institute on the 13th October [1940]'. Undated but written soon after the concert.

166 Llano, 2002, p. 190.

167 *Ibid*, p. 192.

168 TNA BW 82/9, British Council's Quarterly Report for April-June 1943, p. 18.

169 CAC MALT 1, Mallet, unpublished memoir, p. 143.

170 Tennant, 1992, p. 40.

171 *Ibid*, p. 267; RI W L BRAGG 70B.

172 RI W L BRAGG 70A/83, Bragg, 'Preliminary Report on tour in Sweden', 1943.

173 Glover, 2011, p. 72 – on the importance of science in Swedish culture.

174 RI W L BRAGG 70B, Bragg, diary entry for 17 April 1943. Bragg's emphasis.

175 RI W L BRAGG 70B, Bragg, diary entry for 19 April 1943.

176 'Inblick i allt mindre världar. Föredrag i Hälsingborg av nobelpristagaren sir Lawrence Bragg' *Oresund's Posten* 7 May 1943. Copy available in RI W L BRAGG 70A/263; RI W L BRAGG 70B Bragg, diary entry for 19 April 1943.

177 RI W L BRAGG 70B, Bragg, diary entry for 19 April 1943.

178 TNA FD 1/6665, McCance to Mellanby, 12 November 1942.

179 TNA FD 1/6665, 'Report of Dr. R. A. McCance on his visit to the Iberian Peninsula', undated but covering the period February–March 1943, p. 2.

180 *Ibid*, p. 3.

181 *Ibid*, p. 8.

182 *Ibid*, p. 10.

183 *Ibid*.

184 'O sábio Prof. McCance realizou ontem a sua primeira conferência', *Diário de Coimbra*, 20 February 1943. 'Conferências do Professor Inglês sr. dr. Robert McCance', *O Primeiro de Janeiro*, 21 February 1943. 'Prof. Alexander McCance', *O Comércio do Porto*, 21 February 1943.

185 TNA FD 1/6665, 'Report of Dr. R. A. McCance on his visit to the Iberian Peninsula', undated but covering the period February–March 1943, p. 2.

186 *Ibid*, p. 3.

187 *Ibid*.

188 Photograph from Michael Grant's personal photograph album.

189 KCA STE 2/2/4, Steegman, diary entry for 11 January 1944.

190 *Ibid*, entry for 9 February 1944.

191 *Ibid*, entries for 27, 28 and 29 February 1944.

192 TNA BW 56/10, Bridge-Adams to Blake, White and Longden, 5 May 1942.

193 KCA STE 2/2/4, Steegman, diary entries for 31 December 1943, 3 January 1944, 4 January 1944 and 9 February 1944.

194 TNA BW 57/4, Review of Swedish newspapers titled 'Exhibition of English Water Colours in Sweden, 1943', undated, author unclear but written by either the British Council or British Legation.

195 TNA BW 52/12, List of works being exhibited titled 'British Council: Exhibition of British Graphic Art, Lisbon, 1942'; Also see Corse, 2011, Appendix G.

196 TNA BW 56/10, Steegman, 'Madrid Exhibition of Historical Prints', undated but around August 1942.

197 *Ibid*.

198 TNA BW 56/10, 'Engraved portraits passed to Mr. Read for dispatch, 5th October, 1942 – Roll 3'.

199 TNA BW 56/10, Advertisement for Steegman's lectures by the British Institute in Madrid, November 1942.

200 KCA STE 2/2/2, Steegman's, diary entries for 19, 21 and 22 November 1942.

201 TNA BW 57/4, Bottrall to Longden, 26 May 1943.

202 *Ibid.*

203 TNA BW 57/4, Bottrall to Longden, 31 May 1943.

204 TNA BW 57/4, Bottrall to Longden, 18 June 1943.

205 TNA BW 57/4, Review of Swedish newspapers titled 'Exhibition of English Water Colours in Sweden, 1943', undated, author unclear but written by either the British Council or British Legation.

206 TNA BW 57/4, Maclagen to Longden, 18 June 1943.

207 TNA BW 57/4, Longden to Wettergren, 21 June 1943.

208 TNA BW 57/4, Bottrall to Longden, 12 July 1943.

209 TNA BW 57/4, Maclagen to Longden, 5 August 1943.

210 For example RAS P3206, Hildeby, Cleve, Nydahl and Jonsson, 'P. M. angående brittiske undersåten Kimmins', 25 February 1943.

211 RAS P3206, [Name of author difficult to read, but possibly 'Tuva Welanson'], note of monitoring that took place on 9 February 1943 at the National Museum in Stockholm, 9 February 1943.

212 TNA BW 57/4, Longden to Bottrall, 18 March 1943.

213 TNA BW 57/4, Bottrall to Longden, 2 April 1943.

214 TNA BW 82/9, 'The British Council, Report for the Fourth Quarter, 1942', January 1943, p. 3.

215 Shown in photographs from Michael Grant's personal photograph album.

216 Grant, 1994, p. 72.

217 TNA BW 52/8, 'Report of the Visit to Portugal of a delegation from the University of Oxford to confer the degree of D. C. L. on Dr. Salazar', 6 May 1941; Also see RAS P3206, [Name of author difficult to read, but possibly 'Tuva Welanson'], note of monitoring that took place on 9 February 1943 at the National Museum in Stockholm.

218 Grant, 1994, p. 79.

219 *Ibid*, pp. 78–9.

220 CAC BRCO 1/1, Robertson to Mallet, 21 September 1942; and CAC BRCO 1/1, Robertson to Mallet, 2 November 1942.

221 'London 1942'. British Council video channel on Vimeo.

222 'History of the English Language'. Vimeo.

223 'Country Town'. Vimeo.

224 'Steel goes to sea'. Vimeo.

225 'We of the West Riding'. Vimeo.
226 'Island People', Lowland Village', and 'Market Town'. Vimeo.
227 TNA BW 52/12, 'Report by Professor B Ifor Evans on the British Institute, Madrid, January 1942', 28 January 1942.
228 Hurtley, 1992, p. 31. Original Spanish: 'la adopción de Janés de una estraegia maquiavélica en unas circunstancias determinadas'.
229 *Ibid*, pp. 107–9.
230 *Ibid*, pp. 121–2.
231 *Ibid*, pp. 179–80.
232 *Ibid*, pp. 221–3.
233 *Ibid*, pp. 242, 260.
234 CAC BRCO 2/1, Churchill to Robertson, 29 September 1943.
235 Baldwin, 1941.
236 Hamilton, 1940a.
237 Robson, 1940a.
238 Keith, 1942.
239 Keith, 1940, p. 11.
240 *Ibid*, p. 16.
241 *Ibid*, pictures between pp. 16–17, and pp. 32–3; Keith, 1942, pictures between pp. 16–17, pp. 32–3, and pp. 48–9.
242 Churchill, 'This was their finest hour', 18 June 1940. Reproduced in MacArthur, 1999, p. 191.
243 Keith, 1940, p. 16.
244 Stamp, 1940, p. 11.
245 Lewis, 1940, p. 35.
246 *Ibid*, p. 39.
247 'Kultursändebud och känd skald lämnar Sverige' and 'Bibliotek på 3.000 band Kom med Englandsflyget', *Dagens nyheter*, 1 September 1944. Newspaper cutting in RAS P3206.
248 Unwin, 1960, p. 421.
249 For example, RAS P3206, Hildeby, Cleve, Nydahl and Jonsson, 'P. M. angående brittiske undersåten Kimmins', 25 February 1943.
250 Coombs, 1988, p. 13.
251 'Kultursändebud och känd skald lämnar Sverige' and 'Bibliotek på 3.000 band Kom med Englandsflyget', *Dagens nyheter*, 1 September 1944. Newspaper cutting in RAS P3206.
252 Coombs, 1988, pp. 13–14.
253 *Ibid*, p. 12.

Chapter 6

1 Grant, A., telephone conversion with author, 2 July 2008; Bottrall, A., e-mail to author, 29 September 2008.

2 TNA BW 57/1. Orton to Braden, 16 February 1943; TNA BW 57/1 Braden to Bottrall, 17 February 1943.

3 Baroja, Pío Caro. Interview with Iñaki Estaban in Estaban, 2006. Original Spanish: '. . .él fue anglófilo desde el principio, en contra del ambiente germanófilo y fascista de España'.

4 Ley, 1981, p. 10. Original Spanish: 'un triunfo decisivo'.

5 Burns, 1993, p. 102.

6 RI WL BRAGG 70A/63, Bragg to Blake, 14 May 1943. (Bragg arrived back in Britain on 13 May).

7 Grant, 1994, p. 72.

8 TNA BW 82/13, Lloyd, report of visit to Spain, diary entry 23 October 1939.

9 MAEC AG Leg R 5261/8, Lloyd to Alba, 14 February 1940; Alba to Beigbeder, 15 February 1940.

10 TNA BW 82/13, Lloyd, report of meeting with Franco on 23 October 1939, p. 7.

11 TNA BW 82/13, Lloyd, report of meeting with Beigbeder on 23 October 1939, p. 6.

12 Bowen, 2006, pp. 33–4.

13 *Ibid.*, p. 34.

14 Burns, 1993, p. 102; also see Burns, 2009, p. 252.

15 MAEC AG Leg 5261/8, Valera to Beigbeder, 19 May 1940. Original Spanish: 'que Sr. Starkie es católico e indiscutiblemente reúne méritos que en principio permiten considerarle como persona grata al Estado español'.

16 *Ibid.* Original Spanish: 'No obstante y aunque en este Departamento no obra ningún antecedente desfavorable sobre la conducta y actitud del Señor Starkie durante el Movimiento Nacional. . . [yo] suscribe estima conveniente que antes de dar repuesta a la Embajada de la Gran Bretaña se oiga el parecer del Señor Embajador en Londres'.

17 MAEC AG Leg R 5261/8, Beigbeder to Alba, 24 May 1940. Original Spanish: 'si, a su juicio, habría alguna objeción que formular contra dicho candidato'.

18 MAEC AG Leg R 5261/8, Ontiveros to Beigbeder, 14 May 1940. Report on article titled 'Offer of post in Spain for Dr. Starkie', *Irish Independent*, 14 May 1940.

19 See for example, Llano, 2002, p. 215.

20 TNA KV 4/429, Brooman-White, note for B.1.G., 8 December 1942; Bevan to 'General', 10 December 1942.

21 MAEC AG Leg R 5261/8, Alba to Ministro de Asuntos Exteriores, 6 May 1938.

22 MAEC AG Leg R 5261/8, El Subsecretario, telegram titled 'Asunto: Relaciones Culturales Inglaterra', 13 June 1938, referencing an earlier telegram of 25 May 1938.

23 MAEC AG Leg R 5261/8, Alba to Beigbeder, 15 February 1940. Original Spanish: '[L]a forma como interpretará este Gobierno nos neguemos a conceder el permiso para la apertura del Instituto Británico, he tratado de reflejar la impresión secada durante mi conversación con Lord Lloyd, quién me ha dicho que aquella negativa se consideraría aquí como gesto muy poco amistoso por nuestra parte, pues no se comprende la razón por la cual no se autoriza a Inglaterra lo permitido ya a Alemania y a Francia, sobre todo si se considera la actitud de la última hacía el Glorioso Alzamiento Nacional, en nada mas favorable a la observada por la Gran Bretaña'.

24 MAEC AG Leg R 5261/8, Alba to the Ministerio de Asuntos Exteriores, 27 May 1940. Original Spanish: 'Considero muy acertado nombramiento profesor Starkie, católico gran defensor de nuestra causa en la prensa desde el primer momento, españolista de siempre muy conocedor nuestra idioma y autor excelentes obres sobre España, académico corresponsal de la Lengua'.

25 MAEC AG Leg R 4009/1, Alba to Garvin, 14 June 1940.

26 MAEC AG Leg R 5261/8, Spanish Foreign Ministry to British Embassy, Madrid, 5 June 1940.

27 TNA BW 56/2, Reavey to Campkin, 14 June 1940.

28 TNA BW 56/2, White to Lloyd, 25 June 1940 quoting telegram from Samuel Hoare.

29 *Ibid.* with note from Lloyd to Cadogan attached at the end.

30 TNA BW 56/2, Cadogan to Hoare, 27 June 1940.

31 TNA BW 56/2, Alba to Lloyd, 27 June 1940.

32 TNA BW 56/2, Starkie to Lloyd, 23 July 1940.

33 TNA BW 56/2 'Translation of Note Verbale No. 27 addressed to His Majesty's Embassy by the Ministry of Foreign Affairs, dated: 16th February, 1940'; see Corse, 2011, Appendix I.

34 Roberts, 2008, p. 52; TNA KV 4/429 'Contacts of the Portuguese Ambassador Dr. Armindo Monteiro' undated but attached to Brooman-White, 'D. B. through B.1.A. Major Robertson [no relation to Sir Malcolm]', 10 November 1942.

35 Telo, 1990, p. 50 Original Portuguese: 'onde a inciativa é bem acolhida e encontra um público numeroso'.

36 TNA BW 52/8, 'Dr. Salazar's Speech', document undated, but delivered on 19 April 1941 at the University of Coimbra.

37 TNA BW 52/8, Campbell to Eden, 26 April 1941.

38 TNA BW 52/8, 'University of Oxford Delegation to Portugal', 28 April 1941, p. 3.

39 For example: 'A delegação de Universidade de Oxford que vem homenagear o sr. dr. Oliveria Salazar é esperada em Lisboan a Segunda-feira', *O Século*, 11 April 1941; and 'Salazar – Doutor "Honoris Causa" pela Universidade de Oxford', *Diário da Manhã*, 20 April 1941.

40 TNA BW 52/3, Harlech to Bridge, 10 March 1940.

41 TNA BW 52/3, West, translated letter to H. E. The Minister of Education, Ministerio de Educação Nacional, Lisboa, 23 November 1939.

42 TNA BW 52/3, Pacheco, memorandum, 23 November 1939. Quoted by Riler de Motta, translated letter to West, 4 December 1939.

43 TNA BW 52/3, West to Bridge, 6 December 1939.

44 TNA BW 52/3, 'Report on the Visit to Portugal of the Rt. Hon. Lord Harlech P. C. G. C. M .G. 22nd February–5th March, 1940 – Programme in Lisbon' – clearly mentions the Minister of Education 'chairing' the lecture given by Harlech.

45 Roberts, 2008, p. 61.

46 RNCM PN/154, 'Philip Newman in Portugal', undated and author unknown p. 3.

47 *Ibid.*

48 TNA BW 52/13, Gogay to Robertson, 6 November 1942.

49 Monteiro to Salazar, 26 October 1942 reproduced in Rosas, Oliveira and Barros, 1996, p. 346. Original Portuguese: 'Retorquiu Sir Malcolm, visivelmente agitado, que não concebia como a organização oficial da "Mocidade" de um país aliado da Inglaterra podia, num momento destes, aceitar convites para visitar Berlim, depois de ter feito uma peregrinação ao Marrocos de Vichy'.

50 *Ibid.* Original Portuguese: 'ataque de fúria'.

51 *Ibid.*, p. 347. Original Portuguese: 'em certo modo é seu subordinado'.

52 *Ibid.*, p. 348. Original Portuguese: 'está em vésperas de entrar na Lista Negra'.

53 'Tysk Misstänksamhet mot British Council', *Dagens Nyheter*, 19 December 1941, p. 11.

54 *Ibid.* (103 words) and 'Engelsk kulturcentral har öppnats i Stockholm', *Dagens Nyheter*, 18 December 1941, p. 19 (395 words).

55 'Tyskt angrepp på statsrådet Bagge', *Aftonbladet*, 18 December 1941. Newspaper cutting in RAS P3206. Original Swedish: 'Tyskt angrepp på statsrådet Bagge. Efterspel till öppnandet av British Council-byrån: Politisk kullerbytta'; Also see 'Brittiskt kulturinstitut öppnat i Stockholm'. Unclear which Swedish newspaper the cutting is from, but dated 18 December 1941 – newspaper cutting in

RAS P3206; and 'Berlin vädrar Secret Service bakom teaparty'. Also unclear which Swedish newspaper the cutting is from, but dated 17 December 1941 – Newspaper cutting in RAS P3206.

56 Grafström, 1989, p. 375 – entry for 18 December 1941. Original Swedish: '1. Svenske ecklesiastikministern plägar som en självfallen hövlighetsåtgärd närvara vid olika utländska kulturella manifestationer i Stockholm. Sålunda var han som bekant närvarande vid den tyska bokutställningen samt vid invigningen av den tyska skolan. 2. (i Berlinmeddelandet hade bland annat stått, att British Council vore en spionericentral) Intill dess att motsatsen bevisas eller göres sannolikt har svenska regeringen ingen anledning att misstänka på neutral svensk botten verksamma kulturella utländska institutioner för illegal verksamhet. 3. Sveriges förbindelser med The British Council äro äldre än våra förbindelser med Akademischer Austauschdienst och beröra frågor angående studentutbyte och föreläsningsverksamhet. Enligt de officiella försäkringar svenska regeringen erhållit angående B.C. – byråns verksamhet här kommer denna att bedrivas enligt dessa linjer'.

57 Arnstad, 2006, p. 89.
58 *Ibid.*, pp. 86, 89.
59 *Ibid.*, pp. 407–8. Original Swedish: 'Av svenskar har en viss känsla av skam när vi ser på våra grannländer och brödrafolk som lever under tyskt förtryck'.
60 *Ibid.*, pp. 160.
61 *Ibid.*, pp. 228–9.
62 CAC MALT 1, Mallet, unpublished memoir, p. 66.
63 Tennant, 1992, p. 31 and Arnstad, 2006, p. 299.
64 CAC MALT 1, Mallet, unpublished memoir, pp. 157–8.
65 'Engelsk poet föreläser här', *Dagens Nyheter*, 21 April 1942, p. 1; 'Fyra miljoner hus skall byggas i England', *Dagens Nyheter*, 10 October 1942, p. 12; '"Den måste jag se närmare på"', *Dagens Nyheter*, 10 February 1943, p. 1; 'Yngste Nobelpristagaren krigsutbildar naturvetare', *Dagens Nyheter*, 18 April 1943, p. 5.
66 Grant, 1994, p. 68.
67 KCA STE 2/2/4, Steegman, travel diary entry for 29 December 1943.
68 Grant, 1994, p. 71.
69 CAC BRCO 2/6, Yücel to Robertson, 11 April 1943.
70 CAC BRCO 2/6, Grant to Robertson, 15 April 1943, attaching *ibid*.
71 'HALKEVLERİNİN KURULUŞU VE ÇALIŞMALARI', particularly footnotes 21 and 22.

72 CAC BRCO 2/1, Deedes to Robertson, 7 July 1943; CAC BRCO 2/2, Grant to Robertson, 23 September 1943.

73 CAC BRCO 1/2, Grant to Robertson, 30 August 1943.

74 Bali, 2007, pp. 74–5.

75 TNA BW 56/6, Starkie to White, 27 August 1940.

76 TNA BW 56/2, Starkie to Lloyd. Undated, though clearly late September 1940 from dates of handwritten notes on the telegram.

77 Hoare, 1946, p. 71.

78 See, for example, 'La entrevista de Hitler y el Sr. Serrano Suñer', *ABC*, 18 September 1940, p. 1; Also see other newspapers such as *Arriba* through September 1940.

79 Hoare, 1946, p. 75.

80 Serrano Suñer, 1977, p. 266. Original Spanish: 'capaz de mil locuras'; and 'exaltado germanófilo en los primeros meses de la guerra mundial, y anglófilo luego seducido por Sir Samuel Hoare'.

81 TNA BW 56/3, Starkie to Lloyd, 15 January 1941.

82 *Ibid.*

83 TNA BW 56/2 Starkie, 'The British Institute in Madrid' – article for *The Times*, undated but late 1940.

84 MAEC AG Leg R 1012/244, Starkie to Serrano Suñer, 17 April 1942; MAEC AG Leg R 1012/260, British Embassy in Madrid, note 441 (70B/6/42) to Spanish Foreign Ministry, 15 May 1942; MAEC AG Leg R 1012/260, Spanish Foreign Ministry, Nota Verbal to British Embassy in Madrid, 30 May 1942; MAEC AG Leg R 1317/13, British Embassy in Madrid, Note 818 to Spanish Foreign Ministry, 15 October 1941; MAEC AG Leg R 1317/13, Spanish Foreign Ministry, Minuta Num 649 to British Embassy in Madrid, 30 October 1941.

85 MAEC AG Leg R 1317/13, Spanish Foreign Ministry. Minuta Num 649 to British Embassy in Madrid, 30 October 1941. Original Spanish: 'tiene la honra de significarle que, por el momento y en principio, no existe inconveniente en que se celebren las conferencias sobre Alpinismo y Poesía Británica a cargo respectivamente de Mr Hugo Ruttledge y Mr Laurence Binyon, en la inteligencia, claro es, de que llegado el momento oportuno se solicitaran por el Instituto Británico en esta capital las correspondientes autorizaciones reglamentarias para cada una de las conferencias aludidas'.

86 TNA BW 56/3, Starkie to Robertson, 17 September 1941.

87 RAS P3206, Danielsson to von Döbeln, 12 February 1942. Original Swedish: 'Av tillgängliga tidningsfotografier synes Bottrall vida jude'.

88 RAS P3206, Cassel, 'P. M. ang. Francis James Ronald Bottrall', 21 September
    1942. Original Swedish: 'Omkring 190 cm. lång, small, dålig hållning, går med
    lån steg, tämligen kort hals och runt huvud, näsan är lång ocg small och verkar
    inslagen, (se ill.) ögonen utstående med tun ögonlock och något melankoliska,
    munnen plutig och stor. Kal hjässa. Han uppträder ovådat vid bordet, sitter
    krokig, talar med mat i munnen, är högljudd etc., (iakttaget vid lunch)'.

89 RAS P3206, 'Avskrift ur P. 262', 7 January 1942; 'Avskrift' 20 February 1942.

90 RAS P3206 [Name of author difficult to read, but possibly 'Tuva Welanson'],
    Report on the opening of the British Council's watercolour exhibition, 9
    February 1943. Original Swedish: 'Bland de första som infunnit sig var Mr. och
    Mrs. Mallet. Vidare märktes Mr. Bottrall och en dam, som troligen var hans fru,
    samt Mr. Urquhart och Mr. Hinks. Genom en bekant fick undertecknad höra,
    att Mr. Hinks eller Direktör Roger, som hon kallade honom, kände väl till konst
    och hade en konstandel eller något dylikt i London. Så småningom samlade
    sig en hel mängd personer, både svensk och engelsmän, men undertecknad
    kände ocke igen och lyckades icke uppfatta namnet på några flera. Med största
    sannolikhet kan fastställas, att chefen för British Council i London, som
    väntades till Stockholm, icke var närvarande. Det skulle i så fall ha märkt vid
    Kronprinsens och Kronprinsessans ankomst, då han väl i så fall skulle ha blivit
    presenterad för dem. Det var emellertid huvudsakligen minister Mallet ensam,
    som visade dem omkring'.

91 Grafström, 1989, p. 516 – diary entry for 24 October 1943. Original Swedish:
    'Nicolson är lika fascinerande som sällskapsmänniska och föreläsare som han
    är i sina böcker, varav jag läst de flesta. När han talar om traditionen i engelskt
    liv – han gör det med intensiv sakkunskap och behärskat patos – tycker man sig
    bättre förstå de egenskaper, som gjort britterna till de skickliga imperiebyggare
    de äro'.

92 'Ransonering i England en tid efter kriget slut', *Dagens Nyheter*, 20 October
    1943, p. 1; 'Reorganisation av Europa skall föregå fredsslutet: Harold Nicolson
    har inte mött krigströtthet hos det engelska folket', *Dagens Nyheter*, 20 October
    1943, p. 4; 'Den lilla ön utanför Holland födde fem stora nationer. Harold
    Nicolson om revolutionen i brittiska imperietanken', *Dagens Nyheter*, 22
    October 1943, p. 7.

93 Nicolson, H., letter to Nicolson, B. and Nicolson, N., 7 November 1943
    reproduced in Nicolson, 1970, p. 328.

94 Zahavi and Zahavi, 1997; Wight, 2007, p. 20.

95 TNA BW 56/4, Starkie to White, 19 January 1942.

96   MAEC AG Leg R 1317/13, The British Embassy, Note No. 787 to Spanish
      Foreign Ministry, 13 October 1941; 'The British Institute. . .' invitation to a
      concert with Astra Desmond, November 1941; Starkie to 'Marquis' [unclear who
      this is but referred to in the letter as a relative of 'Juan Valera'], 13 November
      1941. TNA BW 82/9, 'The British Council: Report for the Second Quarter, 1942',
      July 1942, p. 3.
97   TNA BW 56/4, Starkie to Blake, 12 May 1942.
98   Hoare, 1946, p. 164.
99   *Ibid.*, pp. 165–6.
100 *Ibid.*, p. 176.
101 Monteiro to Salazar, 26 September 1942 reproduced in Rosas, Oliveira and
      Barros, 1996, p. 306. Original Portuguese: 'inesperada modificação'.
102 *Ibid.* Original Portuguese: 'a Espanha é um país que, tendo partido de posições
      inimigas dia a dia se aproxima de nós; o seu interesse para a Inglaterra *está a
      subir. Portugal, pelo contrário, apesar dos Tratados de aliança, tende a afastar-se
      de nós'.* Emphasis as in Rosas.
103 *Ibid.* Original Portuguese: 'intervenção de estações mais altas'.
104 TNA BW 52/13. Gogay to Robertson, 6 November 1942.
105 TNA BW 52/8. Read to Spanish Consulate-General, 8 April 1941.
106 TNA BW 52/8. Entwistle to White, 22 February 1941.
107 Roberts, 2008, pp. 55–6.
108 KCA STE 2/2/2, Steegman, travel diary entry for 13 November 1942.
109 'Instituto Alemán de Cultura – Concierto de canto', *ABC,* 13 February 1943,
      p. 10. Original Spanish: 'junto con destacadas personalidades de la vida cultural
      española'.
110 KCA STE 2/2/2, Steegman, travel diary entry for 13 November 1942.
111 Ley, 1981, p. 11. Original Spanish: 'Todos van cambiando con las circunstancias
      hasta que yo tenga que acabar por no venir aquí'.
112 Bottrall, e-mail to author, 29 September 2008.
113 KCA STE 2/2/2, Steegman, travel diary entry 1 December 1942.
114 MAEC AG Leg R 5261/9, 'Libros Prohibidos en España', 17 February 1944.
      Original Spanish: 'En Inglaterra causa muy mal efecto'.
115 TNA BW 56/6, Starkie to Blake, 5 July 1941.
116 TNA BW 56/6, Starkie to White, 29 March 1943, referencing a meeting with
      Conde de Jordana in November 1942.
117 TNA BW 56/6, 'Professor Starkie's Official Report on the arrangements made
      for starting the new Institute in Barcelona', 25 August 1943.

118 TNW BW 56/6, Hoare to Jordana, 6 July 1943; and TNA BW 56/6 Translation of letter from Jordana to Hoare, 20 August 1943.

119 AGA 54/6839, Pastor to Mamblas, 1 March 1943 attaching report titled 'Informe relative a las posibilidades de expansion de las relaciones culturales entre España y la Gran Bretaña'. Also see note titled 'Relaciones Culturales Entre España y Gran Bretaña', 22 July 1943.

120 Glover, 2011, pp. 27–33.

121 Eastment, 1982, p. 103.

122 TNA BW 56/7, Starkie to Mallet, 11 January 1946.

123 Glover, 2011, p. 72.

124 RI W L BRAGG 70B, Bragg, diary entry for 7 May 1943, p. 19.

125 'Yngste Nobelpristagaren krigsutbildar naturvetare', *Dagens Nyheter*, 18 April 1943, p. 5.

126 RI W L BRAGG 70A/63, Bragg to Blake, 14 May 1943.

127 RI W L BRAGG 70A/21, Quensel to Bragg, 19 March 1943.

128 RI W L BRAGG 70B, Bragg diary entry for 17 April 1943, p. 3.

129 RI W L BRAGG 70A/58, Hedvall to Bragg, 30 April 1943; and 70A/50 Pettersson to Bragg, 16 April 1943.

130 RI W L BRAGG 70A/177, Bragg to Quensel, 14 September 1943; 70A/185, Hedvall to Bragg, 23 September 1943; 70A/192, Quensel to Bragg, 4 October 1943; 70A/227, Hedvall to Bragg, 28 January 1944.

131 KCA STE 2/2/4, Steegman, diary entry for 26 February 1944.

132 *Ibid*, entry for 16 February 1944.

133 *Ibid*, entry for 17 February 1944.

134 *Ibid*, entry for 23 February 1944.

135 *Ibid*, entry for 1 March 1944.

136 TNA FD 1/6665, 'Report of Dr. R. A. McCance on his visit to the Iberian Peninsula', undated but covering the period February–March 1943, p. 2.

137 *Ibid*, p. 3.

138 *Ibid*, pp. 3–4.

139 *Ibid*, pp. 3, 5.

140 'Conferencia del profesor Alexander McCance', *ABC*, 13 February 1943, p. 10.

141 'Sesión de la Academia Médico-Quirúrgica Española', *Arriba*, 13 February 1943, p. 2; 'Académica Medico Quirúrgica', *Ya*, 13 February 1943, p. 2.

142 TNA FD 1/6665, 'Report of Dr. R. A. McCance on his visit to the Iberian Peninsula', undated but covering the period February–March 1943, p. 15.

143 *Ibid*, pp. 15–16.

144 'Exposicion del Libro Alemán en Madrid', *Ya*, 19 November 1940, p. 3; 'Inauguración de curso del Instituto de Cultura Italiana', *Arriba*, 15 January 1941, p. 3; 'El Instituto Alemán de Cultura inaugural reunions de estudiantes españoles y alemanes', *Arriba*, 12 September 1941, p. 3; 'Inauguración del año académico en el Instituto de Cultura Italiana', *Ya*, 21 November 1941, p. 4; 'Instituto de Cultura Italiana', *Ya*, 6 April 1942, p. 2; 'Música en el Instituto Alemán de Cultura', *Ya*, 7 April 1942, p. 2.

145 'Leslie Howard, en Madrid', *Ya*, 15 May 1943, p. 4; 'Perecen Leslie Howard y doce pasajeros más en ataque aéreo', *Ya*, 3 June 1943, p. 1; 'El avión en que viajaba Leslie Howard, derribado en el golfo de Gascuña', *Arriba*, 3 June 1943, p. 1; Ruiz, 1943, p. 4. Original Spanish: 'originalidad y por su calidad', 'Su comprensión de Dickens er perfecta', 'Excusado resulta decir que el libro es importante y digno de ser leído'.

146 'Conferencia de mister Frank Wallace', *Ya*, 19 January 1945, p. 2; 'En el Instituto Británico', *Ya*, 8 March 1945, p. 2; 'Instituto Britanico: Conferencia de mister Woodruff, sobre el cardinal Newmann', *ABC*, 4 March 1945, p. 36. Original Spanish: 'El confenciante fué muy aplaudido por el selecto público'.

147 'Declaraciones del director del semanario inglés "The Tablet" ', *La Vanguardia Española*, 20 March 1945, p. 2 Original Spanish: 'se ha creado un ambiente general favourable'; Also see 'Estancia de Mr. Douglas Woodruff en Barcelona', *La Vanguardia Española*, 9 March 1945, p. 10.

148 'Engelsk poet föreläser här', *Dagens Nyheter*, 21 April 1942, p. 1. Original Swedish: 'Engelsk poet föreläser här'.

149 'Engelsk förläggare får poem från fronter runt jordklotet', *Dagens Nyheter*, 21 April 1942, p. 11. Original Swedish: 'Han torde vara den störste engelske kritikern sedan Coleridge'; 'T. S. ELIOT Till skaldens Sverigebesök: DIKTER' – Advertisement by Bonniers – *Dagens Nyheter*, 25 April 1942, p. 8.

150 'Engelsk förläggare får poem från fronter runt jordklotet', *Dagens Nyheter*, 21 April 1942, p. 11. Original Swedish: 'Förläggarna har det ganska svårt, papper är det ont om, och man har få arbetare'.

151 'Fyra miljoner hus skall byggas i England', *Dagens Nyheter*, 10 October 1942, p. 12. Original Swedish: 'Det finns gator där endast ett par hus äro förstörda, och här gäller det att bygga de nya husen så att de helt smälter in i den gamla gatubilden. Sedan har vi distrikt där mycket förstörts, och här måste vi riva ned det gamla och göra helt nya kvarter i modern stil. Så har vi områden där knappt hälften bombats, och då får vi gå varligt fram, så nybggnaderna inte blir för extremt moderna. Vi är inga älskare av skyskrapor. . . '.

152   CAC BRCO 1/2, Robertson to Mallet, 4 December 1942.

153   'Diário de Coimbra – Lord Harlech', *O Comercio do Porto*, 1 March 1940. Original Portuguese: 'ao terminar a sua bela lição, foi muito aplaudido'; and 'Lord Harlech', *Diário de Coimbra*, 11 February 1940. Original Portuguese: 'Lord Harlech é também uma autoridade reconhecida acerca dos monumentos nacionais de Inglatrra, tendo escrito um importante Guia dos monumentos, em 3 volumes, que é justamente considerada uma das melhores obras no género'.

154   MAEC AG Leg R 3575/69, Castaneda to Serrano Suñer, 11 May 1942.

155   MAEC AG Leg R 3541/80, Maura to Jordana, 18 December 1943.

156   MAEC AG Leg R 3541/80, Valera, 'Nota para la Secretaria particular del Excmo. Sr. Ministro de Asuntos Exteriores', 27 December 1943. Original Spanish: 'En cuanto a los Sres. Don Walter Fitzwilliam Starkie y don Francisco Pietro, habida cuenta de que el primero es Agregado Cultural de la Embajada Británica y el segundo Embajador de Francia, y, por otra parte, en atención a las actuales circunstancias, parece oportuno que se aplace la tramitación de sus nombramientos mientras ostenten sus aludidos cargos oficiales o, cuando menos, hasta tanto que las aludidas circunstancias cesen'.

157   MAEC AG Leg R 3541/80, Casteneda to Ministro de Asuntos Exteriores, 19 June 1945; Casteneda to Subsecretario del Ministerio de Asuntos Exteriores, 4 July 1945; MAEC AG Leg R 2473/44, El Subsecretario de Asuntos Exteriores to El Subsecretario de Educación Nacional, 6 June 1945; El Subsecretario del Ministerio de Educación Nacional to El Subsecretario del Ministerio de Asuntos Exteriores, 10 April 1945.

158   Balson, e-mail to author, 27 May 2008.

159   *Ibid.*

160   TNA BW 82/9, 'The British Council – Report for the First Quarter, 1941', April 1941, p. 6; TNA BW 82/9, 'The British Council – Report for the Third Quarter, 1942', October 1942, p. 2.

161   TNA BW 82/9, 'The British Council – Report for the First Quarter, 1945', April 1945, p. 4; TNA BW 82/9, 'The British Council – Report for the Second Quarter, 1945', July 1945, p. 4.

162   Ley, 1981, p. 64. Original Spanish: 'La mayor parte de los asistentes no estaban de acuerdo con mis métodos de profesor que decían ser muy lentos en vista de que después de dos o tres clases, no habían llegado a tener un conocimiento profundo del idioma. "A mía no me interesa esencialmente la lengua inglesa, observó Victor Ruiz Iriarte, sólo quiero aprender un poco para leer con cierta facilidad a Shakespeare en el original"'.

163 Wight, 2007, p. 31.

164 *ABC* is available at http://hemeroteca.abc.es/; *La Vanguardia Española* is available at www.lavanguardia.es/hemeroteca. The 'Española' was dropped from the title after the Second World War.

165 For all figures see Corse, 2011, Appendix J.

166 *Ibid.*

167 TNA BW 82/9, 'The British Council – Report for the First Quarter, 1943', April 1943, p. 2.

168 For all figures see Corse, 2011, Appendix J.

Chapter 7

1 White, 1965, p. 123 (Appendix C).

2 *Ibid.*, p. 32.

3 TNA FO 370/634, Eden to Churchill, 20 May 1941; TNA PREM 4/20/3 Duff Cooper to Churchill. 7 February 1941.

4 CAC BRCO 2/5, Robertson to Riverdale. 14 July 1943.

5 Monteiro to Salazar, 26 October 1942 reproduced in Rosas, Oliveira and Barros, 1996, p. 346.

6 White, 1965, p. 49.

7 CAC BRCO 1/4. Desmond to Robertson, 2 April 1945; HKRC TGA 8812/1/1/17, Longden to Clark, undated but between two related letters dated 6 and 20 December 1943 in the file.

8 Coombs, 1988, p. 13.

9 TNA BW 61/4, 'Mr. C. A. F. Dundas's Report on his tour of Turkey, August, 1940'.

10 CAC MALT 1, Mallet, unpublished memoir, p. 75.

11 Roberts, 2008, pp. 59–60.

12 Burge, 1945, p. 311.

13 Monteiro to Salazar, 26 September 1942 reproduced in Rosas, Oliveira and Barros, 1996, p. 306.

14 TNA BW 56/8, Reavey to Wiggin, 28 October 1940.

15 TNA INF 1/443, Halifax to Simon, 12 January 1940; TNA FO 370/634, Eden to Churchill, 20 May 1941; Unwin, 1960, p. 437; White, 1965, p. 32; TNA PREM 4/20/3 Duff Cooper to Churchill, 7 February 1941; TNA FO 954/23A, Hoare to Robertson, 12 November 1941; TNA BW 61/12 Grant to Blake, 19 February 1941.

16 Unwin, 1960, p. 419.

17 *Ibid.*, p. 422; Coombs, 1988, p. 12.

18 Grant, 1994, p. 65.

19 RI W L BRAGG 70A/248, Hägg to Bragg, 25 December 1944.

20 Stamp, 1940, p. 11.

21 KCA STE 2/2/2, Steegman, travel diary entry for 13 November 1942.

22 RI W L BRAGG 70A/63, Bragg to Blake, 14 May 1943.

23 KCA STE 2/2/4 Steegman, travel diary entry for 29 December 1943.

24 'Instituto Alemán de Cultura – Concierto de canto', *ABC*, 13 February 1943, p. 10.

25 TNA BW 52/10, Campbell to Eden, 22 February 1945; TNA BW 61/7, Extract from the Draft Minutes of the 99th Meeting of the Finance and Agenda Committee held on 8 February 1944. Comments by Blake on agenda item 'Turkey: High School for Girls, Istanbul'; TNA BW 56/10, Steegman, 'Visit to Spain and Portugal: Final Report', 3 March 1943.

26 See Bogart, 1995, p. 56.

27 KCA JDH 26/9, Bottrall to Hayward, 26 December 1942.

28 Unwin, 1960, p. 421.

29 Richards, 2005.

30 Bogart, 1995, p. 91.

31 TNA BW 82/9, 'The British Council – Report for the First Quarter, 1943', April 1943, p. 2.

32 'Tyskt angrepp på statsrådet Bagge', *Aftonbladet*, 18 December 1941. Newspaper cutting in RAS P3206; KCA STE 2/2/2, Steegman, travel diary entry for 13 November 1942; Grant, 1994, p. 72.

33 TNA BW 56/7, Starkie to Mallet, 11 January 1946; Eastment, 1982, p. 103.

34 TNA BW 56/2, Reavey to Campkin, 14 June 1940.

35 TNA BW 82/9, 'The British Council: Report for the First Quarter, 1941', April, 1941, p. 6; TNA BW 82/9, 'The British Council: Report for the Third Quarter, 1942', October, 1942, p. 2.

36 See Corse, 2011, Appendix J.

37 Hoare, 1946, p. 75.

38 TNA BW 82/9, 'The British Council: Report for the First Quarter, 1942', April, 1942, p. 2; TNA BW 82/9, 'The British Council: Report for the First Quarter, 1943', April, 1943, p. 3; TNA BW 82/9, 'The British Council: Report for the Third Quarter, 1943', November, 1943, p. 2; TNA BW 82/9, 'The British Council: Report for the Second Quarter, 1944', July, 1944, p. 3; TNA BW 82/9, 'The British Council: Report for the Third Quarter, 1944', October, 1944, p. 2.

39 See Corse, 2011, Appendix D.

40 TNA BW 82/9, 'The British Council: Report for the First Quarter, 1942', April, 1942, p. 4; TNA BW 82/9, 'The British Council: Report for the Fourth Quarter,

1943', January, 1944, p. 4; TNA BW 82/9, 'The British Council: Report for the
First Quarter, 1945', April, 1945, p. 5.

41 TNA BW 82/9, 'The British Council: Report for the Fourth Quarter, 1943',
January 1944, p. 3; TNA BW 82/9, 'The British Council: Report for the First
Quarter, 1945', April 1945, p. 4.

42 TNA BW 57/4, Bottrall to Longden, 12 July 1943.

43 TNA FD 1/6665, 'Report of Dr. R. A. McCance on his visit to the Iberian
Peninsula', undated but covering the period February–March 1943, pp. 15–16.

44 RI W L BRAGG 70A/63, Bragg to Blake, 14 May 1943.

45 Drout, 2006, p. 16.

46 Stamp, 1940, p. 11.

47 Blackmore, 1999, p. 65.

48 Unwin, 1960, p. 422; Coombs, 1988, p. 12.

49 Donaldson, 1984; Taylor, 1981; Hurtley, 1992; Berdah, 1993; Roberts, 2008.

50 Eastment, 1982; Ellwood, 1982.

51 'Instituto de Cultura Italiana: Conferencia del professor Tamberlini', *ABC*,
3 February 1943, p. 7; 'Concierto en el Instituto Alemán de Cultura', *ABC*,
19 November 1942, p. 12; 'Concierto en el Instituto Alemán de Cultura', *ABC*,
15 April 1943, p. 14. Original Spanish: 'Autores españoles y actores italianos
en el siglo XVI'.

52 Bogart, 1995.

53 Glover, 2011, pp. 27–33; AGA 54/6839, Pastor to Mamblas, 1 March 1943
attaching report titled 'Informe relative a las posibilidades de expansion de
las relaciones culturales entre España y la Gran Bretaña'. Also see note titled
'Relaciones Culturales Entre España y Gran Bretaña', 22 July 1943.

54 'Russia to limit British Council', *BBC News Website*, 12 December 2007. http://
news.bbc.co.uk/1/hi/world/europe/7139959.stm; 'British Council in Iran
'illegal' *BBC News Website*, 5 February 2009. http://news.bbc.co.uk/1/hi/world/
middle_east/7872525.stm; 'Attack on British Council compound in Kabul kills
12', *BBC News Website*, 19 August 2011. www.bbc.co.uk/news/world-south-asia-
14585563.

55 Tennant, 1992, p. 263.

56 Cull, No date.

Bibliography

Author's correspondence

Balson, M., 27 May 2008.
Balson, M., 20 June 2008.
Balson, M., 27 October 2008.
Bottrall, A., 29 September 2008.
Collins, L., 24 May 2008.
Gordon, D., 11 September 2009.
Gordon, D., 20 May 2008.
Thirsk, B., 17 August 2008.
Thirsk, B., 16 September 2008.

Interviews

Estorninho, C., interview by T. Smith, early 2005. My thanks to Alison Roberts for sending me a copy of the interview transcript.
Grant, A., telephone conversation with author, 2 July 2008.

Archives

Archivo General de la Administración, Madrid, Spain.
Churchill Archives Centre, Churchill College, University of Cambridge.
Hyman Kreitman Research Centre, Tate Britain, London.
King's College Archive, King's College, University of Cambridge.
Ministerio de Asuntos Exteriores y de Cooperación, Madrid, Spain.
The National Archives, Kew.
Riksarkivet, Stockholm, Sweden.
Royal Institution Archive, Royal Institution, London.
Royal Northern College of Music, Manchester.

Private collections

Michael Grant's personal photograph album of his time in Turkey (1940-45). I am very grateful to his son Antony for allowing me to view and use this photograph in my book.

Electronic Databases

British Council Portugal, Historical Archives CD-ROM. My thanks to Sofia Leitão at the
British Council in Lisbon for sending this to me.
British Council video channel on Vimeo. http://www.vimeo.com/britishcouncil.
British Council video channel on YouTube. http://www.youtube.com/user/britishcouncil.
British Film Institute, Film & TV Database. http://www.bfi.org.uk/filmtvinfo/ftvdb/.

Books and articles

'A fundação do Instituo Britânico em Portugal vem preencher uma falta que há muito se
fazia sentir nas relações culturais entre os dois países aliados', *República*, 22 November
1938.
'A visita de "Lord" Lloyd', *Diário de Manhã*, 23 November 1938.
'Académica Medico Quirúrgica', *Ya*, 13 February 1943.
Adams, R. J. Q. (2004), 'Hoare, Samuel John Gurney, Viscount Templewood (1880–1959)',
Oxford Dictionary of National Biography. Oxford: Oxford University Press (online
edition January 2008). www.oxforddnb.com/view/article/33898.
Alexander, S. (2003), *Foreign Strands: A British Council Journey*. Bristol: Merriotts Press.
Allison Peers, E. (1948), 'The teaching of English in Spain', *ELT Journal*, II, (5), 129–34.
Allport, G. W. and Postman, L. J. (1964), 'The basic psychology of rumor', in Katz,
D., Cartwright, D., Eldersveld, S. and McClung Lee, A. (eds), *Public Opinion and
Propaganda*. New York, Chicago and San Francisco: Holt, Rinehart and Winston.
Amat, C. G. (2008), 'Turina, Joaquín, §1: Life', *Grove Music Online*. Oxford:
Oxford University Press. www.grovemusic.com/shared/views/article.
html?section=music.28603.1.
Amos, M. (1940), *British Justice*. London: Longmans Green & Co Ltd.
Arnstad, H. (2006), *Spelaren Christian Günther: Sverige Under Andra Världskriget*.
Stockholm: Wahlström & Widstrand.
'Art as Propaganda', *The Language Business*, 25 March 2007. http://www.dblackie.blogs.
com/the_language_business/2007/03/art_as_propagan.html.
'Attack on British Council compound in Kabul kills 12', *BBC News Website*, 19 August
2011. www.bbc.co.uk/news/world-south-asia-14585563.
Aunger, R. (ed.) (2000), *Darwinizing Culture: The Status of Memetics as a Science*. Oxford:
Oxford University Press.
Baiôa, M., Fernandes, P. J. and Ribeiro de Meneses, F. (2003), 'The political history of
twentieth century Portugal', *e-Journal of Portuguese History*, 1, 2, Winter, 1–18. www.
brown.edu/Departments/Portuguese_Brazilian_Studies/ejph/html/issue2/pdf/baioa.pdf.
Baker White, J. (1955), *The Big Lie*. London: Evans Brothers Limited.
Baldwin, S. (1940), *The Englishman*. London: Longmans Green & Co Ltd.
— (1941), *El Hombre Inglés*. London: Longmans Green & Co Ltd.
Balfour, J. (2004), 'Campbell, Sir Ronald Hugh (1883-1953)', rev. A. Adamthwaite, *Oxford
Dictionary of National Biography*. Oxford: Oxford University Press (online edition
January 2008). www.oxforddnb.com/view/article/32273.
Bali, R. N. (2007), 'II. Dünya Savaşi Yillarinda: Türkiye'de Amerikan Propagandasi',
Toplumsal Tarihi, 158, Şubat [February] 2007, 74–5. www.rifatbali.com/images/stories/
dokumanlar/turkiyede_amerikan_propagandasi.pdf.

Barrio, A. M. (1989), 'La etapa de Ramón Serrano Súñer en el Ministerio de Asuntos Exteriores', *Espacio, Tiempo y Forma, Series V H.o Contemporánea*, 2, 145–67.

Beevor, A. (2007), *The Battle for Spain: The Spanish Civil War 1936–1939*. London: Phoenix.

Belen, S. (2008), 'The Behaviour of Stochastic Rumours', PhD Thesis, Australia: University of Adelaide, http://www.digital.library.adelaide.edu.au/dspace/bitstream/2440/49472/1/02whole.pdf.

Berdah, J.-F. (1993), 'La "propaganda" cultural Británica en España durante la Segunda Guerra Mundial a través de la acción del "British Council": Un aspecto de las relaciones Hispano-Británicas (1939–1946)', in Tusell, J., Sueiro, S., Marín, J. M. and Casanova, M. (eds), *El Régimen de Franco (1936–1975) Congreso Internacional Madrid, Mayo 1993: Tomo II*. Madrid: Departamento de Historia Contemporánea UNED.

— (1998), 'La propaganda culturelle britannique en Espagne pendant la seconde guerre mondiale: ambition et action du British Council (1939–1946)', *Guerre Mondiales et Conflits Contemporains*, Mars 1998, 189, 95–107. http://www.gernika.free.fr/GM%26CC.html.

Biagetti, M. (2010), *Walter Starkie: Escritor, Academic, Peregrine*. Pomigliano d'Arco: Edizioni Compostellane.

'Bibliotek på 3.000 band Kom med Englandsflyget', *Dagens Nyheter*, 1 September 1944.

Black, J. and Potts, J. (2003), *Swedish Reflections, From Beowulf to Bergman*. London: Arcadia Books.

Blackmore, S. (1999), *The Meme Machine*. Oxford: Oxford University Press.

Bogart, L. (1995), *Cool Words, Cold War: A New Look at USIA's Premises for Propaganda*, revised edition, abridged by A. Bogart. London and Washington: The American University Press.

Bowen, W. H. (2006), *Spain During World War II*. Columbia, Missouri: University of Missouri Press.

Brady, K. (2008), 'Rumor Models' at http://www.people.clarkson.edu/~jhowell/teaching/bradyproj.pdf. 14 December 2008.

Brass, D. (1941), 'Shine, Sir?', *Anglo-Portuguese News*, 13 September 1941.

Bribiesca, L. B. (2001), 'Memetics: a dangerous idea', *Interciencia*, enero 2001, 26, 1, 29–31.

British Council (1941), *Report of the British Council 1940–1941*. London: British Council.

— (1955), *The British Council 1934–1955: Twenty-first Anniversary Report*. London: British Council.

— (2007a), *Annual Report 2006/07*. London: British Council. www.britishcouncil.org/annual-report/pdfs/BC-Annual-Report-2006-07.PDF.

— (2007b), *Grove Music Online*, Oxford: Oxford University Press. www.grovemusic.com/shared/views/article.html?section=music.04011.

'British Council in Iran 'illegal', *BBC News Website*, 5 February 2009. http://www.news.bbc.co.uk/1/hi/world/middle_east/7872525.stm.

'British Council in Russian test', *BBC News Website*, 3 January 2008. http://www.news.bbc.co.uk/go/pr/fr/-/1/hi/world/europe/7169940.stm.

Brown, A. C. (1982), 'The Czechoslovak Air Force in Britain, 1940–1945', PhD Thesis, University of Southampton. www.ssci.freeserve.co.uk/airmen/Part1.pdf and www.ssci.freeserve.co.uk/airmen/Part2.pdf.

Burge, M. R. K. (1945), 'The British Council', *The Political Quarterly*, 16, (4), October, 307–15.

Burns, J. (2009), *Papa Spy: Love, Faith and Betrayal in Wartime Spain*. London, Berlin, New York: Bloomsbury.

Burns, T. (1993), *The Use of Memory: Publishing and Further Pursuits*. London: Sheed & Ward.

Butler, E. (1963), *Amateur Agent: A Story of Black Propaganda during World War II*. London: George G. Harrap & Co Ltd.

Cañas, G. (1987), 'La venta del archive de Walter Starkie se hizo al margen de sus herederos', *El Pais*, 5 February 1987.

'Cassandra', *The Daily Mirror*, 14 June 1941.

Chaves, I. (2008), 'Criação do Instituto Britânico desponta em Coimbra', *Campeão das Províncias Online*, 12 March 2008.

'Chegou hoje a Lisboa o sábio inglês dr. McCance', *Diário de Lisboa*, 16 February 1943.

Clark, K. (1977), *The Other Half: A Self-Portrait*. London: John Murray.

Cole, R. (1987), 'The Other "Phoney War": British Propaganda in Neutral Europe, September–December 1939', *Journal of Contemporary History*, 1, 22, 455–79.

— (1990), *Britain and the War of Words in Neutral Europe, 1939–45: The Art of the Possible*. London: Macmillan.

— (1996), ' "Good Relations": Irish Neutrality and the Propaganda of John Betjeman, 1941–1943', *Éire-Ireland*, Geimhreadh-Winter, 33–46.

'Concierto en el Instituto Alemán de Cultura', *ABC*, 19 November 1942.

'Concierto en el Instituto Alemán de Cultura', *ABC*, 15 April 1943.

'Conferencia de mister Frank Wallace', *Ya*, 19 January 1945.

'Conferencia del profesor Alexander McCance', *ABC*, 13 February 1943.

Conradi, P. and Stoddard, M. (eds) (1999), *Cold War, Common Pursuit: British Council Lecturers in Poland, 1938–1998*. London: Starhaven.

Conte, R. (2000), 'Memes through (social) minds', in Aunger, R. (ed.), *Darwinizing Culture: The Status of Memetics as a Science*. Oxford: Oxford University Press.

Coombs, D. (1988), *Spreading the Word: The Library Work of the British Council*. London and New York: Mansell Publishing Limited.

Corr, W. (1998), Book Review of Iriye, A. (1997), *Cultural Internationalism and World Order*. Baltimore, MD: John Hopkins University Press in *Journal of World History*, Fall, pp. 303–5.

Corse, E. (2008), 'British propaganda in neutral Eire after the fall of France, 1940', *Contemporary British History*, 22, 2, 163–80.

—. (2011), 'Cultural propaganda: The British Council's activities in neutral Europe 1939–1945', Unpublished PhD Thesis, University of Kent.

Cross, J. A. (1977), *Sir Samuel Hoare: A Political Biography*. London: Jonathan Cape.

Cruickshank, C. (1976), *Special Operations Executive in Scandinavia*. Oxford: Oxford University Press.

Cull, N. J. (No date), 'Propaganda?', *British Council website*. www.britishcouncil.org/history-why-propaganda.htm. Unclear date but accessed 2007.

— (1995), *Selling War: The British Propaganda Campaign Against American 'Neutrality' in World War II*. Oxford: Oxford University Press.

— (2008), *The Cold War and the United States Information Agency: American Propaganda and Public Diplomacy* (paperback edition 2010). Cambridge: Cambridge University Press.

Cull, N. J., Culbert, D. and Welch, D. (2003), *Propaganda and Mass Persuasion: A Historical Encyclopaedia, 1500 to the Present*. California: ABC-CLIO.

D'Abernon, Viscount (1929), 'The economic mission to South America: address given on October 29th, 1929', *Journal of the Royal Institute of International Affairs*, 8, (6), November, 568–82.

Daley, D. J. and Kendall, D. G. (1965), 'Stochastic rumours', *IMA Journal of Applied Mathematics*, 1, 42–55.

Dalton, H. (1957), *The Fateful Years: Memoirs 1931–1945*. London: Frederick Muller Ltd.

Dawkins, R. (1976), *The Selfish Gene*. Oxford: Oxford University Press.

— (1982), *The Extended Phenotype*. Oxford: Freeman.

— (2006), *The God Delusion*. London, Toronto, Sydney, Auckland, Johannesburg: Bantam Press.

'Declaraciones del director del semanario inglés "The Tablet" ', *La Vanguardia Española*, 20 March 1945.

Del Pino, R. (1996), 'Walter Starkie: entre la manigua y el British Council', *La Opinión da Granada*, 23 Julio, 1996, 39. www.manueldafalla.com/falla/website/noticias_falla_pdf/105.-%2023-07-2006.pdf.

Deletant, D. (2002), 'The British Council and Romania: 1934 to the present', in Michelson, P. E. and Treptow, K. W. (eds), *National Development in Romania and Southeastern Europe*. Iaşi, Oxford: Center for Romanian Studies.

Delgado Gómez-Escalonilla, L. (1994), 'Las relaciones culturales de España en tiempo de crisis: de la II República a la Guerra Mundial', *Espacio, Tiempo y Forma*, Serie V, Historia, Contemporánea), 7, 259–94. http://www.62.204.194.45:8080/fedora/get/bibliuned:ETFSerie5-96DDBE83-B02B-AD03-16E2-864A3C904A55/PDF.

'Den lilla ön utanför Holland födde fem stora nationer. Harold Nicolson om revolutionen i brittiska imperietanken', *Dagens Nyheter*, 22 October 1943.

' "Den måste jag se närmare på" ', *Dagens Nyheter*, 10 February 1943.

Denniston, R. (2004), 'Bazna, Elyesa (b. 1903)', *Oxford Dictionary of National Biography*. Oxford: Oxford University Press. www.oxforddnb.com/view/article/60870.

Deringil, S. (1982), 'The preservation of Turkey's neutrality during the Second World War: 1940', *Middle Eastern Studies*, 18, 1, 30–52.

'Diário de Coimbra – Lord Harlech', *O Comercio do Porto*, 1 March 1940.

Dimitrov, V. (2002), 'Bulgarian neutrality: domestic and international perspectives', in Wylie, N. (ed.), *European Neutrals and Non-Belligerents during the Second World War*. Cambridge: Cambridge University Press.

Donaldson, F. (1984), *The British Council: The First Fifty Years*. London: Jonathan Cape.

Doob, L. (1950), *Public Opinion and Propaganda*. New York: Henry Holt and Company Inc.

— (1964), 'Goebbels' principles of propaganda', in Katz, D., Cartwright, D., Eldersveld, S. and McClung Lee, A. (eds), *Public Opinion and Propaganda*. New York, Chicago and San Francisco: Holt, Rinehart and Winston.

Drout, M. D. C. (2006), *How Tradition Works: A Meme-Based Cultural Poetics of the Anglo-Saxon Tenth Century*. Tempe, Arizona: Arizona Center for Medieval and Renaissance Studies (ACMRS).

Duff Cooper, A. (1953), *Old Men Forget*. London: Rupert Hart-Davis.

Dunstan, R. (1982), 'The rumour process', *Journal of Applied Probability*, 19, 4, 759–66.

Eastment, D. (1982). 'The policies and position of the British Council from the outbreak of war to 1950', Unpublished PhD Thesis, University of Leeds.

'El avión en que viajaba Leslie Howard, derribado en el golfo de Gascuña', *Arriba*, 3 June 1943.

'El 'British Council' abandona Europa para concentrarse en los países islámicos y en la lucha antiterrorista', *20minutos.es*, 26 February 2007. www.20minutos.es/noticias/206149/0/british/council/cierre/.

'El Instituto Alemán de Cultura inaugural reunions de estudiantes españoles y alemanes', *Arriba*, 12 September 1941.

Ellul, J. (1973), *Propaganda: The Formation of Men's Attitudes* (translated by K. Kellen and J. Lerner). New York: Vintage Books.

Ellwood, D. W. (1982), 'Showing the world what it owed to Britain: foreign policy and cultural propaganda 1935-1945', in Pronay, N. and Spring D. W., (eds), *Propaganda, Politics and Film, 1938-1945*. London: Macmillan.

'En el Instituto Británico', *Ya*, 8 March 1945.

'Engelsk förläggare får poem från fronter runt jordklotet', *Dagens Nyheter*, 21 April 1942.

'Engelsk kulturcentral har öppnats i Stockholm', *Dagens Nyheter*, 18 December 1941.

'Engelsk poet föreläser här', *Dagens Nyheter*, 21 April 1942.

Englekirk, J. E., Barcia, J. R. and Robe, S. L. (1977), 'Walter F. Starkie, Spanish and Portuguese: Los Angeles', *Online Archive of California*. http://www.content.cdlib.org/xtf/view?docId=hb1199n68c&brand=oac.

'Está em Lisboa o maestro inglês Malcolm Sargent', *Diário de Lisboa*, 11 January 1943.

Estaban, I. (2006), 'Pío Baroja molestaba a los politicos por su sinceridad', *El Correo Digital*, 4 February 2006. www.elcorreodigital.com/vizcaya/pg060204/prensa/noticias/Cultura_VIZ/200602/04/VIZ-CUL-000.html.

'Estancia de Mr. Douglas Woodruff en Barcelona', *La Vanguardia Española*, 9 March 1945.

Ewen, S. (2008), 'The changing face of consumer marketing', *Where the Truth Lies: A Symposium on Propaganda Today*. New York: School of Visual Arts. Published as videos on iTunes. Also see www.wherethetruthlies.org.

'Exposicion del Libro Alemán en Madrid', *Ya*, 19 November 1940.

Foot, M. R. D. (1992), 'Preface', in Tennant, P., (ed.), *Touchlines of War*. Hull: Hull University Press.

— (1999), *SOE: Special Operations Executive*. London: Pimlico.

Forbes Adam, C. (1948), *Life of Lord Lloyd*. London: Macmillan.

Foss, B. (2007), *War Paint: Art, War, State and Identity in Britain, 1939-1945*. New Haven and London: Yale University Press.

'Fyra miljoner hus skall byggas i England', *Dagens Nyheter*, 10 October 1942.

Gardner, A., Loren, S. and Heston, C. (1986), 'El hospital Anglo-Americano pasará a depender del Ministerio de Educación y Ciencia', *El Pais*, 22 February 1986.

Garnett, D. (2002), *Secret History of PWE: The Political Warfare Executive, 1939-1945*. London: St Ermin's Press.

Glover, N. (2011), *National Relations: Public Diplomacy, National Identity and the Swedish Institute 1945-1970*. Lund, Sweden: Nordic Academic Press.

Gordon, D. (2008), 'Walter Starkie and the greatest novel of all', *First Principles: ISI Web Journal*, 10 April 2008. www.firstprinciplesjournal.com/print.aspx?article=5798&loc=b&type=cbtp.

Grafström, S. (1989), *Anteckningar 1938-1944* (Utgivna genom Stig Ekman). Stockholm: Kungl. Samfundet för utgivande av handskrifter rörande Skandinaviens historia.

Grant, M. (1994), *My First Eighty Years*. Henley-on-Thames: Aidan Ellis Publishing.

Greig, B. (1944), 'It's funny, but it's rather foolish, too', *The Daily Mirror*, 20 November, 2.

Guha, R. (1999), *Elementary Aspects of Peasant Insurgency in Colonial India*. Durham, NC and London: Duke University Press.

Hale, W. (2000), *Turkish Foreign Policy 1774-2000*. London: Frank Cass.

Hales, J. E. (1940), *British Education*. London: Longmans Green & Co Ltd.

'HALKEVLERİNİN KURULUŞU VE ÇALIŞMALARI' at http://www.w3.balikesir.edu.tr/~mozsari/Halkevleri.htm. Undated.

Halman, T. S. (2003), 'Hasan-Ali Yücel: Minister of Enlightenment', *The Turkish Times*, 14, 318, May 2003. www.theturkishtimes.com/archive/03/0503/f-yucel.html.

Hamilton, C. (1940a), *La Mujer Inglesa*. London: Longmans Green & Co Ltd.
— (1940b), *The Englishwoman*. London: Longmans Green & Co Ltd.
Haycraft, J. (1998), *Adventures of a Language Traveller* (edited by M. Woosnam-Mills). London: Constable.
Hayes, B. (2005), 'Rumours and errours', *American Scientist*, 93, 3, May–June, 207.
Heine, C. (2008), 'Campo, Conrado del', *Grove Music Online*. Oxford: Oxford University Press. www.grovemusic.com/shared/views/article.html?section=music.04698.
Henn-Collins, P. (1943), 'The British Council and music in Cairo', *The Musical Times*, July, 218.
Hernández-Sandoica, E. and Moradiellos, E. (2002), 'Spain and the Second World War, 1939–1945', in Wylie, N. (ed.), *European Neutrals and Non-Belligerents During the Second World War*. Cambridge: Cambridge University Press.
Hess, C. A. (2007), 'Falla, Manuel de, §5: The Republic and the Civil War', *Grove Music Online*. Oxford: Oxford University Press. www.grovemusic.com/shared/views/article.html?section=music.09266.5.
Hoare, S. (1946), *Ambassador on Special Mission*. London: Collins.
Holt, T. (2004), *The Deceivers: Allied Military Deception in the Second World War*. London: Weidenfeld and Nicolson.
Hornby, A. S. (1996), 'Looking back', *ELT Journal*, XXI, 1, 3–6.
Howe, E. (1982), *The Black Game: British Subversive Operations Against the Germans During the Second World War*. London: Michael Joseph.
Hurtley, J. (1992), *José Janés: Editor de Literatura Inglesa*. Barcelona: PPU.
— (2005), 'Wandering between the wars: Walter Starkie's di/visions', in Tazón-Salces, J. E. and Carrera Suárez, I., (eds), *Post-Imperial Encounters: Anglo-Hispanic Cultural Relations* (Studies in Comparative Literature 45). Amsterdam and New York: Rodopi.
'"I penned negative Amazon reviews" – Historian Figes', *BBC News Website*, 24 April 2010. http://news.bbc.co.uk/1/hi/uk/8641515.stm.
Illich, I. and Sanders, B. (1988), *ABC: The Alphabetization of the Popular Mind*. San Francisco: North Point Press.
'In full: British Council statement', *BBC News Website*, 17 January 2008. http://news.bbc.co.uk/go/pr/fr/-/1/hi/uk_politics/7193954.stm.
'Inauguración de curso del Instituto de Cultura Italiana', *Arriba*, 15 January 1941.
'Inauguración del año académico en el Instituto de Cultura Italiana', *Ya*, 21 November 1941.
'Inblick i allt mindre världar. Föredrag i Hälsingborg av nobelpristagaren sir Lawrence Bragg', *Oresund's Posten*, 7 May 1943.
Inkeles, A. (1964), 'The Bolshevik agitator', in Katz, D., Cartwright, D., Eldersveld, S. and McClung Lee, A. (eds), *Public Opinion and Propaganda*. New York, Chicago and San Francisco: Holt, Rinehart and Winston.
'Instituto Alemán de Cultura – Concierto de canto', *ABC*, 13 February 1943.
'Instituto Britanico: Conferencia de mister Woodruff, sobre el cardinal Newmann', *ABC*, 4 March 1945.
'Instituto Británico', *Diário de Notícias*, 19 November 1938.
'Instituto de Cultura Italiana: Conferencia del professor Tamberlini', *ABC*, 3 February 1943.
'Instituto de Cultura Italiana', *Ya*, 6 April 1942.
Jeffery, K. (2010), *MI6: The History of the Secret Intelligence Service, 1909–1949*. London, Berlin, New York and Sydney: Bloomsbury.
Jennings, W. I. (1938), 'British organization for rearmament', *Political Science Quarterly*, LIII, 4, December, 481–90.

Jiménez Losantos, F. (2001), 'Un gran libro contra Baroja', *La Ilustración Liberal*, 9, September 2001. www.libertadigital.com:83/ilustracion_liberal/articulo.php/163.

Jordana, Conde de (2002), *Milicia y diplomacia: diarios del Conde de Jordana, 1936–1944*, estudio preliminary, Carlos Seco Serrano; selección y glosas, Rafael Gómez-Jordana. Burgos: Editorial Dossoles.

Jowett, G. S. and O'Donnell, V. (1999), *Propaganda and Persuasion* (third edition). Thousand Oaks, London and New Delhi: Sage Publications.

Keith, A. B. (1940), *The British Commonwealth*. London: Longmans Green & Co Ltd.

— (1942), *Det Brittiska Samväldet*. Stockholm: Calson Press Boktr.

Kendall, D. G. (1956), 'Deterministic and stochastic epidemics in closed populations', *Proceedings of the 3rd Berkeley Symposium on Mathematical Statistics and Probability*, 4, 149–65.

Kenyon, F. M. (1943), 'The British Council and music in Cairo', *The Musical Times*, October 1943, 316.

Kershaw, I. (2008), *Fateful Choices: Ten Decisions that Changed the World 1940–1941*. London: Penguin Books.

Ketola, H.-M. (2004), 'Teaching 'correct' attitudes: An Anglican emissary to Sweden and Finland in 1944', *The Journal of Ecclesiastical History*, 44, 75–101.

'Kind wishes from The Rt. Hon. Sir Malcolm Robertson, G. C. M. G., K. B. E., M. P., Chairman of the British Council', *Anglo-Portuguese News*, 17 June 1941.

Knatchbull-Hugessen, H. (1949), *Diplomat in Peace and War*. London: John Murray.

'Kultursändebud och känd skald lämnar Sverige', *Dagens Nyheter*, 1 September 1944.

'La entrevista de Hitler y el Sr. Serrano Suñer', *ABC*, 18 September 1940.

Langhorne, R. (2004), 'Hugessen, Sir Hughe Montgomery Knatchbull- (1886–1971)', *Oxford Dictionary of National Biography*. Oxford: Oxford University Press (online edition, January 2008). www.oxforddnb.com/view/article/31319.

Larson, C. (1941), 'The British Ministry of Information', *Public Opinion Quarterly*, Fall, 412–31.

Lefevre, C. and Picard, P. (1944), 'Distribution of the final extent of a rumour process', *Journal of Applied Probability*, 31, 1, 244–9.

'Leslie Howard, en Madrid', *Ya*, 15 May 1943.

Levine, P. A. (2002), 'Swedish neutrality during the Second World War: tactical success or moral compromise?', in Wylie, N. (ed.), *European Neutrals and Non-Belligerents During the Second World War*. Cambridge: Cambridge University Press.

Lewis, M. (1940), *British Ships and British Seamen*. London: Longmans Green & Co Ltd.

Ley, C. D. (1981), *La Costanilla de los Diablos (Memorias literarias 1943–1952)*. Madrid: José Estaban, Editor.

Liborio, E. (1943), 'O Recital Philippe Newman a favor da Cruz Vermelha Portuguesa', *Diário de Manhã*, 3 July 1943.

Llano, S. (2002), 'Starkie y el British Council en España: música, cultura y propaganda', in Suarez-Pajares, J. (ed.), *Música Española entre dos Guerras, 1914–1945*. Granada: Publicaciones del archive Manuel de Falla.

Lloyd-Jones, H. (2008), 'Grant, Michael (1914–2004)', *Oxford Dictionary of National Biography*. Oxford: Oxford University Press (online edition, January 2008). www. oxforddnb.com/view/article/94333.

'London Day', *Daily Telegraph*, 8 March 1940.

'Lord Harlech', *Diário de Coimbra*, 11 February 1940.

Lundkvist, A. (1940), 'Romaner från England', *Bonniers Litterära Magasin*, årg IX, Nr. 6, June–August, 455–60.

Lysaght, C. E. (1979), *Brendan Bracken*. London: Allen Lane.

MacArthur, B. (ed.) (1999), *The Penguin Book of Twentieth-Century Speeches*. London: Penguin Books.

Mackenzie, W. J. M. (2002), *A Secret History of S.O.E.: The Special Operations Executive 1940–1945*. London: St Ermin's Press.

Maki, D. P. and Thompson M. (1973), *Mathematical Models and Applications*. Englewood Cliffs, New Jersey: Prentice-Hall.

Malvern, S. (2004), *Modern Art, Britain and the Great War: Witnessing, Testimony and Remembrance*. New Haven and London: Yale University Press.

Martin, D. (2004), 'Michael Grant, who wrote histories of the ancient world, is dead at 89', *New York Times*, 25 October 2004.

Martinez de Vicente, P. (2005), 'The secret Spanish evasion routes to save refugee Jews from the holocaust', *The International Raoul Wallenberg Foundation* website, 28 June 2005. www.raoulwallenberg.net/?en/highlights/secret-spanish-evasion-routes.2898. htm.

McLaine, I. (1979), *Ministry of Morale: Home Front Morale and the Ministry of Information in World War II*. London: George Allen & Unwin.

Mercier, A. (2008), *Guilhermina Suggia: Cellist*. Aldershot: Ashgate Publishing Ltd.

Messinger, G. S. (1992), *British Propaganda and the State in the First World War*. Manchester: Manchester University Press.

'Michael Grant', *The Times*, 13 October 2004.

Michels, E. (2004), 'Deutsch als Weltsprache? Franz Thierfelder, the Deutsche Akademie in Munich and the promotion of the German language abroad, 1923–1945', *German History*, 22, 206–28.

Michelson, P. E. and Treptow, K. W. (eds) (2002), *National Development in Romania and Southeastern Europe*. Iaşi, Oxford: Center for Romanian Studies.

'Min. of Inf. is angry', *Daily Express*, 12 June 1941.

Miner, S. M. (2003), *Stalin's Holy War: Religion, Nationalism and Alliance Politics*. Chapel Hill: University of North Carolina Press.

Monterrey, T. (2003a), 'Los estudios Ingleses en España (1900–1950): contexto ideológico-cultural, autores y obras', *Atlantis*, 25, 2, 71–96. www.atlantisjournal.org/Papers/25_2/071-096%20Monterrey.pdf.

— (2003b), 'Los estudios Ingleses en España (1900–1950): legislación curricular', *Atlantis*, 25, 1, 63–80. www.atlantisjournal.org/Papers/25_1/063-080_Monterrey.pdf.

'Música en el Instituto Alemán de Cultura', *Ya*, 7 April 1942.

Niblo, S. R. (1983), 'British propaganda in Mexico during the Second World War: the development of cultural imperialism', *Latin American Perspectives*, 10, 114–26.

Nicolson, H. (1955), 'The British Council 1934–1955', in British Council, *The British Council: 1934–1955 – Twenty-First Anniversary Report*. London: British Council.

Nicolson, N. (ed.) (1970), *Harold Nicolson: Diaries & Letters 1939–1945*. London: Fontana Books.

Niño, A. (1996), 'Los condones del pequeño noble: La reina de Inglaterra concede la Orden del', *El Pais*, 18 June 1996. www.elpais.com/articulo/madrid/ESPAnA/REINO_UNIDO/MADRID/REINO_UNIDO/condones/pequeno/nobel/elpepuespmad/19960618elpmad_15/Tes?print=1.

'No Instituto Britânico: Inaugurou-se ontem a exposição de traduções portuguesas de livros Britanicos', *Jornal do Comércio*, 14 March 1944.

'Nya utländska böcker', *Bonniers Litterära Magasin*, årg IX, Nr. 6, June–August 1940, 502–4.

Nye, Joseph S. (2004), *Soft Power: The Means to Success in World Politics*. New York: Public Affairs.

'O dr. Malcolm Sargent chefe de orquestra inglês a quem se deve o desenvolvimento das massas corais nos últimos anos, está em Lisboa onde vem dirigir a Orquestra da Emissora em três concertos em São Carlos', *Diário Popular*, 11 January 1943.

Ó Drisceoil, D. (1996), *Censorship in Ireland 1939–1945: Neutrality, Politics and Society*. Cork: Cork University Press.

'O Instituto Britanico em Portugal: A Inglaterra deseja tornar ainda mais solida a antiga aliança luso-britanica declarou-nos hoje lord Lloyd of Dolobran', *Diário de Manhã*, 24 November 1938.

'O prof. Dr. McCance falou, ontem, no Hospital de Santo António sôbre a «Fisiologia da infância e a sua relação com a medicina preventiva', *O Comércio do Porto*, 26 February 1943.

'O violinista Philippe Newman no Instituto Britânico', *Jornal do Comércio*, 19 March 1944.

Ogden, C. K. (1930), *Basic English: A General Introduction with Rules and Grammar*. London: Kegan Paul & Co. Ltd.

O'Halpin, E. (2002), 'Irish neutrality in the Second World War', in Wylie, N. (ed.), *European Neutrals and Non-Belligerents During the Second World War*. Cambridge: Cambridge University Press.

Orwell, G. (1946), 'Politics and the English language', *Horizon*, April, 13, 252–65.

— (1949), *Nineteen Eighty-Four*. London: Martin Secker & Warburg (reprinted by Penguin Classics, 2000).

Osei, G. K. and Thompson, J. W. (1997), 'The supersession of one rumour by another', *Journal of Applied Probability*, 14, 1, 127–34.

'Our vision, purpose and values', *British Council website* www.britishcouncil.org/new/freedom-of-information/information-guide/who-we-are-and-what-we-do/vision-purpose-and-values/.

Pearton, M. (2002), 'Romanian neutrality, 1939–1940', in Wylie, N. (ed.), *European Neutrals and Non-Belligerents During the Second World War*. Cambridge: Cambridge University Press.

'Perecen Leslie Howard y doce pasajeros más en ataque aéreo', *Ya*, 3 June 1943.

'Professor Michael Grant', *Daily Telegraph*. 7 October 2004.

Pronay, N. and Spring, D. W. (1982), *Propaganda, Politics and Film, 1938–1945*. London: Macmillan.

Pronay, N. and Taylor, P. M. (1984), ' "An improper use of broadcasting. . .". The British government and clandestine radio propaganda operations against Germany during the Munich crisis and after', *Journal of Contemporary History*, 19, 1, 357–84.

'Ransonering i England en tid efter kriget slut', *Dagens Nyheter*, 20 October 1943.

'Reorganisation av Europa skall föregå fredsslutet: Harold Nicolson har inte mött krigströtthet hos det engelska folket', *Dagens Nyheter*, 20 October 1943.

Resina, J. R. (1998), 'Historical discourse and the propaganda film: reporting the revolution in Barcelona', *New Literary History*, 29, 1, 67–84.

Rey-Ximena, J. (2008), 'Leslie, lo que Franco se llevo', *El Mundo*, 5 October 2008. www.elmundo.es/papel/2008/10/05/cronica/2513564.html.

— (2009), *El Vuelo de Ibis: Leslie Howard al Servicio de Su Majestad Británica*. Madrid: Ediciones Facta s.l.

Richards, L. (2005), 'Whispers of war – the British World War II rumour campaign', *Psywar.Org website*. www.psywar.org/sibs.php. Originally published in *Falling Leaf*, 183.

Ritchie, S. (2004), *Our Man in Yugoslavia: The Story of a Secret Service Operative*. London: Routledge.

Roberts, A. (2008), *Um Toque Decisivo: A Small But Crucial Push. British Council – 70 Years with Portugal*. Lisbon: Medialivros, Actividades Editorials SA.

Robertson, F. A. de V. (1940), *British Aviation*. London: Longmans Green & Co Ltd.

Robson, W. A. (1940a), *O Sistema Governativo da Grã-Bretanha*. Lisboa: Conselho Britânico das Relações Culurais [The British Council]. Undated but early 1940s.

— (1940b), *The British System of Government*. London: Longmans Green & Co Ltd.

Rogers, T. (2003), 'The Right Book Club: Text wars, modernity and cultural politics in the late thirties', *Journal: Literature & History*, 12, 2, 1–15.

Rohrer, F. (2009), 'The perils of five-star reviews', *BBC News Magazine*, 25 June 2009. http://www.news.bbc.co.uk/1/hi/magazine/8118577.stm.

Rosas, F. (2002), 'Portuguese neutrality in the Second World War', in Wylie, N. (ed.), *European Neutrals and Non-Belligerents During the Second World War*. Cambridge: Cambridge University Press.

Rosas, F., Oliveira, P. de, and Barros, J. L. (1996), *Armindo Monteiro e Oliveira Salazar: Correspondência Política 1926–1955*. Lisboa: Editorial Estampo.

Rossignol, D. (1991), *Historie de la Propagande en France de 1940 à 1944: L'Utopie Pétain*. Paris: PUF.

Ruiz, N. G. (1943) 'G. K. Chesterton: "Vida de Dickens"', *Ya*, 7 October 1943.

'Russia row offices "to stay shut"', *BBC News Website*, 17 January 2008. http://www.news.bbc.co.uk/go/pr/fr/-/1/hi/uk_politics/7193186.stm.

'Russia to limit British Council', *BBC News Website*, 12 December 2007. http://www.news.bbc.co.uk/1/hi/world/europe/7139959.stm.

Sanders, M. L. (1975), 'Wellington House and the British propaganda during the First World War', *The Historical Journal*, XVIII, I, 119–46.

Schneider, I. S. (1994), 'La propaganda alemana en España 1942–1944', *Espacio, Tiempo y Forma*, Serie V, H.a Contemporánea, t. 7.

— (1999), 'La propaganda alemana en la Segunda República Española', *Historia y Comunicación Social*, 4, 183–97.

'Scholar Gypsy', *Time*, 11 January 1937.

Serrano Suñer, R. (1977), *Entre el Silencio y la Propaganda la Historia como fue Memorias*. Barcelona: Editorial Planeta.

'Sesión de la Academia Médico-Quirúrgica Española', *Arriba*, 13 February 1943.

Spears, E. (1956), *Assignment to Catastrophe*. London: Reprint Society.

Stamp, L. D. (1940), *The Face of Britain*. London: Longmans Green & Co Ltd.

Starkie de Herrero, A. (1986), 'Aclaración sobre Walter Starkie', *El Pais*, 1 March 1986.

Starkie, W. (1934), *Spanish Raggle-Taggle: Adventures with a Fiddle in North Spain*. Harmondsworth: Penguin Books (Reprinted 1961).

— (1940), *The Waveless Plain: An Italian Autobiography*. London: The Travel Book Club.

— (1948), 'The British Council in Spain', *Bulletin of Spanish Studies*, 25, 100, 270–75.

— (1953), *In Sara's Tents*. London: John Murray.

— (1963), *Scholars and Gypsies: An Autobiography*. Berkeley and Los Angeles: University of California Press.

Stone, G. A. (2005), *Spain, Portugal & the Great Powers, 1931–1941*. Basingstoke: Palgrave.

Suarez-Pajares, J. (ed.) (2002), *Música Española entre dos Guerras, 1914–1945*. Granada: Publicaciones del archive Manuel de Falla.

Svartengren, T. H. (1948), 'English language studies in Sweden', *ELT Journal*, II, (6), 153–62.

'T. S. ELIOT Till skaldens Sverigebesök: DIKTER' – Advertisement by Bonniers – *Dagens Nyheter*, 25 April 1942.

Taylor, P. M. (1980), 'The Foreign Office and British propaganda during the First World War', *The Historical Journal*, 23, 4, 875–98.

— (1981), *The Projection of Britain: British Overseas Publicity and Propaganda 1919–1939*. Cambridge: Cambridge University Press.

— (2003), *Munitions of the Mind: a History of Propaganda from the Ancient World to the Present Day* (third edition). Manchester and New York: Manchester University Press.

Tazón-Salces, J. E. and Carrera Suárez, I. (2005), *Post-Imperial Encounters: Anglo-Hispanic Cultural Relations* (Studies in Comparative Literature 45). Amsterdam and New York: Rodopi.

Telo, A. J. (1990), *Propaganda e Guerra Secreta em Portugal (1939–1945)*. Lisbon: Perspectivas & Realidades.

Tennant, P. (1992), *Touchlines of War*. Hull: Hull University Press.

'The British Council cooks the books', *The Language Business*, 26 March 2007. http://dblackie.blogs.com/the_language_business/2007/03/the_british_cou.html.

Thierfelder, F. (1940), *Englischer Kulturimperialismus: Der 'British Council' als Werkzeug der Geistigen Einkreisung Deutschlands*. Berlin: Junker und Dünnhaupt Verlag.

Thistlewood, D. (1994), 'Herbert Read (1893–1968)', *Prospects: the Quarterly Review of Comparative Education (Paris, UNESCO): International Bureau of Education*, 24, 1/2, 375–90. www.ibe.unesco.org/publications/ThinkersPdf/reade.pdf.

Tomes, J. (2004), 'Lloyd, George Ambrose, first Baron Lloyd (1879–1941)', *Oxford Dictionary of National Biography*, Oxford: Oxford University Press (online edition, January 2008). www.oxforddnb.com/view/article/34567.

'Turco-British relations in all dimensions', *Turkish Daily News*, 21 July 2001.

Tusell Gómez, J. (2005), *La España de Franco*. Madrid: Biblioteca de al Historia, Alba Libros, S.L.

'Tysk Misstänksamhet mot British Council', *Dagens Nyheter*, 19 December 1941.

'Tyskt angrepp på statsrådet Bagge', *Aftonbladet*, 18 December 1941.

Unwin, S. (1960), *The Truth About a Publisher*. London: Allen & Unwin Ltd.

Walhbäck, K. (1967), 'Sweden: secrecy and neutrality', *Journal of Contemporary History*, 2, 183–91.

Webb, D. (2006), 'Inflation: the value of the pound 1750–2005', *House of Commons Library, Research Paper 06/09*, 13 February 2006. www.parliament.uk/commons/lib/research/rp2006/rp06-009.pdf.

West, S. G. (1938), 'The present situation in Portugal', *International Affairs (Royal Institute of International Affairs 1931–1939)*, 17, 2, Mar-Apr, 1938. Address given at Chatham House on October 28th, 1937 with Sir Claud Russell KCMG, in the Chair.

Westrup, J. A. (1944), 'The British Council and music', *The Musical Times*, August, 236–7.

Wheeler, D. L. (1983), 'In the service of order: the Portuguese political police and the British, German and Spanish intelligence, 1932–1945', *Journal of Contemporary History*, XVIII, 1, 1–25.

White, A. J. S. (1965), *The British Council, the First 25 years: 1934–1959 – A Personal Account*. London: British Council.

Wigg, R. (ed.) (2005), *Churchill and Spain: The Survival of the Franco Regime, 1940-45*. (Canada Blanch Studies on Contemporary Spain) Where: Routledge.

Wight, R. (2007), *The Peacock's Tail and the Reputation Reflex*. London: Arts and Business.

Williams, B. (2002), *Truth and Truthfulness*. Princeton, NJ: Princeton University Press (Paperback 2004).

Wylie, N. (2001), ' "An Amateur Learns his Job"? Special Operations Executive in Portugal 1940-42', *Journal of Contemporary History*, 36, (3), 441–57.

— (2002), 'Switzerland: a neutral of distinction?', in Wylie, N. (ed.), *European Neutrals and Non-Belligerents During the Second World War*. Cambridge: Cambridge University Press.

'Yngste Nobelpristagaren krigsutbildar naturvetare', *Dagens Nyheter*, 18 April 1943.

Young, K. (ed.) (1980), *The Diaries of Sir Robert Bruce Lockhart – Volume Two: 1939–1965*. London: Macmillan.

Zahavi, A. and Zahavi, A. (1997), *The Handicap Principle: The Missing Piece of Darwin's puzzle*. Oxford and New York: Oxford University Press.

Živojinovic, D. R. (2002), 'Yugoslavia', in Wylie, N. (ed.), *European Neutrals and Non-Belligerents During the Second World War*. Cambridge: Cambridge University Press.

Index